BELFASTMEN

BELFASTMEN

AN INTIMATE HISTORY OF LIFE BEFORE GAY LIBERATION

TOM HULME

CORNELL UNIVERSITY PRESS
Ithaca and London

This book is freely available in an open access edition thanks to the generous support of the Arts and Humanities Research Council (AH/V008404/1) and Queen's University Belfast. The open access edition is available through the Cornell Open Initiative.

First published 2026 by Cornell University Press

Librarians: A CIP catalog record for this book is available from the Library of Congress.

ISBN 9781501786440 (hardcover)
ISBN 9781501786457 (paperback)
ISBN 9781501786471 (pdf)
ISBN 9781501786464 (epub)

GPSR EU contact: Sam Thornton, Mare Nostrum Group B.V., Mauritskade 21D, 1091 GC, Amsterdam, NL, gpsr@mare-nostrum.co.uk.

For Cormac McAteer; we are now Belfastmen together

Contents

Abbreviations viii

Note on Terminology ix

Introduction 1

1. The Intimate Queer City 21

2. The Queer Irish World 56

3. Sexology, Religion, and Reading Queer in Ulster 80

4. Boys, Friends, and Lovers 106

5. Families, Neighborhoods, and the Public 133

6. Ulster's Manliness on Trial 156

Conclusion 184

Acknowledgments 189

Notes 193

Bibliography 247

Index 289

Abbreviations

AGDC	Arthur Greeves Diary Collection
BBC	British Broadcasting Corporation
BSSSP	British Society for the Study of Sex Psychology
CIYMS	Church of Ireland Young Men's Society
GPO	General Post Office
GRONI	General Register Office of Northern Ireland
HMS	Her/His Majesty's Ship
JP	Justice of the Peace
MA	master of arts
MP	member of Parliament
MV	Motor Vessel
PC	Privy Council
PDDS	Personal Diary of David Strain
PRONI	Public Record Office of Northern Ireland
QC	Queen's Counsel
RIC/RUC	Royal Ulster Constabulary/Royal Irish Constabulary
RMS	Royal Mail Ship
SS	steamship
USA	United States of America
YMCA	Young Men Christian's Association

Note on Terminology

Naming conventions are fraught with tensions when it comes to the history and present of the island of Ireland. The partition of the country in the early 1920s created a jurisdiction—Northern Ireland—that a significant proportion of the population still consider to be occupied by the British state and thus refuse to legitimize by name. I use a schematic that I think best captures the specificities of the everyday context in which same-sex desire was experienced, understood, and regulated rather than signaling my personal politics. First, the regional culture of which Belfast was the heart, regardless of whether I am describing before or after partition, is *Ulster* or *the north of Ireland*. After partition, the polity—that is, the government, its legislation, and bureaucratic structures—is Northern Ireland. Second, and from a similar logic, I predominantly refer to the rest of the island as *the south of Ireland* and the polity after partition as the Irish Free State (1922–37) or Republic of Ireland (1937–), though I recognize a history just as complex there too.[1] Finally, the United Kingdom is used—and only rarely—as a political and legal denominator while *Britain and Ireland* is a geographic descriptor to discuss cultural developments that affected both.[2]

The language of sexuality and identity is no less complex. I have chosen to use *queer* to describe men and sexual practices that fell outside of the expected norms of society unless—as was sometimes the case later in the period—my subjects actually used *gay* or *homosexual*. I recognize that to gay people of a certain generation, *queer* might be painfully remembered as a slur, though it was used by some Belfastmen to describe themselves by at least the 1930s. For some activists, *queer* recalls a radical historical process of reclaiming and defying heteronormativity after the gay liberation movement of the late 1960s and 1970s. Historians, following the rise of queer theory in the 1990s, instead find *queer* useful because of its indeterminacy: it captures historical impulses and understandings of sex, gender, and desire that were inconsistent with and different from any modern homosexual/heterosexual binary or indeed the more recent umbrella term LGBTQIA+.[3] This is my own aim in using the term: a way to appreciate the historical nuances of the period without backdating our own understandings of sexual desire and identity.

Introduction

Thomas Henry Gibney was born in Belfast in 1868. His family lived on Green Street, a small row of terraced houses occupied by laborers and tradesmen just a stone's throw away from the busy Donegall Quay. Even though Belfast was a town rapidly becoming a prosperous city in the second half of the nineteenth century, existence could be mean and short for the working classes, who toiled in often-dangerous industries and lived in overcrowded, unsanitary districts. The patriarch of the Gibneys had work as a skilled bootmaker but died in 1878 of pneumonia and tuberculosis, aged just forty. His wife, Eliza, an illiterate shopkeeper, was left to bring up several children on her own.[1] Life went on until, some twelve years later, a tragedy of a different sort struck the family. Unbeknown to Thomas Gibney, now aged twenty-one, detectives of the Royal Irish Constabulary had been secretly watching him for over six months. Finally, in February 1890, they broke cover to arrest him and eleven others on charges of buggery and gross indecency. All these men—who were shop assistants, clerks, and amateur actors—had allegedly been having sexual affairs with each other in locations across the city, from public urinals in the dockside Queen's Square to bars in the Catholic stronghold of the Falls Road in the west.[2]

Even though Eliza Gibney was unable to read the daily papers, there is no doubt that news of her son's arrest would have soon reached her through the gossip that easily circulated in Irish working-class neighborhoods. She may have heard that part of the charge related to how her son and other men were purportedly distributing lewd photographs and running a brothel, or perhaps she had already known that her son was supplementing the meagre family income by selling sex. Even if the accusations were true, the profits of this enterprise were not enough for what he needed now; unlike some of the better off men who were caught up in the case, Thomas Gibney and his family were unable to find bail money and remained in custody until the trial some months later. But if Eliza Gibney was embarrassed or even ashamed by her son's behavior, it did not stop her from fulfilling her maternal duty. She bravely came to court to give a character statement, probably explaining to the jury the difficulties of the family's economic situation or how her son was *usually* a good boy.[3] The judge was still whipped into a frenzy by the magnitude of the scandal and railed against the immorality of the accused and the "plague" they had brought to his city, comments that were then reproduced in the local press. A prison sentence of eighteen months was passed down to seven of the men, with the added punishment of back-breaking hard labor. Thomas Gibney's treatment was at least slightly more lenient; the young man had persuaded the authorities that he was seventeen at the time of the crimes rather than twenty-one, or perhaps he just struggled to keep track of his own age, given he was seemingly illiterate like his mother. Either way, it was enough for the judge to deem him not as bad as those old enough to know better but still deserving of twelve months in the Crumlin Road Gaol.[4]

If the experience of trial and prosecution had shaken the Gibney family, in the essentials Thomas Gibney's life continued in much the same way after he was released from prison. He went back to the same working-class district where many of his relatives also lived and found work as a laborer, probably in the booming shipyards nearby. When Eliza Gibney died of bronchitis in 1906, aged fifty-six, her other now-adult children continued to support their brother; he went to live with his married sister and her son, who were running a small boardinghouse for industrial workers less than a hundred feet away from the original family home. Less than a decade after his mother's passing, Thomas Gibney was dead too, at just forty-six. He succumbed to a heart attack after weakening from a combination of the same respiratory illnesses that had taken his parents. Perhaps the involuntary time spent in an often-overcrowded prison had contributed to his poor health, much in the same way as it had for the more famous martyr Oscar Wilde.[5]

Whether Thomas Gibney continued to have sexual relationships with other men after his conviction in 1890 is now knowledge lost to time, though he was seemingly not arrested in Belfast again. But there are suggestive echoes of male intimacy in the historical record. When the Census recorded his household in 1901, the only other occupier apart from him and his mother was a young single man noted by the enumerator to be a "friend." The man present at his death was another bachelor, who had been sharing the same boardinghouse for several years.[6] Either way, Thomas Gibney's very public brush with the law had not been enough to have him cast out by his family or community—not in life nor in death. A simple obituary in the *Belfast Telegraph* in February 1914, one of many newspapers that had reported his trial almost a quarter of a century before, records the hopes of the surviving siblings that their friends would join them as they finally put to rest their "dearly beloved brother."[7]

Writing Intimate Queer Lives

This book is made up of many life stories like Thomas Gibney's, woven together across the eight or so decades that saw the recriminalization of sex between men in Britain and Ireland in the 1880s and the emergence of a mainstream debate about homosexuality in the 1950s.[8] I have used *intimate* in the book's title to signal how this is not a top-down or political history of the regulation of sex and sexuality in that era but rather about everyday encounters and relationships and how they were experienced. For that reason, and like the other books that take similar approaches, this is an intimate history in terms of its subject. But as I researched and then began to write the book, it became clear to me that there was a second type of intimacy guiding my hand: what I can now see as an affective method or, more loftily put, "historical praxis."[9] My connection to Belfast and its queer past was transformed by the experience of being a gay man who had relocated there from London in 2016 to teach history at one of the region's universities. As I got to know the city, began to search for echoes of the queer past, and started to get involved in local history and activist communities, I found myself becoming deeply invested in the personal stories of long-dead Belfastmen. Leaning into that emotion rather than trying to stay academically detached or objectively aloof has shaped my historical approach: what I chose to cover, where I looked for my sources, and how I have tried to describe the lives I uncovered.

After beginning this intimate research journey as a relative newcomer to queer history, I realized that I was treading in the deep footsteps of previous waves of gay and lesbian scholars. During the bloom of homophile activism in the decades after the Second World War, these forerunners sought to reclaim lost or forgotten "homosexual" or "gay" lives because of the power they held for connecting the persecuted past to the political present.[10] In the late 1970s and continuing into at least the 1990s, debates raged about whether such recovery histories of an innate, timeless, or essential homosexuality should be replaced by "social constructionism": the idea that sexual identities, practices, and even desires were a cultural product of different times and places.[11] The more recent rise of queer theory and its destabilizing of any sense of a clear binary between homosexuality and heterosexuality—including in my own lifetime—has been even more challenging to a belief in historically stable sexual identities.[12] Though gay histories for a popular audience can happily collapse the distance between then and now, most academic historians would now agree that we need a "critical queer history": an approach that is not about an easy lineage to the present but rather the "unknowability and indeterminacy of the sexual past."[13] This theoretical shift in the work of historians has meant that the deeper I got into my research of Belfast's queer men, and the more familiar their lives began to feel, the more problematic my affinity became. That is hardly an experience unique to those who study sexuality, admittedly; many writers, in their micro-historical or biographical approaches, have risked clouding their judgment by loving their subjects too much.[14] But the stakes, not to mention the rancor of the academic debate, have been higher in queer history than in many other subdisciplines, probably because of the culture wars that still impinge on the lives of sexual and gender minorities.

Even a novice therapist can tell you that the first step to resolving a problem is to recognize that you have one. I know that these queer men of the past were not gay like I am today, even if it sometimes feels like it; they lived in a different context and were without doubt formed by it. My book accepts the critical perspective of queer theory and resists trying to shove any historical figure into a homosexuality-shaped hole. But, like the historians of emotion who are the most open-minded about intimate methods, I did not know how to write the history of queer Belfastmen without forming a relationship with them.[15] I am not the only one to grapple with these issues in queer history, nor the first to come out in favor of recognizing our common aspirations and connections across time. There is no doubt either that these concerns will continue to haunt the field for years to come, as we continue to move further away from the past and our own understanding of LGBTQIA+ identities evolves.[16] I aim purely to add to the conversation by showing a fresh method for writing about historical queer lives—one that allows us to get even closer to our subjects, especially those who have left only faint archival traces. If this intimate approach still risks collapsing the objective or emotional distance between then and now, I can only swear that the benefit outweighs the costs: a far richer account of the intricacies of being a queer man in an era before gay rights.

The bulk of the material for *Belfastmen* originates from a source familiar to most historians of sexuality: the criminal archive. In any local or national jurisdiction, the style of contemporary policing and later archival practices determines how much evidence, if any, survives. For many parts of Britain and Ireland there is little to no descriptive material, but for the city of Belfast historians are relatively fortunate. There are comprehensive records of trials, with charges, lists of those who spoke in court, witness statements, and final judgments. These cover almost every incident of gross indecency (any sexual contact or even the suggestion of it) or buggery (anal sex) that made it to trial at the Belfast Assizes or Recorder Court (later City Commission) between 1891 and 1958, totaling around sixty relevant cases. I supplement these court documents with prison registers. These are patchy for the period before 1908 and much of the late 1930s onward too, but between those dates are a fairly complete record of arrests. When locals and visitors alike were booked into custody, their biographical details—occupation, family, religion, address—were logged, probably by a police officer or clerk. Physical characteristics were then noted by a prison guard or doctor, such as height, weight, and hair color or the tattoos and scars that were etched into their bodies. Even if an arrested man was later discharged before or after trial, these large, heavy, and unfortunately decaying books are an unrivaled way to learn more about those who were believed to be engaging in same-sex encounters.

Putting together these various legal sources enabled me to start telling stories of where and how queer Belfastmen lived their lives, but relying on the criminal archive still presents problems for a self-consciously intimate history. Witness statements especially are rarely just a clear window onto a culture of men who desired other men. Cases of sex between adults, whether fleeting or part of a longer relationship, were tried under the same laws that punished the clear sexual abuse of children and sexual assaults of (usually younger) men. In between the two poles of clearly consensual acts and the horrible violent abuse of children there were a range of encounters that fall into a difficult gray area of interpretation. There were no legal male sexual relationships at the time, and our own understandings of childhood, desire, and consent do not map onto the past so easily. We must tread carefully when thinking and writing about those who would fall below age of consent laws today but were still active and sometimes enthusiastic participants in historical male queer scenes.[17] This tricky issue is taken up more fully in chapter 4, but it is worth insisting up front that we cannot appreciate the complexity of past queerness if we simply backdate our own moral perspectives or legal strictures. The result is that some of my intimate stories do involve adolescent boys whom we would rightly see today as too young to consent in the manner defined by our own society.

Witness statements, whether from boys or young men, are also not always the repository of facts they claimed to be.[18] Anyone who had taken part in an illegal sexual encounter had good reason to be dishonest, and we know that the police encouraged witnesses—especially the younger ones—to tell stories the jury wanted to hear, whether about regret or being led astray.[19] The most critical theorists and historians have urged us to be wary about the truths that such materials might promise to contain. Legal proceedings were part of a process of creating modern sexual categories out of a complex world of encounters and understandings and do not simply reveal the preexistence of something easily defined as homosexuality.[20] I take these concerns about using legal sources seriously: I question why some sexual and romantic encounters, and the men who took part in them, were exposed to the legal system and why others were not; and I point out where the evidence was mediated through the lens of other witnesses or the perspective of the court. At the same time, I treat the stories that witnesses crafted as representative of the possibilities of queer life that existed. Whether sexual encounters always did happen exactly in the way they were described by witnesses is less important than the fact that they feasibly could.[21]

It is important for an ethics of historical research to acknowledge that all these criminal sources have come to me through a process of detection, observation, and arrest that could ruin a man's life. They often detail the shame and anxiety that queer men could feel and document the physical attacks they sometimes faced from members of the public and the police. "Every historian of the multitude, the dispossessed, the subaltern, and the enslaved," as Saidya Hartman puts it in her beautiful reconstruction of the intimate lives of Black American women, "is forced to grapple with the power and authority of the archive and the limits it sets on what can be known, whose perspective matters, and who is endowed with the gravity and authority of historical actor."[22] I have grappled with this question too and the risk that the inherent violence of the criminal archive might reinscribe a viewpoint of queer men that reduces their lives to sex or the moment that they were exposed. I could claim benevolent objectives of socially recovering unfairly forgotten lives, but the result might be the same: a kind of amateur pathologization of same-sex desire that even punishes victims of state oppression by revealing their public disgrace a second time.[23] My decision to name my subjects where legally possible, partly out of a desire for historical traceability for other historians but also as a political act of visibility and to actively reject any shame about sex between men, only makes this issue more pressing.[24]

My solution to overcoming a criminalizing viewpoint is to try to find out far more about the subjective experiences of any queer man who was arrested, as I began to demonstrate in my opening vignette of Thomas Gibney's life. In practice and effect, I have returned to the long-established approaches and ethos of the social historians of the 1960s, echoing their aim to restore agency to disenfranchised groups as well as emulating their enthusiasm for reconstructing a richer picture of everyday life.[25] At the same time, I have turned to digital genealogy and family history methods to gain this longer and deeper human perspective, trawling sources like the census and records of birth, marriage, and death, documents relating to travel or citizenship, and newspapers from all over the world.[26]

In tune with the queer intimacy of my book, I have allowed myself to speculate on the feelings and thoughts of men in Belfast.[27] Writing imaginatively, or reading between the lines when a historical source is only blunt or partial, might risk the accusation that an analysis has elements of historical fiction. I am not overly concerned about that possibility and would argue that often the only difference between academic works that do and do not claim absolute historical truth is how the latter are just more reflexive about their subjective positionality (or, to put it in laymen's terms, we all do it but only some of us admit it!). At any rate, I have buried myself in contemporary sources beyond criminal records to make my speculation less about how *we* would feel in the same situations today and more how people in the past *might* have felt, given the cultural context in which they lived. Memoirs, contemporary novels, oral histories, reams of the local press: they provide not just color but also the emotional nuance that is often lacking in the criminal record. The result of combining these different approaches is a historically informed method of imagining the lives of queer men who barely left any evidence of their own print on the past.[28]

Speculation is necessary for reconstructing the lives of some queer men, but not all. Worth noting at the outset is how lucky I have been to chance upon the personal archive of perhaps one of the richest yet unacknowledged individual sources of queer history. David Harbison Strain was born in 1896 into a family with long-established Ulster roots and grew up in Galwally Park, a small middle-class suburb on the expanding southern edge of Belfast.[29] As the oldest of three boys, he was destined to eventually take over the family's linen merchant business in the center of the city, but already in his early twenties he was aware that he was the black sheep of the family, or a *confirmed bachelor*, as he put it delicately in 1921.[30] After Strain died in 1969, his extensive archive was deposited into the Public Record Office of Northern Ireland, with whom he had been communicating since at least the early part of the decade. Alongside the detailed business records of the W. J. Strain & Son's linen firm and other family ventures are personal items such as letters, photo albums, newspaper clippings, and Strain's own attempt to write a genealogical history.

At the heart of the David Strain collection are forty-three diaries, covering 1920–43 and 1962–69 and totaling what I would estimate to be around two million words. The first series of diaries are unrivaled in their richness. Until the Second World War and the experience of the Belfast Blitz interrupted his flow, Strain wrote an entry every day, regularly as much as five to ten pages in a careful cursive hand. To describe him as fastidious does not go far enough. Strain prided himself on attention to detail and documented in exceptional depth the conversations he had, almost in screenplay style, as well as the minutiae of his day-to-day life, even when it was hardly a flattering portrayal of his own somewhat snobbish foibles. For most of the 1920s, he describes confused attempts to build friendships with male youths and other men, both of his own class and those who labored below. After 1931, the year in which Strain discovered books that were frank about his hero Oscar Wilde as well as newer scientific understandings of homosexuality, the diaries become a remarkably probing description of contemporary queerness: daily walks around the city looking for male partners, romantic and eventually sexual affairs, discussions of the latest queer novels, and remarks about how his family and friends responded to his discovery that he was different from most men. I use this rich diary throughout my book to understand the process of modern queer self-making—how Strain practiced his daily reflective entries as what cultural historians call "a technology of the self"—but also as an unrivaled if subjective window onto a forgotten social world.[31] The fact that Strain went back in his old age to correct his illegible youthful handwriting suggests he wanted the diaries to be read. But apart from Denys Blakeway's book *The Last Dance* (2010), which drew on Strain's diary from 1936 as just one of many to describe all aspects of a "pivotal year for Britain," these rare writings seem to have lain almost entirely unused.[32]

By creating many small queer histories that do not just begin and end when a man was arrested, whether pulled from the criminal archive or the pages of David Strain's diary, I try to restore a degree of agency and dignity to men who have long since been forgotten or were recorded only at their most vulnerable point.[33] At the same time, I aim to make a broader thematic contribution to the history of sexuality: an intimate approach, I suggest, might help us understand the experience of male queerness in new and exciting ways. Historians, when looking at male urban scenes, have tended to focus mostly on the moments of sex, arrest, and exposure because they are what created archival traces and would seem to offer the most hope for understanding historical desires. Drawing productively on the insights of feminists, queer theorists, and geographers, these historians have now built a rich historiography about where queer men met, what they did together, and how the law and the newspapers responded to their desires. I focus on these areas too but argue that by looking beyond policing, and even the experiences of the queer scene itself, we can gain a clearer sense of the other more mundane ways that men were situated in their society.

Encounters with the law and even the pursuit of sex were only relatively fleeting in a man's life; more time could be spent at work, socializing with friends, attending church, or fulfilling family obligations. But rather than this being a separate world, it often actively crossed over into the intimate queer lives of men too, sometimes with negative results but just as often positive ones. When we look away from the courts, the sensationalist press, and the queer scene, we find not just men who desired men but respected colleagues, popular neighbors, much loved brothers, and even devoted husbands. Appreciating these perhaps paradoxical truths helps us to see a more vibrant and hopeful tapestry of everyday queer life in the past—and even in places where we might not have expected to find one at all.

Belfast: City of Conflict?

There are now literally hundreds of studies of historical urban sex scenes: ancient to modern, Western to Global South, covert to gloriously open. That Belfast has not yet had its own is surprising at first glance: the late Victorian city was already the sort of urban-industrial capital that historians have found to be home to queer subcultures. Size and density, regional pulling power, commercial leisure zones, deviant dockside districts: all these urban characteristics encouraged or enabled male intimacies elsewhere.[34] It cannot be a simple question of sources; as I have already described, there was a remarkable richness of catalogued material just waiting to be used. The historiographical and popular dominance of the Troubles—the ethnonationalist conflict that erupted in the late 1960s until it ended, formally at least, with the Good Friday Agreement in 1998—might be one obvious reason that historians have been less interested in many social aspects of Belfast in the slightly more peaceful eras before. But of greater importance, if rarely stated openly, is an assumption that the city simply could not be home to flourishing queer lives because of its peculiar social and cultural circumstances. To put it bluntly, Belfast has more often been stereotyped as Bigotsborough, as the journalist and novelist James Douglas unkindly dubbed it in 1907, than as a city of brotherly love.[35]

To appreciate how Belfast arrived at this reputation—and to suggest a queerly surprising alternative—requires a brief journey back to the city's founding. Entwining processes of English settler colonialism and religious conflict, joined later by rapid urban and industrial development, created a unique social structure in the northeast of Ireland. Though there had been a small fortified settlement at the end of the medieval era, the foundations of the modern city—socially, politically, physically—were laid during the Ulster Plantation of the early seventeenth century. When Sir Arthur Chichester was granted the area by James I in 1603, he set about building a town that was incorporated ten years later. In 1660, about a third of the population of Belfast was Catholic, the dominant religion of Ireland, but by 1757 it had fallen to less than 7 percent. The original English and Manx settlers had been followed by Scottish, firmly setting the character of Belfast as Protestant and predominantly Presbyterian.[36]

Migration from the surrounding countryside was more prevalent in the eighteenth and nineteenth centuries, and only then did the Catholic population begin to recover. By 1808, this mostly poor community was already concentrated in the west of the town, having reached around four thousand people, at that point roughly 15 percent of the total. Belfast Protestantism was not free of conflict between and indeed within its various denominations, but ecumenical relations with the still-small Catholic community remained generally amicable and even supportive.[37] This situation began to change in the late eighteenth and early nineteenth centuries. The Catholic population had continued to grow, reaching a third of the total of Belfast by the 1830s, and on the national stage demands for full Catholic political rights were becoming urgent. Tensions were deepened by the growth of reactionary doctrinal tendencies in both religions, from the evangelicalism of Protestantism to the authoritarianism of Catholicism. Protestant fears of engulfment—or, more accurately, the loss of its unfair political and economic hegemony in the region—began to manifest and only worsened with the Irish Home Rule crises from the 1870s. Preexisting residential patterns in Belfast now facilitated semi-regular outbreaks of violence between ethnoreligiously segregated working-class districts.[38]

The legacy of sectarian conflict in the nineteenth century was a profoundly divided city into the twentieth, with essentially two separate civic cultures existing side by side. The 1901 census demonstrates that around

60 percent of the population were living on streets where 90 percent of the residents were either Catholic or Protestant.[39] A new low in communal tensions came with the upheavals of the early 1920s. The partition of the island of Ireland, after a decade of world war, revolution, and civil war, created Northern Ireland. Made up of six of the nine counties of Ulster, it was a gerrymandered de facto unionist Protestant jurisdiction, with Belfast as its capital and the United Kingdom as its parent. The worsening conditions of a postwar economic slump and the continuing sociopolitical fallout then led to the first conflict to be dubbed the Troubles. Almost five hundred were killed in around two years, with ten thousand expelled from work and twenty-three thousand evicted from their homes. Roughly three-quarters of these victims were Catholic, despite making up only a quarter of the population.[40] By the late 1960s, the eve of the second and much longer-lasting Troubles, segregation had grown to reach 67 percent.[41] In this context, unions between Catholic and Protestant men and women were vanishingly rare. Roughly 1 percent of marriages were mixed in Ireland in 1911 and under 2 percent in Belfast; given the far larger non-Catholic population of the city, they were clearly subject to stronger disapproval there than in the rest of the country.[42]

Despite this deeply rooted modern experience of segregation and division, one of the most prominent activist memories of the gay liberation movement in Belfast is of how the scene that emerged in the 1970s and 1980s was largely unaffected by sectarianism. Already beyond the pale of polite society, gay men and lesbian women were drawn together by their common experiences and goals rather than divided by their ethnoreligious affiliation; they even reveled in their ownership of the otherwise deserted and semi-militarized city center. There are naturally caveats to be made to this broadly shared recollection of harmony. Tensions around the national question often bubbled below the surface, sometimes erupting in activist groups or in bars, and nationalists could feel the gay rights movement was effectively unionist because of its orientation toward initially achieving legal change through the British government.[43] Even so, it seems accurate that there was far more social mixing between gay Catholics and Protestants than there was in wider society.

Why, if a queer scene could exist in the 1970s and even be relatively non-sectarian, would the possibility of such a world in the era before be forgotten or ignored? First, it is worth noting that by no means is queer historical amnesia unique to Ireland. A memory of the pre-gay liberation era as one of silence, shame, and invisibility was a common trope in the first activist-written histories in the 1960s and 1970s; the challenges of their present, as American scholars were arguing in protest already in the 1980s, was projected back into an "abysmal past."[44] But given how common the language of darkness, invisibility, and hiddenness has been in making sense of Ireland's difficult modern history, it is no surprise that its own queer histories have fallen deeper into this trap.[45] Studies of Irish queer life tend to begin with the well-known scandals of the 1880s to early 1900s and the Dublin-based revolutionaries of 1916 before galloping across the next sixty years to the more well-documented activism that began in the early 1970s, and many begin their timelines in that later period altogether. Only Averill Earls's recent pioneering work on Dublin has attempted to reconstruct everyday Irish male queer life in the mid-twentieth century.[46]

An additional cloaking layer to Belfast's queer history results from the recent divergence of Northern Ireland's politics: first, in comparison to Britain, especially after the partial decriminalization of sex between men in England and Wales in 1967, where the path to more liberal laws has been somewhat less difficult; and second, since the 1990s, the Republic of Ireland too, which has become a European leader in LGBT acceptance. The latter's recent Decade of Centenaries has even included more official recognition of the role of queer people in the formation of its modern state.[47] As I will detail more fully in later chapters, the post–Second World War period in Belfast saw a rise in public information about a dreaded new social problem termed homosexuality, mostly a fear that was being replicated from larger debates taking place in Britain. Institutions and individuals were now forced into a confrontation with a subject that had barely been mentioned before. In another universe, a Christian message of love and acceptance could have won, but the largest Irish churches, which were intensely conservative on social issues, were mostly unreceptive. The outbreak of the Troubles only made the situation worse, as suspicion, distrust, and outright hostility toward social difference exploded.

The British government recognized the internal opposition from Irish religious leaders, and indeed the region's politicians too, and decided not to bring the laws regulating male sex into line with England and Wales, despite governing the jurisdiction under Direct Rule after the collapse of Northern Ireland's parliament during the Troubles. The very suggestion that Westminster might legislate led to the creation of a grotesque Save Ulster from Sodomy campaign by the Reverend Ian Paisley, the founder of the Free Presbyterian Church and leader of the newly formed Democratic Unionist Party. Even after the gay rights activists took matters into their own hands, with decriminalization being achieved via the European Court of Human Rights in 1982, the homophobic chill remained. From the 1980s to early 2000s, Belfastmen were surveilled by the police in numerous sting operations of often secluded sites, and if arrested could expect to have their names and faces splashed across the tabloid media. Paisley and his political descendants have also not been shy about the supposed abomination of homosexuality.[48] To this day there are still several unsolved murders of gay men in recent decades, as well as countless stories of suicide or forced emigration. In 2015, the year before I moved to Belfast, the BBC could still ask if the city was the worst place in Europe to be gay.[49]

Belfast's experience provides a powerful example of what Zavier Nunn has termed the "anticipatory impulse" in queer history: the mistake of looking back from a difficult present to antedate the same sort of past, or at least to search for its origins.[50] Is it that surprising that those queer Belfastmen who grew up in the worsening culture of the 1950s and 1960s, whether they then fled to more tolerant cities abroad or stayed behind to fight, have not imagined a more humane response to their situation? Or even that sociologists or political scientists, who are best versed in the dynamics of the Troubles-era city, have assumed that homophobia was always lurking below the surface of such a deeply religious society? Perhaps not. But the reality of Belfast's experience, as we will see, was far more complex.

Secrecy, Silence, and the Lives of Queer Belfastmen

If we try to ignore the impulse to anticipate the awful homophobia that developed in the second half of the twentieth century, we can see a different and, in some ways, more positive experience of queerness in Belfast in the era before. Partly this was a result of the city's middling size, which at its largest was only roughly four hundred thousand people. The history of urban sexuality has commonly been seen through the lens of the world's exceptionally big capitals and follows a paradigm set out by the pioneering historian-theorist-activist John D'Emilio over forty years ago. He powerfully argued that the continued rise of the capitalistic wage economy and urbanization of the late nineteenth and twentieth centuries freed men from the bonds of their families and so provided the bedrock for the formation of modern homosexual communities.[51] Many unaccompanied rural queer migrants found their way to Belfast, but the city always had the feel of a large comprehensible town instead of a major unknowable metropolis. By the early twentieth century there was an intricate network of pubs, cafés, shops, and even churches where queer Belfastmen could create social networks, but these spaces were always shared with the rest of society. To survive without scandalous exposure, the queer scene had to remain visibly respectable. But in other ways this everyday familiarity could also be useful.

Predictable daily patterns of work and leisure brought the same men into repeat contact in ways that helped them discover the desires of others more slowly and carefully. These contradictions of the middling city make it a specific urban typography rather than just a shadow or poorer cousin of the liberatory big city, and appreciating that distinction might help renew the queer urban paradigm in novel ways, given how there are far more small cities than metropolises.[52]

Belfast was intimate in other ways that challenge us to think about the divisions and experiences of its modern experience. When I was searching for the queer scene, I was vigilant for echoes of sectarianism, and not just because of the obvious role it played in broader society. Race and ethnicity have sexually structured segregated cities elsewhere in the world, whether the cultural power of these categories led to totally separate scenes or an erotically charged slumming by White queers into predominantly Black neighborhoods.[53] Though there is some evidence that the scene was unequal in Belfast too because of the poorer socioeconomic status of Catholics, the middling size of the city and the visually indistinct nature of the two communities ensured that relationships across the divide were almost an inevitability. At the same time, the intimacy of Belfast meant that friends, family, and neighbors often knew about the queerness of their men. Intense connections of kin and community had survived in urbanizing Ulster precisely because they were so vital for the everyday navigation of a sectarian culture—a necessity to maintain the safety and solidity of their religious and political community. But when other members of society were confronted with the fact of a man's same-sex desire there could still be benevolent toleration: an acceptance of sexual difference, if not the sort of celebration that is today called Pride.[54] Given the close connection between queer men and their families, the relative visibility of their social networks within the city, and even a nonsectarianism, Belfast before the 1950s confounds any expectations we might have had of only oppression, difficulty, and isolation.

The city's exceptional imbrication in a web of unique imperial, political, and religious forces both allowed for and even encouraged this ambiguously intimate middling experience. Ireland technically became a part of the United Kingdom after the Acts of Union in 1800, but the history of English colonial settling, as well as the pseudo-scientific racism that positioned "Celtic" peoples as lower than "Anglo Saxon," meant it was hardly an equal partner. Ireland still had an active role in supplying soldiers and administrators for colonial exploitation elsewhere, however, and were received as White in those places rather than Other. Yet experiences in Ireland differed by social class or region too, most obviously in Ulster, where there were far stronger emotional links with Britain and its sovereignty remains. Ireland's colonial history—like the history of all places that found themselves encountering European powers—was unique, as has now long been recognized by historians.[55] Asking whether Ireland was a colony or not has become too simple a question—a framing that does not capture the complexities and paradoxes of how historical colonial cultures worked, nor how they were actually experienced.[56] The island has grown more diverse over the last two decades, with globalization and greater European integration transforming the demographics of the south especially. Irish historians have responded by working with a consciously decolonizing lens, emphasizing how the structures of colonialism have continued to influence the country far beyond the classic era of empire.[57]

The colonial and then partially postcolonial relationship between Britain and Ireland in the late nineteenth and twentieth centuries certainly structured both the representations and realities of Irish queerness. The Victorian laws that regulated same-sex encounters in Ireland originated from Westminster, with the most prominent, the Criminal Law Amendment Act of 1885, being passed in response to moral panics about prostitution and child sexual exploitation in London and remaining on the statute book in both jurisdictions after partition. That said, this law was only rarely used in Belfast to punish men who had sex with men, with rarely more than one or two cases in most years, a rate that was roughly three times lower than the British capital at the turn of the twentieth century.[58] A degree of regional autonomy over the legal system also meant that the Vagrancy Law Amendment Act of 1898, which was used extensively in London to arrest men for soliciting, was not extended to Ireland until 1912, and even after that date it was almost never put to work against queer men in the north.[59] The British Empire may have shaped the legal definition of same-sex desire, but how the police and courts then applied it remained a local matter.

There were similar complexities in how the discourse of same-sex desire worked in Irish cultural politics. Public debates about queerness were infrequent or euphemistic on both sides of the Irish Sea, but a series of outrages—notable among them the Dublin Castle Scandal (1884), London's Cleveland Street Scandal (1889), and the infamous downfall of Oscar Wilde (1895)—shaped a range of contradictory understandings about "unnatural crimes." British commentators were happy to stereotype the Irish as irrational, which included their sexual behavior, but this narrative was not surprisingly rejected in Ireland. Instead, the evolving anti-colonial and revolutionary position was that same-sex desire was essentially alien to their country. In this rhetoric, or perhaps genuine belief for some, it was obviously the sexually impure British who were to blame. Their soldiers paid "fallen women" for sex in Irish garrison towns while the dissolute governing class corrupted the working Catholic lads of Dublin—as was the story publicly weaved about the Dublin Castle Scandal. In both cases, the morality of the Celt was endangered by imported Anglo-Saxon lust.[60] Irish nationalists responded to these anxieties by building a movement rooted in male power and pushing back on the colonial stereotyping of Ireland as inferior or feminized by its relationship to Britain.[61] Resisting accusations of savagery and sexual immorality meant denying the existence of queerness before colonization and stressing its foreignness in the present and was a useful political tool for insisting on self-governance, as contemporary nationalists in African and Arabic nations also recognized.[62]

Unionists and Protestants in the north of Ireland had an uneasy position in this discourse of imported sin and, as we will see later, could find themselves attacked by nationalists for the same sexual hypocrisies as the British. Probably as a response to this possibility, the governors of Belfast preferred to ignore or actively suppress any evidence that same-sex desire was a normal part of life in their city. After the creation of Northern Ireland, this situation of tacit silence only heightened. The governing class remained emotionally and politically wedded to Britain but insisted their corner of the United Kingdom reigned morally superior.[63] A pious self-image now set paradoxical limits on what the government and leading institutions were willing to say or do to tackle sexual crime, with the police force and local unionist-dominated press largely falling in line. There was probably a hostility from the educated leaders of this deeply religious society toward the idea that sex between men could ever be normal or acceptable, but they were caught in a bind: trying to root it out or even talk about the problem was tantamount to accepting it existed at all. When part of the rhetoric about unnatural perversions had long been that they were foreign in origin, admitting such crimes still existed in semi-self-governing Northern Ireland would have been worse than overlooking them altogether. Occasional outbursts in the newspapers were the only moments that the open secret was spoken, and only ever in relation to the specific details of court trials rather than as a broader social conversation. When it came to same-sex desire, the approach was unstated ignorance rather than public revelation.[64]

Given the cultural power of silence, it is no surprise that there is little evidence of a cohesive field of knowledge about sexuality in the north of Ireland before the late 1950s. This *Scientia sexualis*, as in Michel Foucault's famous schema, had begun to emerge on the European continent from the eighteenth century but by the final third of the nineteenth was breathlessly categorizing a range of deviant behaviors, desires, and bodily understandings, from sadism to psychical hermaphroditism.[65] In the south of Ireland, the political and social power of the Catholic Church was too dominant an influence to allow such a conversation to flourish, and individual sin rather than innate sexuality remained the way that society officially thought about men who had sex with men.[66] Though the Catholic Church obviously held less sway in Ulster, the Protestant churches in the region played much the same role in discouraging an academic field about homosexuality to develop. One renegade Belfast Methodist minister, about whom we will learn more later, recognized in the late 1930s that most of his colleagues still did not have a clue about the latest medical thinking on what he called homoeroticism.[67]

The obsession of the Irish churches with female morality only compounded their blind spots about male desires. In the Victorian era, women were categorized in both pseudoscientific and religious thought, Catholic and Protestant, as being blessed with a moral superiority when it came to sex. If women ignored that natural impulse, such as by conceiving a child outside of marriage, they could find themselves cast out into reformatory homes or shamefully sent out of the community to have their babies. Men instead were supposedly driven by a carnality that they were helpless to control. Their sexual indiscretions were mostly ignored or blamed on external factors, like the wayward women who tempted them or the effects of the demon drink.[68] Into the mid-twentieth century, this gender hypocrisy only strengthened. The anxieties of the postcolonial Catholic moral project in the Irish Free State were fixated on pure women as the guardians of the nation, and that rhetoric proliferated in response in Northern Ireland too.[69]

It was mostly those who paid women for sex who benefited from Ireland's gendered moral hypocrisy, but some queer men in Belfast were also able to act outside of oppressive cultural norms. Even if they were publicly exposed for having sex with other men, they seemed to have a better chance of recovering from that social stigma than the unfortunate women who offended the rigid Irish moral code.[70] Unfortunately, these divergent expectations have also made the experiences of queer women difficult to uncover. Women were far less free to create the same sort of social and sexual environments as men, which has had the effect of making queer women "twice marginal and twice invisible" in Ulster.[71] Unlike in other more permissive European and North American scenes, it was not until the 1960s and 1970s, with the gay and women's liberation movements, that they began to share urban social spaces with queer men and become more visible in the historical record.[72]

Policing approaches in Belfast reflected the gendered double standard as well as the powerful culture of purposeful silence about queerness. The police certainly knew that men who had sex with men walked among them. Why else would they record as evidence how they had found products that could be used as lubricants, such as Vaseline or cold cream, in the pockets of men they arrested? When they gave their witness statements to the courts, they described in gripping detail the mechanics of how men were meeting men in public toilets.[73] Constables were also close enough to the neighborhoods they patrolled—indeed, often living in them—to be aware of the family secrets and gossip that could circulate about queer men.[74] But arrests for gross indecency or buggery remained low until the late 1950s, still rarely being more than a couple of men each year and often none at all. In fact, there was only one case, during the mid-1920s, where a constable seemingly returned purposefully to the alleys in Belfast that many knew were being used for casual sexual encounters. He told the court, perhaps with some pride, "I had a similar prosecution before about 12 months ago. I got men in a urinal."[75] Almost every other occasion that a man ended up in court was instead the result of an unexpected discovery of public sexual indiscretion.

Life may have been tough for queer men in Belfast in many respects, but it was arguably not as hard as in Dublin in the mid-twentieth century, where there were periodical campaigns of police entrapment or surveillance, or even in the much smaller city of Cork, where a special vice squad operated for a time.[76] There was certainly nowhere near the same sort of consistent monitoring, harassment, and prosecution of men that could be found in Paris in the 1870s, London in the 1930s and 1940s, or West Germany in the decades after the Second World War.[77] It was also exceptionally rare for any evidence to be gathered about queer sex that had happened behind closed doors or as part of a long-term more discreet relationship. Between 1890 and 1958, just six court cases of sex between men in Belfast involved encounters in a private house, and in three of these the evidence was only gathered after complaints about public sex. The home and a man's authority over it was often assumed as being beyond the remit of the law in Ireland, a society where privacy was fiercely protected. But when it came to other sex-related crimes, such as infanticide or the concealment of birth, the police *did* breach the domestic boundary to monitor the behavior of women—just another example of the gendered double standard.[78]

The police in Belfast had other pragmatic and ideological reasons for not wanting to uncover what queer men did in alleyways or urinals, let alone how they behaved behind closed doors. Before the 1920s, the Royal Irish Constabulary was under-resourced and overworked, demoralized by low pay, and ground down by trying to keep a lid on a tinder box ready to ignite. After partition, the financial situation improved for the reformed Royal Ulster

Constabulary, but there were renewed risks from nationalist paramilitaries, especially in the early years of the new jurisdiction. The seeming absence of any public debate in Northern Ireland's parliament and no directive to crack down on queer men in public gave the individual policeman a justification for his discretion. Without a firm steer from politicians, he could prioritize policing behavior that directly endangered the public, property, or security of the province. Those crimes that had more obvious victims were a higher priority than those that did not, which is one explanation for the high level of evidence of sexual offences against children or younger men in the criminal archive. But above all, containing the dangerous and aggrieved Catholic minority in their midst was the new police force's primary directive from the Protestant unionist administration.[79]

Turning a blind eye or simply moving men on, which certainly happened in other cities in Britain and Ireland, was probably an attractive option for the constable on his beat in Belfast.[80] A time-consuming moral crusade was never going to be rewarded by a political administration that was happy to experience ignorance as bliss when it came to queer sex. Constables also knew that their own word as a witness was often not enough to secure a conviction in a guilt-beyond-doubt legal system, especially if the accused were smart enough to not say anything incriminating and no other witnesses came forward, both of which were common in Belfast. In that context, there was little to be personally gained for a constable from revealing sexual acts that almost always took place out of public view.

An absence of evidence is not evidence of absence, however, and the lack of a regional conversation about male sexual deviance did not preclude its expression. In fact, and somewhat paradoxically, secrecy and silence only enabled more diverse experiences of same-sex desire in Belfast, because there was no strong legal or medical discourse of pathological homosexuality.[81] As we will see, it was only after the Second World War that the relationship between divergent sexual desires and societal silence began to break down, with devastating consequences for queer intimacy in Belfast. But until that point, a multitude of rich and often contradictory ways to be queer had room to flourish—a scene that *Belfastmen* will reconstruct in all its vibrant color.

I first came across Thomas Gibney in 2017 when I was word-searching digital newspaper archives for Irish examples of "unnatural crime." He appeared in several articles about the so-called Belfast Scandal, an event that rocked the city and was a hot topic of discussion in both Britain and Ireland, though entirely forgotten today. The reports could tell me what the unfortunate arrested men had been doing with each other, if only in euphemistic language, but Thomas appeared as just a name: a man without a history, caught in a desperate moment and seemingly destined for a miserable future. After gathering more basic genealogical detail from the criminal archive, I searched backward and forward in time for other sources of information about his life, from birth certificate to obituary. Less than a generation ago, reconstructing this life would have taken years and a good deal of luck too, if it was ever feasible at all. But now, because of mass digitization, a story of an unremarkable and forgotten working-class man could be wrenched away from sensational reporting and the cold legal gaze of the state. There was simply far more to Thomas Gibney's life than just what he did with other men in public toilets or backstreet bars. Over the following chapters of this book, I trace how this life and many more challenge us to reconsider what it meant to be queer in a middling Irish city in the time before gay liberation.

Chapter 1

The Intimate Queer City

Joseph "Wilson" McCullough was born in 1920 and grew up in a working-class district of west Belfast, where his father and uncle ran a small grocer's shop.[1] Instead of following them into the family business when he left school, McCullough first found a job in Henry Matier's, a well-known manufacturer of linen handkerchiefs. At the age of eighteen, he then took up a position in Clifford's, a British company that sold the "unmistakable London cut" in men's clothing on affordable credit to provincial shoppers.[2] When he was not working in the High Street store, McCullough was a familiar face on Belfast's queer scene. In 1938, he was picked up by David Strain. The older man had been driving his car on July 12, while trying to avoid the marching Orangemen who took over the city on that date, when he met the eyes of McCullough—tailoring scissors still in his top pocket—from across the street. McCullough confidently went over to the driver's side to make conversation and happily accepted the offer of a lift. Before dropping McCullough off a couple of streets from his home, Strain took the young man's hand and found his caresses eagerly returned. "Do you know," Strain remarked, "I think we will become good friends—at least I hope we will, because I like you." After complimenting the older man on his beautiful eyes, McCullough made his own feelings clear by leaning in to receive a kiss on the forehead before promising they would meet again soon.[3]

Just under a week later, David Strain took Wilson McCullough out to his country hut, where they kissed more passionately after talking about Oscar Wilde and their shared experiences of trying to find partners in the city. "Have you had any men friends?" Strain tentatively asked. McCullough admitted that not only had there been others but there was one at that moment too.[4] The lover in question was Charles O'Hara, who was almost double McCullough's age. He was the son of a Ballymena man who had moved into the city in the 1890s to work as a clerk in the busy asylum on the Falls Road. Though the patriarch of the O'Haras had managed to obtain decent white-collar work, his early death in 1907 from tuberculosis, when Charles was just four years old, left the family in financial trouble. In 1911, when the census was taken, an enumerator recorded how a young widow was supporting herself and four children under the age of twelve on a linen smoother's wage.[5]

Whether Wilson McCullough and Charles O'Hara had met fleetingly on the streets or by another method is long forgotten, but perhaps their Presbyterian religion, origins in the west of the city, and working-class backgrounds were a few things that kept them together. A shared love of literature was certainly another bond. Kenneth Matthews's *Aleko* (1934) was one book they read and passed around to other queer men. It told the story of an English teacher in Greece and his "pure" love for one of his pupils, and perhaps these two lovers felt it relevant to their own intergenerational relationship. *The Flame of Freedom* (1936), by Reginald Underwood, was a pulpier tale of complex desires, unrequited passions, and the inevitable suicide; at the least, it gave a clearer glimpse into the kind of queer subculture that the two men wanted to inhabit.[6]

David Strain never warmed to Wilson McCullough's boyfriend. He found Charles O'Hara abrasive and even sarcastic and was offended when this somewhat secretive man refused to sign a visitors' book at the country hut. By then O'Hara was working as a clerk and was presumably worried about what might happen if the police found this list of only male friends next to a bookcase heaving with rare queer novels from all over the world. More than a hint of jealousy runs through Strain's description of their love triangle too, which is probably why he stopped seeing McCullough over the winter of 1938. When he then spotted the young man back on "the prowl" in one of the city's more notorious alleyways early the next year, he was surprised. "So that's what Wilson is doing now," he wrote in his diary before speculating, perhaps smugly, "Evidently he and Charles are through."[7] As a romantic idealist—or a bit of a prude, depending on your views of nonmonogamy—David Strain thought it impossible that a committed love could coexist with casual sex with other partners. But he was wrong.

By the mid-1940s, Wilson McCullough and Charles O'Hara had moved to London and were rooming together in the grand Victorian development of Lancaster Gate that overlooked Kensington Gardens, and both were doing white-collar work. Apart from some time spent in Canada in the late 1940s and possibly elsewhere in the British Empire in the early 1950s, they carried on living in Notting Hill for over two decades. In 1972, O'Hara died of cancer. On the death certificate, his lover of about thirty-five years officially recorded their relationship as cousins. Even though sex between men had been legalized in England five years previously, if not yet in their native Northern Ireland, McCullough had perhaps still been compelled to try to keep their relationship secret.[8] He stayed in the south of England for the rest of his life, moving at some point to the quieter town of Worthing, but echoes of his Ulster origins and lasting connections remained. Sometime after he died in 2012, at the age of ninety-two, a family gravestone was placed in Belfast's Roselawn cemetery; it memorializes Wilson McCullough not as an ambitious queer migrant but simply as a "beloved son."[9]

Wilson McCullough's queer life revolved around the city. When he was not cruising—that is, looking to make contact and even have sex with other men in semipublic places—he was visiting them at their places of work for passionate trysts. At other times, he simply socialized with queer friends at the theater or the cinema or had dancing classes alongside his older male lover.[10] For historians of queerness, this lifestyle will not be that surprising. It is more evidence of two linked arguments of a now well-established scholarship: Past metropolises could house vibrant cultures of men who desired men long before gay liberation; and, through its specific built environment and layout, the city shaped how those modern understandings and experiences of sexuality were formed.[11] Even if this is a familiar story, the absence of its telling for Belfast—or the assumption that it did not exist at all—is an oversight worth correcting.

In this chapter, I show how men who desired men were active all over the city, from streets to social clubs, cinemas to shops, and parks to public libraries. They were even a mundane presence, not yet a source of moral panic. A few parts of their lives remained mostly invisible, like the sexual encounters hidden in the dark of alleys and public toilets, but many of the spaces they used were shared with the rest of the population who lived, worked, and played in the city. This world came into being after the intense urbanization of the mid- to late nineteenth century and the creation of economic and social cultures where men were separated from the watchful eyes of rural or small-town life (and often women too). At the same time, queer Belfast was supported not just by the anonymity of a growing metropolis but also by the everyday opportunities for familiarity that an intimate middling city provided. The result was a complex world where public and private, social and sexual all overlapped—and often in plain view.

Street Life

The Victorian era was famously characterized by the advent of "shock cities": settlements that seemed to spring from nowhere to triple or quadruple in size in a matter of decades. For writers and thinkers at the time, such places were a vantage point to understand a new age that could frighten yet fascinate.[12] But this general trend of urban-industrial growth was barely apparent in Ireland. Over the course of the nineteenth century, accelerating especially after the Great Famine (1845–1852), most long-established towns—not to mention rural areas—were losing rather than gaining people as the overall population of the country essentially halved. British colonial rule exploited and extracted wealth, and there was little domestic industrial development. Irish migrants used their labor to fuel the booming cities of North America and Britain instead of those in their home country. Even Dublin, the seat of British administrative power, had just a modest climb in its metropolitan population from around 252,000 people to 404,000 between 1841 and 1911, with much of the growth being suburban. Dublin was not a manufacturing base, and its port had relatively little to process too, given the ongoing struggles of the agricultural economy.[13]

Only the northeast of Ulster, and its capital of Belfast especially, managed to buck these trends of industrial and demographic malaise. Even if its peculiar socioreligious culture marked Belfast as unique, the city had more in common economically with similarly growing British provincial centers like Manchester, Glasgow, and Birmingham than it did with Dublin, Cork, or Galway. Unskilled labor was abundant and cheap, there was easy access to the centers of heavy engineering and raw material in northern England and Scotland, and there were close ancestral links to those areas too. Shipbuilding flourished at the turn of the twentieth century, and the older, established linen manufacturing—if volatile—also continued to contribute. The effect of industrial growth on the urban environment was striking. The port teemed with dockers and sailors from all over the world while predominantly Protestant migrants from the surrounding Ulster countryside poured into the factories and shipyards. The population of "Linenopolis" or "the Athens of the North"—satirical sobriquets of the eighteenth century that were still adopted unironically by some at the turn of the twentieth century—exploded from 75,000 in 1841 to a startling 387,000 in 1911. If the metropolitan area is included in those statistics, the region was touching half a million people. On the eve of the First World War, Belfast was comfortably the largest city on the island and had entered the top ten for Britain and Ireland.[14]

For scholars of sexuality, this type of rapid demographic growth and its concentration in urban areas has long been seen to have consequences for sexual behavior. Men of all classes, and in ever increasing numbers, were now drawn away from the old certainties of country life. Without the surveillant eyes of home, church, and family, some were freer to have sex with other men and even build fledgling cultures based around a shared recognition of that desire.[15] Though Irish men were never truly separated from their families, as we will see later, some certainly found freedom in the city. By digging into the backgrounds of those arrested for cruising, we can glimpse this pull of the city as early as the 1890s. William Christie, for example, was born into a family of farmers in Antrim in 1850. He moved to Belfast to look for work in his early forties, finding a job as a butler and lodging in a small house next door to a pub in the rowdy dockside district of Sailortown.[16] When he was not working, Christie spent some of his time on the cruising scene. Late one evening in January 1892, he found himself in trouble after approaching Allen Shaw, a seventeen-year-old industrial worker traveling home from seeing friends in east Belfast. Walking down Victoria Street on the northern edge of the city center, Christie apparently tried to pull the youth into a doorway, grabbed at his privates, and exposed his own too. When Shaw succeeded in brushing him off, Christie followed him further down the street, suggesting they go for a drink or back to his lodgings. When those offers did not work, Christie told the youth that he "could meet him on the street any night" before finally bidding him goodbye.[17]

Other men in the north of Ireland in the late nineteenth and early twentieth centuries made the same journey as William Christie. Young farmers from County Antrim, adolescent laborers from County Tyrone, and middle-aged postmen from County Down all came into Belfast to take up work and cruised in the time they now spent away from their families.[18] Their motivation to migrate was probably primarily economic; after all, only 20 percent of the city's household heads had been born there when the census was taken in 1901, and it is safe to say that the other 80 percent were not predominantly queer.[19] Even so, it was the changing nature of the modernizing city that enabled these men to fulfil different sorts of sexual desires.

In the mid- to late nineteenth century, the dazzling profits from industrialization had helped create a new and self-satisfied bourgeoisie, and their demands for a metropolis that reflected the might of its merchants reshaped the central urban district. Old housing was gradually swept away and replaced with large commercial buildings while the gaps were filled in with grand hotels, ornate theaters, and spacious department stores. Royal Avenue (fig. 1.1), a wide boulevard laid out in the 1880s, stood at the heart of the new city and was eventually crowned with an imposing Baroque-style city hall in 1906. The old town hall had only been officially opened in 1871; Belfast's ascendancy was so rapid that this restrained red brick and sandstone building was now a reminder of the limits of previous ambition.[20]

Belfast, for all its enterprising growth, was still neither beautiful nor refined in the eyes of many onlookers. Cathal O'Byrne, a romantic Irish nationalist, described it as "one of the ugliest cities in the world" in his reminiscing historical portrait of 1946, while the popular novelist St. John Ervine had already dubbed it an "upstart city . . . without breeding and tradition" and home to people "full of contempt for those who have not made money." But these negative writers could not help but be fascinated by Belfast's infectious energy.[21] Even against the backdrop of the Great Depression, which was hard on the old heavy industries of the northeast of Ulster, the central streets could heave with pedestrians, many of whom had been brought in on a modern transport system from the growing suburbs. In the run-up to Christmas in 1930, a journalist in *Ireland's Saturday Night*, a popular weekly entertainment newspaper, described the scene around the main shopping district (figs. 1.2 and 1.3): "a mass of people overflowing the pavements . . . a sea of heads . . . alive with movement against a background of bright and gaily coloured windows." This "Castle Place crawl," as the newspaper dubbed it, was "the only way to get along."[22]

Countless historians and literary scholars have demonstrated how it was this sort of creation of a modern urban center and its bustling streets that brought forth opportunities for men to meet other men. Anonymously lingering among lively crowds and waiting for a glimpse that confirmed a mutual recognition provided men with a chance for clandestine erotic expression.[23] A few in Belfast were brazen enough to publicly touch those they thought were reciprocating their signs of interest. In 1928, for example, Hugh Stitt—a married industrial worker—was in a large mass that had gathered to hear an open-air Salvation Army service when he realized a man in front was feeling his crotch. "I had you well on there," this man boldly told his quarry, presumably having noticed a growing lump in Stitt's trousers. Stitt must have been conflicted, because he told the cruiser that he ought to be ashamed of himself and then led him into the arms of the police, despite his seeming erection.[24]

Figure 1.1. A view of the main streets of Castle Place and Royal Avenue. A. R. Hogg, *From Donegall Place. Trams* (1914), BELUM.Y1732. Courtesy of National Museums NI, Ulster Museum Collection.

Much of the surviving criminal archive evidence of street cruising in Belfast is about unwanted, aggressive, or ambiguous advances because they were the encounters that were most likely to end with a man being reported to the police, who were then duty-bound to investigate. Through more personal sources such as diaries, which have the benefit of not being directly refracted through the criminalizing lens of the legal system, we can see how most encounters on the streets were usually more careful. By the early twentieth century, cruising was so formulaic and ritualistic that those in the know in Belfast were even amused when they were approached. As just one representative incidence, take this interaction between David Strain and a young man in February 1939. Strain was making his usual route around the city center when he saw Hugh Herron walking ahead. After following at a

FIGURE 1.2. The busy area of Castle Junction. *High St. from Castle Place. Belfast* (1939), HOYFM.BT.315, *Belfast Telegraph*. Courtesy of National Museums NI, Ulster Folk Museum Collection.

distance for a while, he finally approached and asked for a light. Herron, who was a working-class lad aged just twenty, understood what was happening; he laughed and struck a match and accepted the offer of a cigarette too. After chatting while walking together, they made a future date at Strain's suburban home. Just a few weeks later, Herron confessed his feelings to Strain in a letter: "to be so much in love with you and see you so seldom is heart-rending," he insisted.[25]

Many other queer encounters in Belfast began and ended in this way. Cruisers approached those they believed were lingering in doorways or next to lampposts, and asked simply where they were from or what they thought about the weather. Others waited until they noticed a man gazing curiously at them, whether openly or in the reflection of shop windows, before starting a conversation. A chance connection, easily made as the other users of

FIGURE 1.3. The reverse view down Castle Junction. *High St. to Castle Place, Belfast* (1928), HOYFM.BT.314, *Belfast Telegraph*. Courtesy of National Museums NI, Ulster Folk Museum Collection.

the city continued with their daily business all around, could then result in a sexual liaison or a friendship developed somewhere more private.[26]

Most of the queer cruising took place in roughly one square mile of the small city center (see fig. 1.4), bounded in the east by the River Lagan that flowed into Belfast Lough, in the north by the working-class Sailortown district that lay just beyond Corporation Square, in the south by the gleaming new City Hall, and in the west by the large shops of Royal Avenue. Within this zone, there were a couple of areas that were especially well frequented. Queen's Square (fig. 1.5), named for the royal visit of Queen Victoria in the 1840s and later home to the Albert Clock, was in the oldest part of Belfast and on the edge of the commercial district. It was a central node for transport: just across the bridge from the major rail station of Queen's Quay that brought in commuters to the east of the city, right in the path of disembarking sailors and passengers from daily steamships, and the terminating point for several suburban tram lines. Boisterous pubs lined the southern edge of the square, and there was a large and particularly well-known public toilet.[27]

Movement, alcohol, semipublic spaces: all these were the necessary ingredients for casual queer encounters. We know, for example, that the strikingly handsome British-diplomat-turned-Irish-revolutionary Roger Casement probably made good use of the Queen's Square area in the early twentieth century. His scandalous diaries have been contentious for over a century, with some still believing a conspiracy theory that the British state fabricated them to dissuade public support for a repeal of Casement's death sentence for his role in the Easter Rising of 1916. Forensic expertise and contextual research, however, have demonstrated the authenticity of the writings as well as recognizing the politically homophobic reasons why some nationalists have wanted to put this Irish hero back into the closet.[28] Any squeamishness of that kind would certainly be compounded by an entry from May 1910, when Casement recorded how he had met a man near the Albert Clock whose penis was "huge and curved," and the owner was "awfully keen" (at least for the price of just over four shillings).[29] Other queer men prowled the streets around this area and set dates in some of the bars and hotels. Late at night, when the major businesses had shut, sexual liaisons happened in the dark of nearby doorways or alleys.[30]

Though not mentioned by Roger Casement, there was another location a stone's throw away from Queens's Square that lay at the heart of the city's cruising culture for probably a century or more. The Belfast Entries are a cluster of alleys, some partly covered, that date back to the early eighteenth century. They link together Ann Street and High Street, between Cornmarket and Church Lane. Originally, they were convenient walkways through the gardens of the houses that fronted these main thoroughfares, but eventually they began to facilitate trade, playing host to workshops and offices as well as shops and pubs. From their earliest days they were also residential, especially for merchants but also the poorer classes who toiled in the growing city. After the rich began to leave the dirty industrializing city for more distinguished suburban surroundings in the mid-nineteenth century, the demographic began to lean more heavily toward the disreputable. In 1852, the Reverend W. M. O'Hanlon described Hudson's Entry, for example, as "a complete den of vice and uncleanness, probably unsurpassed in what is called the civilized world."[31] Inebriation, violence, and female prostitution, he lamented, were endemic. Urban redevelopment gradually cleared away some of the worst housing of the Entries, and there was always a romantic appreciation for the historical events that had taken place in some of the old

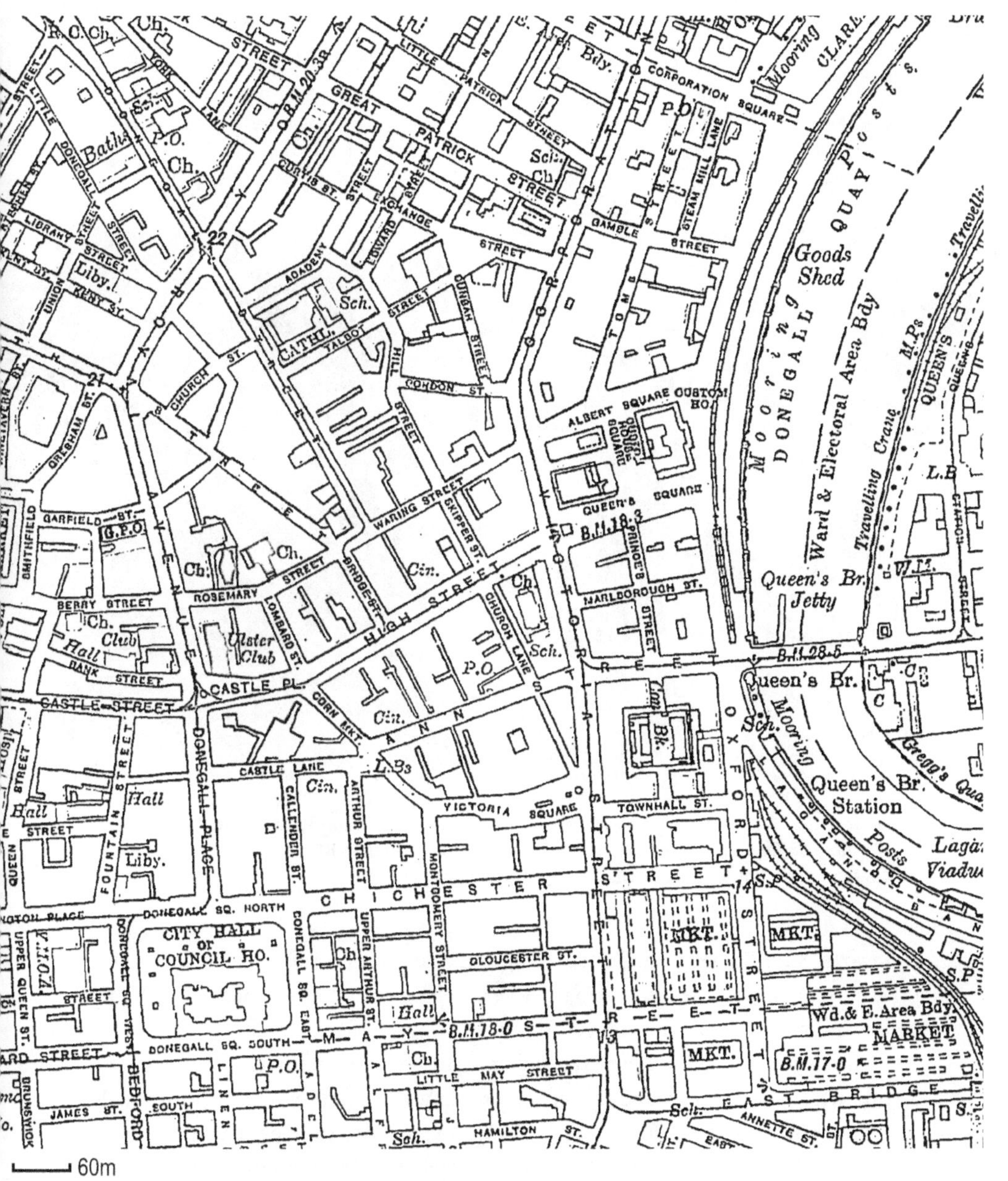

FIGURE 1.4. Map of Belfast's city center. Adapted by Cormac McAteer from the Department of Agriculture for Northern Ireland Ordnance Survey Northern Ireland Map (1923), which was scanned and georeferenced by Conor Graham and Lorraine Barry, LPS/OSNI MOU203, GIS Unit, CDDA, School of GAP, QUB Belfast © 2015.

FIGURE 1.5. A sailor lurks suggestively outside a bar. *Queen's Square, Belfast, with Sailor in War Time Uniform, Horse and Cart, Air Raid Shelter* (1943), HOYFM.BT.390, *Belfast Telegraph*. Courtesy of National Museums NI, Ulster Folk Museum Collection.

taverns (the Society of United Irishmen was founded in Crown Entry, for instance). Still, it was well into the twentieth century before these alleys truly lost a reputation for deviance.[32]

If the unruly character of the Belfast Entries made them attractive for anyone who sought to escape respectable society, their design and location made them especially good for queer cruising. By the late nineteenth century, the sensibilities and the senses of upright Victorians were becoming offended by working men who urinated in the streets. In response to a public health drive, toilets were now erected in growing cities. In Belfast, the Entries were reimagined as an ideal out-of-the-way site for corrugated iron pissoirs. Though these urinals did limit street peeing, they had an unintentional effect: the creation of a public-private or gray area space where men could legitimately have their penises out.[33] Larger public toilets existed in other areas of the city center but were locked at night and often had uniformed attendants in the daytime.[34] The

Entries were instead more open and naturally harder to police (see figs. 1.6 and 1.7). There was little space for a constable or member of the public to set up watch, and there were usually at least two routes to pass in or out when a cruiser's suspicions were raised. If the space offered a degree of seclusion, the Entries were also right in the middle of a bustling zone of shops and department stores that provided crowds to disappear into. In late 1931, one policeman explained to a probably shocked courtroom just how the entry urinals could be used. Constable James Rutledge had been patrolling Hamilton Court at about seven o'clock in the evening when he heard a shuffling noise in a urinal directly behind the Hemisphere pub. Moving closer, and helped by a streetlamp above, he spied two men masturbating each other in one of four small compartments. Each time the culprits heard someone come into the entry, they stopped and "took up positions as if they were using [the urinal] in the ordinary way." They then went to the door to watch the interlopers leaving before retaking up their sexual encounter. Unfortunately, on this occasion they did not spot the constable and were arrested after a few minutes of his watching.[35]

There were other public urinals dotted about the city center that were suitable for cruising, and men sometimes toured between them.[36] The large and ornate stalls of the Great Northern Railway station, at Great Victoria Street on the eastern edge of the city center, relied on the transience of travel to cloak queer activities, for example, while a urinal behind the Central Library just off Royal Avenue also seems to have been notorious from at least the 1890s, perhaps helped by its proximity to the raucous boardinghouse districts of the docks and Carrick Hill.[37] But none of these conveniences were as popular as the network of urinals between High Street and Ann Street. Between the 1890s and 1930s, various men were discovered here, from adolescent boys who sold sex to older middle-class men to drunken working-class lovers who could have been at home with their wives.[38] Even the police were apparently not protected from being propositioned by queer cruisers if they ventured down the alleys; in 1892, one soldier-chef received a slap on the ear after apparently demanding a constable "show me the size of yours" outside a Crown Entry urinal and was later discovered being penetrated by another soldier in a urinal a few streets away.[39] Little wonder that the prudish David Strain could complain so viciously in the early 1940s about "all the scum flitting about or loafing about the various entries" and warned his young lovers off the area.[40] Despite his moral misgivings, public toilets provided a space for self-fulfillment, even if it was brief when compared to relationships that could take place behind closed doors, though the latter could sometimes follow on naturally from the former.[41]

Desires for respectability and public hygiene had unintended effects: they put bodily functions out of sight but created new sites of sexual intimacy.

Figure 1.6. The dimly lit Crown Entry. A. R. Hogg, *Looking to Ann Street, Showing Cave Bar* (1914), BELUM.Y1860. Courtesy of National Museums NI, Ulster Museum Collection.

Public parks—envisioned as the healthy lungs of the city and an opportunity to civilize working-class leisure time—give us another example of the same process.[42] The expanse of open space coupled with private thickets made them relatively hard to police. Cruising depended on watching and being watched; lingering suggestively while looking at the flowers, eyeing passersby and trying to catch a glance, striking up a conversation before moving out of sight.[43] The first municipal green space in Belfast, Ormeau Park, was

FIGURE 1.7. Pottinger's Entry—a site of many popular pubs. A. R. Hogg, *Towards Ann Street* (1939), BELUM.Y2553. Courtesy of National Museums NI, Ulster Museum Collection.

laid out in the 1870s to the expanding suburban east of the city and was a useful combination of open vistas and secluded groves (see fig. 1.8). It seems to have been Belfast's busiest green space for cruising, if only rarely revealed to the authorities.

One court case from 1937 demonstrates how encounters could happen in Ormeau Park. Liam Murphy, a seventeen-year-old working-class boy, explained to the courts that he had entered the park with an older man late

FIGURE 1.8. Several men suspiciously eye a photographer. Robert John Welch, *View on One of the Main Paths, Near the River Lagan*, (1928), BELUM.Y.W.10.60.12. Courtesy of National Museums NI, Ulster Museum Collection.

one afternoon. Sitting on a bench along one of many winding paths, the more experienced man told the youth to read his newspaper while looking around to see if anyone was coming. They then masturbated each other. When a group of women walked past, the lovers buttoned up and walked a bit before coming back to the same seat to resume. Unfortunately for Murphy, a park ranger had been keeping watch, and he was caught. The older man was luckier, running out of the park to disappear into the surrounding working-class neighborhood.[44]

There are more examples of men who usually managed to find partners in parks, both in Ormeau and others across the city. They had sex hidden from view in ditches or behind bushes, chatted in summer houses before finding privacy in a urinal, or simply reveled in the erotic acknowledgment of other cruisers who tried to catch their gaze.[45] In an era when the police were not on the lookout for male sexual transgressions, most of this culture went unnoticed or uninterrupted; it was just an everyday fact of Belfast's queer life. For some of the many Irish men who migrated to the city, the streets, toilets, and parks enabled and even encouraged a casual culture of queer cruising and sex. This was often a fleeting or transient experience, shaped by the cloak of relative anonymity that the busy city provided, if never without a total lack of physical and legal danger. At the same time, as we will now see, there was much about Belfast that was *not* anonymous—and that experience had its role to play in queer life too.

Sectarianism, Integration, Familiarity

Many of the dynamics of Belfast's urban cruising were broadly the same as other metropolises of this era. That said, there were elements of idiosyncrasy that are worth considering too. Like in almost every other aspect of everyday life in Belfast, the differences and power relations between Catholics and various denominations of Protestants also structured sexual encounters. On the one hand, the two communities were visually the same unless adorned in the parading gear of Orangeism or clutching rosary beads. The city center was relatively unsegregated too, if assumed Protestant and unionist in its loyalties, as demonstrated by the flying of the Union flag and prominent statues of British monarchs. Long before the heightening of tensions that came with the outbreak of the Troubles, the queer scene brought men from different ethnoreligious backgrounds into direct communication in a way that was less likely in sectarianized workplaces or neighborhoods.

When the Belfast Scandal broke out in 1890, after a male brothel was discovered just a stone's throw away from the ornate and imposing building that housed the city's governing harbor commissioners, it became clear that working men from both communities were not just having sex with each other. The six younger defendants, split equally between Catholic and Protestant, were also socializing in pubs that were technically in mostly segregated areas, like the Falls Road.[46] Some of the men were even in a romantic Irish nationalist troupe, the Emerald Minstrels, without that being an obstacle to queer friendship. The anonymity of the cruising scene, and some of the rowdy pubs and oyster bars down the alleyways of the city center, also brought men of different backgrounds together, if only for a fleeting moment. As just one example, in August 1925, a middle-class Presbyterian in his midforties was discovered having sex with a Catholic laborer of a similar age. They had met just after midnight, outside a dockside urinal. Both men had much to lose by being caught in a same-sex encounter: the former was a bachelor but had a good job in the civil service, whereas the latter had been married for twelve years.[47] Now exposed for having "grossly indecent" sex, and in public too, the fact that it had been with someone of a different religion hardly mattered at all.

Other queer men disobeyed the sectarian lines of the city, if only in the secretive cruising space of the urinal or over pints of stout in more socially permissive pubs.[48] But we should be careful of proclaiming sex across the divide a harbinger of a queer nonsectarianism. There were often clear power and class imbalances in these encounters. When relations took place between men of different religions, the paid participant was usually Catholic.[49] Two of the men charged in the Belfast Scandal, for example, lived in the predominantly Protestant Shankill neighborhood, and it was in their houses that some of the offenses allegedly took place. They were both older and better off and seemingly paid younger Catholic men for sex.[50]

Economically discriminated against in the city, Catholic youths and men certainly had a reason to sell their time or their bodies, and many Protestant men had the money to buy. Even so, as we will see more in chapter 4, these boys were not without agency, and the cash nexus allowed some Catholic youths to invert the usual classed and ethnoreligious dynamic.[51] Whether the latter were targeting the former out of an eroticization of the Other and not just their immediate availability is harder to know. Certainly, eroticization did happen in London and New York, where the rough-and-tumble Irish laborer was thought to be particularly virile and open to same-sex encounters by middle-class Englishmen and Americans.[52] But the writings of queer Protestants from Ulster—like the memoirist Robin Bryans, diplomat Roger Casement, and linen merchant David Strain—have only hints at cross-religion attraction. These men briefly mention being curious about the "brogue" or look of "Irish" youths but more because of an idealized masculine rural or nonpoliticized Celtic character than strictly religious identity.[53]

Life amid the gangs of sex-selling youths was mixed when it came to religious backgrounds, as we have already seen with the boys of the Belfast Scandal in 1890, but evidence of longer-term relationships or friendships between queer men of different religions is harder to come by, as are longer-term relationships in general. There are at least hints that the sectarian boundary could be breached, if not always without trepidation. When he was first exploring his queer desires, David Strain's closest confidant was a sympathetic Catholic hairdresser whom he even accompanied to mass, though not without privately recording how unimpressed he was, as a Reformed Presbyterian, with the Catholic idea of worship.[54] Another long romantic obsession with a shop-boy was also hampered because he suspected the youth's

Catholicism made him disloyal to Northern Ireland (and the boy certainly was open with and proud of his nationalism). As a result, Strain recorded, he felt an "inward urge to try and get a Protestant or at any rate one who does not show hate of his country." Though the friendship continued, it was ultimately held back because of how their different faiths and upbringings informed their political allegiances.[55]

All of David Strain's close friends were instead Protestant men. That said, in a city where Protestants outnumbered Catholics three or four to one and the former were far more likely to share Strain's middle-class business and linen industry background, circumstances could be as important as sectarianism. Toward the end of the 1930s, which not coincidentally was when Strain more fully embraced queer sex as well as platonic love, he does seem to have then started associating with more Catholic men. In 1941, for example, he entertained two seemingly queer Catholic friends at his home, and in 1943, he had a sexual and romantic relationship with another Catholic working-class youth.[56] Catholic men, if mostly from Dublin, were also a part of the group of friends that coalesced around Walter Smith and Cecil Bond (both of whom we will meet properly in chapter 4).[57] Sexual and social patterns were shaped by the political and territorial conflicts of the north of Ireland, but not to the extent that there were two totally separate queer communities in this era. In a city the size and character of Belfast, it would have been difficult and even undesirable to have such a division.

If the navigating of sectarianism made life in Belfast different for same-sex desiring men, so too did its relatively conservative mainstream culture. Men did not face extensive persecution, but the strength of moral puritanism and an awareness of the possible punishment meant a microcosm of the infamous scenes of legally permissive Paris or avant-garde Weimar Berlin was unlikely to develop in Ireland.[58] Thankfully, Belfastmen knew that the predictable patterns of everyday life gave them other ways to figure out the potential openness of men to a romantic or sexual approach. In 1921, the author Hugh A. MacCartan captured well the repetitive daily nature of industrial Belfast and the types of men who lived there. "The mazes of red-brick houses have sprung to life with the morning itself," he wrote in his admittedly boosterish *The Glamour of Belfast*, "artisans and labourers in dungarees filling the trams or footing it briskly to the foundries and shipyards; clerks and traders fingering the keys of those mammoth warehouses beside the docks; captains of industry from the palatial villas." For MacCartan, these rituals (see fig. 1.9) indicated the economic health of his bustling city. But for queer men, the rigors of the capitalist workday had a more important function: an opportunity to gradually learn more about a potential cruising target.[59] Men could assess

FIGURE 1.9. Workers stream across a bridge into the city. W. A. Green, *Queen's Bridge, Belfast* (n.d.), HOYFM.WAG.3728. Courtesy of National Museums NI, Ulster Folk Museum Collection.

each other's desires in a situation where outright rejection or violence was unlikely and were able to prejudge what might happen if they suggested a more intimate setting for a future conversation.

Walking, for all the technological advancement of the Victoria era, was still how most men moved around the center of this small city.[60] For cruisers, initial contact was often as others went about their daily routines, traveling to and from work especially. The first stage was to catch a glance or a smile, maybe when waiting patiently at the traffic lights or stuck in a queue for the shop. A second meeting might be a brief exchange of pleasantries, perhaps about the weather or the busyness of the streets. Men now became "nodding acquaintances," as David Strain put it in 1936.[61] Minor meetings gradually developed into longer casual conversations about shared interests—music, theater, the cinema. If everything was still proceeding amicably, questions could be asked about a man's home life, even how he felt about love and romance. Finally, a date could be set to meet elsewhere—a café, perhaps, or a private home.[62] Not all these encounters necessarily led to sex or romance, of course; there was still an ambiguity around categories of sexuality that meant the boundaries between friendship and desire were not so firmly set, as we will see more later. The result was that youths and men alike seemingly did not see anything strange about agreeing to meet again a man they had not previously known. Either way, the sheer possibility of queer intimacy—embedded deeply into the urban experience—was fundamental to everyday life in Belfast.

If walking was still common, urban and technological progress created some new spaces where queer daily routine also thrived.[63] Public transport, in Belfast as elsewhere, provides the best example. Belfast's first horse-drawn tramline arrived 1872; just over two decades later, there were six lines, twenty-four miles of track, and over eleven million annual passengers. The first half of the twentieth century, after the city corporation bought and electrified the network, then saw almost uninterrupted growth. By 1945—the peak of the system—there were 160 million annual rides across over thirty different routes as well as about sixty million on the trolleybus system that had begun at the end of the previous decade.[64] Trams played an important role in the everyday life of queer men in Belfast. After a connection had been made on the busy streets, it was easy to jump on one and travel to somewhere more private, whether a house or just wooded ground that lay near the end of the line.[65] Trams also provided a space where it was considered normal to pass the time by chatting with other passengers—an experience that was probably more likely in an intimate city like Belfast than it was in a heaving metropolis like London. But the intimacy of trams was not without its risks; in 1949, for example, one middle-aged schoolteacher traveling into Belfast from Bangor found himself led into the clutches of the police by a youth with whom he had started a suggestive conversation and to whom he later unwisely sent a romantic letter.[66]

David Strain was well-off enough to have his own motorcar as early as 1920, but he was also a frequent user of the trams, commuting from his suburban home to his work premises on Bedford Street. In his diaries, he describes countless occasions where he made a connection with youths or young men on the Ormeau Road route, chatting about the weather or the latest films. Sometimes these conversations led to future meetings, but his familiar visibility on public transport also made him open to cruising approaches elsewhere.[67] In early 1940, for example, Strain approached a man who was standing at a street corner in the city center and asked for a match. After the man accepted the return offer of a cigarette, they chatted about the weather and the blackout before taking a walk together. Eventually, the man agreed to go to Strain's office, where he admitted he already knew the queer proprietor because he had often seen him taking the tram.[68]

Even if men had not actually come to know each other gradually, this sense of familiarity could be performed as part of the cruising ritual. In 1934, David Strain described how he was walking away from Queen's Arcade, another known meeting site for queer men just off Royal Avenue, when he felt someone take his arm. When he turned around, he found a well-dressed gentleman clutching a bottle of whiskey. "Aren't you Penge?" the drinker asked tentatively. If Strain had reacted angrily, this would have been the end of the meeting. Instead he laughed and said no, which opened an avenue for a reply: "Gee but you are like him. I'm awfully sorry for making the mistake." Friendliness now confirmed, and potential queerness assumed, an invitation to move to the more intimate setting of a restaurant could be made (if rejected on this occasion, because Strain was into handsome youths and not older or stoutish men).[69] Not surprisingly, Strain learned from encounters such as these and brought the same tactic into his own cruising repertoire. In 1936, for example, he spotted a youth on the tram whom he already knew by sight and introduced himself. "Have you got a brother here representing a Manchester textile house?" he asked. The youth replied that he had no brothers but smiled as he did so, "so now the way is prepared for him to acknowledge me again when he sees me," Strain noted.[70]

In a larger and more anonymous metropolis, this approach would have been curious at best or suspicious at worst. But in a more middling-sized city, familiarity was a reasonable assumption to make. Men were given the opportunity of denial, but how they made it was more important than the fact that they did not know each other at all. Late one evening in 1937, for example, David Strain noticed a man in his midtwenties looking at his car as he drove down one of the main streets of the city center, so he pulled up to the curb and waited for the conversation to begin. "Oh! I am sorry; I thought it was another chap I knew," Strain tried as his opening gambit. When the youth laughed and replied "very sissily" that it was not a problem, he was invited into the car where they could talk more privately.[71] On countless occasions, Strain ran into youths or men he had previously met, whether during his everyday "town tour" or "prowl," as he put it, or through replies to his surreptitious personal adverts in the *Belfast Telegraph*.[72] Sometimes the repeat meeting was something to be quickly avoided or delicately negotiated, especially if a relationship had turned sour. But it could also be an opportunity to chat again or journey to somewhere more private to rekindle an old flame.[73] Some queer men even traveled around the town together, usually with men of their own class or milieu, to try to spot these examples of "that" or "it," as they euphemistically termed queerness. In doing so, they doubled their potential knowledge of the regular "downtown wanderers."[74]

The relative smallness of Belfast's queer scene made it easy to navigate while the lack of policing and public interest in what queer men were doing meant that the geography of cruising remained relatively stable in comparison to other cities, where there was a cat-and-mouse game between the police and their victims.[75] A final example of the familiarity that was available to those who chose to look for it would be Tommy Millar. He was a happy-go-lucky type and very active on the cruising scene. David Strain first met him late one night when driving down Rosemary Street in the central shopping district of the city. Millar was apparently so confident that he simply got into the car and laughingly asked the older man how he had known him. On their way to Strain's country hut, the youth described many failed attempts at love but promised, "If you stay by me, you'll find I can stick by you!" It turned out that he already had two male lovers—one aged forty-two and the other aged twenty-eight. Over the next couple of years, David Strain could hardly go into the city center without bumping into Tommy Millar. He was hanging around the Entries, probably using the urinals for illicit pleasures; cruising the shop windows, like Dolcis Shoes (fig. 1.10), a recently opened London chain with a strikingly modernist frontage; or simply parading down the High Street, "looking very swish" in his silk suit.[76]

Histories of urban cruising have tended to focus on the practice as primarily enabled by the anonymity of the city: "the stuff of fleeting, ephemeral moments."[77] But in Belfast it was actually through an everyday familiarity—a culmination of moments that eventually ceased to be ephemeral—that a visible queer world began to take shape.

A Social and Commercial Scene

Given the centrality of street culture to queer life, one could be forgiven for assuming that Belfastmen spent all their time cruising outside, which would be no mean feat in a place as soggy as Ireland. There were certainly no exclusively gay venues before the 1960s, but that does not mean that men desiring men were not already using the commercial leisure scene of the city. The interwar decades were economically difficult for Ulster, but there was growth in urban retail, service industries, and public employment as a consumer society continued to emerge. New shopping areas were built, such as the North Street Arcade, and the city wholeheartedly embraced the revolution in cinemas and dance halls (if not without religious panics about their moral effects).[78] Cruisers, friends, and lovers adapted to these shifts

FIGURE 1.10. A strikingly modern shop frontage with opportunities for gazing at reflections. A. R. Hogg, *Dolcis Shoes, no. 28–30. Shopfront* (1933), BELUM.Y1746. Courtesy of National Museums NI, Ulster Museum Collection.

and "reterritorialized the city" to make it their own, even as other urbanites moved around them.[79]

One location that epitomized the shifts toward a modern shopping experience in Belfast was also a central site for men looking for other men. Woolworth's, an American company, opened its first store in England in

1909, with its Irish location following in 1915. When a fire ripped through the small and nondescript Victorian building in 1928, there was an opportunity to build a new and much larger premises (fig. 1.11).[80] The store that reopened in 1930 was now spread across four floors, two of them carrying an immense and varied assortment of goods; it also housed a self-service cafeteria. Department stores had existed in the city since the 1880s, like the grand Robinson and Cleaver's on Royal Avenue, but the modus operandi of the American company made it different. Woolworth's had long pioneered a "five-and-dime" model of retailing, where a variety of everyday items were sold at cheap fixed prices, and the Belfast store—where all items were three or six pence—was no different.[81] In comparison to the longer-established and more highbrow establishments, there was a diversity to its customers. "Everybody goes to Woolworth's," as the newspaper reported, "and you have as much right [to be] there as anybody else."[82] The result of this shoppers' social democracy was a natural diversity of "Belfast types": "the poor woman in a shawl, buying a rag doll for a dirty-faced baby . . . the cautious tradesman, selecting something from the tool counter . . . cores of "flappers" . . . revelling among the cosmetics . . . other[s] simply shuffling around and having a cheap entertainment seeing what was to be seen."[83] Such flow, movement, and glamour were enticing for anyone who was seeking romance. The large open staircases and the aisles piled high with the latest modern goods made Woolworth's the ideal place to strut and catch a glance. Men who were out on the town with their friends, for example, could now play a game of "spotting talent" among the young women who crowded the cosmetic counters.[84]

For those seeking same-sex encounters, the same highly charged energy and diversity of Woolworth's made it an excellent place for casual cruising. David Strain may have been staunchly middle class but he also appreciated a bargain, so he had been shopping for flowers, crockery, and paint in Woolworth's since the 1920s. But after he began making more ambitious queer friends in the mid-1930s, he found a new appreciation for the store's erotic potential. In 1938, for example, he was going up the central stairs when he spotted a sailor youth he knew; their chat ended with a promise to see each other again before the lad went back to sea. On his way down the stairs later the same day, Strain then saw a different fresh-faced youth going in the opposite direction. When Strain reached the ground floor, he looked up to spot the youth, now on the second flight of stairs, smiling back down at him. After striking up a conversation, using his *Have I met you before someplace?* approach, Strain's target agreed to meet him anytime he liked. A date was set to reconvene outside another department store a few evenings later.[85] Many of David

FIGURE 1.11. Woolworths, the queer hotspot of the 1930s. A. R. Hogg, *F. W. Woolworth and Co. Ltd.* (1930), BELUM.Y2397. Courtesy of National Museums NI, Ulster Museum Collection.

Strain's friends—young and old, poor and rich—could be found making the same intimate connections both outside and inside the store.[86]

I have already hinted at the role that alcohol played in cruising cultures, and that will be a recurring theme. Even in a city that had a reputation for God-fearing temperance, pubs were a central part of everyday life; in the Edwardian era, there was at least one per 328 inhabitants.[87] In the urban center, many pubs were socially mixed venues that brought together men of different classes, politics, and religions. The often-rowdy energy of these social institutions paradoxically also provided a more relaxed environment for a degree of same-sex intimacy. In 1924, for example, eighteen-year-old Ernie Richardson was out for a drink with an older friend from his neighborhood and drinking around Winecellar Entry when he was approached by another man. Edward Summers was in his midtwenties and was locally well-known as a pianist, whereas Richardson was currently out of work, so when the better-off man offered to buy him a beer in the nearby Rosemary Bar, he was happy to say yes. But once they were sat down to drink, Richardson found his leg being felt while an unfamiliar face leaned daringly close to rub against his own. They then left together in search of a private urinal where Summer promised payment, but Richardson's friend came back on the scene to violently interrupt the encounter.[88] It is no coincidence that the pubs that backed directly onto the Entries, like the Rosemary Bar, feature so often in these witness statements of men who were propositioned or discovered having sex in Belfast.[89]

Queer men of all types used pubs for their own purposes and had various goals. Young men passed around titillating photos suggestive of sexual acts between men. Working-class lads in backstreet drinking dens were not just selling newspapers or fetching taxis for wealthier patrons but advertising their own sexual availabilities. Apprentices enjoyed boozing sessions in the oyster houses, spending their wages as well as money won at horse racing, before taking other drunken men into darkened doorways outside. A few bold cruisers even set evening dates in hotel bars with men they had only just met for the first time on the streets.[90] But there was a social element as much as there was erotic. When they were not selling sex, gangs of rent boys hung out in bars where they did not just gossip about their exploits but also held theater practice sessions. Laborers entertained their friends and lovers by singing in the small concert rooms of dockside bars while milkmen drank together after their rounds before going on to see performances at the local variety theater. A few even shared drinks—and I suspect scandalous stories—with women who were selling sex out of some of the more disreputable venues.[91] These were fairly mundane happenings that took place against the backdrop of the city every day.

There was seemingly a whisper network that helped provide men with more knowledge about which venues in the city were relatively tolerant. One witness who has left us some rare detail of how this happened was actually an outsider to Ireland. Frank Kameny would go on to become one of the most important American homophile activists, cofounding the Washington, DC branch of the pioneering Mattachine Society in 1961, but for a year in the mid-1950s, he lived in Armagh, where he worked as an astronomer at the town's famous observatory. Aged about thirty, he had just had his first meaningful same-sex relationship in the United States the year before. After making a connection with a local man he met in Armagh's Beresford Arms Hotel, Kameny learned there was more to explore in the region. "We had sort of an affair," he explained in an interview a couple of decades later, "and he introduced me to all kinds of other people, and we got to know people in

Belfast, and I used to drive in on a Saturday night. Belfast had its gay life and its gay bars, you know, in a somewhat covert sort of way. But I got to know quite a number of people, and some of us used to take trips. . . . And it was really very, very pleasant."[92]

It was only in the late 1950s or early 1960s that the Royal Avenue Hotel Bar began to attract a more obviously gay clientele—and, for the first time, a few lesbian customers too.[93] The fact that few other bars have survived in the gay public memory of Belfast by name suggests they were simply not known as being exclusively for men looking for men or that their queer character was evident for only a short period.[94] These were tacitly shared spaces where queer men rubbed shoulders with other urban characters, from sailors on shore leave to female prostitutes, who were avoiding the civilizing gaze of both the middle classes and the police.

For working-class men, meetings that began in pubs then became sexual encounters in the darkened spots of the city nearby. But relatively few middle- or upper-class men were arrested in the first half of the twentieth century, probably because their money and respectability allowed them to instead take their street pickups to safer and more private places. For David Strain, as we have already seen, this meant the seclusion of his city center office, where he entertained countless young men in the 1930s and 1940s. As just another example, in 1942 he was making his usual urban routes when he got chatting with a youth in the doorway of Woolworth's. After lighting their cigarettes, they walked back to his office on Bedford Street. "On the whole [he] seems to be a genuine youth," Strain later reported, "although dear knows where he may go at other times." After exchanging names and telephone numbers, he drove the boy to a tram stop and then went home with pleasant memories of their happy evening.[95] Other better-off men did much the same, picking up lads in locations like Smithfield Market or the rough-and-ready Bodega Bar before taking them back to the safety of their suburban homes or grand country mansions.[96]

For those men still too nervous to risk their lovers being seen entering their houses, there were also many hotels serving businessmen or guesthouses for the less well-off. Some were located in more insalubrious parts of town, and the owners likely had an inkling for what purpose their rooms were being used. In 1916, for example, one working-class lad told the police how he had stayed in the grandly named Empire Hotel where he'd had sex with an older wealthier man. In reality, this was more of a lodging house for transient Sailortown workers than a respectable hotel for colonial high society. The landlady, Minnie Cunningham, had already been fined and threatened with imprisonment a few years earlier for using the premises as a "disorderly house"—euphemistic legal language that suggests she was presiding over a brothel.[97] Now back in court as a witness in a gross indecency case, she explained that people often came looking for rooms late at night because the hotel was near the railway. Minnie Cunningham insisted that the older man had told her he was the boy's uncle and promised they would sleep in separate beds, but there was a hint of a suggestion from the youth's witness statement that she had been bribed with a bottle of whiskey for her silence.[98]

Other liaisons took place in accommodations of a much higher status. Roger Casement found plenty of sex outdoors in the city, but he also took his young middle-class boyfriend, Joseph "Millar" Gordon, into hotels too. In May 1910, for example, they stayed together in the Grand Central. By that time the passions of the early part of their intermittent relationship had dampened. But for the "first time after so many years," Casement described, there was again "deep mutual longing." An important British diplomat in his midforties now "rode gloriously" on his "splendid steed." "Grand," the twenty-year-old Gordon exclaimed after they reached their shared climax. The next month they were together again, this time at the Belfast Midland. After dinner they retired to their bedroom for privacy: "In deep & warm," Casement recorded happily in his diary. Now sated, they journeyed back to visit Gordon's mother in well-heeled Myrtlefield Park.[99] Other queer men were doing much the same as Roger Casement. Some checked in as father and son or as uncle and nephew to ward off suspicion, but others openly shared beds, where they took breakfast together that was brought up by maids. Only on the rare occasions that someone told the police about these stays—whether a queer man somewhat unwisely reporting a crime against himself, for example, or trying to distract from his own crimes by offering up another perpetrator—was the implicit privacy of hotels broken.[100] Usually, there was instead an economy of queerness: proprietors of disreputable and decent accommodations alike were seemingly willing to turn a blind eye, whether in pursuit of profit or out of simple deference to their privileged customers.

Hotels and pubs may have had the potential for greater sexual expression, but other venues were also available for everyday socializing. David Strain was a puritanical teetotaler and careful with his money too, so he only rarely stepped inside a pub and never stayed in hotels. But he and his friends, and other men like them, used the many other social and leisure spaces of the city. Cinemas have of course long been recognized as a place for courting couples who could not find privacy at home, straight and queer alike. The intimately charged atmosphere they provided could be erotically conducive, whereas the darkness and warmth could be safer and more attractive than braving the streets.[101] There is little criminal archival evidence of queer men using cinemas in Belfast because the Royal Ulster Constabulary were not actively policing these spaces and neither do there seem to have been any complaints made to them. There is just one case in 1930 in which a fifteen-year-old boy described meeting a man at the Royal Avenue Picture House—one of the largest in the city—and having sex in its restroom.[102] But there are smaller snatches of information that suggest cinemas in Ireland were being used for cruising. The author Kenneth Martin described how his crotch was felt when he was in the Adelphi cinema in his hometown of Bangor, County Down, in the mid-1950s. "I knew what I was getting into when I sat next to that young man: lust radiated from his tight light-colored trousers, his knees spread wide," he recalled.[103] David Strain and his friends attended the cinema countless times in Belfast in the 1930s, and it seems likely at least some of the more adventurous of his circle were doing the same as Kenneth Martin. Strain, though, was primmer; in 1943, he limited himself to holding hands with a young man while they watched *Ship Ahoy* in the Royal Avenue Picture House (though they had already had sex in his office earlier in the day).[104]

It was not just the darkened seating of cinemas that held an interest for queer men in Belfast. As cavernously large venues took off in the interwar golden age of the picture palace, they also began to provide refreshment areas. The Classic opened in 1923 on Castle Arcade with seating for a gargantuan 1,800 people and was supposedly well-known for its romantic atmosphere. When patrons were not in the ornate black and gold auditoriums, they could visit a café on the first floor that held around 250 people, described as "the last word in daintiness" with luxurious style, live orchestral music, and reasonably priced food and drinks.[105] Staying open until 10:00 p.m. each night, it was a perfect place for private conversations to take place in the relative open, especially for the many men in Belfast who were sworn off alcohol for religious reasons. David Strain, for example, was introduced to the Classic Café by one of his younger lovers. He was immediately taken in by the "beautiful surroundings" (see fig. 1.12) and made it a regular hangout; on one occasion in 1937, for example, he described for his diary an afternoon of drinking coffee and eating biscuits as he listened to a queer friend tell another all his woes after being romantically let down by an older suitor.[106]

Other cafés provided the same sort of social experience, even if few were as large as those attached to the main cinemas. The Golden Dawn in Fountain Street, for example, was another haunt of David Strain and his friends. Open from 1927 to 1939, it advertised itself as cozy and comfortable, a place where anyone could "feel at home."[107] Strain certainly did, quizzing new friends and lovers on their favorite queer novels from the United States.[108] At

FIGURE 1.12. Cinema cafés—a useful space for queer socializing. A. R. Hogg, *Classic Cinema. Cafe Interior* (1938), BELUM.Y1726. Courtesy of National Museums NI, Ulster Museum Collection.

the same time, men still had to be careful about how they used these cafés; they were relatively respectable and nowhere near as permissive as the pubs or bars of the docks or the Entries. The Golden Dawn was busy and played host to local associations and clubs as varied as the National Federation of Sub-Postmasters and intercity chess tournaments.[109] Strain, a cautious man, tried to pick tables that were farthest away from the gaze of the public and was embarrassed when acquaintances or colleagues outside of his queer life spotted the "gliding" walk of his more effeminate friends.[110]

If there were always risks to being queer, most Belfastmen managed to integrate into the city in couples or even small groups without causing alarm or even suspicion. They were attending the YMCA to see films like *Kameradshaft* (1931), shown by the Peace League; walking around the Botanic Gardens together and admiring the flowers; visiting shows and exhibitions at the King's Hall or Belle Vue pleasure grounds; or lurking in cheese shops to spy a desired lover who worked behind the counter.[111] As we will see more in chapter 5, there was some public knowledge that they existed in Ulster society, but it was not yet any cause for wide moral concern. That said, queer men did have to remain sensibly careful. It is telling, for example, that even though some—like Wilson McCullough—enjoyed attending the burgeoning dance halls in the 1930s, they knew they had to dance with women rather than with men, even if that meant betraying the "brotherhood" in the eyes of more critical, even separatist, homosexuals like David Strain.[112]

Cinemas, cafés, bars, department stores; urinals, alleyways, and parks: that these sites should form a queer geography in a modern city such as Belfast is hardly surprising, given what historians of other cities have found, not to mention what many gay men today will know themselves through intuition and experience. But it is worth noting how the lack of explicitly queer venues in Belfast meant that even social spaces formed to explicitly reform young men could be queerly coopted.[113] The original goal of the Church of Ireland Young Men's Society was obviously not to be a conduit for queer desire; rather, it was to create a moral environment for unaccompanied rural migrants who were at risk from the "evil companionship" that was found in less wholesome (i.e., more secular) parts of Belfast.[114] The society originally prioritized moral education but by the interwar period also realized that providing entertainment was better than losing youths to the less regulated temptations of the streets, cinemas, or pubs. Bible classes, sermons, and debating societies were now joined by sports clubs, amateur dramatics, and even billiard playing—a pastime that less than a generation before had been seen as a gateway to drunkenness and depravity![115] Yet the comfortable and cheery reading room in the city center (see fig. 1.13), on Donegall Square East, was also a popular venue for queer men; David Strain often hung out with friends his own age there, where they tried to chat up the youths they were all chasing.[116] It seems unlikely that this fact was known to the leaders of the society, though it is possible that they ignored potential transgressions out of a desire to avoid bringing their institution into disrepute.[117]

In much the same way, boarding hostels that sought to get young men away from the insalubrious streets ironically became a site for erotic encounters. In 1923, for example, a thirty-year-old carter was arrested for propositioning men in the Protestant-run Salvation Army Home for working men on Waring Street, not coincidentally next to the cruising hotspot of Queen's Square. A couple of decades later, two seventeen-year-old boys were reported to the police by another boy in the Morning Star Hostel in west Belfast. This Catholic-run institution had only opened in 1939, after several Brothers of the St. Vincent de Paul Society had visited public lodging houses in the city and

FIGURE 1.13. The supposedly morally elevating premises of the CIYMS. A. R. Hogg, *Church of Ireland Young Men's Society. Victoria Memorial Hall* (1917), BELUM.Y2462. Courtesy of National Museums NI, Ulster Museum Collection.

been appalled by the "great number of evils necessarily inherent in them."[118] In the 1950s, another court trial revealed that a gang of rent boys—hailing from Dublin, Belfast, and towns across the north of Ireland—were living in another hostel on Waring Street (bordering the aforementioned Queen's Square).[119] Any institution that allowed for this gathering of young working-class males, especially if it provided spaces of privacy or seminudity, could be turned to the advantage of queerness.

If religious institutions provided spaces for erotic activity, in this deeply pious city they were also a place for genuine queer believers to socialize. David Strain and other men in Belfast continued to attend explicitly religious meetings long after they had discovered and begun to express their sexual desires and sometimes took their friends and lovers along too. They also found potential fellow travelers in the Oxford Group, an evangelical movement founded by the American former Lutheran Frank Buchman, which had some success among the Ulster Protestant middle classes in the 1930s. Cecil Bond—who was certainly economical with his ecumenicism, given he was a Presbyterian who also joined the Church of Ireland Young Men's Society—made friends with men from other chapters of the Oxford Group, who then came to spend the weekend in Belfast.[120] Homosocial religious environments now became a site of emotional as well as sexual fulfilment, regardless of what theology was being preached inside—an important challenge to any memory of religion always being an oppressive influence in the lives of queer Irish men.[121]

Belfast's geography undoubtedly shared much in common with other metropolises. Industrialization, urbanization, modernization—each of these interlocking processes brought more and more men into the city and shaped the built environment in ways that facilitated a queer sexual subculture. The most explicit and sexually immediate cruising happened in the cracks between respectable spaces, most obviously the urinals that were out of sight down the Entries. It is possible that there were other familiar cruising sites too. Bathhouses, for example, were central in other queer cities but have left only tiny traces of evidence for Belfast.[122] To some extent, this is because queer sexual life was both clandestine and relatively unpoliced; we can reconstruct only from what survives, and David Strain—my best historical source—was not a bathhouse user. At any rate, none of the other locations that appear in Belfast's archival record are shockingly original; they were replicated in modern urban scenes across the world. But at the same time, Belfast's scene was also shaped by the intimacy of everyday life in Ireland. Cruising took place in broad daylight, whether men were walking in parks, lingering on corners, or just tramming their daily commute. Rather than just being enabled by the anonymity of urbanity, it was now the predictability of Belfast's middling size that helped men meet other men. Such encounters were less likely to lead to immediate sexual gratification, but they also lowered the chances of assault or arrest.

It was through this interplay of anonymity and familiarity that circles of queer friends came into formation in Belfast. These relationships were not invisible nor hidden but rather woven into the everyday social and leisure scene of the city, from shops to cinemas, cafés and even churches. In traversing Belfast in their pursuit of queer intimacy, some of these men even jumped across the sectarian lines that marked Ulster. Ethno-religious background might shape what sexual role a man took, or maybe how men were eroticized by their lovers. But there is some hopeful evidence that what

David Strain and others dubbed the brotherhood could be more important than local religious or political affiliations. This Belfast—one where same-sex desire flowered and sometimes trumped sectarianism—is a refreshing alternative to what is usually a narrative of segregation, oppression, and violence. The next chapter will show how men in pursuit of this life did not just move in local circles but international ones too. By doing so, the queer scene of Belfast came to bear the imprint of other cultures that were blossoming far beyond the borders of Ireland.

Chapter 2

The Queer Irish World

William Gray was born in 1877 on Baltic Street, just east of the river Lagan. Like the street name suggests, this district was orientated toward the sea; Queen's Quay, a major element of Belfast's Victorian expansion, was less than a five-minute walk away. His father was a seaman and so often away from home, but Gray had eight siblings to keep him company. When he was a child, the family moved slightly farther east to Paxton Street, still near the docks and sailor neighbors, before migrating to the more middle-class Upper Newtownards Road as Gray's father climbed the ranks to sea captain. After his elderly parents died in 1913 and 1920, Gray carried on living in east Belfast but in a furnished flat on Lichfield Avenue, still a bachelor but the very image of an upstanding citizen. He had served in the navy in the First World War, worked before that as a rental agent, and then in the early 1920s obtained a decent job in the Ministry of Home Affairs, the new department tasked with keeping a lid on the bubbling tensions of the region.[1]

The daily tram commute of this now middle-aged man took him across the river Lagan, via either the Albert Bridge or Queen's Bridge, giving him a line of sight across the quays and harbors of his childhood.[2] Maybe William Gray had long ago heard rumors about the erotic possibilities of the docklands or grown fond of manly seamen. On a Saturday night in the summer of 1925, a constable observed Gray accept the advances of a former sailor and follow him into a urinal. When Gray turned around to face the constable peering through the perforated wall of the toilet, he exclaimed, "A nice thing, and me a civil servant."[3] This middle-class status and government job was why Gray was now pilloried in the press, refused bail, and subjected to a tirade of public abuse by the resident magistrate, who insisted it was "a charge of great gravity" and "if such crime existed it was time it was stamped out." Gray's meek excuse that he had drunk so much stout and whiskey that he could not remember having sex did not work: he was sentenced to twelve months with hard labor.[4] Gray's public shaming meant that reintegrating into society after his release from prison in 1927 would be difficult. So, a year later, he obtained an immigration visa to settle in the United States, took a steamer to Liverpool, and then traveled third class across the ocean to land in Boston, Massachusetts. Gray told the border agencies he was neither an anarchist nor a polygamist, which was probably true, but his pen must have wavered before he lied about having been in prison.[5]

William Gray's slightly younger sister had already moved in 1913 to Quincy, Massachusetts, an industrial coastal city with a strong Irish population.[6] Jeannie Gray had possibly made that decision because of a scandal of her own; her seafaring husband seems to have abandoned her after the birth of their children over a decade before, and they later divorced. She did not remarry but, with her children and then grandchildren, became an active part of the Ulster Protestant émigré community.[7] William Gray now depended on the generosity and support of his American family. His sister paid for his passage and put him up in her house, and her son, who had grown up with his uncle in Belfast over twenty years before, was the witness to his American naturalization.[8] A former convict now built a new life, doing annual sea tours as a steward for the United Fruit Company—a homosocial world that may have brought its own opportunities for queer socializing—and working in the local shipyards during the Second World War.[9] When he died in 1948, aged seventy-one, there was a memorial service at a local Congregational church and an obituary in the *Quincy Patriot Ledger*.[10] For two decades, Jeannie and William Gray had lived in a house that looked directly out across the Atlantic. How often had they reminisced about their old life in Belfast or the difficult decisions that had brought them so far away from home?

William Gray's queer life was shaped in myriad ways by an Irish world that existed beyond not just Belfast but the borders of Ireland too. When at home he moved through working-class districts that brought sailors and their lovers together, and when faced with the shame of prosecution, he used the long-established diasporic networks that stretched across the globe. This chapter looks at these and many other forms of intimate links that were forged between Irish men, the maritime experience, and the subcultures of other countries, and brings the importance of movement and travel to the forefront of the story of queer Belfast.[11]

By moving in the scenes of other cities, especially British and American, Irish migrants expanded their horizons of same-sex desire. When they then returned home, they introduced other local men into that world in ways that had important effects on the creation of an intimate cruising culture, especially in the docklands, that endured well into the mid-twentieth century. When the Second World War broke out in 1939, a peculiarly intense moment of male military movement again made the city ripe for queer encounters. Throughout the late nineteenth century and for much of the twentieth century too, the queer experience of the north of Ireland was shaped as much by these transnational networks as it was domestic cultures, experiences, and politics, challenging any notion of an insular "island story."[12]

Queer Irishness Abroad

Irish migration, both short- and long-term, was nothing new by the time that William Gray made the lengthy journey across the Atlantic to the United States. Mass movement had its roots in the seventeenth-century era of settling North America, but was catalyzed specially by the Great Famine (1845–1852). Over two million left the country in that horrific time, and a further four to five million over the next sixty-five years, as the opportunities of Ireland continued to falter under the extractive experience of British colonialism and the social and economic limitations imposed by rigid Irish inheritance customs.[13] Most of these migrants chose prosperous North America, but nearby Britain—the world's first industrial nation—took significant numbers into the early twentieth century as well.[14] The exodus largely followed a rural-to-urban pattern, with the country-born being drawn to areas where industrial employment was most likely to be found. Cities such as New York, Chicago, and Boston or London, Manchester, and Liverpool now became host to large Irish populations. The result was the creation of a diaspora: an ethnic grouping that maintained its links to the ancestral land while forging a new bifurcated identity in their chosen home.[15]

If the reasons for this migration were primarily economic, it still had important social and cultural effects on the Irish experience of queerness. Understandings of same-sex encounters in diasporic communities were often structured by the experiences and class background of migrants.[16] The English raconteur Quentin Crisp, recounting his London life of the 1930s, observed how it tended to be the Irish "down-and-outs" who could be found sexually advertising themselves around the Marble Arch in the city's West End. "In those days there must have been a picture of this monument and a map of the surrounding streets on the wall of every gentleman's lavatory in Cardiff, Glasgow, Belfast and points west," he quipped, "for whenever a ruined Celt arrived in London, this is where he came to rest—or should I say work?" Crisp, who became a well-known makeup-wearing face on this cruising scene, even made claims about a peculiarly Irish culture of soliciting: "They could run up and down the scales of flattery without a hint of *pianissimo*. Though they did this for venal ends, they also enjoyed it. It was the exercise of their native genius. As Italian is the language of song, Irish is the voice of flattery. . . . When they gave it up you knew they liked you. . . . Though mercifully the flattery dies, the hard-luck story never fades. If I were asked what the word 'con' meant, I would say that it was something done by impecunious Irishmen to English queers."[17]

Quentin Crisp's encounters with "ruined Celts" in London are by no means unique; there were many other queer Englishmen—middle class especially—who sought or bought the affections of the rough and tough Irish laborer.[18] Police reports, diaries, and memoirs from New York also suggest that the working-class Irish, both migrants and second-generation, were eroticized by other men and seen as being peculiarly open to sexual advances. Earl Lind was a college student in the city in the 1890s and a self-defined invert or fairy who admitted he "seemed to be especially drawn toward young men of Irish blood." In a 1918 account of his life, he described in salacious depth how he had cruised a drunken gang of Irish and Italian hoodlums with disturbing results. The experience began with Lind covering them with kisses while they "caressed" and called him "pet names" but ended in a violent rape in an alley. Lind escaped, but two of the gang caught up with him. Instead of another assault, they apparently now promised to protect him, and brought their former victim back to the gang where he was "received . . . kindly, petted and soothed . . . as one would a peevish baby." For a year after, Lind continued to visit this gang of adolescent roughs and even became a "husband" of a nineteen-year-old American of Irish descent (whom he described as the most virile and handsome of the lot).[19]

Earl Lind and Quentin Crisp were commercial writers who described these encounters as scintillatingly as possible for the voyeuristic reader, but there are also echoes of a Victorian racialized thinking in their eroticization of Irish sexual immorality. Depictions of the Irish as violent, alcoholic, criminal, deceptive, and prone to uncontrolled emotion were especially powerful in the mid-nineteenth century. Lind was writing at not much historical distance from such stereotypes, and Crisp penned his memoir in another period of Hibernophobia following a renewed exodus from Ireland to Britain in the postwar years.[20] But there is a hint too of the realities of an ambiguous Irish cruising culture: a lack of "homosexual" desire was not an obstacle to an intimate relationship that could have different benefits for each man. Crisp even went on to say that if he "refused them a loan they never turned nasty" and reminisced about how he maintained a pleasant friendship with one Irish migrant for many years after.[21] Irishmen living in British and American cities, in a hypermasculine world of bachelors, were away from the domesticating presence of women and most likely lacked the highbrow medical-legal knowledge of homosexuality. Relationships with other men could easily be an economic or social decision that was not the same as a fixed sexual abnormality. The key, as the historians Matt Houlbrook and George Chauncey have argued for London and New York respectively, was an Irish code of masculinity. Camaraderie between young working-class men, and the gendered performance of physical dominance over their effeminate admirers, could be more important than the sex of their casual partner.[22]

Ireland remained a distinctly rural country in comparison to the rapidly urbanized Britain or United States, but there were certainly parts of Irish cities that were similar, in function if not in size, to the laborer subcultures of London and New York. Most of Belfast lies in County Antrim, which was second only to County Dublin and double most of the other counties of Ireland in terms of the number of boarders and lodgers in the early twentieth century. At the time of the 1911 census, at least 4.68 percent of the county were living in these circumstances, and it was likely much higher in the urban core.[23] Many of these houses were in neighborhoods that had large populations of seafarers and rural migrant laborers, such as Carrick Hill, where transience and the absence of family ties was a fact of life.[24] Ample evidence from Belfast suggests that casual encounters between males were common in such working-class or institutional living spaces.

In the early 1890s, there was a spate of gross indecency trials following encounters in smaller lodging houses, usually reported when working-class adolescents rejected the coarse advances of older laborers (though one case concerned a precocious fifteen-year-old who tried to have sex with the men staying casually in his mother's house).[25] Later in the 1890s, there was a recognition of both the need for more housing and the moral dangers of unregulated lodging residences, if more for vulnerable young women than men. The Belfast local authorities, like those in other cities in Britain and North America, now began to plan their own model boardinghouses that were easier to keep an eye on.[26] It was telling that it was mixed-sex rooms that contravened Belfast city council's regulations; men who were sharing beds for reasons other than economy might still escape detection.[27] Reports of immorality in the institutional spaces of the city now died down, maybe because the local government officials were successful in maintaining propriety over the institutions they inspected, though it is also possible that the willingness to report at the end of the nineteenth century had been a temporary response to the very public discovery of a cluster of Irish and British sex scandals, including several that took place in Belfast.[28]

During the 1930s there was a fresh rise in cases in workhouses, hostels, and boardinghouses. These sorts of cheaper accommodations, needed more than ever during the difficult years of the economic depression, were overcrowded with single men. There was also now growing awareness of same-sex desire and gender transgression in popular culture, which perhaps again resulted in a motivation for witnesses to come forward.[29] One place in which there seems to have been an engrained culture of casual sex between men was the gender-segregated Belfast Union Workhouse on Lisburn Road. In 1935, a seventeen-year-old boy alleged that Edward Graham (twenty-one) and Samuel Currie (twenty-three) had both tried to initiate sex with him in the middle of the night. Currie had apparently cajoled, "Be a good spud, let me put it in between your legs," which suggests he usually expected his sexual camaraderie to be returned. When he was rebuked, he threatened that if he had a knife he would use it on the boy, which bluntly underscores the importance of masculine dominance in encounters that were not necessarily about mutual desire.[30] Currie claimed in defense that the workhouse was riddled with corruption but refused to give the names of other men involved, though he did warn he would tell all if he was dragged into court. The boy, meanwhile, at least according to Currie, was also a hypocrite: he was apparently sleeping with other men in the wards.[31] Three years later one of these men Currie identified did indeed find himself in trouble in the workhouse for the same crime. Joseph Fitzsimons, who was in his early sixties by that time, was caught giving William Erskine, a twenty-three-year-old, just a few pence to let down his trousers. Erskine admitted that he knew what Fitzsimons had wanted but had met with him in a stairwell anyway.[32]

The boardinghouse culture of London and New York, then, had its counterpart in Belfast, and it is just as likely that Irish migrants transported that culture abroad as brought it back home. But if sex could be transactional or free of queer self-making for some working-class migrants who happened to find themselves in all-male circumstances, we should be careful of extrapolating that experience to all Irish travel. There is evidence that at least some men were leaving Belfast with the express motive of visiting other cruising scenes.[33] Working-class Belfast trade wanted to spend the money they had made selling their bodies and so socialized in the leisure resorts such as Blackpool on the northeast coast of England, as did the adventurous queer young men who were unpaid for their sexual favors.[34] Others used lonely-hearts magazines to find queer men in both Britain and Ireland, who could then be visited to forge a long-term romantic relationship.[35] Some particularly active cruisers even relocated to British cities simply to make new sexual connections after they felt they had exhausted Belfast's admittedly small potential. In 1937, for example, one youth complained to David Strain that he had failed to find any partners so was going over to Birmingham in the English midlands, though he left a photo with his address to encourage future contact.[36]

The life of William John Leeburn Knox gives us a rich example of both the possibilities and perils of this migrant experience for queer working-class men. He was already working the streets of Belfast in the early 1910s, when he was just sixteen, and was forced to give a witness statement when a constable discovered him in an embrace in an entry with a man a decade his senior. By the early 1920s, after serving in the First World War, Knox became a regular of the queer hotspots of London. Piccadilly in the West End was one haunt, as was the Union Jack Club in Waterloo, the latter of which he had maybe learned about through his naval comrades. Unfortunately for Knox, the British capital's unofficial vice squad were much more familiar with sexual subcultures than the Royal Irish/Ulster Constabulary. During the 1920s and 1930s, he was arrested and sentenced to prison at least eleven times for importuning other men on London's streets. These determined policemen recorded how Knox used an effeminate voice and even had his camp name, Gertie, tattooed on his arm and subjected him to the degrading treatment of swabbing his face for makeup as a demonstration of sexual deviancy (fig. 2.1).[37]

By the early twentieth century there were seven passenger steamship routes to Britain from Belfast, many of them daily and directly connected to express trains on to the major cities, so there was little obstacle to trying a different way of life, if only for a brief visit.[38] Though some men were traveling explicitly for sex, discovering a queer scene abroad was sometimes just a byproduct of a migration made for a deeper desire for freedom. The city's everyday sectarian conflicts and overbearing religiosity could create a sense of claustrophobia. Belfast was relatively bustling but obviously nowhere near as large as London, and the malaise of its literary and artistic scene was a common complaint. For those who had the talent, the money, or the sheer desire, migrating to the British capital offered a chance to escape and live a

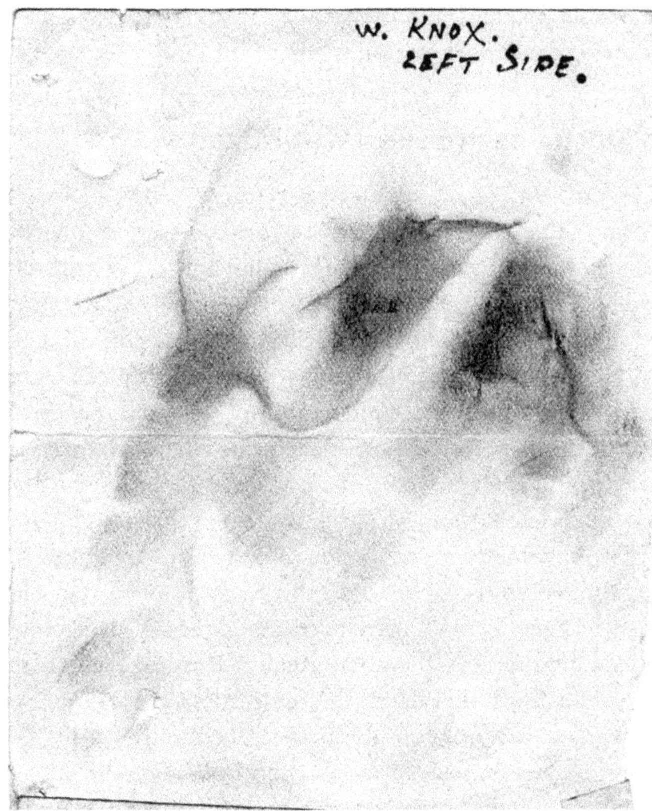

FIGURE 2.1. The makeup swab taken of William Leeburn Knox. "William Knox importuning for immoral purposes 1938," CRIM 1/1041, National Archives (London).

more extroverted life. The author and actor John Keyes, for example, may have known he was sexually different at the age of five, but it was to take a part in London's West End when he was in his late teens that encouraged him to move away from home. It was only then, in the mid to late 1950s, that he met others like himself—such as the famous dancer, John Gilpin—and his queer life could begin.[39]

Other artistic and theatrical types—opera singers, painters, novelists—also left Belfast to make their marks on Britain.[40] Yet technological developments in transport and communication in the nineteenth century did not just take men away easily but brought them back too, especially into port cities like Belfast. John Keyes, for example, returned for good and even in the hardly alluring year of 1969; he "didn't want to miss our Troubles," as he later quipped sardonically.[41] When they came home, even if just for a visit, these Belfastmen brought important cultural and sexual knowledge with them that reshaped the queer social world of the city.

Sex and Slumming in Belfast's Dockland

Over the second half of the nineteenth century, Belfast had transformed from just "an indifferent anchorage" into "a splendid port." Between 1847 and 1897, the number of vessels entering the city doubled (4,213 to 8,763), the tonnage more than quadrupled (538,525 to 2,298,868), and revenue went up almost sixfold (£26,711 to £153,451).[42] Belfast was now not just the foremost harbor in Ireland but the third in Britain and Ireland by profit. A byproduct of this economic progress was the creation of an exciting waterfront culture right in the heart of Linenopolis. Ambitious schemes of urban improvement led to the artificial deepening of the natural inlet from the River Lagan into the lough, reclaimed land was used to create shipyards and other zones of industry, and formerly muddy banks now became energetic quays and docks. Single male workers, such as those who manned the shipyards or the legions of sailors from all corners of the globe, needed somewhere to stay and something to keep them entertained. Bustling districts sprung up in response, straddling both sides of the central docks, and brought together cheap lodgings and raucous pubs for locals and visitors alike.[43]

Belfast's most vibrant waterfront neighborhood, literally dubbed Sailortown, was situated on the northwestern side of the city center. It was a more mixed community than many, though households of the same religion still tended to cluster at the street level.[44] Local histories acknowledge the periods of intense violence that took place there, such as the first Troubles in 1920–1922 or the deadly riots of 1935, but balance the reality of sectarian strife with strong memories of Sailortown's proud tradition of working-class solidarity. They also hint, if a bit more cautiously, at how the residents of the district could tolerate drunkenness, prostitution, and violence in their midst.[45] Local government and the reform organizations run by the churches were concerned about this immorality, though not—at least openly—about sex between men. Seafarers, they believed, were more vulnerable to unscrupulous locals looking to make a quick profit or were the problem themselves: drunk, horny, and disorderly. Sailors' homes, institutes, and churches had sprung up in the mid-nineteenth century across Europe and North America as part of a social purity movement that tried to civilize these transient workers. Belfast was no different: charitable ventures such as the Belfast Sailors' Home on Corporation Street tried—mostly in vain—to mitigate the ever-present temptations of alcohol and commercial sex by substituting God, temperance, and wholesome activities.[46] Sailortown's reputation as a rowdy and permissive district that stubbornly resisted domestication still lasted until the decline of the docks in the later twentieth century.

Every part of the small city center featured in the queer sexual geography in some way, but it was the docklands that saw some of the most open cruising. The reputation of Sailortown was probably well known to queer men, who shared knowledge among themselves, or maybe they recognized the frequency with which the district's main streets appeared in the crime report pages of local newspapers and read between the lines.[47] Whatever brought the district to their attention, visitors and locals alike were compelled to make their way into this rough-and-tumble world to fulfil their own desires.[48] James Douglas gives us an example of one such man. Unfortunately, there is no surviving biographical information that can confirm his background for certain, but the fact that both of his bailers were stationers might give us a clue. No James Douglas in Belfast worked in that trade or similar, but a sixty-two-year-old printer of that name lived in Blackburn, England. He was well-known enough to have a newspaper feature him as a local celebrity, but when he died, in the year he was arrested in Belfast, his son and not his wife was present and there was no press notice, which might suggest his trial overseas had been known.[49] Either way, late one Friday night in November 1894, a James Douglas found himself stood at a lamppost outside a fire station on Great Georges Street and chatting with Archibald Andrews, a local fireman in his early twenties.

James Douglas's opening gambit was probably a classic Sailortown conversation: an observation on a fight that was spilling out of the pub on the other side of the street. After not much more talk, he then made his intentions clear by fumbling with Andrews's trousers. When the fireman asked him what he was doing, he coyly replied, "You ought to know." Andrews claimed that he now played agent provocateur, taking the older man into the privacy of the station and asking him what the payment was going to be for his body. When Douglas then handed him a two-shilling piece, a relatively high amount for this sort of encounter, Andrews responded by punching him and blowing his whistle for the harbor police.

Had Archibald Andrews been interested in queer sex and then changed his mind, or had he been entrapping the unfortunate James Douglas from the start? We will now never know, though the courts were dubious about him taking the law into his own hands. When Andrews later made his detailed statement to the petty sessions clerk, Douglas's solicitor led the fireman to describe how he often gave his coat to young men who were presumably too poor to have their own, though he seemingly did not receive any benefit for the favor. These curious details about interactions with vulnerable youths may have suggested he had ulterior sexual motives.[50] If that was not suspicious enough, his own socioeconomic history and what he said he already knew about the queer world may have raised alarms. Andrews had grown up in one of the more disreputable entries of the city center and left school to join the Royal Navy after the rowdy oyster house his widowed mother ran was lost to a fire and urban redevelopment in the 1880s.[51] On long voyages, he told the court, he had "heard sailors talking about this sort of thing." Douglas had also wanted to "Cobain him," Andrews said—a reference to the east Belfast politician Edward de Cobain, infamously convicted of gross indecency just a couple of years before and humiliated in the press.[52] Andrews lacked the emerging medical-legal language of homosexuality to express what Douglas had attempted, but he knew queer desire when he saw it. He even insisted that he had previously noticed the accused repeatedly going in and out of a urinal on Library Street, which was less than ten minutes' walk away from Sailortown. If Andrews was telling the truth, Douglas was a habitual cruiser and clearly aware of where he needed to go to find willing partners. He had made a mistake in whom he approached on this night, but the boldness of his methods suggests this was a common enough occurrence in the streets of Sailortown, even if it was only rarely revealed to the authorities.

Belfast was never big or bold enough to support exclusively gay bars in its city center in the pre–gay liberation era, and neither could the docks. Instead, and like in other medium-sized port cities, queer men had to share dockside pubs with those who were also beyond the pale of polite society: drunken sailors, unruly laborers, and female sex workers. Du Barry's was Belfast's most infamous example. It was on Prince's Street near the Albert Clock in Queen's Square, a well-known cruising site.[53] A pub had existed there since 1860, and by the early twentieth century it was already rumored to be a popular meeting place for shipowners and their mistresses.[54] In 1930, a local resident magistrate described the surrounding area as being where "cosmopolitan toughs congregate"—a peculiar turn of phrase given how opposite those two descriptors might have seemed.[55] Yet the launch of the Du Barry's brand in the late 1930s by the experienced local publican Peter O'Hara explicitly built on this reputation for forbidden yet sophisticated encounters.

The pub's name referenced Jeanne Bécu, the Comtesse du Barry and royal mistress of Louis XV. Though Du Barry was a long-established character in historical novels, she had also recently featured in a slew of eponymous Hollywood films. *Madame Du Barry* (1934), a "flaming love story [that] rocked a nation and shocked the world," was especially popular in cinemas across

Belfast.[56] The use of Bécu's title for the bar was indicative of the glamour and intrigue of her story, but the tendency of Anglo cultures to stereotype prostitution through the image of Frenchness meant there was a double meaning at work.[57] Promotions placed in the local press suggestively promised "continental comfort, atmosphere, and [the] best liqueur" in an "UNCOMMON bar" and asked "Do you need a change of outlook?"[58] Messages even appeared in the personals column of the *Belfast Telegraph*, promising, for example, "To-night—Du-Barry's . . . 'I'll make you happy.'"[59] By mimicking the mystery and excitement of the lonely-hearts genre, the erotic potential of the pub managed to hide in plain sight.

Du Barry's is still popularly remembered in Belfast as a notorious pub-cum-brothel that was particularly popular with sailors, but it is less commonly recognized that queer men were also attracted to its more tolerant atmosphere.[60] Jeff Dudgeon, a prominent local gay rights activist in the 1970s, has described how Du Barry's was a well-known haunt earlier in the century, a detail he gleaned from a gay man who came of age during the Second World War.[61] During those years, David Strain—something of a puritan—was alarmed when he found out that his latest queer crush, a young merchant sailor, did not just have another lover in the navy but also had been in Du Barry's with his comrades.[62] Perhaps while this young sailor was there he met Gerard Dillon, an Irish artist who was born in the west of the city. Dillon visited the bar with other bohemian friends during the war and drew sketches of American servicemen for the cheap price of a drink. He apparently cruised Dublin's docks too and had spent many years in the more vibrant scene of London, so probably he had been looking for connections in similar places in Belfast.[63] Chasers of "rough trade"—those working men who sold sex—were still visiting Du Barry's until at least the 1960s. The Dolly Sisters, for example—a pair of known "screamers"—apparently preferred this "butch" pub because, as they scoffed, there were no real men in the more exclusively gay space of the Royal Avenue Hotel Bar.[64]

Like in other cities, queer men in Belfast sometimes rubbed shoulders and likely formed friendships with female sex workers in working-class dock spaces, even if they happened to be competing for the same trade.[65] At the same time, the relationship between these diverse urban characters was fragile; after all, one reason we have accounts of cruising queer men is because they were sometimes reported by those they desired. Working-class men may have been amenable on some occasions, but on others they simply refused to be rough trade or turn a blind eye to what was happening in their neighborhood.[66] Even so, at least some cosmopolitan social spaces were ripe for co-option, providing a sexual world that could flourish and satisfy the needs of a range of urban groups.

Sailors and Their Admirers

For those who might have defined themselves as queer or even through the scientific language of homosexuality, it was the ostensibly straight sailors of bars such as Du Barry's whom they were hoping to take home. Naval men—especially in national fighting forces though not exclusively—were lauded in queer culture as emblems of virile masculinity. For their admirers, they expressed a gruff manliness through their uniforms, exotic adventures at sea, and patriotic prowess.[67] The queer travel writer Robin Harbinson, who grew up in east Belfast, hinted at his lust for such men in a memoir of his early life. When he was just in his twenties and traveling to North America after the Second World War, he shared a cabin with Canadian seamen aboard the passenger ship RMS *Aquitania*. "Mama would have swooned in horror," he wrote in mock outrage, "at the sight of thirty young men strutting naked between the cabin and shower-baths, flicking towels at each other's buttocks." "What would she have said about the huge, hairy thighs swinging contentedly over the edge of bunks?" he wondered out loud. Harbinson was writing for a respectable audience at a time when homosexuality was still taboo, so the queer desire of *The Protégé* (1963) is implied rather than explicit. Still, his descriptions of "muscular bodies that wrestled and writhed, panting and sweating, no holds barred, on the cabin floor" leave little to the imagination.[68] For those who moved in queer circles—or at least already knew the rumors of *rum, sodomy, and the lash*—such musings would have been plainly obvious.[69]

The sailor was more than just a symbolic figure of desire, however: he was an important cog in the machine that circulated sexual knowledge on shore in Ireland. His understanding of queer desire, formed on ships and in raucous ports across the maritime world, was imported directly into Irish urban life.[70] One encounter between David Strain and a young man demonstrates how sailors could use their experience of same-sex intimacies at sea as an advertising ploy on dry land. Strain had been an avid enthusiast of motoring since his youth and was a well-recognized sight around the city in his pride and joy: a 1924 Triumph. He lifted the men he came across and dropped them wherever they wanted to go—often just for the fun of it, but also especially as he became more confident in his queer self, because he knew it might provide an opportunity to make a new contact. One afternoon in 1934, he was driving in the countryside when he spotted a fresh face at the side of the road. He stopped and picked up this man, a twenty-five-year-old named John Magee.

David Strain opened his conversation with John Magee with a suggestive justification of why he gave lifts only to men: with a woman in the car, he claimed, witnesses might think they had been "fooling" around together if there was a crash (a not uncommon fear that accompanied the rise of the car in Ireland).[71] Magee read between the lines and offered his own anecdote about how another man had picked him up and began to get "funny." As Strain recorded in his diary, "I felt he was trying to make an opening for a conversation around the one subject." That opening now made, their talk became more explicit. "You see, I was in the navy," Magee revealed, "and I knew all about that kind of thing—'Flying Fish' they were called." The etymology of this phrase is difficult to pin down today, given how queer men across the world used their own terms that never made it into the medical journals or even the popular press, but it perhaps compared sex between men to something else that was humorously unnatural: a fish that could fly.[72]

After an incredulous David Strain asked John Magee if he had met any of these Flying Fish, the younger man explained: "Yes. I remember when I was on the [HMS] Furious at first, I asked one of the chaps one day what it all meant. So, he told me that the first time I wanted a bob[73] or so to come along and let him know and he would explain." Conversation continued—about hobbies, work, and other meetings with men on the prowl—before Magee candidly admitted it had been almost a year since he had been with another man. When Strain asked Magee what was in it for him, he smiled and replied, "What compensation does a prostitute get?" before admitting he was out of work and would be glad of any money or help at all. With both men on the same page, a future date was set.[74]

Ostensibly "normal" sailors were commonly seduced through the promise of money or gifts.[75] They could take part in queer sexual encounters without considering themselves different from the men who did not for two important reasons: first, if they maintained their manhood by taking the masculine role in relationships, or second, by disclaiming physical desire and instead justifying their behavior by being paid. Representation was often as important as reality, though: the *image* of masculinity and sexual disinterest took precedence over what happened between lovers behind closed doors.[76] John Magee's justification fell more into the category of paid sex, though what sort of relationship he was really looking for remained ambiguous. David Strain, after some sleuthing around the village in which Magee lived, found out his new friend in fact had both wife and child. When confronted with this fresh information, Magee sheepishly claimed that he had been legally forced into this marriage after being falsely accused of impregnating a woman who was apparently known to have lots of sexual relationships. He now claimed that all he really wanted was a friend, not being "a bit keen about the other thing"—that is, sex between men. Magee still became a casual companion for a short time, gardening for Strain at his country hut and receiving clothes and money in return. On another occasion in 1942, Strain was picked up by a "working-class type" in the city center; after sex in his private office, the older man was fascinated by the youth happily explaining the tattoos on his chest: evidence of "what he had done when he was serving on a boat!"[77]

We should remain aware of how queer middle-class men such as David Strain could not just be attracted by rough masculinity but still feel tender affection toward their potential lovers.[78] If sailors and other economically vulnerable workers often received compensation for their time, there could be compassion following sex or even no physical encounter at all. These queer relationships do not map onto the gay liberation ideals of the later twentieth century so easily, and especially the ideal of relationships between men who were more equal in their desires and social standing. But they could still be intimate and, for some intellectuals and their followers, even a vehicle for social transformation.[79]

It is easy enough to see why sailors were popular figures on urban queer scenes, but it is worth remembering that they were not always just paid partners for middle-class men. Often they were the ones looking for casual sex too, whether now permanently resident on land or just taking shore leave. Like their comrades who were paid for their bodies, they could justify their own queer desires for a variety of reasons. When they were at sea, men were simply more available than women, and they may have believed that sleeping with another sailor was less immoral than marital infidelity or even sex with a woman before marriage. Queer sex also had the benefit of avoiding unwanted pregnancies or avoiding diseases from women who sold sex (official venereal disease publicity campaigns did not get off the ground in Northern Ireland until the Second World War, but there was still public knowledge of the dangers).[80]

There were also fewer mercenary reasons that some sailors chose to have sex with other men. Edward Irenaeus Prime-Stevenson, a novelist and sexological writer who traveled across Europe and North America, claimed in the early twentieth century that a sea captain had told him homosexuality was rife on English ships. Prime-Stevenson speculated that this was largely a result of the naval environment. Long voyages created a close masculine culture or bachelor state while living in such closeness to the power of nature meant sailors were only "vaguely bound by conventional human notions—if bound at all." Quentin Crisp, in his more colorful manner, suggested that men who ran away to sea abandoned the accepted conventions of society: "after a sojourn in strange ports," he noted, sailors "returned with their outlook and possibly their anus broadened."[81] Sex with other men could be more than just a begrudging necessity, then, born out of a social situation where there were no women. Oral histories, carried out by Paul Baker and Jo Stanley, with British sailors of the postwar years confirmed that men could discover their queerness in naval homosocial environments or were knowingly attracted to such queer possibilities in the first place.[82]

Whatever the cause, criminal archives from Belfast demonstrate that sailors of all ages were indeed open to casual encounters with other males, regardless of their own marital status. They were not just found in dockside districts, either; they were haunting the urinals of the Entries, approaching newsboys on the streets, or having sex in fields with men of their own age and class.[83] When one middle-aged former sailor was caught aggressively trying to encourage a terrified sixteen-year-old boy into a park urinal in 1924, he simply told the police, "I am a naval man, what can you expect!"[84] For middle-class cruisers and sailors alike, the belief in the queer life of seafaring and its lasting influence on land was more than just a stereotype.

Most of the records we must rely on to reconstruct the lives of these queer sailors were created at a moment of pleasure and then pain and reveal only the fleeting or transactional aspects of urban cruising cultures. Reconstructing ongoing relationships and the complexities of intimacy and desire in the manly maritime world is much more difficult.[85] But it is important to know that some Belfastmen did not just find sex at sea but formed passionate long-term relationships too. William "Billy" Nelson was one such man. He was from a respectable working-class district in the north of the city and lived close enough to the docks to hear the horns of the ships. Nelson enlisted in the Royal Navy in 1956, six months before his eighteenth birthday, and trained in Portsmouth in England. After a year of service, he was posted to the HMS *Bulwark*, where he met a Scottish Royal Marine, Alexander Smith, who was around four years his senior.[86] They soon formed a bond that developed into more than just friendship. When they spent time on leave, they shared a bed, a practice that was not necessarily suspicious and so good cover for what became a blossoming sexual relationship. Their trouble instead began when Smith bravely made it clear to his commanding officer that he did not want to be separated from his younger lover. Both were reprimanded, and the Scotsman was transferred to another ship. Seafaring life undeniably provided opportunities for such homosocial bonding and even romantic relationships, but the regimentation and strict hierarchies of the Royal Navy meant there was always this risk of exposure and then punishment.

In his misery and anguish, Billy Nelson took to drinking and cried himself to sleep at night. But the love of these two sailors endured against the odds. Early in October 1958, Nelson could not hide his delight after a letter from Smith arrived for the first time since they were separated. Writing back, he gushed: "Oh Alex, my relief is profound! I thought perhaps they wouldn't let you write and every post before this only brought me bitter disappointment. I can't begin to tell you how much I've missed you, life has been almost unbearable. I often look at our writing on your locker door and find it hard to believe you're gone. I still look for your towel and one night, even went round for you at supper time. After that grim realisation set in." Signing off, Nelson was unrestrained in his emotion: "Take care of yourself and keep faith in me; it won't be unfounded. I love you so very dearly and always my heart and soul are yours." In now frequent letters, Nelson and Smith updated each other on their day-to-day lives, reminisced about their time together in foreign ports, planned future holidays with friends, and relayed their mutual determination that everything would work out alright for their relationship.[87]

When Billy Nelson was on shore leave in England and now lonely without his lover, he was consoled by naval comrades and civilians on the queer scene. Rosie, another sailor, showed him the sights of Portsmouth, like the drag bar Criterion, a hotspot on the south coast, and introduced him to several of his camp friends (who kindly promised to try to help with his naval situation).[88] Finally, in early 1959, after both men had been fully discharged, they were reunited at Nelson's mother's home in Belfast. Unfortunately, the reason a record of this relationship has then come to us is because she reported her son and his lover to the police. The letters were then found in Smith's locker in the sailors' hostel in the city center, and both were hauled into the police station to make statements. The result was jail time for the crime of having a romantic relationship across the maritime world.[89] Though this relationship does not seem to have survived in the long run, Billy Nelson still managed to find love. When he died just a few years ago in the English midlands, after a second career as a nurse, he left most of his money and property to a male partner—on the condition that he cared for their dog Rémy for the rest of her life.[90]

The Queer Opportunity of Global Conflict

Sailors, both in Belfast and beyond, give us clear evidence of the importance to queer men of moving between urban locations to experience different sites of intimate homosocial bonding. Already by the early twentieth century there was a consensus among sexological writers that the all-male world of military cultures could provide similar opportunities for same-sex desiring men.[91] In his sprawling work *The Intersexes* (1908), for example, Edward Prime-Stevenson dedicated an entire section to military prostitution. Young soldiers, he argued, could be constitutionally homosexual, but more likely they were driven by mercenary motives that resulted from the poor pay of the armed forces. The more dedicated Uranian or homosexual was attracted to soldiers because of their excellent physique and youthful openness and the supposed unlikelihood they would be violent or blackmail their admirers. Prime-Stevenson described both soldier-soldier and soldier-civilian relationships as being engrained in queer cultures throughout North America and Europe, including cities in Ireland.[92]

There were barracks in and around Belfast throughout the nineteenth and twentieth centuries, but the exceptional circumstances of global conflict undoubtedly stimulated the queer experiences of men both in and outside of the military. One example from the First World War demonstrates just how important war and movement could be. Vincent Cassidy was the son of a Catholic saddler from Armagh and had already lived in Dublin, London, and New York by his early twenties. When he was returning to Belfast in 1917, he passed through Liverpool, where he made a connection with Jack Fearon, a soldier in the King's Liverpool Regiment. Francis Kavanagh, another young soldier from Cork, had also met Fearon when they had been training together in Formby (a Lancashire town near Liverpool). In early September, Kavanagh and Fearon ran into each other in Belfast, and the latter told the former about a party that was happening in the Imperial Hotel (figs. 2.2 and 2.3). Over several months, Cassidy held intimate queer gatherings where soldiers rubbed shoulders with civilians and drank whiskey cocktails, and he shared a bed with a lover named Hugh Sheehan before the police finally got wind of the affairs and swiftly arrested the ringleader.[93]

The city provided the spaces for queer encounters to take place, but it was the homosocial culture of the military network, which spread across Britain and Ireland, that helped foster and even justify intimate male friendships.[94] The Second World War was an equally transformative moment that has left us much more evidence of both sexual opportunity and the beginnings of a more explicitly gay identity. The close homosocial world of the armed forces again had erotic potential, and queer behavior, from drag performances to casual sex among soldiers, could even be accepted as good for army morale. Young men, in huge numbers, were now pulled away from the influence of the home or small community and given an opportunity to test not just their

FIGURE 2.2. Hugh Sheehan met Vincent Cassidy outside this hotel, and stayed there for several months. A. R. Hogg, *Imperial Hotel, no. 16–18* (n.d.), BELUM.Y1948. Courtesy of National Museums NI, Ulster Museum Collection.

patriotic duty but their sexual prowess as well—though not without the risk of a court-martial and dishonorable discharge.[95]

Conscription was never introduced in Northern Ireland, for both political and pragmatic reasons relating to the substantial Irish nationalist minority, and rates of enlistment did remain lower than in other parts of the United Kingdom.[96] But around thirty-eight thousand men and women still joined up, and there is some evidence to suggest that it was an important moment of sexual realization for some of them.[97] One man, arrested in 1947, told the courts how he understood he was same-sex attracted as young as eleven, but only when he joined the Royal Marines did he "learn a lot on sex life." Another man living in Bangor, County Down, recalled in the 1960s how he had fallen in with "active homosexuals" when he had joined the Gordon Highlanders in 1945 and had learned to accept the same persuasion.[98] To some degree the wartime tolerance for homosexuality could even continue in the postwar

FIGURE 2.3. Hugh Sheehan and Vincent Cassidy probably shared a bedroom of this sort. A. R. Hogg, *Imperial Hotel, no. 16–18. Interior. Bedroom,* (1930), BELUM.Y1954. Courtesy of National Museums NI, Ulster Museum Collection.

decades; the previously mentioned Royal Avenue Hotel Bar, for example, was run by a pair of straight but sympathetic former Royal Air Force men.[99]

Much as was the case with sailors, middle-class queer men tended to eroticize both the masculinity and sexual availability of soldiers.[100] Though nothing as explicit as Robin Harbinson's description of Canadian seamen has survived in personal recollections of servicemen in Belfast, there is evidence that suggests they were cruising targets. Henry Blair, for example, an insurance manager in his late forties who lived alone in Belfast in a bachelor-style flat, was traveling between Liverpool and Belfast in early 1939 when he found himself in trouble after fraternizing with servicemen on the MV *Ulster Prince.*[101] He had booked a double berth cabin under his own name with a Mr. Martin but boarded alone and never asked for a refund; perhaps he had smartly wanted to head off any suspicions that may have arisen if two men were seen entering a room that anyone watching knew had just one bed.

Henry Blair spent the journey across the Irish Sea in the bar with a party of infantrymen from the Second Battalion of the South Wales Borderers, paying for all the drinks and allegedly trying to pick them up. One private said he "took a chance" and went to Blair's cabin because he did not have anywhere to sleep but refused to get in bed with his encouraging host. Undeterred, Blair went back to the bar and managed to persuade another private to join him down below. The first soldier must have told the rest of his pals what he suspected was happening in the cabin because a group of them then tried to get in to rescue their comrade. After much shouting and banging, a partially dressed and likely sheepish Welshman finally opened the door to a ship steward. Blair found the police waiting for him when he disembarked a couple of hours later, who noted in their statement that an incriminating tub of Vaseline was found under his pillow.[102]

The global conflict was important for the queer soldiers who took part but also had transformative effects on the cruising scenes of cities.[103] The north of Ireland was strategically important for the war effort because of both its position in the Atlantic and its use as a launching point for American servicemen. Already by 1941 there were over one hundred thousand British troops stationed in canvas camps, huts, or requisitioned buildings, and between 1942 and 1944 over three hundred thousand Americans also passed through the province. Given the population of Northern Ireland was roughly 1.2 million people, these numbers brought significant changes in day-to-day life.[104]

The exotic and exciting presence of American GIs provoked fears about immorality, but it was women, whose purity was already intensely guarded in the north of Ireland, who found themselves heavily criticized for fraternizing with the "Yanks."[105] The sexual opportunities that American troops brought to Belfast apparently still delighted the queer men of the city, though none of these visitors appear to have ended up in court themselves.[106] In fact, convictions of men who had sex with men remained relatively low throughout the six years of the war, and there was still no discernible moral panic. Reports in the press of the rare cases that did make it to the courts were now even shorn of any reference to the same-sex element, if they were reported at all, reversing the interwar trend for slightly less ambiguous coverage. In religiously superior Ulster, it was perhaps worse for wartime morale—already fragile because of ethnonationalist divisions—to admit the existence of same-sex desire than to try to root it out.[107]

If the authorities continued to remain tight-lipped about queer encounters in Belfast, servicemen, whether on leave or passing through on journeys to other bases, were undoubtedly an important and visible part of the urban sexual geography. It was a relatively exciting and liberating time in the city. Nevill Johnson, an English artist who had moved to the region in the 1930s, described how even in "sturdily provincial Belfast . . . in nests of anarchy and deviation . . . orgies took place and mayhem prevailed."[108] Whether any of the orgies Johnson was referring to involved man-on-man action is knowledge lost to time, though the painter did have several male queer friends.[109] Another Belfastman did recall that the urinals were especially full the morning after the unexpected and devasting Luftwaffe raid in 1941; perhaps the horror of destruction paradoxically led to a devil-may-care sexual attitude among those who usually managed to contain their desires.[110] In the docklands, as we saw with Du Barry's, the bustling clubs and bars certainly brought military men into contact with Belfast locals while the darkness of the Blitz provided a degree of cover for quick illicit encounters.[111]

Cavorting with servicemen may have been an attractive way to spend the hours in the dark, but it could still get a man arrested or badly assaulted. John Hughes found this out to his detriment in November 1939 after bringing a soldier home to his aunt's house for tea. The young man maintained that Hughes had touched him and asked him about his own sexual history with women, but Hughes countered that his guest had exposed himself and exclaimed "I have been dying for a bloody buck all night" before attempting to rape him. The soldier did admit to assaulting Hughes but was adamant he did so because his host had "tried to do a dirty trick" on him.[112] This case reached the courts only after the victim's cousin went to the police, Hughes perhaps being too concerned that the police might ask why he would bring home a young man he had just met on the street. Regardless, his experience suggests that the opportunities of the war still had to be balanced with the risks of urban cruising. In fact, it might have even been the case that the seemingly greater visibility of queerness was making negative public responses more likely than before.[113]

A lot more common than arrest or assault, though, were both transactional and medium-term liaisons between civilians and servicemen. Snippets from David Strain's diaries suggest that soldiers were objects of desire for him and his friends. In April 1942, for example, he picked up a young serviceman in Smithfield Market and later took him to his house for tea, where they had a pleasant time chatting about poetry.[114] Strain entertained other soldiers at his house, including some Americans, and often gave them lifts in his car, though it is unclear whether these friendships always had a romantic element.[115] The amount of cruising servicemen on the streets of the city was so high that Strain now found he even had stiff competition for the younger men he preferred. On one occasion he ran into a lad he had been chasing for some time outside the queer hotspot of Woolworth's, but his invite for an evening out was turned down because his target had already arranged to meet an air force officer and then skipped off with another who just happened to be passing. Later the same night, after meeting no one around the city, Strain decided to go back to the High Street, where he saw another young man he knew, again outside Woolworth's. They chatted for a short time before a youth in the air force, whom Strain's friend seemingly knew, came along and took him out of sight.[116] Into the postwar period, servicemen stationed in Belfast remained a part of the cruising culture—especially for those who were willing to pay with money or access to the rarefied world of the higher social classes. In 1952, a mini Belfast scandal was made public in a British tabloid paper, *The News of the World*, when men of elite classes were found to have been picking up English soldiers outside of City Hall and taking them back to their country mansions.[117]

Early in the war there had been concerns that hundreds of servicemen were aimlessly wandering the streets of Belfast with nothing to entertain them, especially on the Sabbath when the leisure venues of the city closed their doors. The Reverend W. S. Kerr, preaching in St. Anne's Cathedral and appealing to the "fathers and mothers whose own sons may be to-night in strange cities," made it clear that the dangers were sexual. "Our young soldiers and sailors are on Sundays exposed to peculiar moral temptations," he insisted. "Many are lying in wait to lure them into evil. Agents are busy to attract them to dens of iniquity where the loss of their money is not the worst disaster."[118] Whether Reverend Kerr realized it was not just the pimps and female prostitutes who had their eyes on servicemen is not clear, but the Women's Volunteer Patrol—set up in 1943—was concerned only with regulating the behavior of young women.[119] Either way, for Belfast's queer men, the streets thronging with impressionable young soldiers was an exciting prospect, not a moral conundrum—and there were financial and social benefits to their foreign lovers too.

Wartime Belfast was undoubtedly not as busy or as radical as the "paved double bed" that Quentin Crisp described for London during the Blitz, but pockets of a more cosmopolitan and sexually adventurous culture did exist, encouraged by the paradoxically socially relaxing influence of global conflict.[120] But if the war had stimulated a carpe diem attitude for Belfast's same-sex-desiring men, the queerness of the city had already been marked by international dynamics for at least sixty years before. Queer lives were not only determined by a man's immediate surroundings but often lived across multiple destinations and shaped by the international sharing of intimate sexual knowledge. Life at sea, and on shore leave in exotic ports, could introduce young sailors to ways of life that they brought back to their home country. Maritime spaces of movement and transition now became an important part of Belfast's cruising scene, before and even after the slow emergence of more explicitly homosexual bars in the postwar decades.

What marked out dockside areas as sites of potential encounter was a generally disreputable or more permissive character: one that allowed for male intimacy and socializing, if not without the risk of discovery, assault, or arrest. Irish experiences—whether in Belfast, London, or New York—were undoubtedly shaped by class. "Ruined Celts," as Quentin Crisp put it, may have justified sex with another man as an economic or simple physical transaction rather than an expression of innate identity and so distinguished themselves from the middle-class men who sought out their bodies. That said, working-class youths could also learn about desire through their engagement with queer men in towns and cities outside of Ireland, embodying an increasingly modern sense of queerness that was defined by self-realization and not just sexual behavior. The next chapter explores in more depth the range of queer models that were developed or brought into Belfast long before the gay rights movement and how they could coexist, overlap, or conflict until at least the postwar decades.

Chapter 3

Sexology, Religion, and Reading Queer in Ulster

Arthur Greeves was born in an affluent east Belfast suburb in 1895. As the son of a successful linen industrialist, he had a privileged life: regular trips to the opera, days spent painting or lunching with friends, and little expectation that he would contribute to the family business. Even with all this good fortune, Greeves struggled to be happy and by his early twenties was tortured by feelings of loneliness and desires for other men that he did not yet understand.[1] Finding the work of the radical socialist Edward Carpenter in 1918 was a turning point. This Englishman's four-volume prose poem *Towards Democracy* (1883), which had been republished the previous year, contained a description of the Child of Uranus: a misunderstood outcast who had a "Woman-soul within a Man's form dwelling."[2] Greeves now found hope. Carpenter, he reflected in an entry in his pocket diary, was "the first man I have ever heard of who I think would understand me properly."[3]

Inspired by this discovery, Greeves soon acquired Carpenter's more recent book, *The Intermediate Sex: A Transitional Study of Some Types of Men and Women* (1908), in which the author continued to flesh out his theory of healthy and normal men who were nonetheless attracted to their own sex.[4] Greeves deemed the work "most interesting" and spent a whole day familiarizing himself with the ideas of his "wonderful" prophet.[5] He continued to read other relatively recent medical or philosophical works about sexuality, finding his way from Carpenter to the rarer writings of John Addington Symonds and Havelock Ellis. Such books did not just relay the latest thinking about homosexual desire but also described historical examples of male love in both fact and fiction from across the world.[6] Greeves could now follow one of Carpenter's suggestions and borrow a work by Michel de Montaigne from a friend. The effects of studying this French Renaissance philosopher were so sexually startling that his twentieth-century reader could not sleep that night until he had masturbated. He was also excited to learn that Christopher Marlowe was "very that way" but was alarmed by his writings too: reading the early modern playwright was such an intense experience that Greeves exclaimed it took "too much out of me!"[7]

Arthur Greeves had entered a different queer world through literature but was never truly content with what he found. In the summer of 1918, he lapsed back into depression. "Why are we Urnings persecuted like this?" he asked his diary, using a terminology he had recently learned through Edward Carpenter, before adding, "Oh why can't I die?"[8] In 1922, while living in London and visiting friends at the University of Oxford, he was delighted to find a way out: the promises of Freudian psychoanalysis. One doctor acquaintance told him to try "flirting" with women to "encourage anything in the right way," meaning heterosexuality, and gave him a copy of *New Psychology and the Teacher* (1921) by Hugh Crichton-Miller. Greeves then moved onto R. H. Hingley's *Psycho Analysis* (1921) and was excited to find that the author seemed "very hopeful . . . [of] helping and in fact curing cases like myself!!" Through these recently published texts, one Belfastman began to engage with ideas that were at the very cutting edge of psychiatry. The Victorian language of Uranians or Urnings and their healthy same-sex love was now replaced in his diary with more modern ruminations on his subconscious mind and battles to sublimate his desires and fantasies about "ravishingly beautiful" male youths.[9] Whether he was successful we will probably never know; Greeves's diaries end suddenly in 1922 without resolution.

The ability of Arthur Greeves to travel through a range of old and new sexual models—some positive, some negative—is a recent phenomenon in historical terms. It was only in the final decades of the nineteenth century that doctors, psychologists, and psychiatrists began to catalogue and categorize a full spectrum of deviance. The new discipline that emerged was dubbed *sexology*: the science of sexuality. Men and women, and those who troubled the gendered binary, could now be labeled by their internal condition and not just the sexual encounters they had. *Homosexuals* were a group or class defined by psychological and/or physiological attraction to their own sex. Their impulses were obviously nonreproductive and so departed from those who would soon be defined as *heterosexuals*. For some sexologists, these queer individuals were the worrying signs of a degenerating society, whether the result of a poisonous urban environment and contagion or biological hereditary unfitness. For others with a more forgiving or at least self-interested mindset, those who embodied same-sex love and desire were an eternal minority, one that was unfairly oppressed by law, church, and society.

When the theorist, philosopher, and historian Michel Foucault famously proclaimed how "the sodomite had been a temporary aberration" before the late nineteenth century but "the homosexual was now a species," he was primarily making a point about the birth of this specific medical and legal category. Popular attitudes toward same-sex desire or how men actually felt about and understood their desires were not strictly a part of this shift—something that has often been forgotten or just ignored in histories of sexuality.[10] If the understanding had shifted significantly at an intellectual level, it could take a long time for these startlingly modern ideas about same-sex desire to become embedded in the popular consciousness. Even in those countries that produced pioneers of sexology there was no simple before and after the late-nineteenth century "invention" of the homosexual. Older ways to understand or embody same-sex desire were not so easily replaced by scientific or medical models, and different national and regional cultures shaped how theoretical writings about queerness were received by the men they concerned.[11]

In Ireland, the medical infrastructure was less developed, and public knowledge about bodily desires was held back by the oppression of the state and church. Queerness was instead translated through the intense religiosity and prudery of the region or simply overlooked altogether. As my opening vignette of Arthur Greeves's life begins to suggest, men who diverged from the supposed norm had to make a journey of discovery on their own, with the result that there was a diversity of ways to be queer. This chapter explores three different models through which queer desire was understood in Belfast: scientific frameworks of inversion and homosexuality; Christianity, with both positive and negative interpretations of the Bible; and popular literature, especially English and American. Though I show how these models ebbed and flowed at different points, they could also overlap or simply coexist. This fact means there was no definite way to conceive of same-sex attraction until at least the 1950s, when a more concrete understanding of homosexuality emerged in the culture of the north of Ireland.

Sexology, Psychiatry, and the Irish Homosexual

In Britain, the imperial power that shaped many though not all of Ireland's legal and governmental institutions, there was relatively little open discussion of homosexuality before the mid-twentieth century. Pioneering sexological texts, mostly published first in French or German, were stifled by the country's medical and legal bodies and difficult to obtain.[12] At the end of the nineteenth century, those English authors who had the literary connections and language skills to obtain and read rare Continental texts were still uneasy about their ideas being accessible in a hostile moral environment. John Addington Symonds was the author of *A Problem in Greek Ethics* (1883) and *A Problem in Modern Ethics* (1891), both of which were later acquired by Greeves. While he was alive, Symonds had instructed his small network of fellow travelers to *not* share his privately printed work more widely. All the first editions of *Sexual Inversion* (1897), which he cowrote with Havelock Ellis, were bought up and destroyed at the behest of his widow, and the second edition, with Symonds's name taken off, was subjected to a successful obscenity trial in 1898. Even after *Sexual Inversion* was finally republished in Britain in 1928 it remained expensive and difficult to obtain for medical professionals, let alone the general reading public.[13] The decades between the world wars did see some tentative moves toward more public knowledge of the theories of homosexuality, but organizations such as the British Society of the Study of Sex Psychology kept a relatively low profile, bickered internally about how far they should try to reach the masses, and were wary of the latest Freudian developments.[14]

Even if the situation in Britain had been more advanced, the new jurisdiction of Northern Ireland would not have provided a fertile ground for sexology. There was a lack of funding for psychiatry in the economically and politically difficult decades after the violent partition of the island and only slow or inadequate reform of the health system in general. Professional medical thinking remained more in tune with the nineteenth-century approach of simply containing the "insane" in poorly maintained institutions, and using modern methods of treatment for mental health conditions was rare.[15] In 1938 a government report lamented how Northern Ireland was many years behind Britain when it came to the law and mental deficiency and suggested the formation of a psychological clinic to help understand juvenile offenders in particular. The following year the resident medical superintendent of the Down Mental Hospital was similarly disappointed by how most medical students in the region were still being taught nothing about neuroses and so tended to regard Freudian theories as "nonsense."[16]

Medical ignorance was compounded by the veil of moral silence that covered the public conversation. Before the 1950s, homosexuality was mentioned a total of only four times in the *Belfast Telegraph*, the leading title of the region, and not even in relation to anything that was happening in contemporary Ireland.[17] Criminal trials were usually reported, but there was no direct discussion—even in euphemistic language—about the social world of same-sex-desiring individuals. There was still some public knowledge about the general existence of men who had sex with men because of the English newspapers that circulated in the region, but reading the Belfast press would have led to a sense that the authorities barely knew such men lived in their own city.

If scientific understandings of same-sex desire were rarely expressed in public before the 1950s, there is some evidence that there was still a casual knowledge of such concepts in Belfast among both queer men and those who witnessed their presence in public. Theories on the European continent in the late nineteenth century had been produced through the mutual interaction of doctors with their "abnormal" patients, so it is not that surprising that the language of sexologists roughly aligned with what queer men in Ireland were also thinking and saying.[18] Sexual inversion—the idea that same-sex desire was due to a man's innate femininity, whether biologically or spiritually—had some purchase on the cruising scene. In 1890, for example, one young man refused the request of his older partner in crime to join him in the same prison cell after they had been arrested together. "No," he said within earshot of the police, "you are a woman and I am a man."[19] A couple of decades later, another working-class youth told the police that he had heard that the man who had cruised him was a hermaphrodite, which was a variant of inversion that the psychiatrist Richard von Krafft-Ebing had defined in his foundational work *Psychopathia Sexualis* (1886). This young man in Belfast probably lacked access to such medical texts, but he had traveled the world as a sailor; perhaps he had picked up some understanding from those who had read the original German or learned about it through a sexological popularizer such as Edward Carpenter.[20] At any rate, in both these cases of urban subculture, younger working-class men used a casualized language of medical theories to explain why they were different—more *normal*—as compared to the older middle-class men they had sexually satisfied.

Gender transgression had in fact long been a part of the city's queer scene, even before it could be named in the scientific language of inversion. When the Belfast Scandal of male prostitution erupted in 1890, the press chose not to reveal how one of the accused had an adopted name of Kathryn. Still, they did report how the youths—many of them actors—had attended masquerade balls where one had acted as master of ceremonies.[21] Astute readers would have seen the similarities between these details and the reports of trials of scandalous cross-dressing, female impersonation, and theatrical campness in other places in Victorian Britain and Ireland and may have understood the suggestion that such behaviors were linked to same-sex perversions.[22] By the 1920s and 1930s, the sense that gender deviancy and desire were a related phenomenon was growing. Some of those members of the public who reported queer men to the Belfast police now mentioned womanly mannerisms or "unnatural looking" faces.[23] There were also veiled references in the local newspapers to the problems of effeminate "pansies" or "milksops" who were an affront to the famed manly stoicism of the Ulsterman.[24]

Though little self-reflection from the scene has survived, we should not discount the possibility of a transgender reading of how queerness was (and was not) being expressed in Belfast.[25] In such an intensely masculine and often violent society, demonstrations of potentially transgressive gender could sometimes lead to awful repercussions. In 1908, for example, one young military recruit found this out when he was viciously attacked by a policeman simply for cavorting on the street in women's clothing.[26] Little wonder, then, that there is not enough evidence of a trans subculture in Ireland to rival that of Weimar Berlin or post-Prohibition San Francisco. Though in these examples abroad there were still obvious limits to social tolerance, conservative gender norms in Belfast kept this sort of experience almost entirely in the shadows.[27] What is more, as we will see in the next chapter, many of Belfast's queers could be openly disdainful of those they felt were not living up to their status as Ulstermen.

Nonetheless, after physically and mentally broken soldiers returned from the First World War, the now obvious fragility of masculinity did encourage a more public debate about the past, present, and future of gender norms, as did the effeminizing effects of unemployment in the 1930s and the signs on the horizon of another world war.[28] The heightening of a modern beauty industry for men, which in part was a response to the psychological unease about male inadequacy, elicited a counter-discourse, in Belfast as elsewhere, of fears that the distance between the sexes was narrowing. Newspapers were now used as a method of reminding Ulster's men of their duties to remain as manly, or even manlier, than their cousins across the Irish sea. Those who used cosmetics were marked out as being especially vulnerable to sexual deviance.[29] Still, many in Belfast remained ignorant of these shifts in their perceptions of men and women. Terms like *pansy* could denote effeminacy without necessarily same-sex desire, for example, and even a *ladies' man* whose sexual appetite had led him into a commercialistic obsession with fashion.[30]

We can only wonder how many men in Belfast repressed same-sex desires because of the intensely masculine culture of Ulster; it is easier to find evidence of those who embraced their queerness than those who ignored it. Some queer men certainly understand that what they did with other men was not just criminal but could be socially distasteful too. Negative feelings about physical desire held them back from consummating their romantic love with other men, and when those who did take part in urban cruising found themselves in the hands of the police, they often expressed shame. Some even admitted, in their moment of exposure, that they "deserved to be punished."[31]

Still, we should be careful of always accepting at face value the declarations of guilt or an eagerness for a cure when men were desperately trying to avoid prosecution. One example of a consensual encounter, first spied on by a vigilant member of the public in 1927, hints at the ambiguities of claiming remorse. Edward McLoughlin was a middle-aged married baker and his lover a munition worker from Glasgow. At first McLoughlin apologized to the police and claimed he would not do it again if he could be let free. But when the younger man protested he was an orphan and blamed McLoughlin for calling him into the toilet where the sex had taken place, the older man changed tack. "Yes," McLoughlin now responded more honestly, "and we got to understand one another as we both felt the same way."[32] In another startling display of manly defiance, a middle-aged salesman even drunkenly turned up at a police station in 1912, hammering on the barracks door, and challenged the constable who had landed him in court for gross indecency just a couple of months before.[33] Even during a moment of potential social downfall, some queer men rejected the disgust of those who judged them.[34]

Eventually the power of Freudian ideas did begin to grow in Belfast, and with it more internalized self-loathing about same-sex desires. When one man was arrested in 1947, for example, he explained how there was something "abnormal" about himself from early adolescence, a problem that had only been awoken further when he was serving in the hot climate of India during the Second World War. Blaming the weather for his same-sex attraction may have been a response to the writings of the explorer Richard Francis Burton. His concept of the Sotadic Zone (1885) suggested that "pederasty" was more prevalent in hot climates; similar claims were made in Havelock Ellis's *Sexual Inversion*. Regardless, by using books that dealt directly with sex, this man in Belfast had "discovered the class" under which he came and said he was now seeking a cure—unsuccessfully, given he had been discovered in a toilet sexual encounter with an adolescent boy. This man's description of his self-discovery and diagnosing of a psychological problem was not enough to sway the judgment of the court; he was sentenced to nine months in prison, along with his name and address being printed in the newspapers next to the description of an "indecent offence."[35]

It was only with developments in the medical structure of Northern Ireland that the pathologization of homosexuality could truly take root. The Westminster creation of the National Health Service in 1948, and a new Mental Health Act for the province soon after, transformed local hospital provision. Psychiatry was now empowered to finally find its way into the courtroom. In late 1949, Charles B. Robinson—a prominent local physician and later chairman of the Irish branch of the Royal Medico-Psychological Association—was called upon by the prosecution to provide the first medical profile used in a queer trial in Belfast. The physician, echoing the Freudian model, dated the onset of the accused's "abnormal sexual impulses" to boarding school and suggested they were the result of an overbearing mother. The prognosis for curing this "sex perversion" was not good, Robinson told the jury, because the man had been indulging his dysfunctional desires for decades. The man may have needed alcohol to go through with the sexual act, he surmised, but the drinking was more for courage than it was the cause.[36] Just a year or so later, another arrested man told the police he was willing to undergo any treatment for a cure. The judge accepted, and an admitted homosexual was thus sent to a hospital instead of prison for the first time in the region's history.[37] A few others were given the same punishment into the 1950s and 1960s, as the availability in the province of conversion therapy—both voluntary and mandated—began to grow.[38]

Still, we should not overestimate the spread of such medical understandings of desire in the city. Even in the postwar period, by which point the discussion of homosexuality in the English-speaking world had become more open and articulated in the language of psychoanalysis, most observers in Belfast stayed tightlipped.[39] In 1958, Charles Robinson could argue that the prudish religious culture of the region was still causing an aversion to Freudian theories, despite his best educational efforts. "Ulster people," he reflected, thought it better to either endure or pray their way out of mental troubles.[40] This wariness of psychiatric models of homosexuality—in the classroom, the courtroom, and even the hospital—left a space for other ways to understand same-sex desire in Belfast until at least the 1960s. Different sorts of experts were able to step in and provide their own interpretations, and some, as we will see, were eager to take on that task.

Religion for Controlling *and* Expressing Sexual Desire

The undeniable religiosity of Ulster shaped experiences and understandings of same-sex desire in complex and sometimes contradictory ways. If same-sex crimes were discussed in the local press, biblically sanctioned beliefs were naturally one frame of reference to understand what had happened. During the Belfast Scandal of 1890, for example, the assizes judge drew on a language of "plague" to describe the existence and potential influence of young men who sold sex to other men.[41] The phrase "not to be named among Christians" often prefaced the unspeakable sin of "buggery" in legal documents and, before the second half of the twentieth century, "unnatural crime" was sometimes euphemistically used to report trials in the press instead of the more legalistic "gross indecency."[42] Sex between men, as a transgression of God's natural law, could simply never be doctrinally justified by the local leaders of Catholicism or Protestantism, and that was reflected in how the state—if only rarely—spoke about the problem too.

Religious disapproval was not the same as regular condemnation, however. For most of the period there was no enthusiasm from the churches to have an open theological discussion about abnormal male desire. The north of Ireland was not unique in this respect. If there is evidence that "sodomites" were already a recognizable social group in the eighteenth century in cities such as London, and even the origins of what were later called homosexuals, silence and confusion could generally surround the specifics of sodomy itself well into the twentieth century.[43] Biblical condemnations of unnatural or even sodomitic sins could still signify other nonprocreative acts, from bestiality to abortion, or indeed nonsexual sins altogether.[44] Only after the Second World War did anal sex and the still-emerging pathological category of the homosexual become more commonly and urgently entwined in Christian teaching. Beginning with the writing of sexologists in the late nineteenth century and continuing in the evangelical politics of the present day, there has been a forgetting of this complexity of religious belief. Instead, we are often left with a simple assumption: that homosexuals have existed front and center in Christianity's social critique forever.[45]

The north of Ireland has suffered more than most in terms of this "theological amnesia,"[46] largely because of the historically clouding effect of the extreme homophobia of the Reverend Ian Paisley's Free Presbyterian Church. But before Paisley took it upon himself to Save Ulster from Sodomy in the late 1970s and early 1980s, most Christians in Belfast were concerned more with illegitimate children than the existence of queer men.[47] In England, there had been a White Cross Society that ensured the sexual morality of male youths and even ran a reforming hostel for rent boys, but the suggestion that a Belfast branch be formed in 1903 came to nothing.[48] Other religious organizations did target adolescents, such as the Young Men's Christian Association or the Church of Ireland Young Men's Society, but they were more social than surveillant: they encouraged a muscular Christianity that elevated mind and body but did not directly educate youths on the danger of same-sex desires.[49] By the early 1940s, one woman who sat on the committee of the Church of Ireland's Moral Welfare Association privately lamented how they were failing to do much at all about the problems faced by boys. Instead, she noted in their committee meetings, most of their time was focused on dealing only with unmarried expectant mothers.[50]

Youths and men of all faiths were certainly warned by schoolmasters and the clergy, if in mostly hushed tones, about the dangers of using their body for promiscuous nonreproductive pleasure. But the subtext was really the forbidding of birth control and—for public schoolboys especially—the perils of masturbation. Same-sex desires and behaviors were barely visible or only implicit in these moral panics. Maurice C. Hime, for example, a schoolmaster of the Foyle College in Derry in the northwest of Ireland, wrote many dense and theologically informed screeds against "self-pollution" in the late nineteenth century. He did hint at some concern about what boys did together and not just alone but thought it better to not directly describe the behaviors to his pupils in case he inadvertently provided sexual guidance. Over forty years later, lectures by clergymen for the Moral Welfare Association in Belfast, on topics such as "sensuality" and man's "nature," had not moved much beyond this anti-masturbation panic.[51]

In England, a more professionalized social hygiene movement, eventually supported by the state, was redefining understandings of sexual difference, satisfaction, and pleasure by the early twentieth century, even if it had nothing positive to say about homosexuality. But Northern Ireland's government was far less interventional, which simply allowed an older religiously sanctioned politics of social purity to last much longer than across the Irish Sea.[52] In effect, homosexuality remained unspoken, and succumbing to same-sex desires was representative only of a personal failing: an individual lapse into temptation rather than any broader social problem. Silence, embarrassment, or only vague and sporadic denouncements were consequently the main responses from moral puritans to the existence of queerness in Belfast.

Ulster was undoubtedly devout, at least in the ways that can be easily measured by historians.[53] Even as the signs of secularization began to grow in Britain in the mid-twentieth century, the three main denominations in Belfast—Presbyterian, Church of Ireland, and Catholic—maintained a strong grip on local culture.[54] Given the instability of the region both before and after it was partitioned in the early 1920s, the various churches had to serve as an anchoring moral force. Proclamations about purity and sin seeped out from the pulpit and informed the policies of government while the churches provided many social services as well as the ethos for reforming associations and almost every aspect of everyday life was colored by Christian principles, from the organization of education to the purposes of sport and leisure.[55] But if Christianity had the steer on the social morality of Belfast, there were still blind spots in its purview.

If this was the general picture in the north of Ireland, there is one extraordinary exception that proves the rule. William Lovell Northridge was born in County Cork in the south but trained and served as a minister in Belfast from 1910, later becoming the president of the Methodist Church of Ireland. By the time he retired in the 1950s he was rightly celebrated as one of the most distinguished members of this nonconformist Protestant denomination.[56] The intellectual work he carried on outside of the church was just as important as his leadership in securing this reputation. In 1918 he graduated with an undergraduate philosophy degree from Queen's University Belfast before studying for an MA at the University of London. He finally returned to Queen's to earn a PhD in 1922 with a thesis on modern theories of the unconscious.

In his landmark work *Psychology and Pastoral Practice* (1938), William Lovell Northridge embraced medical models and the teachings of Freud in particular. Homoeroticism, as he usually termed homosexuality, required a modern treatment and "much more sympathy and understanding" than the church or law was willing to give.[57] Most homosexuals were made and fixated at the immature stage of preadolescence, he argued, so they could be *unmade* too, through a combination of religious pastoral support and the medical wonders of psychiatry. Northridge's treatment of same-sex desire had responded to modern scientific understandings of desire yet still found a place for the power of Christian faith, demonstrating how clearly different regimes of sexual knowledge could overlap and even work together in this era.[58]

The aim of the Freudian impulse was the release of a healthy heterosexuality rather than the acceptance of homosexuality though Freud himself remained ambivalent about the possibility of changing a patient's sexuality.[59] William Lovell Northridge was also nuanced in his beliefs; though he believed the vast majority of homoeroticism was acquired, there was at least a minority whose desire for other men was innate and unchangeable. "Our duty as ministers," he explained, "is not to add to the difficulties by unsympathetic handling, but to explain that some are born in this way, that there is no disgrace in it, that many of the finest characters and most creative minds are homosexual, and that, if they will accept themselves fully, they will be able, without difficulty, to exercise due control and carry out sublimation. Any other attitude on the part of the spiritual adviser will only create barriers to happiness and to the progress of the soul's life."[60] In his insistence that homosexuality could be inborn and deserved sympathy, William Lovell Northridge was remarkably at the forefront of emerging Christian ideas about how to deal with same-sex attraction. At the same time, and even though he recognized same-sex encounters were "punishable by law with great severity," he did not suggest that the law should be reformed—a position that the Anglican Church, in contrast, was now gradually moving toward, if only in private at this point.[61]

William Lovell Northridge wanted his book on pastoral practice to be a tool for education. He dedicated it to the ministry of the Irish Methodist Church and described how it was written in a language that was as non-technical as possible.[62] His reputation and career in Belfast did help him put these ideas into action. He was a tutor at the Edgehill Theological College from 1926, then principal from 1943 to 1957, and taught many ministers-in-training to use psychology in their future pastoral work.[63] Though the Methodists were one of the smaller Protestant denominations, making up less than 5 percent of the population, Northridge also had some impact outside of his own circles. *Witness*, the periodical of the much larger Presbyterian Church of Ireland, took notice of his ideas. They positively reviewed Northridge's book and tentatively repeated his suggestions that occasional sermons could be preached on themes such as "religion and sex" or "God and our bodies."[64] Some local Bible class students were using *Psychology and Pastoral Practice* from its first publication, and early versions of his lectures on psychology were also shared with an interfaith group of interested readers.[65] When William Lovell Northridge died in 1966, the moderator of the Presbyterian Church could rightly declare the minister had been "too big for any denomination" and "belonged to us all."[66]

We should naturally be careful of confusing one case of personal expertise for a broader religious compassion toward homosexual men in Ireland by the late 1930s. The section on homoeroticism was less than 5 percent of *Psychology and Pastoral Practice*, and William Lovell Northridge recognized how difficult and "almost unconceivable" the subject was to "the sexually normal." The minister also lamented how his ecclesiastical colleagues generally saw psychology as being out of their purview and described the "negative, repressive, and extremely puritanical" spirit that had undoubtedly made life hard for those who came to him to seek sexual advice.[67] These more nuanced ideas about homosexuality were always on the far fringes of public

Christian debate, let alone in the conservative churches of Ireland. Even so, the sympathetic tone of Northridge's writing, and the lack of any moral public outrage about his advice, suggests there could be some delicate tolerance of queer Protestant men, if only those who agreed to suppress their urges through a combination of religious devotion and psychological therapy.[68]

For the most part, queer men in Belfast had to navigate both the silences and the oppressions of religion to come to their own understanding of same-sex desire. For Catholics this was a particularly tough task. There was little difference in the basics of Irish denominational understanding between their religion and Protestantism: sex, above all, was for reproduction. But the unnegotiable nature of a centralized doctrine from Rome, and the church's intense distrust of Freudian theories well into the mid-twentieth century, made it virtually impossible for Catholics to develop a local approach or conversation about homosexuality.[69] In moral theology textbooks—such as those written by an Englishman, Henry Davis, but used for teaching in the 1930s at St. Patrick's, Maynooth, the primary Catholic seminary in Ireland—sexual sins were so disgusting that they could only be described in Latin.[70] William Lovell Northridge was critical of the Catholic conception of sinning, which he summarized as being "contempt for God the Law Giver, disobedience to His precepts." Such an understanding, he suggested, positioned God as more of a Judge than the Father. The guilt and penances of confession only attacked the symptoms of homosexual desire, he argued, while "leaving the disease itself and its causes unaffected."[71]

Denominational arrogance and sectarianism made ecclesiastical figures like William Lovell Northridge more likely to criticize non-Protestantism, but historians have also noted how Irish Catholic bishops tended to negatively follow the dogma of the Christian message instead of its more benevolent *love thy neighbor* spirit.[72] Theology in Ireland had been especially puritanical before the twentieth century, but the postcolonial project of the Irish Free State added just another set of barriers to the open discussion of same-sex desire. The Catholic Church retained overwhelming power and confidence in driving forward the agenda of the state, and the open hostility of clerics to outside modern influences formed the basis for campaigns against even simple pleasures such as dancehalls and the cinema. When a governmental investigation in Dublin into the operation of the criminal law in the early 1930s provided scandalous evidence of moral laxity, including sexual encounters between men, its report was hastily blocked and remained unpublished.[73] In this context, Catholic priests in Belfast were even less likely than their Protestant counterparts to be doling out sympathetic psychiatric advice.[74] In the dark booth of the confessional, they instead instilled a private sense of shame and guilt about most sexual desires and disciplined their parishioners in the name of God and the Irish nation. If questions to their Father could be a way for some queer men to surreptitiously gain sexual knowledge, the fears of eternal damnation after committing a mortal sin were unfortunately very real.[75]

The life of two brothers, brought up in a devoutly Catholic west Belfast household, illustrate what were likely common experiences for those who were bold or desperate enough to seek religious advice. Joseph Dillon had considered joining the priesthood before embracing a queer life in London in the 1930s and then back in Belfast in the 1940s. But by the 1950s he returned to celibacy and the Catholic fold as the fear of meeting his maker grew stronger—though he did maintain his daringly camp persona.[76] Joseph Dillon's similarly effete younger brother, the famous painter Gerard Dillon, went in the opposite direction. When he sought theological guidance at the age of eighteen and explained he could not change his nature, the priest who heard his confession reacted angrily, warned him of the waiting pits of hell, and threatened to throw him out of the faith altogether. Gerard Dillon then disavowed churchgoing and, almost half a century later, lamented how he had failed to stop his great-nephew from entering the priesthood himself. Both Dillon brothers, it seems, struggled to reconcile their faith with the physical expression of same-sex desires.[77] It would not be until the 1960s—with the disappointment of Vatican II's unchanging position on contraception and the beginning of challenges to the moral authority of the church in Ireland—that a more open acknowledgment of same-sex desire became possible in Catholic communities.[78]

If some men found organized religion an obstacle to sexual fulfilment, there were others who actively turned to their faith to understand queer difference.[79] A "life in the pew" could be more about an individual interpretation of theology than it was highbrow denominational debate.[80] Even the Bible—the supposed eternal source of homophobia—was ripe for queer reinterpretation. The story of David and Jonathan, and the former's lament after the latter's death, already had a well-established pedigree among popularizers of sexology. John Addington Symonds led the way in Britain, transforming the story into a poem in line with his Hellenic thinking, before Oscar Wilde more famously referenced the "great affection of an elder for a younger man as there was between David and Jonathan" in his court defense of 1895. Even so, David and Jonathan's story remained ambiguous enough that it could also feature in mainstream children's books throughout the twentieth century.[81]

In 1932, the Reverend McIlroy, almost certainly unaware of any queer undertones, preached at the Newtownbreda Presbyterian Church in Belfast how David and Jonathan's love for each other was the same as man's love for God. David Strain, who was by then aware of both old and new models of sexuality, described it as "a terrible ordeal . . . seeing that my love is for a male." This devout Reformed Presbyterian now bitterly recognized how his fellow worshippers could accept historic male love but not its contemporary expression.[82] Gradually, Strain learned to find solace in the story of David and Jonathan and to see his own desires as part of this longer biblical tradition. He later reflected that he was ashamed only of the ignorant who insulted him with terms like fruit-merchant: "the unintelligent mind knows nothing of David and Jonathan," he defiantly told his diary.[83] Strain even used the story as a way to court young men, reading the relevant passages aloud from the book of Samuel, whether from the Bible in his family home or when visiting other churches.[84]

By harking back to an idea of a male spiritual comradeship that had lost power after Oscar Wilde's downfall, David Strain's understanding may seem old fashioned or out of touch with emerging ideas of modern sexuality. At the same time, it was the ability of this powerful religious understanding to combine with other models of desire and queer sociability that still made it useful in the twentieth century. It provided a defense against popular charges that same-sex desire was only physical and so inherently morally lower than romantic relationships between men and women.[85] For that reason, Strain also worried about the lustfulness of the street youths he sought to educate and seduce and was conflicted about how far his own desire for the male body was allowed to go under the constraints of his religious beliefs. "I am not a sodomite," he reflected in 1933, "but after all if I met a fellow who would return my love, I cannot see why we should not kiss and caress one another if we wished." By the end of the decade, Strain was willing to do even more than just that as he accepted that his sincere spiritual love had a necessary physical component, though he still was sometimes frustrated by his "puritanism!"[86]

Unfortunately, not all queer men in Belfast were able to balance or combine their faith with medical models of desire. Arthur Greeves was also deeply religious; before he discovered sexology, his diary entries refer to his attempts to "keep pure minded" or to be forgiven when he could not. He struggled with a failure to control masturbatory urges, recorded in his diaries euphemistically as Went North, even as he described more openly his attraction to multiple young men. At this point his relationship with Christianity was more complex than just condemnation. Greeves even sought solace in his faith, thanking God for bringing Carpenter into his life and asking for divine intervention when planning a date with another man in 1918.[87]

The Religious Society of Friends—or Quakers—could even help this devout Plymouth Brethren worshipper on his journey. Introduced through his older cousin to a Dublin group of these relatively liberal nonconformist Protestants, Greeves was taken cycling, lunching, and worshipping. He now fell in love with one young man of roughly the same age and class, who it seems his matchmaking cousin had hoped would be a suitable acquaintance. When that did not work out, another Quaker was sympathetic. "He is a real decent sort," Greeves told his diary, "[and] helped me a lot."[88] At the same time, when Greeves discovered psychoanalysis this sort of rumination on religion and its benefits disappeared from his diaries. As Greeves's life progressed, he struggled to stay committed to one nonconformist denomination and even became interested in the Baha'I faith, which certainly was *not* accepting of homosexuality.[89] Whether he continued to try to have relationships with men in this era is unfortunately not recorded.

In the wake of gay liberation politics, in Ireland as elsewhere, these queer religious cultures could seem antithetical to the virtues of being "out and proud." Middle-class religious men tended to not directly challenge the homophobia of their surroundings but rather sought public respectability through the contradictions of the "stained glass closet."[90] Christian beliefs provided a way of understanding same-sex desires and were not always a solely repressive influence; rather, they changed and adapted to the new category of sexuality at the same time as they shaped that category too.[91] Men like David Strain or Arthur Greeves experienced varying degrees of "queer martyrdom": a self-expression, even erotic, that combined their suffering with the "spiritual possibility of redemption."[92] The relative cultural lag in Belfast in terms of a medical discourse of homosexuality may have even helped such divergent experiences of spiritual queerness outlast other societies. In Britain, modernist writing influentially criticized religious morality as an obstacle to sexual knowledge. But in Belfast, there was no strong modernist tradition. When coupled with the suppression of sexual information and clerical silence, religion could still be a way to understand queer desire with tentatively positive results.[93]

Unfortunately, from the mid-1950s, this situation did begin to change. The direct impetus for religious discussion of same-sex desire came from Britain, where the Church of England had by this point recognized same-sex desire as a condition and concluded that men who gave into it were sinners but not criminals. They were called to give evidence to the Wolfenden Committee, which had been partially tasked by the British government with examining the laws concerning men who had sex with men, which then recommended decriminalization of acts in private. People in Belfast now needed guidance on homosexuality and other pressing social issues and naturally looked toward their religious leaders. The Protestant sister churches in Ireland were duty-bound to respond.[94]

At a Diocesan Synod of the Church of Ireland in Armagh in 1957, the Archbishop John Gregg made it clear that Christians across the sea had gone too far. He argued that removing punishment was like substituting "condonation for condemnation" when it came to "un-natural conduct." The risk was simple: the spread of behavior that was both "anti-social and corrupting" to a pure and moral society.[95] The Presbyterian Church of Ireland was more tentatively accepting. It did not discuss the Wolfenden Report at its General Assembly, but *Biblical Theology*, the house journal of the Union Theological College in Belfast, carried an article in response to the proposed legal change. Written pseudonymously, suggesting an unease about openly confronting the topic, the author insisted that "homosexual vice should not be given either too little or too much attention" because it was "confined to a small minority"—an echo of how unnatural desires were still seen as being foreign to the region. Still, the statement of the facts of Wolfenden were accepted by the Presbyterian commentator, and by extension the distinction between legality and morality. But there was still a fear of letting "the incorrigible . . . infect the healthy members of society," demonstrating that the new pathological model of inborn homosexuality had not totally overcome older ways of thinking about immorality.[96] Like it had throughout the century, the Catholic Church in Ireland chose to not say anything public at all.[97] Religious models of sin or temptation—or the privacy and secrecy that did not allow for discussion at all—were simply no longer a fit approach for dealing with the social problem of men who had sex with men in Belfast.

Reading Queer Books

Old religion and new psychiatry eventually produced explanations of same-sex desire that could be expressively homophobic, but even before that point queer men could subversively read between the lines to access the information and affirmation they needed. Popular literature provided a similarly ambiguous route into queer learning but was more diverse in terms of the genres, periods, and places it covered. It was also far easier to access. In Belfast, like elsewhere in Britain and Ireland, the spread of highbrow medical or scientific texts never approached that of Victorian aesthetic poetry or even the daring pulp novels of the American Jazz Age. It was the ability of such works to translate the sexological and religious ideas of same-sex desire to a lay audience that made them so powerful. At the same time, they often went beyond these individualistic ways of understanding queerness by also demonstrating a new model for men who loved men: a community or quasi-ethnic group that could be found in the modern city. Belfastmen now had more emotive and exciting treatments of sex and romance that they could import into their everyday lives. By engaging with these books, they reshaped their own queer selves and began to understand how to find and have intimate relationships. The result, long before the gay liberation movement, were the beginnings of positive models of selfhood for men who loved men.[98]

One of the most important forms of queer literature was also the oldest. For those in the know, literary classics provided an established language of male love and romantic friendship that took on new meanings after the late-Victorian medical discussion of homosexuality. Looking to history, for both sexologists and everyday readers, could provide a sense of same-sex desire as perennial or essential and thus be used to create a shared identity in the present too.[99] When David Strain discovered in the early 1930s that others had spotted the same allusions as himself, he described it as "quite a wonderful thing . . . to learn that my interpretation . . . should be exactly correct. . . . No wonder I found such delight and pleasure, although mixed with pain . . . in Shakespeare's sonnets, [in Tennyson's] *In Memoriam* and most of Wilde's poems—what a revelation!"[100]

David Strain was notable in that he made these connections on his own. Other men instead found out about literary or historical sources through the compendium approach of books written by sexological popularizers. We have already seen how this was the case for Arthur Greeves, a man of an elite background, but men from the lower social classes could follow the same route. A young Belfast library assistant named Ernie Smyth provides one detailed example of a working-class enthusiast for queer books.[101] He mentioned Carpenter's *Intermediate Sex* (1908) to most of his queer pen pals and even sent copies to those who could not get their hands on one of their own.[102] Carpenter's undeniably popular, literary, and relatively accessible works were distinguished by their compassionate and supportive stance on same-sex love, even if they were not entirely frank about the physical form that such love might take.[103] Still, men in Belfast were able to read between the lines to use his works as a justification for sexual relationships. Smyth described in his letters how he was "very affectionate" and longed to give "love in the most intimate way," though he did insist that same-sex relationships had to be more than just "mechanical pleasure."[104]

Ernie Smyth also appreciated the American poet and queer prophet Walt Whitman, but—for him as for many others—it was the infamous aestheticism of Oscar Wilde that provided the biggest inspiration.[105] Smyth's description of his personal taste, in a letter to a potential lover, could have been taken from *The Picture of Dorian Gray* (1891). "I am very fond of artistic surroundings, beautiful colours in furniture and curtains and softly shaded lamps," he cooed, as well as "flowers, perfume, colour, [and] beautiful scenery"—"all those beautiful things which appeal to the refined tastes of an artistic mind." Smyth's insistence on his elevated sensibility was likely again informed by Carpenter, who had suggested in *The Intermediate Sex* that Uranians were naturally of a more intellectual and sensitive disposition.[106] In effect, this was Ernie Smyth's attempt to consciously create a domestic queer aesthetic that had a dual purpose: reaffirming his cultural and sexual self-fashioning and advertising himself to likeminded men.[107]

It was common in the first half of the twentieth century for queer men in Belfast to search even further back in time for models of same-sex love, a way to give their own desires in the present a historical basis.[108] Ernie Smyth, just like his queer idols, also professed to be an enthusiast of Ancient Greek and Roman marbles. He used the postal service to acquire cards and drawings from London, which he kept in his bedroom on a respectable upper-working-class street in south Belfast, and even doodled to make them more sexually explicit. There were other queer men in the city who similarly incorporated flourishes from antiquity into their queerness.[109] Walter Smith, for example, may have looked like an upright masculine clerk at first glance, but he enjoyed campily signing off his letters to friends in the 1930s as Eros and Endymion.[110] Arthur Greeves also found inspiration in the ancients. After receiving an elite education at Campbell College in east Belfast he would have already had some understanding of classics, but it was only when he found out from Edward Carpenter about the organization of sexual behavior among the Dorians that he pulled up early Victorian works on the topic to learn more.[111] But the most serious Belfast enthusiast of the Greeks was the well-known author Forrest Reid. His tales of boyhood are also the only real candidate for a local queer literature in this period, though the Uranian longing of his novels, such as *The Garden God: A Tale of Two Boys* (1905), is mostly implicit.[112] Forrest Reid's Hellenism did skate close to the edge of public respectability at some points, however. In the early 1940s it seems that either he or an editor toned down the queer undertones of his *Poems from the Greek Anthology*, and some of his more famous contemporaries, such as Henry James, were worried about being linked publicly with the pederastic themes of his stories.[113]

By the time that Forrest Reid was writing there had long been a public knowledge of the potential for immoral influence that lurked in Greek writings or indeed Victorian aestheticism, strengthened especially when Oscar

Wilde made the link between the two so clear during his courtroom defiance in the 1890s.[114] But there was no attempt in Northern Ireland to prevent anyone from reading what were now canonically recognized works. As one politician put it in 1924, in relation to how libraries in the region selected their books, the government did "not want to banish classics" though newer "trashy" or "pernicious" books were fair game.[115] Even so, discovering the veiled homophile themes of classic literature was only easy for those of a higher social class, who were more likely to have been introduced to such writings during their elite education.

Thankfully, by the interwar period, a more accessible and obviously queer literature could also be found in Belfast. Very little of it came from within Ireland itself, however. Political and religious moralists in the Irish Free State, particularly after the Censorship of Publications Act (1929), attacked homegrown authors who were deemed to have published indecent works, and that included even brief mentions of same-sex desire.[116] There was never a clamor in Northern Ireland to emulate this rabid censorship— a proud point of difference for many Ulster Protestants, even if it emanated more from a desire to stay closer to the ad hoc censorship culture of Britain than any homegrown liberality of thought.[117] Still, it would have been a brave author indeed who decided to try writing a queer Belfast novel. In general, the culture of the north was conservative, less open to experimentation, and—according to its critics—consequently lagged behind the literary trends of other countries that allowed for sexual experimentation.[118]

Instead of a regional queer literature, two distinct genres of foreign writing dominated the scene in Belfast. First was the English public school or university coming-of-age story. These novels center on adolescent or young men who fall hopelessly in love with other boys, though most steer away from the modern concepts of inversion or homosexuality. In effect, they are descendants of the late Victorian Hellenic-inspired ideals of manly romantic friendship, and for that reason the storylines are peppered with references to the Ancient Greeks. The physical desires are usually cloaked or at least unconsummated—hidden in the innocence of youth—though astute critics and everyday readers were aware of the implication. David Strain described E. F. Benson's *The Inheritor* (1930), which focused on a Cambridge student tormented by his feelings for male friends, as being "one of if not the most beautiful story" he had ever read. When he then picked up a copy of Derek Walker Smith's *Out of Step* (1930) at Smithfield market, he recognized how it was similarly the "story of a boy at a public school with my troubles—love for other boys." Thankfully, it also contained "wonderful descriptions" of Strain's "own feelings."[119]

A second literary paradigm entered Ireland from the other side of the Atlantic. These middlebrow-at-best novels focused on seamy urban subcultures, especially in New York, and captured the dangerous excitement of crime, drugs, and gender transgression.[120] But a greater openness about queerness came at a literary cost: the salacious content could only be justified to publishers and critics if the protagonists met their moral comeuppance. As E. M. Forster sardonically noted, his own optimistic novel about love between men could only have been published during his lifetime "if it ended unhappily, with a lad dangling from a noose or with a suicide pact."[121] Actually published stories from the United States at least still popularized sexological ideas, and showed how some men could subversively embrace queerness despite the moral and social risks. In that respect, they were far more useful than the staid and often hand-wringing English schoolboy stories.

The experiences of one young Belfastman can tell us more about this culture of reading. Harry Ritchie was the son of a soldier and lived with his widowed English-born mother in a working class-district in the east of the city.[122] He had already found himself caught up in a same-sex crime court case in Belfast in 1931, when he was just fifteen and in a relationship with a laborer around ten years his senior, and had seemingly left Ireland not long after to spend time in London.[123] It may have been in the British capital that he first came across queer novels, but he was still eager to discuss them when back in Belfast and on coffee dates with older men. He was a fan of André Tellier's *Twilight Men* (1931), for example, a melodramatic morality tale that took place across London, Paris, and New York and ended with the effeminate protagonist bashing in his father's head. Even so, Ritchie described it as "a very beautiful book" and speculated that "the writer must have been of the brotherhood to have been able to know so well what to write about."[124]

Harry Ritchie was also an enthusiast of Blair Niles's *Strange Brother* (1931), a novel that featured a young New Yorker discovering Edward Carpenter, Walt Whitman, and the Harlem drag balls before killing himself out of a fear of being publicly exposed as a homosexual. Such was the popularity of this pulpy tale in Belfast in the 1930s that the title was used as a self-identifying label by some queer men. Even street youths, approached at random, could be expected to have heard of the book. In 1937, for example, David Strain struck up a conversation with a lad who was watching the Orangemen parading on the twelfth of July. When asked if he had read *Strange Brother*, the youth replied immediately. "Oh, yes," he exclaimed, "by that Niles woman . . . a very remarkable book, but a very sad ending—I did not know there were such people until I read that book."[125] Slumming tales in the ethnically diverse neighborhoods of the modern American city may have been exotic in a region where White

Christians made up the overwhelming majority of the population, but this context was not that important to Belfast's men. Their interest was instead piqued by the sexual and social element, which proved there were men like themselves all over the world—an international brotherhood, as they termed it—who were trying and even succeeding in building their own queer world.[126]

Brief and careful adverts in periodicals like *John O'London's Weekly*, such as stories about the "intermediate sex," were one initial way to find out what had been published.[127] Even the reviews in the daily press that damned novels were another useful indicator of queer content. Richard Rumbold's *Little Victims* (1933), for example, centered on the protagonist's life—and one suspects the author's too—at public school and then Oxford. It was frank about homosexuality, which was suggested as the result of hereditary degeneration and, in the Freudian sense, an overbearing mother/difficult father. The story ends with the student's seduction by other Oxonians and then a despairing suicide. Reviewers predicted it would be controversial and were proven right. Some months later, Rumbold was refused Holy Communion at Oxford after the Archbishop of Birmingham had told the priest of the private chapel about the objectionable content of the book. The young author even went to Rome to appeal to the Pope about his excommunication but returned home unsuccessful.[128] An early review in Belfast's *Northern Whig* had sensed the distastefulness of the topic and ended by suggesting the "hero" should "obviously . . . never have been born."[129] David Strain noted in his diary just a couple of days later how he had now ordered this book because it concerned his "kind of person."[130] Those who were less avid readers of the newspapers could also expect to find out about books by cruising and talking with other queer men, who were more than happy to recommend their favorites.[131]

By the 1920s and 1930s, these sorts of literary descriptions of same-sex desire could be picked up all over Belfast. Armed with the knowledge of what existed, queer men made their way to the two best-known bookshops in the city—Erskine Mayne's (fig. 3.1) on Donegall Square North and Mullan's on Donegall Place—who stocked the latest titles or were happy to order them in.[132] Perhaps the proprietors were unaware of what lay behind the dust jacket, being too busy to check everything that passed through their catalogue. The British government did not advertise what books were banned, and booksellers were usually mindful of only the more obviously illicit titles.[133] But they may have just been unbothered: profit was profit, ignorance was bliss, and the sexual foibles of a few men were not their business. As long as formal state censorship of sexual discussion remained lax in Northern Ireland, there was no need for fairly discreet booksellers to worry.

FIGURE 3.1. Bookshops like Mayne's sold queer novels throughout the 1930s and 1940s, seemingly without fear (or perhaps knowledge). A. R. Hogg, *W. E. Mayne, Bookshop, No. 3, Window Display with Advertisement for 'A Century of . . .'* (1934), BELUM.Y2097. Courtesy of National Museums NI, Ulster Museum Collection.

In conservative Belfast, there were some who were even successful in pushing the limits of what could be sold without facing conviction. The Progressive Bookshop, in the city center though not on a main thoroughfare, was opened in the late 1920s by the left-wing organizer Davy McClean. It was probably modeled on the bookshop of the same name in London, which had been founded in 1918 and brought together radicals and bohemians from across the political spectrum while serving also as a metropolitan hub for the surreptitious distribution of works being challenged by obscenity laws.[134] Belfast's iteration proudly advertised itself as being the only place in the city that catered exclusively on topics like socialism, evolution, Esperanto, and philosophy.[135] This was certainly accurate. The radical scene of Belfast was stymied at this time, especially by unionist political dominance. McClean's venture, which later hosted the monthly Left Book Club, instead became home to a small group of progressive artists and intellectuals. The influential poet John Hewitt memorialized the scene in 1929: a "Mermaid Tavern of Belfast" where "the young men come to argue, talk, and show/brave lyrics to their friends."[136]

By at least the early 1930s, the Progressive Bookshop was selling books and pamphlets about the lives of famous queer men. Works on Oscar Wilde featured heavily, such as Charles Joseph Finger's *The Tragic Story of Oscar Wilde's Life* (1923) and *Recollections of Oscar Wilde* (1906) by Ernest La Jeunesse, André Gide, and Franz Blei. Wilde's own poetry was available too, as were the famous works of Walt Whitman. Displaying these titles in the shop window alerted queer men to the potential that more daring works were inside.[137] William J. Fielding's *Homo-Sexual Life* (1925), an American and Freudian pamphlet that named and discussed same-sex desire, if not with any positivity, was one such text.[138] McClean seemingly also personally kept an open mind on matters of sexuality. In the 1940s he employed Terence Pim as a shop manager, who used to "strut around in enormous polished-leather boots" and sported bleached blond hair. The novelist Brian Moore found this brave young man so fascinating that he used him as inspiration for a flamboyant homosexual character in his Belfast wartime-set *The Emperor of Ice Cream* (1965).[139]

Visiting bookshops to buy or request explicitly sexological literature could be a daunting experience, especially for those Belfastmen who were outside of radical political circles. Thankfully, publishers and distributors could be contacted directly by post to send titles in the return mail. Just a few examples of avenues we know men in Belfast took in the 1920s and 1930s: Denny's in London supplied both classic literature and the newer works of Edward Carpenter; Harrods sent translated German works such as Ernst Glaeser's *Class 1902* (1929); and John Grant's in Edinburgh provided various works by or about Wilde.[140] Even obscure tracts from Robert Sherard's Corsica-based Vindex Publishing Company found their way into the city, such as those that vociferously defended dear Oscar's reputation.[141] Most of these works fell into a gray area of regulation that enabled them to avoid detection; they were niche, cheap, and not important enough to be banned but not so obscure that they were impossible to locate or were only privately shared among an exclusive literary class.[142]

Even works that had been explicitly prohibited could still trickle into the region.[143] In 1929, for example, the *Belfast Telegraph* reported how one "English-banned book"—Radclyffe Hall's *The Well of Loneliness* (1928)—was "circulating freely." Though not prohibited in the United States and Europe, this infamous novel was still expensive to obtain, so a circle of interested readers in Ulster had clubbed together to find the money and then passed it around the province.[144] Like the daring American novels that managed to fly under the radar, *The Well of Loneliness* popularized understandings of inversion that were translated directly from sexological works and dared to depict fulfilling relationships for its female protagonists. At the same time, it also gave a glimpse of male "inverts" and their community in Paris's café scene. Though no reflection on what the Ulster readers thought about this novel has survived, both these depictions of queer life must have been a valuable lesson for those men in Belfast who were searching for the same.

Until funding began to flow from Britain to Northern Ireland after the birth of the Welfare State in the late 1940s, there was almost no medical infrastructure in which the relatively new theories of homosexuality could be embedded.[145] The local press, the legal system, and most ecclesiastical figures remained tight-lipped too, partly from a general ignorance about emerging modern ideas but also from a prudish fear of what might happen if sexual topics were broached publicly. But not everyone in Belfast was languishing in ignorance. The city may have been a traditionalist stronghold, unlauded for its artistic or literary scene, but it was not entirely closed off from wider cultural currents. There were numerous sites where queer men could find useful information, from bookshops and libraries to markets and mail order. Some sexological thinkers had an impact in the region, such as Edward Carpenter and Havelock Ellis and, in the postwar period especially, the followers of Sigmund Freud. But models of inversion or homosexuality were always more likely to be translated through the easier availability of novels and poetry than strictly medical texts. Oscar Wilde, not surprisingly, was a major influence on Belfast's men as he was on many others elsewhere. More surprising is how the slumming novels of the Harlem Renaissance found an audience in the Irish city. Though extensive reflection on these latter texts has not survived, the importing of the terminology of brotherhood into the everyday language of Belfast's queer men suggests it was the social group model of American urban life that was most attractive, the idea that same-sex desire was not something to be confronted on one's own.

Reading was only a starting point for queer men: a way to begin using new ideas to explain and express their sense of sexuality. They could take away the aspects of queerness that suited them, modifying for their own context, but were free to leave behind those bits that did not.[146] In practice, this entailed a mixing of different sexual models: taking spiritual or biological inversion and combining it with psychoanalytic theories of delayed development but not forgetting the colorful descriptions of Victorian poets or even the lessons of the Bible. The result was a lack of one simple or definite way to understand same-sex desire, no evolution from religious sin to criminality to sexological difference but rather a crossing over of each or even none.[147] In a sense, the ambiguity of Belfast's cultural position and its reception of ideas of same-sex desire were even novel. There was a peculiar lack of modern sexological thinking that reflected the intense religiosity of the island of Ireland. Yet, at the same time, the desire to remain close to Britain and the long-existing connections to the United States meant that queer literature flowed into the province in remarkably accessible ways. The result was a regional exceptionalism that defies any stereotype of the north of Ireland as being a backward-thinking and entirely repressed region.

To illustrate the intricacies of these models of sexuality in Belfast—the possibilities, limitations, and conflicts—my next chapter goes beyond the theories of same-sex desire to think about the realities. Physical and romantic queer relationships could be informed by what men had read but in practice were also shaped by a diverse range of everyday motivations and popular understandings of manly behavior. By digging deeper into this complex and contradictory world in Belfast, the past instability of the modern binary of homosexual and heterosexual comes even further into the light.

Chapter 4

Boys, Friends, and Lovers

In September 1919, Frederick "Howard" Aicken was born to a cooper and his wife in Newtownards, a small town about ten miles east of Belfast. The family of five endured poverty in the economically difficult decades of the interwar years. Food was scarce, and one daughter died at the age of ten from tubercular meningitis that had been exacerbated by malnutrition. Given his start in life, there was almost no chance that Aicken could have progressed to a higher formal education, despite leaving technical college at the top of his class at the age of sixteen.[1] In 1936, against the backdrop of the continuing depression, he was instead looking for work and thinking of taking a clerkship in a solicitor's office. Trawling the Situations Vacant on the front page of the *Belfast Telegraph*, Aicken spotted an advert for a different job: "Youth required as Apprentice by old-established business concern. Applicants must state age, qualifications, religion, and salary expected for five years' apprenticeship."[2] He wrote in reply, and the following week traveled—with his mother—to W. J. Strain & Sons linen merchants in the center of Belfast. The proprietor, David Strain, was impressed with the boy: "tall, good appearance, age 17, and signs of culture." Aicken later remembered that this meeting had been more like a fashion parade of young men being vetted than it was an interview. He got the job after a second round of interrogation and started work a few days later.[3]

David Strain was quickly smitten with his bright new employee and began to see him outside of work too. After just a couple of months, he dared to dream that Howard Aicken could be the special male friend for whom he had been desperately searching, despite being over twice the youth's age. He tested the water by reading Aicken portions of books about male love, like Lionel Birch's *Pyramid* (1931), a novel that described a public schoolboy's romantic infatuations, and Alfred Tennyson's more well-known poetic elegy for his friend, *In Memoriam* (1850). Eventually, after he had been introduced to *The Ballad of Reading Gaol* (1898), the young employee asked his older teacher why the author Oscar Wilde had been imprisoned. Strain explained that some were simply born with a love for boys or men. "I suppose you have already guessed that I am one of those people?" he added tentatively. Aicken smiled knowingly. When Strain finally made his move and a "feast of kisses" ensued, Aicken responded in kind. "I always wanted you to do this," the youth sighed, "but I was backward at showing you I loved you."

Little did his employer-now-lover know, but Howard Aicken had already been introduced to the queer world. When he was just sixteen, a visiting South American had told him about the curious men of that country who painted their lips and took boys to bed. Aicken was also hanging around in places where encounters might begin, like Bangor—a hedonistic resort town, at least by Irish standards—and Belfast restaurants where hopeful cruisers offered him cigarettes. He then discovered the sexual pleasures of urinals through an encounter with an older man in a dimly lit entry before becoming the lover of a former soldier in his late twenties who had met his gaze staring into a High Street shop window.[4] When David Strain slyly read the youth's diary in the late 1930s, he was disgusted to discover this blossoming enthusiasm for cruising. Their relationship was damaged, and, after a few tumultuous months of broken promises, arguments, and affairs, the young man was fired from his job.

Howard Aicken remained a familiar face on Belfast's scene for the next few years—frequently haunting the city center until late at night and replying to suggestive personal adverts in the newspaper—and had become "notorious" even before his eighteenth birthday.[5] Ireland, unsurprisingly, could not contain him. After working in a local factory office during the Second World War, he moved to Ilford in east London and then in the 1950s emigrated to Brooklyn to be with another man. Later in life he moved again, back to England, to be closer to the sister who had shared his difficult upbringing in Belfast; he died in 2007 at the age of eighty-seven.[6]

There was an economic self-interest in Howard Aicken's behavior; he was given money or other gifts and taken about the cafés and cinemas of the city by better-off men. But there was reciprocity too, despite his tender age. He recorded in his diary how one lover nearly cried when receiving a thoughtful present and waxed lyrical about the beautiful voices of men who chased him. He was also keen on "the love usually shown by younger for those older than themselves," as he put it, and jealous when the attentions of these mature men were wandering to other youths. Aiken, in summary, was defiant: why should he not love and have sex with who he wanted?[7]

This chapter digs deeper into how other youths and men experienced their queerness, from adolescent sex work to chaste intergenerational friendships, brief physical encounters to complex bonds of love. Understandings of same-sex desire in Belfast, as we have already seen, were shaped by the lack of wide access to the latest sexological knowledge. This gray area extended into the practicalities of actual relationships too but could provide opportunities as much as it did restrictions on what males did together. The boundaries between sex, romance, friendship, and intimacy may have been beginning to harden in the early twentieth century as a response to fears of effeminacy and even pathological homosexuality.[8] But in Belfast—for the time being—they also remained porous. The result was an ambiguous sexual culture that defied any strict dichotomy of homosexual and heterosexual until the social scene of love and courtship began to shift in the post–World War Two era.[9]

Working-Class Youths and Sex Work

The most ambiguous character of Belfast's past sexual subculture is one of the most globally common: the rent boy.[10] Transactional encounters were a facet of almost every aspect of queer life in this period, from cruising to the longer relationships that continued beyond the toilets. Poor and working-class boys and young men in Belfast sold sex in locations as diverse as city center alleyways, ice cream shops, and public parks and can be found in archival records from the 1890s until at least the 1960s. It is not surprising that the first real public conversation about queerness in the city also came with the scandalous discovery of a circle of sex-selling friends in 1890.[11] In Roger Casement's diaries too, the casual encounters recorded between males in the city are accompanied by the fastidious noting of money exchanging hands. In 1911, for example, Casement spent eight shillings on a Dungannon "boy" found on the Ormeau Road; the youth apparently said he "like[d] it rightly."[12] There has been disquiet about Casement's choice of sexual partners, even though his moral compass meant he limited actual sexual liaisons to older boys who—if his description of erections and activities can be trusted—at least returned his desire.[13] Either way, to understand the queer world of pre–

gay liberation Belfast we have to tackle intergenerational and paid relationships head-on.

The Criminal Law Amendment Act of 1885 had raised the age of consent between males and females to sixteen in Britain and Ireland. It stipulated no legal age for sexual contact between males and conflated all physical acts together—consensual and nonconsensual, paid and unpaid.[14] Even if the law had been more precise, the social and economic context of the modern industrial city blurred any obvious graduation from the innocence of youth to the self-determination of adulthood. Boys technically left school at age fourteen but often before in practice. Attendance rates in Belfast were especially low before the partition of the island, exacerbated by an underfunded education system. Even after reform and a building program in the late 1920s and 1930s, youths in Northern Ireland were less often in school than their counterparts across the Irish Sea.[15] Working-class boys were not usually skipping school but taking paid work out of necessity. Well into the twentieth century, they were expected to give up at least some of their income for the family budget. They were sent abroad for economic opportunities, took up lowly paid and underregulated work locally as street sellers and messengers, or worked as apprentices alongside men. Yet despite their participation in the labor market, before 1934 they were not eligible for unemployment insurance until they reached sixteen (though rates of juvenile unemployment in Belfast were still lower than for adult men). By combining a degree of economic independence and familial responsibility, boys often reached some markers of adulthood before full emotional or physical maturity. At the same time, they had freedom to traverse all parts of the city at all times of day, from dark alleys to raucous pubs. Often they considered themselves to have become men long before the arbitrary date of their eighteenth birthday.[16]

A striking portrayal of this transition from youth to quasi-adulthood can be found in Joseph Tomelty's Belfast-set novel *The Apprentice* (1953). The protagonist, Frankie Price, a Catholic boy, endures cruelty at the hands of an aunt who begrudgingly takes him in after the premature death of his parents. Tomelty had himself worked as an apprenticed house painter in the 1920s, lodging in a Belfast boarding hostel on the Falls Road, though there is no suggestion that his own childhood was abusive. Even so, there is an authenticity and rare honesty to his portrayal of the pitfalls and possibilities of working-class life.[17] For Price, starting work at age fourteen brings economic freedom from poverty, though he is forced to turn over most of his meager pay to his tyrannical aunt. But working with men of both religions still gives him an education in life, love, and even sex. After a workmate notices Price quizzically looking at his loyalist tattoo, for example, the man explains how "they say King William was a fruit merchant." When Price is puzzled, the man elaborates. "Aye, he was a 'poof' so they say. I got that on my arm over twenty years ago; I was in the Navy then. I had little sense. Nothing short of a blow lamp would take it out."[18]

By the time that Tomelty was writing this novel he would have been more than familiar with men who desired men, and not just because vitriol toward homosexuality was growing in the 1950s: Tomelty had been a cofounder in 1940 of the Ulster Group Theatre, which was a welcoming home for some of the city's more daringly camp actors.[19] Whether he had also been told about queer men during his own apprenticeship has not survived in the historical record, but we do know that happened for other local boys. One makeup-wearing youth who was working the streets of Belfast in 1938 described to David Strain how he had heard of "other fellows doing it" when he was employed at the machine makers of Combe, Barbour and Combe. After gaining that knowledge, he had decided to follow their lead.[20]

When we look more intimately into the personal backgrounds of those boys and young men who admitted selling sex in Belfast, it is plainly and painfully clear that many had difficult lives. They grew up in inadequate institutional homes, lived in poor and overcrowded conditions, and struggled with unemployment. In an era where the welfare safety net was patchy, they suffered the exploitation that came with unregulated urban capitalism. Still, we should appreciate the differences between the tough choices they made and the horrible experiences of those who had no choice at all. The clear grooming and sexual assault of children of all ages happened in many locations in Belfast. From the family home to workhouses, churches, and schools, or sometimes rough ground in less well-policed neighborhoods, children were never safe from abusive men. These cases tended to reach the courts after the signs of physical harm became visible on the victims' bodies, or they told a parent or other adult, despite the threats of the perpetrator. Even so, the infamous shame and silence that surrounded sexual abuse in modern Ireland likely led to many more assaults being covered up by church or family than those who were brought to justice. If a case did make it into the courts, young children who were confused and traumatized were then coaxed by the police and solicitors to make their testimony. They had only naïve sexual language to describe the violent acts carried out upon them.[21]

Those boys who sold sex tended to be aged fifteen to twenty, though there are examples of those as young as twelve or thirteen doing the same. Still, in their behavior and their own words, all these boys demonstrated how they were different from children who were abused. They expressed a casual familiarity with sexual anatomy and acts and were usually brought into the legal system when found with an older man in city center cruising spots. In the moment of discovery, they sometimes claimed to be unwilling participants. But witnesses to the sexual encounter rarely described coercion, and protesting victims sometimes appear again in gross indecency trials years later, and even as the accused rather than a victim or witness.[22]

There were also boys who admitted to the policemen or court that they had not been pushed into a sexual encounter. Late one evening in July 1939, for example, the police spied on a working-class boy just short of his sixteenth birthday wandering around the city center and going into several urinals with Arthur Patterson, a drunken sailor. When the constables interrupted the two embracing in an entry, the boy claimed that it was the man who had made all the sexual suggestions. But he also relayed how Patterson had said "I won't harm you" and had offered him about seven shillings and later admitted that no force had been used.[23] Other boys even described how they had managed the dynamics of their sexual encounters, whether by bartering for more money or setting up repeat meetings with their customers.[24]

Newsboys, a poorly paid subgroup of streetworkers, give us an insight into the motivations and experiences of adolescent sex work. Chroniclers of everyday life, in Belfast as elsewhere, saw these unmissable youths as emblematic of romantic urban character. Child-saving campaigners, however, worried more about the newsboys' vulnerability to the temptations of alcohol, gambling, and vice. Less sympathetic observers instead bemoaned how their rowdy horseplay or "corner boy" behavior brought down the respectability of their proudly moral city.[25] Whether loved, lamented, or loathed, the knowledge and accessibility of the streets that newsboys needed for their job also clued them into the everyday patterns of men who were seeking intimacy.[26] Sometimes newsboys were willing to have sex for money and only produced evidence for the prosecution after being caught. Other times they reported unwanted sexual advances to passing policemen, which nonetheless suggests that queer men believed newsboys were *usually* available for pay.[27] There were almost seven hundred of them aged sixteen or younger working in Belfast in 1902—well over half of all the street trading children—which equated to a lot of potential sexual trade.[28]

The extent of this casual culture of selling sex came briefly into view in 1916 after a wealthy industrialist in his late twenties was discovered to have been paying multiple newsboys for brief encounters over the course of many months. These young friends and colleagues were aged between fifteen and sixteen. They described how the older man hung around the pubs near the busy Great Northern Railway Station and frankly admitted that they took the lead in striking up a conversation before leading him into a local ice cream shop, where they gave furtive hand jobs in a semi-private booth for five shillings. They demonstrated little to no fear or shame about what they had done. The insistence that they had also seen the same happening between this man and other newsboys again suggests the availability of these precarious workers was a well-established fact.[29] At the same time, the economic circumstances of the boys suggest that they were selling sex at least partly because of challenging circumstances. Albert McCutcheon, accused of being the ringleader by his friends, was from a poor background. His father, a sawyer, was a County Tyrone migrant whereas his mother was a Belfast-born illiterate domestic servant. He was the third youngest of seven living children, nine of his siblings having died, and the family grew up in a four-room house on Matilda Street in the inner-city neighborhood of St. George's. By the time the court case came around in 1917, McCutcheon could not appear in court to give testimony: he had already been put in a boys' home in Glasgow for stealing.[30]

Quick encounters that followed street pickups were the most obvious manifestation of male sex work in Belfast, but there were also longer and more complex intergenerational relationships that only began in public places. Working-class youths and young men usually lacked domestic privacy, whether they were living in poor overcrowded homes, insalubrious lodging houses, or tightly regulated barracks. An older wealthier man could be a passport—or at least a temporary visa—to a better life.[31] In 1952, for example, one nineteen-year-old English soldier was court-martialed after he admitted being ensnared in Belfast by a rich man in his late thirties. "It was not vice which attracted him," the solicitor claimed, "but rather the things given in return."[32] The defense was likely telling the court what they wanted to hear: that this was not a crime of homosexuality, by then front-page tabloid news, but the lesser charge of avarice. Even so, there are many other examples of boys and young men in Belfast who sold their time or body for more than just money. They were taken to the theater or the cinema, treated to nights in hotels, and given gifts from football boots to full suits.[33] If only for a short time, they were able to escape the monotony and troubles of a laboring life to enjoy social pleasures that would have otherwise been out of reach.

A queer culture of casual prostitution was so common in Belfast that there was a camaraderie between those boys who took part. The youngest rarely had sexual encounters alone. Having a trusted friend alongside may have made sexual acts less laborious, but it also provided some safety when physical power dynamics were stark. In 1910, for example, two boys, aged fourteen and fifteen, had over twenty sexual encounters with a middle-aged laborer in a shed on the edge of the city. They also attended the theater with the man and stayed overnight together in a hut on a local golf course. In the court depositions there is no sense that the boys had already known each other, but the fact that they were apprenticed in the same trade and living in the same working-class district is suggestive of a friendship.[34] Such partnerships were formed on the central streets or in the familiarity of their own neighborhood, where the everyday rhythms of life could be observed. At the same time, transitioning into working life aged fourteen—and the growth of modern transport networks—gave many youths the freedom to move around the rest of the city without adult supervision.[35]

In this context of urban learning and movement, boys were able to share information about older queer cruisers. In late 1937, one seventeen-year-old orphan, who was living in a boardinghouse, walked uninvited into David Strain's workplace and successfully asked for financial help. When they next met on the street, the youth provocatively asked, "Do you not get a different one every night?" The older man's feigned ignorance failed to convince; he admitted "maybe so" and took the orphan back to his office. On future occasions he gave clothing to the boy, who continued to come back to ask for more.[36] By this point, Strain was such a well-known cruiser that many other poor or working-class youths flagged him down in his car or even approached him at home, and many were willing to give him the physical intimacy he desired. Only once in his diaries did he wonder out loud "why they accosted" him, but knowing now the backgrounds and networks of similar boys it seems obvious.[37] In navigating a difficult and often violent world, they were prioritizing those customers who were safe and reliable. The intimate size of Belfast encouraged the identifying of such men and the passing around of street knowledge as creative strategies for surviving an often-dangerous urban world.[38]

Young males who sold sex were, of course, at risk from violent men, but they understood that they held their own power too. The Criminal Law Amendment Act was known as the "blackmailer's charter" for good reason. Because it recriminalized and clearly defined any contact between males as being potentially illegal, producing the necessary evidence to prosecute queer men had technically become easier. The difficult life of Francis Wadman demonstrates the ensuing dangers of the city's commercial sex scene for older men. Wadman had grown up in England, in a staunchly religious middle-class family, but moved to Belfast in the early 1930s to find work as a schoolteacher. By the time he was arrested in 1949, then aged fifty-one, he had for decades been drunkenly picking up "undesirable characters" in the city center and paying them to whip or penetrate him. These young men, mostly aged around eighteen, were willing and brought their friends too. In the months following each encounter they plagued Wadman, at home and at his school, for more meetings and money. The Belfast head constable who eventually arrested the teacher accepted that his prisoner was being blackmailed and was sympathetic. Wadman had "been making an honest effort to break off his associations with these people," the policeman told the court, but they were "trying to frustrate those efforts."[39] There are other examples of youths and young men admitting they had kept coming back to conflicted queer men who had told them to stay away. If their age and lack of wealth made them vulnerable in some ways, their ability to reveal a man's queerness to his neighborhood or the authorities subverted the usual workings of the cross-class relationship.[40]

Boys and young men also exerted more agency by having their say about how relationships developed, both emotionally and physically. They were usually clear with the men who paid them about what they would and would not do for money. In 1917, for example, one sixteen-year-old orphan explained to the court that he had refused to let an older richer man penetrate him but confirmed that he had let him thrust between his thighs until ejaculation.[41] The reticence of this young man to take part in certain sexual acts was probably not a fear of same-sex intimacy as such. Working-class boys and men were used to living and working in proximity to other men, often in varying states of nudity. Without a strong public understanding of what homosexuality meant or entailed, physical affection was not necessarily suspicious. But there were still lines to be drawn around desire. The more intimate acts of receiving anal or giving oral were far rarer than acts like mutual masturbation because they could be seen as emasculating: a reversal of the physical power that working-class males were meant to hold over their middle-class admirers. Even so, it was the public performance of masculinity that remained most important, rather than what could stay a private secret.[42] Many young men on Belfast's cruising scene, when seemingly consenting to sex and even occasionally the receptive role, only complained about being "made a woman" when their behavior was exposed to the police or members of the public.[43]

Perhaps more surprising to our contemporary mores is how it could be the milder displays of desire that were most distasteful to working-class youths and men. One of David Strain's young lovers was happy to lie in the older man's arms while they read novels or listened to records, for example, but still refused to be kissed. "That's enough now," he warned on one occasion, "it's a woman you want." Another admitted he could not stay away from the older man and had no objection to being fondled but again drew the line at kissing. "Don't," he told a disappointed Strain, "it's soft to do that." Kissing was even just "a girls' game," as yet another youth told him.[44] In a society where being deemed manly was so prized, these tamer forms of intimacy could be more suspect than physical sex because they denoted romance, which was coded as feminine, rather than sexual release or camaraderie, which was coded as masculine.[45] At the same time, there were never firm rules when it came to what level of physical touch was allowed in working-class rules of masculinity. Strain's encounters with laborers or servicemen in his office could be intimate in all respects, especially toward the end of the 1930s and the early 1940s when he had embraced the bodily expression of male love. Even though some of these young men lacked enthusiasm, they still "obliged," as he recorded in his diary with some disappointment.[46]

Most of these intergenerational encounters went undiscovered by the authorities in Belfast. There was little sustained moral panic about the sexual dangers of the city for male youths, certainly not in comparison to the supposedly waning purity of modern girls, and the sites where boys could encounter cruising men went largely unregulated by the police.[47] Still, the fact that many adults saw no problem in paying poor youths for brief sexual encounters poses an ethical dilemma for us today. The reclamation urge of gay and lesbian activism can be to find historical forebears, tracing backward how "we" have always existed. The homophile movement of the 1950s and 1960s and, to a lesser extent, gay liberation that followed in the 1970s also promoted an enduring ideal of loving relationships between social and economic equals as a defense against accusations of social deviancy.[48] But we cannot understand the complexity of past queer life if we ignore the historical ordinariness of boys and young men who sold sex. Such encounters were a part of a moral economy that was legitimate under the economic and cultural conditions of capitalism at the time.[49] For the boys who sold sex, it may not have always been pleasurable, but neither was it necessarily experienced as abuse. Instead, it was simply a quick and relatively easy means to a financial or social end.

Growing Up and Becoming a Man

Mutual danger was always present in transactional relationships, but that was not the only dynamic at work. Older men—even when recognizing the social difference between them and the youths they paid—still experienced these relationships as romantically intimate. When prosecution was potentially upon them, some could not hide their feelings of love and responsibility for their boys. In 1931, for example, a laborer in his late twenties was adamant that he was willing to take the blame when he was discovered in a urinal with a fifteen-year-old. The two had met several weeks before and spent time in the cinema and strolling along the river or in the park glasshouse as well as having sex in clandestine locations. "I don't want the little boy touched," the older man instructed the park ranger who had detained them, offering himself as the one who should be punished.[50] Others in Belfast—and even those who had been blackmailed or burgled by their younger lovers—also took the blame on themselves or tried to keep a boy out of trouble.[51]

Neither did the transactional or unequal nature of a relationship preclude emotional feeling in the other direction. We have already seen how Howard Aicken (figs. 4.1 and 4.2) was intellectually enthusiastic about the eros of age-differentiated relationships even before he turned eighteen—what some queer men, most obviously the Uranian poets, had long positioned intellectually as the inheritance of an ancient Hellenic tradition.[52] Other less book-learned working-class youths simply enjoyed queer relationships on their own merits, and even those motivated partly by money could become romantic and last far longer.[53] David Strain's diaries describe countless friendships that began on the cruising scene but continued across cinemas, theaters, and social circles entertained at home. Youths professed their fondness, sent him love letters, and even intimately embraced when they saw him in public. But the same young men still carried photos of women in their wallets, made it clear that their affections were divided, and turned down dates because—as one grinned and put it in 1939—"that's the night I see the girl." Strain's attempts to convert these youths to strictly male relationships for life steadfastly failed. "We can get married," he suggested hopefully to one romantic nineteen-year-old in 1938. But when he also proposed "give up the girl and I'll love you," he was rebuked.[54]

Contemporary understandings and experiences of masculinity could allow for these sorts of queer relationships but were by no means static; they developed through time, as men negotiated the different stages of their life cycle and the often-changing society around them. What it meant to be a man was a process of constant self-remaking.[55] In Belfast in the first half of the twentieth century, there was a clear sense that—for most working-class youth—there was a time or situational limit on how long or in what context romantic male relationships were acceptable. Working-class lads were hardly shy about carrying on with men as well as women, but most still knew that they would eventually do what their families and society expected of them. It was not the fear of homosexuality that ended a relationship; that was not a terminology or state of being that many working-class youths would have understood. Rather, it was meeting a woman and making the conscious decision to honor

FIGURE 4.1. Howard Aicken with an American serviceman during the Second World War. Courtesy of Basil Abbott and Simon Abbott.

the social and sexual responsibilities of their union: settling into a more home-centered life with children. The experience of sex and romance was shaped by a nebulous understanding of age and maturity that set the adolescent phase of life apart from the adulthood sexuality that came after.[56]

Maurice Neill, a hairdresser, provides a good example of how a shift from male to female partners happened in practice. He first met David Strain on

FIGURE 4.2. Howard Aicken with his sister at David Strain's country hut (1937). Courtesy of Basil Abbott and Simon Abbott.

a tram; Strain then took him on dates to the cinema, the theater, and local cafés. Eventually, one evening, their relationship became physical when they parted at the older man's suburban home. "We got to the front door in the porch," Strain described, "[and] I took his hand in mine and was bidding him 'goodnight' when my control completely gave way. Taking him in my arms I kissed him on the cheek. 'Do you mind?' I whispered. 'No,' he replied, and turned his face so that I kissed him on the lips." David Strain wrote romantically, using his diary to imagine a relationship that would have a happy ending. Yet later in their yearlong friendship, Strain was puzzled about why Maurice Neill had stopped reciprocating his passions. "Although he has no objection to my kisses," he recorded, "I miss his caresses, as that is foreign to him . . . if he only loved me as I love him." A few months later, the now-twenty-one-year-old revealed his girlfriend, "and so," Strain lamented, "has ended my affair with Maurice."[57] How Neill's future romantic life might have developed we will never know; he died, still a bachelor, when serving in the air force during the Second World War.[58]

Many youths disappear from Belfast's criminal archive after a difficult day in court explaining their motivations for having sex with an older man, or indeed from the pages of David Strain's diaries after a romantic relationship broke down. But eventually they turn up again in the more mundane records of the state, such as the census. Now in steadier employment, they had married and set up their own home. There are countless examples from the late nineteenth to the mid-twentieth century, from the twenty-five-year-old found drunkenly having sex in a field with a better-off man in 1891 who settled down after fifteen years of soldiering to marry and have a child to the eighteen-year-old discovered selling sex in the Ormeau Park toilets in 1937 who then married in his early twenties.[59] For some young men, selling sex or just enjoying male intimacy—whether at sea, in boardinghouses, or in the private offices of their older lovers—was a temporary behavior, not a lifelong defining habit.[60] Their queer romantic and physical relationships were reasonable when they were young but had to end when they reached the next stage of their life.

Some men managed this natural jump from mixed partners to just women without any problem. But there were many, of course, who did not. It was common for older cruisers arrested in Belfast in the first half of the twentieth century to be married, some having been with their wives for decades and having multiple children.[61] In some cases, their life-stage decisions certainly had been made because of social pressure rather than desire. The expectation that men would transition into a domesticity centered on marriage and children could be powerful and indeed oppressive in Ireland.[62] Though the rate of marriage overall was among the lowest in Europe, it was relatively high in urban Belfast. The sanctity of the family home was also a central projection of the public image of both jurisdictions after partition.[63] Even the most flamboyantly open queer Belfastmen—those with multiple lovers, an enthusiasm for homoerotic novels, or a predilection for cosmetics—could make this decision to conform.[64]

Queer men may have consciously married to hide what they increasingly understood as their nature in some cases, but some sincerely hoped that the power of true love would effect a cure. We already saw how Arthur Greeves had been encouraged by a doctor friend in London in the early 1920s to try flirting with women to kick-start any latent heterosexuality. When Greeves mentioned psychoanalysis to male friends at home in Belfast who were struggling with the same problems, some were wary of the theory but in practice were already following that advice. One told Greeves that the safest way to avoid temptation was marriage and children, leaving subconscious needs to titillating books and plays.[65] William Lovell Northridge, the Freudian Methodist minister, certainly understood that some men took this route. He related in 1938 how one man he knew had married after being released from prison for same-sex crimes and tried to have affairs with women too—"desperate efforts on his part to escape from his constitutional disability," Northridge concluded. At the same time, Northridge seemed to suggest that marriage *could* help a man overcome his "homo-erotic practices."[66] Even as medical understandings of homosexuality increased in the province, this was still an option that men took. In 1947, one young man in Belfast told the police of his constant battle to cure himself, from trying to keep his mind fully occupied with work and exhausting his body through exercise to even considering chemical castration. "But it was always the same," he lamented. "Every time I had any time to think, my mind and sexual feelings turned to my own sex." After he was released from prison less than a year later, he moved to England and, now in his early twenties, took a new approach: he found a wife. The union did not last.[67]

Even a man as self-definitively homosexual as David Strain could consider courting a woman. His trials and tribulations after meeting Ethel Norwood, the daughter of a farmer and family friend, are suggestive of how deeply heteronormative romance ideals had penetrated popular culture in the 1930s. Around the time they first started to see each other properly, when she was just eighteen, Strain was having a torrid time of unrequited love with the similarly young Jack Murray. He never stopped trying to seduce this newsboy, somewhat dubiously imagining their relationship as a reincarnation of sorts of Oscar Wilde and Alfred "Bosie" Douglas. But Strain also began to meet Norwood, usually after she finished work at a factory in town. After he drove her home a few times, they kissed in his car for the first time. "I was disappointed," Strain reflected, "disappointed with the kiss, disappointed with myself for yielding. And yet I would glory in a kiss from Jack—it would seem to be more real." And so began "a farce" of kisses, handholding, and tiffs that lasted almost a year. In his diary, Strain often quoted screenplay-style their torturous conversations about love, in a probably subconscious replication of the melodrama of romantic Hollywood films he had seen.[68]

Ethel Norwood was a smart young woman. She sensed it would not be a blossoming relationship early on, despite David Strain's insistent chasing, and tried—unsuccessfully—to gently let him down by suggesting that they would make better friends than lovers. But Strain convinced himself he had fallen in love, despite never stopping his city center cruising and even proudly self-defining as "a woman hater." When he too finally realized the relationship was doomed, he told Norwood he would not marry her yet tried to impose constraints on who she might otherwise see. Thankfully, and with some relief, she now had the excuse she needed to escape the controlling situation. Sometime after their last romantic meeting, David Strain admitted his mistake. "If I ever had any feelings . . . towards her," he mused, "it must have simply been the outpourings of a pent-up passion that should have been spent on Jack Murray."[69]

Many outwardly conforming relationships in Belfast were damaged by a man's lusting after other men, long before moral panics about homosexuality in the 1950s made the public more aware that queerness could hide in the family home. In the years after an exposure in the courts and local newspaper, some men appear to have moved in with other relatives rather than continue living with their wives, who were likewise back living with their own parents. These women were then not present at their husbands' deaths or chose not to publicly memorialize the events; presumably they were only too aware of the hypocrisy of keeping up appearances in their neighborhood after the crimes had scandalously become public knowledge.[70] Middle-aged husbands too certainly understood that they had broken societal rules when they were discovered cruising. As one exclaimed when he was arrested in the early 1890s, "My God what will the wife say!"[71] Being exposed to friends, family, or the law was a constant risk to be negotiated, especially by those who were only living a queer life secretly. When a man failed to keep desires and relationships private, the result could be public shame, marital separation, and even forced emigration.[72]

If there were some men in Belfast who knowingly used women and marriage as either a shield or a potential cure, for others there were more ambiguous experiences of queerness at work. In an era when definitions of sexuality were still in flux, especially in working-class cultures, men could have sex and even romantic relationships with other men without seeing those desires as conflicting with marriage and children.[73] Self-reflection on this sort of situation in Belfast is sparse, given the Irish societal secrecy around sexual desire in general. But one trial during the First World War does provide a glimpse into the realities of men who were happy to court both genders. Hugh Sheehan was a medical student in his early twenties when he found himself tied up in a case of gross indecency. Fortunately for him, he was called only as a witness: the police were trying to pin a different man as the ringleader, a cosmopolitan migrant who was only recently back in town. Without the possibility of conviction, Hugh Sheehan was freer to be blunt about his sexual appetite. He had "read a little about medicine," he told the court, and said he fell into the category of "a young blood about town." Sheehan did admit his "abominable conduct," perhaps following the coaching of the police, but his statement reads more like the boasting of a young man who had discovered his own power of attraction. He had not only had anal sex with his male lover, he now related to an undoubtedly shocked courtroom, but had also "been with music hall girls."[74] Sexual practices and intimate relationships could be fluid, then, and not limited by any broader sense of shame about queerness.

Whether Hugh Sheehan continued to sleep with men after he married and emigrated to the United States a few years later is unknowable today.[75] But the life of another man in the same era demonstrates how some of these queer complexities continued into middle age for working-class men. When Samuel McGowan was arrested in 1927, he was already in his midthirties. In one of their less euphemistic moments of reporting, the press relayed the judge's damning comments that it was "a disgusting offence, a case of the grossest indecency" and deserved "heavy sentences." McGowan's wife, Mary, bravely appeared in court for his defense, but he was still sentenced to nine months with hard labor.[76] When Samuel McGowan was released, he went back to the marital home in east Belfast. They had gotten together after Mary's first husband died in the Great Influenza epidemic of 1918 following just three months of marriage, and McGowan had brought up her infant son on his laborer's wage before the couple had children of their own.[77]

From the late 1950s, Samuel McGowan became a frequent letter writer to the *Belfast Telegraph*, reminiscing about a life well lived, from colorful childhood characters and London trips with his wife to nostalgic "magic smiles and tears of an Irish summer shower in County Down." When McGowan died suddenly in 1968 in his late seventies, the same newspaper was full of heartfelt memorial notices from his by-then large family.[78] We cannot know what Mary McGowan had thought about her husband of three years being discovered with a nineteen-year-old in a city center entry, or if this was only a one-off sexual encounter that did—or did not—bring feelings of guilt. But it seems that even a powerfully shaming moment of exposure had not heralded the end of their union or stopped them from creating a loving family that was so publicly recalled at his death.[79]

Like Mary McGowan, other women in Belfast stood by their men after they were exposed for having queer sex. For some, that may have been because the alternative was worse. Divorce was difficult to acquire and heavily stigmatized in Ireland, so vanishingly rare.[80] But wives may have also been swayed by the continuing positives of their relationship. Marriage could be a path to independence away from parents and, for women especially, a way to gain a higher social status.[81] Working men who were arrested also invariably continued to support their dependents—economically, for certain, and probably emotionally too—for decades after their exposure. When they died, notices in the local newspaper memorialized the contributions to their families they had made.[82] We must avoid the temptation to define all these marriages between queer men and women as just a false "lavender" front, whether conscious or not, for stigmatized desires that stopped them from being a "real man." In practice, for most men and some of their wives too, love and domestic responsibility could coexist with queer expression, even if moments of exposure and prosecution made that more difficult.

Eventually this ambiguous situation of intimacy and desire began to firm up in the postwar era, with consequences for Belfast's culture of casual queer sex. In Britain, ideals of companionate marriage and responsible fatherhood had already been growing in power for some time, with couples getting married younger, helped by a buoyant economy and a more generous welfare system that made setting up a home easier. Young men were now spending more of their social time in the company of women in commercial venues rather than on the streets or in all-male spaces.[83] These developments came slightly later in the north of Ireland, and there are caveats too: the marriage rate was starting from a comparatively lower point, and the average age at marriage was historically higher too; the impact of affluence was not as obvious in a city where the old industries were vulnerable and wages remained comparatively low; the newly founded British welfare state had decades of local inertia to overcome in building suburban public housing in Belfast; and sex and gender norms remained conservative in a religious society, which meant lower levels of mixing in venues like pubs and youth clubs.[84] In both Britain and the north of Ireland there were also many who failed to live up to the new gendered ideals or actively contested them, including queer men.[85] Even so, by the 1950s the direction of travel in Belfast was clear: when marriage, home, and family were the goal above all else, casual relationships between men were now damningly homosexual rather than just a fact of everyday life.

Embracing a Gay Self

If a stricter binary of homosexuality and heterosexuality eventually took root in Belfast in the second half of the twentieth century, we should be careful to not assume that men who understood themselves to be solely same-sex attracted had not existed in the era before, even if it was not the language of *homosexuality* or *gay* they used. In not just their sexual acts but their internal sense of self, they saw themselves as different because of their homoerotic and romantic desires. By at least the 1920s, such men were seeking each other out and creating their own brotherhood, locally in Belfast but with links stretching across borders. They were not just looking for casual encounters, either. Like their friends and even lovers who were mostly interested in romance with women, they wanted to build enduring and even domestic partnerships of mutual desire. To do so required the use of imaginative methods and the support of other queer men around them: in other words, the beginnings of an identifiable community long before gay liberation.[86]

Ernie Smyth, the young library assistant from Belfast we met in the last chapter, was introduced to the queer world through personal adverts. The snippets he and other men placed in the London-based magazine *The Link* were so blatant that the magazine was subject to a scandalous trial in 1921 and shut down.[87] Closer to home, more careful men were able to use the classifieds section of the *Belfast Telegraph* in much the same way. Suspicious personal adverts begin to appear in the newspaper as early as the 1910s. "CHUM—Young Man, at business, companionable, would like to meet another for walking, amusements, holidays, &c. Reply, in confidence," which was published in 1914, provides one early example.[88] In the 1930s, the number of queer personals exploded, probably in response to the models and languages of queer life that were becoming available through popular novels. Placing an advert was cheap: just three pence per word with a one shilling minimum, the equivalent of just two or three pounds today.[89]

Most of the adverts in the *Belfast Telegraph* were generic. Asking for friendship was an obvious start, so there are countless men who were looking for "chums" or "pals." An additional wishing for "companionship," though, indicated something more romantic. Drawing attention to the trustworthiness of the advert placer—his "genuine," "sincere," or "confidential" intent—also signaled intimate desire. Finally, in case the queer reader was hesitating to reply out of fear for the response, adverts could confirm that their author was "cultured [and] happy-tempered," "broadminded," or "tolerant." Euphemism was used to circumvent the editorial eye or could provide plausible deniability if any suspicions were raised. For that reason, it can be difficult to draw a clear boundary today between the queer and not-queer—much like in other relationships that existed on the scene. But some adverts could be daringly obvious. In 1932, one thirty-two-year-old chum-desiring chap described how he was "quiet [and] musical." Connections between queerness, sensitivity, and the arts—including music—was by then a common conviction of sexologists and laymen alike, and most queer men would have recognized the allusion.[90] But it was this advert placer's admission that he "dislike[d] girls" that made it clear that any queer reader had found the right advert![91] More cloaked at the time but recognizable to historians today was a 1937 personal of a man who labeled his "intermediate temperament." If just a short phrase, it almost certainly referred to Edward Carpenter's *The Intermediate Sex*, an influential book for men who loved men.[92]

We know the author in the case of some personals, which helps confirm that the intention was explicitly queer. David Strain's experience suggests that most readers at the time were able to make the connection, even with the most euphemistic of adverts. He was replying to men as early as 1921, but only in the early 1930s did he build up the courage to meet a correspondent and then place a brief notice of his own. "Young man fond of country and quiet life, wishes to meet another as companion" was the typically careful wording used by this steadfastly respectable Reformed Presbyterian. More than ten men wrote in reply, with details of their age and occupation, and sometimes attaching a photograph. One even bluntly confirmed "girls are taboo!" Strain then traveled into the city to meet his respondents, usually outside well-known shops, before moving on to a quiet café to chat about their hopes for love and friendship as well as gossiping about the other men they had already met using the same tactics.[93]

David Strain's positive experience of placing personals hints at just how common it was for queer men to hide in plain sight, nestling themselves between job notices and commercials for miracle cures on the front page of the best-selling newspaper in the region. Whether the editors ever knew is unclear, but they do not appear to have done anything to stop the slew of adverts in the mid-twentieth century. Not everyone in Belfast was so naive, of course. In 1930 one journalist coyly noted how he "always associated these people who are seen to be hanging around the Castle Arcade with the 'personal' ads in the *Telegraph*, I don't know why."[94] Given how important we have already seen that area around Woolworth's and Castle Place was for cruising men, perhaps these queer adverts were not euphemistic enough.

Out of meetings that resulted from personals, as well as those that developed more organically on the cruising scene, intimate networks of friends and lovers came into formation in Belfast. These existed already before the 1930s and continued to exist in the decades after, but it is only through the diaries of David Strain that they can be reconstructed in their full complexity. Two of his more outgoing acquaintances were central to how this queer community developed in an intimate city. Walter Smith was born in 1898 into a large Presbyterian family in north Belfast. His father worked in the linen industry as both a clerk and a bleacher but progressed enough in his career to move his family to a larger house in south Belfast while Walter was still a boy.[95] Cecil Bond instead had a childhood of relative social decline rather than climbing. He was born in New Zealand in 1900 to well-off English emigrants, but not long after his mother brought him and his siblings back to England. She soon remarried a Presbyterian minister almost three decades her senior and relocated a newly formed family back to her husband's home country of Ireland.[96] By the 1920s, Walter Smith and Cecil Bond occupied roughly the same rung of the middle class, working as clerks or similar. David Strain only left the island of Ireland once in the 1920s and 1930s, to visit Manchester for work (where he was shocked to see personal adverts by queer men not in the newspapers but etched into toilet doors). But his friends were eager to travel and make connections in larger queer networks. Both had acquaintances in Dublin, some through the Oxford Group, and often traveled through London too.[97]

Matchmaking was a crucial social role of queer friends, helping to mitigate the lack of definite social venues in Belfast. In 1935, for example, Walter Smith helped David Strain become acquainted with a cultured middle-class youth he had spotted on the street. Smith realized that this lad, Arthur Fitzsimons, was a friend of a friend and reported back to Strain that the young man shared his interests in music and reading (figs. 4.3 and 4.4). "Really an intelligent chap, David," Smith promised. "I am sure you would like him." Even though it became apparent this man was not interested in a romantic relationship, he became a close friend and ally in the social group nonetheless.[98] The following year, Cecil Bond tried to help Strain too by bringing his young friend Tommy McMeekin into W. J. Strain & Son's linen merchants. At first the choosy Strain was not interested. He unkindly described the youth as "quite an attractive manner but not good looking" in his diary and complained about his bad breath. But Bond did not give up. The following week he called in again to encourage Strain to ring the young man on the phone. When he answered, McMeekin professed his eagerness; he apparently "said he had been in a rotten state not having heard from me and had consulted the telephone book several times with the idea of ringing me up," Strain reported. The two men now began a relationship.[99]

Given the relatively small size of Belfast's scene, there was an element of competition inside these intimate social circles, often playful but sometimes serious. David Strain smugly wrote in his diaries how delighted he was when his similarly aged friends were surprised or jealous at his success in chatting up attractive young men at flower shows or in Woolworths. But he was also defensive, even angry, when he found out that he was not the only older man in the life of the young "whelps" he had been courting, using frantic writings in his diary as a way of convincing himself that he was not upset by their disloyalty.[100] Still, the solidarity and mutual aid of queer friendships was usually more important than the rivalry. It was difficult for both working- and middle-class men to conceal queer relationships in Belfast, given

FIGURE 4.3. Friends of David Strain (Walter Smith [*left*] and Arthur Fitzsimons). "Photograph album containing photographs of members of the Strain family, of their residences at Ouley, Carryduff, and 5 Galwally Park, Belfast . . . ," *Photograph Albums of the Strain Family and Related Families*, D/2585/4/1, the Public Record Office of Northern Ireland.

the closely knit nature of neighborhoods and the business world too, which meant a queer man needed allies. In his early years of dating, David Strain tended to hide himself from view when out in public, often with farcical results—covering his face when he spotted a family friend coming closer, for example, or having a younger man walk a few paces ahead when they left his office together. Even so, by the later 1930s there were rumors about how he entertained young men at his country hut, where he warned them against marriage. Now, his friends leapt to his defense. When Cecil Bond was asked at his lunch club by one of the older diners whether David Strain was "a bit queer," he responded defiantly. "I don't see anything queer about him," Bond snapped, and cattily added, "but perhaps he would see something queer in you!"[101]

Figure 4.4. David Strain (*left*) with his friend Arthur Fitzsimons. "Photograph album containing photographs of members of the Strain family, of their residences at Ouley, Carryduff, and 5 Galwally Park, Belfast . . . ," *Photograph Albums of the Strain Family and Related Families*, D/2585/4/1, the Public Record Office of Northern Ireland.

Friends got together to gossip about how their dates had gone, consoled each other when their romantic lives faltered, and accompanied each other as they trawled the city in the hope of making new contacts.[102] When socializing together, whether in private homes or city center cafés, these men swapped and talked about the latest queer novels or read aloud to each other from new and old volumes of homoerotic poetry.[103] For younger working-class men especially, these meetings with older, more knowledgeable men served as an induction into the queer world.[104] They, in turn, spread this information to their own contacts on the scene and even paid in kind by introducing their older teachers to younger men they knew were willing to be casual lovers. In 1934, for example, a newsboy who had become friends with David Strain alluded in conversation to young friends of his who seemingly sold sex. The older man was intrigued and said he would be interested in learning more. "You really would like to meet one?" the newsboy asked. "Yes," Strain replied, "that is if he is really genuine—I don't mean a dirty beast of an individual." The newsboy assured him that he knew just the fellow and could put them in touch.[105]

Friendships usually began in pursuit of sex or romance but were strengthened through a growing sense of queer culture. Camp, of course, was crucial to solidifying a sense of defiant difference. Men in Belfast sent letters to each other that nodded toward icons like Oscar Wilde or delivered gifts with a knowingly flamboyant edge such as rosebuds with a card inscribed "the promise of fresh blossom."[106] Camp culture also went beyond the privacy of letters or poetry groups. When the police picked up young working-class Belfastmen in Britain, they sometimes described how they were painted with makeup, were wearing fake beauty spots, or had tattoos of their female names.[107] Certainly there was no equivalent in Belfast to the outrageous effeminate behavior of the Dilly Boys of interwar London or the *tetki* of Tsarist St. Petersburg, or at least it was not mentioned by the more innocently naïve Royal Ulster Constabulary.[108] But the same sort of culture did exist in microcosm.

As early as 1890, the courts recorded that one of the young men of the Belfast Scandal went by the name of Kathryn, and many of the youths caught up in the Dublin Castle Scandal the decade before had camp names too, such as the delightful Maid of Athens.[109] In the 1940s, as a more mundane example, there was a well-known "haunter of the cottages" in Belfast who adopted an alias name of Jane Withers. In contrast to that famous Hollywood child actress, this Irish version was unfortunately a short and stout countryman who wore a dust coat and paddy hat.[110] Other men in the city made their sexual and romantic intentions clear by talking like a "sissy" and using Polari slang such as "fairy" (an effeminate queer man) or "chicken" (a younger queer man or youth). Some wore makeup, if only in limited amounts, but a few even dared to hint to potential lovers how attractive they looked in their "lovely green frock."[111] Feminine affectations had probably been picked up in more vibrant urban subcultures abroad or from accessible pulp-novel depictions of queer life. Either way, camp formed the basis for a small but visible culture of queer men in the north of Ireland.[112]

If performing femininity was a way for some to affirm or advertise their same-sex desire, we should not discount the possibility that it was a more embodied—if oppressed—expression of transgender feeling.[113] As we have already seen, the violence and gendered suspicion of Belfast society was actively helping to constitute a more bounded category of what it meant to be a man in the early twentieth century. The same influences were apparent on the queer scene too. A gender-based model of sexual encounter, where relationships were structured or even sanctioned by an understanding that the effeminate and receptive partner was "womanlike" in their desires and self-expression, does not seem to have been predominate in the north of Ireland. In New York in the same era, encounters were usually between either "normal" or "queer" masculine men and such effeminate "fairies." But in Belfast there were only exceedingly rare references from younger men to their "husbands"—and seemingly without describing themselves as corresponding "wives."[114]

Some men who wholeheartedly adopted homosexuality in Belfast were even openly disdainful of the effeminate, insisting that their erotic attractions were solely from and toward masculine men.[115] Effeminacy was not natural for these queer Belfastmen but instead a result of the corruption of what it meant to be manly. David Strain, for example, was conflicted by his desire for youths he thought spoiled their appearance with powder and rouge and embarrassed by the effeminate mannerisms of otherwise close friends.[116] In his opinion, too much learning from the science of sexuality had been a bad thing. They had become "infatuated" with the idea of homosexuality, he reflected negatively, and so "magnified" their "feminine traits . . . into grotesque realities."[117] Strain's concern here was probably not the nuances of the relationship between biological determination and gender, even though he had read some sexological literature. Instead, it was the fragility of his own middle-class status. Strain saw himself as the *good homosexual*: different only because of his choice of sexual object. The *bad homosexual*, in contrast, upset public norms of gender presentation and was less of a man: an embarrassment to those who sought to fit into respectable society. David Strain was not alone in feeling this way. When homosexuality became front-page news in the early 1950s and the Wolfenden Committee was formed in Britain to investigate the scale and nature of the problem, this distinction was embedded into the politics of homosexual law reform and arguably inflected Northern Ireland's gay rights movement well into the 1970s.[118]

Whether they embraced or rejected femininity or faced violence and oppression for their desires, there are many examples of men in Belfast who were enthusiastic about queer romance in the mid-twentieth century. They cruised the city with their friends, read daring and exciting novels from New York, and kept in touch by sending gushing letters about their "dream man" or how it felt to be deeply in love.[119] If some were wracked by shame, there were others who enjoyed their freedom and lived a more liberated queer life. Some had multiple partners at once, maintaining one steady relationship while cruising for more casual lovers. Queer experiences may have begun and ended in youth for some, but for others they continued over a whole life. Belfastmen like this, in the language of more recent eras, were gay, even if that was a terminology they would only begin to use in the later decades of the twentieth century: in trying to live their lives, they did so by accepting their same-sex desires and creating a culture and community around that recognition of difference.

In the era before a gay rights movement began to explicitly bring different sorts of sexual and gender minorities together under one political umbrella, Belfast housed a truly queer world in which a variety of types of men and their romantic or sexual behaviors overlapped.[120] For at least some youths, especially those of the working classes, intimacy with other men did not need to be strictly defined. Sex or companionship could be sold to those willing to pay, whether with money or access to their more rarefied social circle. But there could still be a mutuality to relationships that belied their transactional origins. Young men were fond of their older middle-class lovers at the same time as they decided what level of physical interaction allowed them to maintain their own sense of being a man, even when they kept up courtships with women.

Some working-class men left the queer scene behind when they married and set up home, but others led a double life, with or without the knowledge of their wives. Middle- and upper-class men could feel the same pressures and make the same decisions as the male youths they had sought, though their financial access to private housing or hotels helped them avoid the risk of exposure. There were a multitude of different sorts of domestic arrangements, shaped as much by class and the expectations of the life cycle as they were sexual desire.[121] As we already saw in chapter 3, there was no uncomplicated or contextless binary of heterosexual and homosexual in the works of sexologists or novelists, just waiting to be internalized by men who desired other men. For that reason, we should not be surprised that neither was there a stable queer subject—in Belfast as elsewhere—that can be so easily discovered by historians today.[122]

If ambiguity and complexity in queerness were the mainstays of everyday experience, there are two Irish distinctions worth noting. First, many queer men successfully resisted the domestication of marriage, if not the apron strings of their mothers. The bachelor was a common figure in modern Ireland, given long-established patterns of rural land inheritance and emigration. If sometimes seen as a symbol of demographic malaise, he was not necessarily coded as queer, as had started to become more common elsewhere.[123] At the same time, the official public secrecy about sexuality in the north also gave another reason to tastefully avoid confronting male family members about why they would not marry.

Second, there were social and romantic experiences that cut across men of all classes and ages. There has been a tendency to see modern queerness as structured predominantly by social hierarchies, with working-class men less likely to be interested in understanding their desires through sexological models in comparison to middle-class men—a finding already noted by the sexologist Magnus Hirschfield around the turn of the twentieth century and supported by historians more recently.[124] Though that classed disparity is evident to some degree in Belfast too, the city's small and intimate nature brought people closer together than it kept them apart. Middle-class men were educating their younger working-class lovers about understandings of same-sex desire, both historical and contemporary, and personal diaries show just how many were eager to receive that knowledge. The result, by at least the 1930s, was a small but vibrant cross-class queer culture in the north of Ireland. An element of secrecy ruled this world, at least when it came to hiding sexual facts and acts from church and state. But there was a surprising degree of knowingness too. The next chapter turns toward the important and often ambiguous roles of such outside society in the everyday lives of queer men.

Chapter 5

Families, Neighborhoods, and the Public

George Hogg had a difficult start in life. He was born in 1889 in the Lisburn workhouse, with the whereabouts of his father, a boiler maker, then unknown.[1] His parents must have got back together because six more children were born over the next decade. But the marriage remained fragile. In 1901, mother and father were recorded as living in separate boardinghouses in Belfast, without their children. Hogg and his siblings could have been living with relatives, but their absence from the census might suggest that their parents had been forced to leave them in the workhouse as a desperate temporary measure.[2] A decade later, Hogg was twenty-three and living with his mother and younger brothers in a small but decent house in a working-class Protestant district on the southern side of the city center. Four siblings had not survived infancy, and the matriarch now listed herself as a widow, even though her husband was actually living in a boardinghouse in a small coastal town. Maybe she did not know he was alive, or perhaps she preferred the fiction of death over shameful separation. George Hogg, now working as a laborer, had become the de facto head of the household and was likely bringing in the most money, though his mother still had to work too.[3] At some point in the 1910s, he began a new job as a baker and moved his family to a slightly bigger house nearby.[4] Finally, in 1919, Hogg married Mary McCleery—from rural County Tyrone, who had migrated along with five of her siblings—and they set up home in the respectably working-class Holy Land district of south Belfast.[5]

Life continued for George Hogg and his new family until he was suddenly arrested in 1925 for the crime of gross indecency. He insisted that his accuser, a seventeen-year-old apprentice at the Ormeau Bakery where they both worked, had encouraged him in the staff lavatory and that was why he had invited the lad over to his house one August evening. The alleged victim swore he had no idea that his colleague would be waiting—undressed—to aggressively seduce him.[6] Wherever the truth lay, Hogg found himself in custody. He surely must have panicked about how his wife and the Holy Land district would respond to such a shameful allegation. But in this time of need, Hogg's family and neighbors rallied. One of Mary's brothers-in-law, who lived on a more middle-class street on the edge of the district, provided £50 of the bail for her husband's release—not a small sum for a railway guard who would have been paid roughly £4 a week.[7] When Hogg's case was heard at the Belfast City Commission, the arresting officer told the jury how his prisoner did not drink, smoke, or "quarrel with his wife." This sergeant lived just five or so minutes' walking distance away from the Hogg household so likely already knew his prisoner but used this personal relationship and his own authority to soften rather than harden the judgment of the court.[8] The judge admitted that the sentence he passed down would indeed have been a lot longer if the defense "had not been conducted as it was."[9] Even with this supposedly lenient treatment, George Hogg was sentenced to nine months in prison with hard labor, of which he served about seven and a half months.

Those who lived in the Holy Land district did not need to notice that their neighbor was no longer around. All the local newspapers reported the trial, hinted at the sexual nature of the crime, and even printed George Hogg's occupation and address. So as his release date neared, he must have been worried about what the future might hold. But when Hogg walked out of prison in July 1926, his life seems to have carried on essentially much as it had before. He continued to live with his wife in the Holy Land area and by the 1930s had set up his own bakery on nearby Apsley Street.[10] When he died suddenly of a heart attack in 1947, a notice in the *Northern Whig*—one of the newspapers that had reported his trial just over two decades before—told how the passing of this "dearly loved husband" was "deeply regretted by his loving wife" as well as "his loving brother and sister-in-law."[11] A conviction for a same-sex offense, no matter how socially difficult for Hogg and his family, had not been enough to warrant estrangement or to provoke an escape for a new life. Instead, both his wife and community stood by him, and he was reintegrated back into local Belfast society.

The queerness of George Hogg can be found today only through the criminal archive. The witness statements collected by the petty sessions court tell us something about where he may have propositioned other men and how the legal system acted accordingly. But to appreciate how Belfast society responded to the exposure of his desires, we must look beyond the bureaucratic documents of the state and the moment of pain that they detail. The surviving genealogical scraps of Hogg's life in the decades after his arrest suggest something important and perhaps surprising: there could be a supportive communal response to those who were condemned by the law for a supposedly heinous sexual sin. In an era when the policing of morality in Belfast was highly selective and the authorities remained silent about same-sex desire, it was families, neighborhoods, and the public who really decided how queer men would be treated. The moral decisions these different societal groups made, as we will see in this chapter, depended above all on the individual character of each queer man and the interpersonal and intimate dynamics of urban life—with both positive and negative results.

Moral Vigilantes and Neighborhood Purity

The way that George Hogg came to the attention of the police was a common one in Belfast. The one or two gross indecency or buggery cases that made it into the courts each year were twice as likely to be the result of a public complaint than a discovery made by a policeman on his beat. Reporters of sex between men were sometimes quasi-authority figures—such as workhouse attendants, night watchmen, or park rangers—but most were normal working-class men going about their daily business. About half of those who reported the crime had come across a sexual encounter or suspected one was about to happen while the other half were targets of unwanted cruising or applied that victim status to an acquaintance or family member.[12]

Even in an era of censorship of information about queer desire, some members of the public were able to recognize that men were looking for sex with each other in Belfast.[13] They were wary of those who aimlessly wandered around late at night, particularly when they were in a part of the city, such as alleyways or rough ground, where a lack of streetlight could cloak immoral activities.[14] If men were repeatedly going in and out of urinals, especially if they were not alone or money was seen to exchange hands, the alarm bells rang even louder.[15] Witnesses who had been cruised sometimes explained how they knew a man's intentions were immoral because of an effeminacy in mannerisms or clothing. Speaking "like a girl" or wearing a dress, for example, was not always a harmless affectation or a prank but a suspicious sign of sexual deviance.[16] Cruisers did sometimes use bold or leading questions to figure out the desires of their target—testing a young man about whether he had been with a woman before, for example, or if he had ever masturbated or experienced a wet dream. For the men who were interested, the right answer confirmed their openness to a sexual encounter, but those who were not could still grasp the intention of why they were being asked.[17]

It is undoubtable that some witnesses lied when dragged into the court to make a statement about a sexual encounter they had interrupted. Explaining how they had been suspicious of a man could justify after the fact why they were spying on semi-private spaces such as urinals, especially when solicitors for the defense tried to discredit witnesses by suggesting they were "peeping Toms." Publicly accusing someone could also have been revenge or an attempt at blackmail, using the stigma of sexual immorality to bring social disgrace on an enemy and his family.[18] Either way, this sort of witness testimony is more evidence of how there was some public understanding of queer desire in Belfast long before the press and popular literature became more willing to talk about homosexuality in the 1950s and 1960s. There has been a tendency for historians and sociologists of Ireland to conflate the undeniably strong religious and state policy of silence or prudery with the harder-to-access reality of everyday sexual practices. But at best, the rhetoric of moral purity was delusional or even an active attempt to hide the truth.[19]

If we combine the rich descriptions given by reporting witnesses with an intimate reconstruction of their social world, we can get a clearer sense of why some men decided to challenge public sexual encounters. These moral vigilantes in Belfast followed queer men around the city, kept watch through fences or over the dividing wall of urinals, and fetched their friends to help them make citizens' arrests. They made it their civic duty to protect the purity of working-class neighbors, acquaintances, or relatives by bringing usually middle-class corruptors to the attention of the police. When cross-examined by the court, these vigilantes could be openly proud of their actions, bragging about how they refused to be bribed for their silence, had called the accused "all the dirty names" they could muster, or even physically attacked their prisoner. In each case, in the opinion of these reporters if not always the courts, the duty that came with manly prowess was to maintain local propriety, and that meant policing the conduct of other men.[20]

We can see these moral intentions more clearly if we dig into why Charles Bolland, a young mechanic from the north of Belfast, decided to go out of his way to challenge men who were having sex in public toilets in 1909. He had nipped into a urinal after an evening of drinking and had his suspicions raised by two others hanging around inside: Hugh Dunlop, a former sailor in his early twenties from nearby New Lodge, and a better-off grocer in his thirties from an adjacent district.[21] Bolland lived in the same neighborhood as Dunlop and was a similar age and admitted under cross-examination that the two had known each other for a few years. It seems that this personal relationship was why he decided to act.[22] When the two men did not leave because of his presence, Bolland waited outside the urinal until another friend from his neighborhood, Charles Donovan, happened to be passing. Donovan joined the stakeout, then went into the urinal to discover Dunlop being penetrated by the older man. When Donovan failed to lure this man into a fight by jostling up against him, a constable was fetched, and both accused were arrested.

All the men—prisoners, witnesses, police—took a tramcar to the barracks to make their statements. Donovan now demanded that Dunlop explain his behavior. "Why the hell did you let that fellow do that on you? Why didn't he go and get a woman?" he railed before insisting that Dunlop should tell the constable the truth about having been solicited for sixpence.[23] The two friends were angered that a man of their own class and neighborhood would degrade his masculinity by allowing himself to be sexually used like a woman. On another day, working-class witnesses—drunk and ready for violence—may have *themselves* been subjected to the bourgeois morality the police were tasked with ensuring. Yet when it came to same-sex desire, these men had no problem with exploiting the power of the state to make sure their neighborhood stayed morally upright.[24]

Down in Dublin, just ninety miles or so away, members of the public only rarely reported male same-sex crimes. Averill Earls, the leading historian of queerness in that city, suggests that this was because there was a reticence within Irish working-class communities to trust the police, who were seen as outsiders even after independence.[25] Why, in Belfast, was it more socially acceptable for some working-class men to help the authorities pry into queer behavior? The answer might lie in the peculiar circumstances of the north during the constitutional crisis of the late nineteenth and early twentieth centuries. After the imposition of governmental Home Rule had become a political certainty in the 1910s, staunch unionists used the threat of violent insurrection to ensure their corner of the country was not subsumed into an independent Catholic-dominated state. The formation of loyalist paramilitary organizations, most notably the Ulster Volunteer Force in 1912, bolstered a sense of Ulster Protestantism as distinctively masculine and encouraged men to take the law into their own hands to defend their province.[26] When the Northern Ireland jurisdiction was founded amid the violent disturbances of partition, the police were reconstituted into three regiments—full-time, part-time, and reserve—that confirmed the militarization of the province.[27]

Almost all Protestant men could now be called upon to maintain control over every aspect of life, and by violent force if necessary; they became, if only in an official capacity, a de facto mass police force. At the same time, the isolated Catholic population was forced to continue building its own clubs and manly cultures, from charities to sports, that could defend their community and promote the cause of Irish nationalism.[28]

Men on both sides of the religious divide may have now felt more emboldened to intervene in what were usually fleeting, hidden, and victimless sexual encounters. In some cases, they even went out of their way to entrap queer cruisers in a desire to create the evidence the police could then use for prosecution. In 1925, for example, a shipwright in his late twenties was approached by an effeminate nineteen-year-old millworker in the city center. The man agreed to meet the youth later in a nearby hotel bar, but not because he wanted to have a relationship. After they had a drink and the younger man made his sexual proposition, Wesley Reilly excused himself and fetched the police. When cross-examined about why he had arranged to meet the youth at all, Reilly was blunt: "because I wanted to get him arrested [and] I did not see any policeman on the street."[29] There are several other examples of men who were led into the arms of the police, or other authority figures such as boardinghouse attendants, usually after a young man used his own body as bait.[30] Acting on their own motives, these witnesses effectively deputized themselves to ensure the moral reputation of their Ulster.

Still, even with this sort of fortuitous alignment in motives between the police and working men, there were only thirty-seven court cases in Belfast between 1890 and 1958 that arose from reports made by non-police witnesses. There is no doubt that this was a higher level of vigilance than in Dublin, where it was the police who took the lead in the increasing crackdowns on same-sex encounters in public, usually by staking out urinals. The attempt in the new Irish Free State to create a public image of a muscular Catholic morality—an antidote to the effete depravity of the British ruling classes—was mostly targeted at the behavior of women, but queer men sometimes suffered too.[31] Even so, arrests in both territories of Ireland pale into insignificance with the denouncements of queer people that were common, for example, in the fascist and then communist regime in Germany.[32]

Informing the police was only one way that queer desire was challenged in the Irish city, however. Middle-class cruisers especially, who sometimes paid working-class lads for casual sexual encounters, were also at physical risk.[33] The experiences of Joseph Rea provide a rich example of just how dangerous queer life in Belfast could be. He had been married for forty-four years and had ten children and held some civic status in Belfast, being a member of the Crescent Presbyterian Church and vice president of the Young People's Guild, when he was arrested in 1913.[34] He had been spotted acting suspiciously in the Great Northern Railway Station toilets by two industrial worker brothers, whom Rea already knew; they apparently saw him handing over some coins to a young working-class man.[35] This was the only occasion that Rea was arrested but not the first time he had found himself in trouble. A decade earlier he had been doing his work, collecting donations for the Royal Dystonic Hospital, when he met an eighteen-year-old laborer on the street. Even though Rea did not know him, he went with him into a nearby field, where he was jumped by another young man and robbed of his money and jewelry.[36] Just a couple of months later he was again assaulted and liberated of his possessions, this time by a twenty-five-year-old ship laborer he had come across after a day of heavy drinking—a rank hypocrisy, given Rea was an executive member of the Irish Temperance League and had previously campaigned against spirit grocers as "dens of iniquity."[37]

There are other examples of men in Belfast being attacked for expressing their desires: drugged and then sexually assaulted by an acquaintance met in a pub in 1914; brutally beaten by a soldier unwisely invited home for tea during the Second World War; or assaulted and robbed in an alley after buying drinks for sailors all night in the late 1940s.[38] Often, there is an ambiguity to these encounters, with the sexual desires of men who turned violent hidden from our view. In 1927, for example, one man in his late thirties was discovered receiving oral sex from a similarly aged man in a dark corner of a vacant area of a south Belfast neighborhood. Robert Smith told the police that he was waiting until the other man finished sucking his penis and "was then going to give him the boot and take anything he had." When he was arrested for gross indecency nonetheless, Smith expressed surprise. "Am I in it too?" he asked before adding, "I hope you are not classing me with this man. . . . Didn't you see me with my hands in my pockets? . . . It is a good job you came on the job as there would have been a murder."[39] This was partially a performance of masculinity: an attempt to differentiate his own need for easy sexual release from the engrained abnormality of the other man. Even so, it is indicative of how violence against queer men was easily justified. These sorts of ambiguous examples are only the cases where a record survives in the archive because a man was brave enough to go to the law or, as with Joseph Rea, a policeman or someone else witnessed the attack. The actual incidence of assault against queer men was likely much higher.

Belfast bucked the wider trend of a steady decrease in violent behavior over the course of the nineteenth century: the colonial and sectarian context of Ireland, and the north in particular, meant that the broader European experience of a rising middle-class morality around self-control, and its cascading into the lower classes, simply did not happen. Aggression against individuals in public could instead still be used to control community morality and demonstrate an individual's masculine prowess.[40] The city had already seen endemic sectarian rioting in the Victorian era, which embedded something of a working-class tradition of recreational violence.[41] Even in the decades before the prolonged Troubles of the later twentieth century, there were eruptions of communal conflict, with the first Troubles in the early 1920s or the riots of 1935 being only the most extreme instances. It is not surprising that some men felt emboldened to rob and beat up middle-class cruisers or treat them as disposable objects for their own sexual enjoyment.[42] Queer men, in Belfast as elsewhere, were forced to accept that the fulfilment of their desires was always precarious, especially when they were brought into conflict with working-class toughs looking to brutally demonstrate their strength.[43]

Fear, Shame, and Public Exposure

Assault or arrest was only the beginning of the troubles of the cruising queer man in Belfast. If he found himself dragged into a courtroom to explain his urban cruising, he was aware that the public revelation of same-sex desire could bring great social stigma. Though the voices of these unfortunates have only been recorded by the police or witnesses in Belfast, the panic about being exposed comes through strong. Irish men of all classes were afraid of this outcome. Even so, as Charles Upchurch found in a similar study of Britain in the first half of the nineteenth century, a man's social and economic background made a subtle difference in how such fears were articulated.[44]

For the upper middle classes or elites, on the rare occasion that they were arrested, the anxiety was one of "ruin": the end of a prominent public status in Ulster after high society found out about their shameful sexual behavior. Edgar Milligen, for example, had plenty to lose when he was discovered cruising. He was the son of a major industrialist and Orangeman and educated at the elite school of Harrow in England. At the time of his arrest in 1916, he lived in a country mansion in a prosperous village just south of Belfast and was heavily involved in philanthropic work in the city.[45] When he was picked up for having sexual encounters with adolescent newsboys, he apparently replied to the detective: "I am not going to say that I am guilty, although I cannot say I am entirely innocent. I knew something about it. Who is it that is trying to ruin me? Is there are any possible way out of this? If it is made public, I will be ruined."[46]

Unlike nearly all the other men arrested in the first half of the twentieth century, Milligen was powerful enough to seemingly use personal connections to not be named in the newspaper, but knowledge about the trial probably circulated anyway via the members of the public in the courtroom. He was found not guilty, but there were no more notes in the newspaper about his charitable contributions, and he soon left his village to move into the city, probably to avoid the scandal that had enveloped him.

Edgar Milligen was not so lucky after being arrested for gross indecency again in early 1930.[47] A week after his release later that year he was sailing on the SS *Kaisar-I-Hind* from London for Port Said and intending to stay in then-Ceylon for a year.[48] The criminalization of sex between males had been imposed on that island by the British in 1883 but in practice was rarely enforced. Ceylon consequently had a special place in the queer imagination for its beautiful and supposedly less sexually constrained youths—a self-fulfilling prophecy of sorts.[49] Milligen's trip may have partially been about escaping the shame of conviction, but his choice of destination reflected his status as an elite White European: the power structures of the British colonies were a sexual benefit for him rather than any hindrance. At any rate, when Milligen died in 1939, he was living in Slievemoyne Park, north Belfast, in a large, detached property but not as grand as Glenmore House where he had grown up.[50] A few other middle-class or elite Ulster Protestants were not as fortunate as him and had their crimes splashed across the pages of the press. The most prominent was the politician Edward de Cobain, who insisted in the early 1890s that the gross indecency accusation against him was "a trumped-up charge from beginning to end . . . [made] for the purpose of ruining him politically and socially."[51] He was found guilty nonetheless, lost his seat in parliament, and lived out the rest of his days in obscurity. Little wonder that powerful men worried so much about being ruined.

Working-class cruisers, who lacked social and cultural capital, did not speak of ruin, but they were still aware that exposure might mean disgrace in their locality. Thomas O'Connor, a man in his early thirties, was arrested in 1902 for having sex with a younger working-class man he had found while drinking in Sailortown. He bluntly told the police, "All I want is to keep it out of the papers, so that my friends will not know of it."[52] He was right to be concerned. Even though he was found not guilty, the *Northern Whig* still reported how "A man named O'Connor" had been "charged with having committed an indecent offence" as had "another man . . . on a like offence." These details made it fairly clear that something of a sexual nature had taken place. The number of men involved was suggestive, as was the added detail that the crime had taken place in in a house in Clarke's Lane—a notorious street containing brothels.[53]

The language used to describe same-sex cases in the Irish press in the late Victorian era was usually euphemistic and could also be used for other "unnatural" crimes such as infanticide or bestiality. But the rise of the sensational investigative New Journalism, of which the prominent queer Dublin Castle Scandal in 1884 was a driving influence, meant the reading public—which was now almost everyone—was more aware than ever before of what such criminal offenses might be.[54] Working men in Belfast at the end of the nineteenth century knew that queer exposure was a humiliation that might shape their life for decades after. For that reason, one man begged a constable in 1898 "for God's sake not to expose them and disgrace them."[55] There are numerous examples of men trying to resist arrest by running away, offering bribes, or clinging to streetlamps in a desperate bid to delay their trip to the police barracks—bold resistance indeed in a period when the police could be armed.[56]

Belfast's interwar press was still generally reticent to say much in detail about local court cases of sex between men. The topic was best avoided in case it revealed that the moral superiority of Ulster was perhaps not quite as secure as the rhetoric, and there was a pervasive culture of self-censorship of anything that suggested indecent sexual behavior—a lasting vestige of exceptionalism that was engrained in Irish conceptions of difference from Britain in the late nineteenth century.[57] But a hypocritical willingness to report a bit more on English or continental European trials of same-sex crimes or effeminate gender transgression gave an indication of what was occasionally punished in Ireland. Less tight-lipped English weeklies like *The News of the World* circulated in the city too, much to the anger of the local clergy, though in much smaller numbers than the local dailies.[58] Even in the prim Belfast press, silence and euphemism about sexual crimes could momentarily be broken if the accused was of a middle-class background. In 1925, for example, a locally based Scottish Evangelist preacher who was sexually assaulting boys was arrested and found guilty. The newspapers now facilitated a very public denouncement of a man who ought to have the good character to control his base desires.[59]

One of the most notable hellfire-and-brimstone outbursts came during a session of the Belfast Custody Court in August 1925, when two men—one of whom was distinctly middle class—were transferred to a higher court. The subheading to an article in the *Belfast Telegraph* screamed "MUST GO TO COMMISSION, BELFAST INDECENCY CASE" and described with rare bluntness how the crime was "gross indecency in a public lavatory." The resident magistrate of the Custody Court insisted it was "a charge of great gravity" and "if such crime existed it was time it was stamped out." He had been in the role only a few months after previously working as a journalist and now made a show of how shocked he was by the depravity that existed in his city.[60] When the case was then heard at the City Commission, the lord chief justice—on his first day in the job—added his own outrage. "It was a great pity that there were not stocks or pillories nowadays," he lamented, "in order that the prisoners might be made a public example to all decent minded people."[61] Flare-ups such as these were probably galvanized by the moral purity movements that were gathering steam in Dublin, given how such campaigns involved all-Ireland organizations representing both the Protestant and Catholic churches.[62] For brief moments, the goal to publicly shame queer men—a method of warning others what might happen if they committed the same acts—overcame the powerful desire to keep quiet about homegrown immorality.[63]

More alarming for queer men than the degree of discussion, in practical terms at least, was the move in Belfast toward also reporting the ages, occupations, and street addresses of the convicted. Plausible deniability was basically now impossible in an intimate city of this size. Even if the press did not describe in depth what was said in court, the scandalous proceedings could create a sensation that spread by word of mouth. Members of the public clamored to fit into the room, especially when they had heard a rumor that someone important had been arrested. They then laughed or gasped at the details of sex described and sometimes were even sent out by judges who were disgusted by such prurient interest in sex between men.[64]

Michael McLaverty, a novelist of working-class Catholic life in Ulster, gives us a glimpse into how families may have responded to the local gossip that followed an arrest. When, in *Lost Fields* (1941), the adolescent Peter is caught stealing a bicycle and a policeman arrives at the family home in west Belfast, his sister melodramatically cries, "We're all disgraced now. . . . It'll be in the paper and I'll never get to the convent." After Peter is then taken away to the industrial school in the middle of the night as punishment, his mother is relieved that their neighbors would not see and that she could pretend her son was merely convalescing in the countryside. Unease about the lasting effects of shame is also a key part of *The Three Brothers* (1948). Uncle DJ, some thirty years before, is caught embezzling money while working as a young railway clerk. His sin is hushed up by the village priest to stop it from reaching the law or the press, but his brother worries that the local people will never forget the disgrace: "They hold an evil thing in their minds as easily as they remember their prayers."[65] McLaverty, who came to see himself as a distinctively Catholic moral novelist, did not openly talk about sex let alone queer desire, but his stories reinforce the sense of twitching curtains and the importance of working-class respectability that features in other Ulster novels, oral histories, and memoirs.[66]

When men were arrested in Belfast for same-sex crimes, they sometimes invoked family feelings as the main reason they wanted to avoid exposure: the sister devastated to know her brother had been found fellating a man just a few streets away from the family house they shared; the brothers enraged to discover their younger sibling was satisfying much older men for small change; or the widowed mother who would again have her heart broken.[67] If a man ended up having to publicly defend his sexual behavior in court, it brought not just shame on himself but disgrace on his family too.[68] As one supportive reverend wondered in 1953 after a young man from his congregation was arrested, "what is to happen to them and their family if they are branded with disgrace I do not know."[69] English settlement, capitalism, and ascendant Christianity in the early modern period, and then the rise of pseudoscientific and psychological understandings of race and sexual behavior in the nineteenth century, had all led to the continuing celebration of the patriarchal ideal of the family in Ireland.[70] When that public image was at risk, families were right to be concerned.

The courts in Belfast were certainly aware that their legal judgment could have social consequences. When James Sinton was put on trial in 1909, seemingly for importuning in a urinal, his solicitor made it clear that the result "meant either the salvation or ruin" of his client.[71] Unfortunately for the young civil servant, his case received a lot of attention in the newspapers because he dramatically fainted in the dock after being convicted.[72] Sinton successfully appealed his six-month sentence and was released, but just days later he boarded a steamship with his wife and left for Canada, where they moved in with his sister and her family before later settling in their own home.[73] In an era when transatlantic travel was relatively cheap, other men in Belfast—whether humiliated in court for cross-dressing or publicly exposed for cruising in urinals—made the same decision to flee.[74]

Family and Communal Support

There is no doubt that some Belfastmen picked relocation over public humiliation, but there were many more who stayed, whether out of choice or necessity. Once their sexual behavior had been publicly exposed, it was personal and neighborhood connections that determined whether they would receive the support they needed to deal with both the legal system and a return to their local life in the decades after. The family and its extended social networks worked as a complex set of relationships that did not necessarily map onto clearly fixed social roles.[75] The ability of a queer man to draw on the help of this intimate web was not determined by a natural or insurmountable disgust toward the sin of same-sex desire. Instead, it was the often more mercenary question of social and economic reciprocity that came into play. A queer man might receive the backing of his family and neighborhood if he could provide the same sort of support or had done so in the past.[76] Even when he still felt he had to get out of Belfast, it was family members and the diasporic communities in which they lived that helped him get his life back on track.[77]

If the accused wanted to avoid remaining in custody after his arrest, at least until he was brought up at the more serious assizes courts that could be weeks or months later, he had to find bail. Whether he was able to do so depended on his social connections. Just over half of the working-class men caught by the police remained in custody until their trial; none of the thirteen who were arrested for sex in transient or institutional settings, such as lodging houses or the workhouse, were able to find bail; and if one of an accused couple found bail and another did not, the unfortunates were always the younger poorer partner.[78] In contrast, roughly three-quarters of middle-class or elite men found bail, and two of the remaining six who did not had only recently landed in the country and so may have been seen as flight risks (one man arrested for gross indecency was explicitly denied bail for that reason in 1925). Fewer middle-class men were arrested, so there is less evidence to generalize, but they too had found bail money from local acquaintances and colleagues.[79] We cannot know for certain why other men did not obtain financial support from their loved ones, but we could speculate it was for the same reasons they were afraid of being exposed: they did not want to risk moral judgment by asking those closest to them or tried and were rebuked for so publicly failing in their duty as a man.[80]

Where the bailers are named, at least a quarter were relatives and in truth it was likely more.[81] Married women could not act as sureties, so in only one case did a mother fulfil this role—the widowed parent of a laborer in his twenties, arrested in the early 1930s.[82] Yet only two fathers in this period were bailers, one of whom acted for an adolescent son who might more accurately be seen as a victim.[83] Young men were probably afraid of going to their father, the authority figure—especially in working-class families—who maintained morality and discipline in the household, including through dishing out corrective punishment. That this paternal role was becoming increasingly questioned in the first half of the twentieth century likely made the fatherly response harsher rather than softer when their own masculinity was in danger of being embarrassed.[84] In 1908, for example, one father banned his "blackguard" cross-dressing son from living at home while in 1925 another turned up at a workplace to viciously beat a son who was accused of trying to seduce his colleagues.[85] Other male family members were instead one or two steps removed from the patriarch and may have given a more understanding reaction. Uncles already provided lifelong guidance, especially if a father had died, and brothers-in-law, who were more common as bailers than *actual* brothers, may have been encouraged by their more sympathetic wives to help.[86] Belfast was by no means the limit in this respect; country relatives also supplied bail, demonstrating how closely connected families could remain despite the upheavals of internal migration in Ireland.[87]

Family support often overlapped with money from other local sources. In a time before a comprehensive welfare state and when there was a stigma about seeking money from churches or charitable bodies, systems of working-class mutual support were vital for sustaining individuals and their families through difficult times.[88] At least a quarter of those working men who were bailed out after being accused of a same-sex crime received some financial provision from their immediate district and in several cases from their literal next-door neighbors (possibly money that was collected from helpful families throughout the area).[89] Bailers, both within the district and also beyond, often worked in the same or comparable trades as the arrested man: milkmen helping other milkmen, for example, or hotel porters supporting club waiters.[90] On the rare occasions working men found bail from unrelated higher-class men, it was their employer or senior colleague.[91]

Because of the sectarian geography of Belfast, bail in general tended to come from men of not just a similar class and occupation but the same religious affiliation. Whether working-class districts can be termed *communities* has been debated by historians, with some seeing the concept as a nostalgic construct of memoirs or oral histories that assume shared moral values in the past. In Belfast, where group identity and segregation were strong because of sectarianism, *community* as a term is perhaps less problematic, though there were still local socioeconomic gradations. At any rate, there were many ways that segregated neighborhoods could cement their bonds against outsiders, and mutual aid was just another, even when it was given for something that might bring shame on the locality.[92]

One rich example demonstrates the deep and even queerly suggestive connections that bailers could have with those accused of sexual crimes. James O'Neill was a laborer in his late twenties and living in a predominantly Catholic neighborhood in north Belfast when he was arrested in 1927. Part of his bail was supplied by Alexander McDonald, a laborer who had lived on the same street for decades. Both men had served in the Royal Navy, and each had married into the other's family. When the police booked O'Neill into custody, they recorded how his heavily tattooed body included the inked names of both his sister and McDonald, by then his brother-in-law for around fifteen years, so it must have been a close friendship to say the least.[93] O'Neill had apparently told his cruising target, "I can relieve you, I have been with men before." He also poked fun at a courting male-female couple, describing them as "bally fools." O'Neill was a familiar face in the dockside Anchor Bar, where he sometimes sang to entertain the regulars, and had left there earlier in the evening, as he put it, "with three boys whom I had met on several occasions."[94] In these witness statements he comes across as a confidently camp man about town and hardly a victim who was afraid of being exposed. The exact nature of O'Neill's relationship with his bailer is impossible to tease out today, but it seems likely that McDonald had at least an inkling of his brother-in-law's desires.

The negotiation of queer desire in working-class neighborhoods is rarely recorded in contemporary sources because men of that background tended to not keep diaries that have survived. But memoirs written during the social history boom of the later twentieth century do hint at how the open challenging of gender norms could coexist with the masculine expectations of working-class life.[95] The famous flautist James Galway, who grew up in the rough-and-tumble world of Sailortown, related how he may have been small, lacking physical prowess, and an artistic type, but he did not have to put up with bullying or being nicknamed a "cissy." "The important thing," he insisted, "was to be a character of some sort."[96] Another memoirist recalled a character nicknamed Gibby, a 1920s "cross-dresser" who would "saunter past, dressed up to the nines in high heels and a fur coat, carrying his handbag in a most ladylike fashion." But that did not make him a figure of open fun because "underneath" he was "of the tough breed of the Shankill."[97] The potential for queerness to be overlooked, even in notoriously hardworking-class neighborhoods like the Shankill or the Falls, was greater if one was a well-liked character or the opposite: a feared local hardman who was willing to use his fists to defend his honor. But the same was true if a man fulfilled his masculinity in other gentler ways, whether through his local charitable work or steady contribution to the workplace.[98] Diverging from the heteronormativity of the neighborhood was not always enough to warrant public criticism, then, though tongues must certainly have wagged in private.[99]

Even following a trial or an ensuing prison sentence, when the unspoken assumption of queer behavior was now confirmed, many men remained an important part of their family and locality in Belfast. For the less financially secure, this might have been because they had little other choice: the shared domestic economy was a vital resource from which queer men benefited and to which they contributed.[100] After William Seaton was released from his four-month sentence in early 1899, for example, he went back to his widowed mother and older laborer brother and managed to find work in the east Belfast shipyards. His niece lived in their home while her mother was in a different house nearby with her husband and three other children. A decade later, Seaton was in his late twenties and still living with his mother and now two of his nieces and nephews (both his sister and her husband tragically having died).[101] Queer men may have had the status of ex-convicts, but earning and supporting the wider family could be more important than the sexual behavior that had landed them in the dock. It was even better if the man could convince his kin it had only been a one-off sexual encounter. This defense was possible, at least until the rise in Ireland of the distinct category of homosexuality later in the twentieth century, when sexual desires were increasingly seen to be more engrained.[102]

Economic circumstances may have governed the decisions of some queer men, but emotional bonds could also keep families together. There are countless examples of men continuing to live with their families or in the same neighborhood for decades after a conviction or arrest and deep public mourning when they died. Press notices were certainly conventional and unlikely to reveal family schisms, but total silence was always a telling option that could have been taken by a bereaved but still embarrassed relative.[103] Obituaries, in rare cases, could even hint at a man's queerness. When a twenty-one-year-old hairdresser died of pneumonia in 1937, a family memoriam notice included another man as a "dear friend"—the only mourner to be described in that way. This friend was arrested twice for cruising in his life and was three decades older than the deceased, which suggests there may have been an intergenerational arrangement with the hairdresser. At any rate, including his special companionship in the notice was a curious detail that may have suggested the family had a degree of knowledge about their son's potentially transgressive life.[104]

A powerful example of family love and neighborhood respect can be found following the early death of David Purse, a laborer in his late twenties from Sailortown. He was arrested in the notorious Belfast Entries in 1932 but escaped with a suspended sentence of six months.[105] When he succumbed to tuberculosis just six years later, the reporting of his funeral showed his integration into this proud working-class district. Purse had been publicly named in the *Belfast Telegraph* for his "serious charge," but the family now announced the death of their "dearly loved" family member in the same newspaper. The local Orange Lodge, in which the men of the large Purse family were well represented, implored their members to attend the funeral out of respect.[106] The following week, the bereaved parents were moved to place a message of thanks, acknowledging the Lodge along with the other friends and neighbors who had sympathized, sent letters of condolence, and brought floral tributes.[107] We cannot know whether the immediate reaction to David Purse's arrest had been rough, but it seems that the standing of the family within the Sailortown neighborhood had at least warranted a public display of support for the loss of their son.

Those queer men who did not conform to the expected life cycle by marrying instead formed new and long-lasting domestic units with their relatives, usually after their parents had died. Urban experiences of accommodating nonmarried relatives mirrored the pragmatic socioeconomic approach of families in rural Ireland.[108] Sisters especially could be housekeepers and companions who provided a respectable veneer to a queer life, secret or not, or simply the emotional support that was needed after a difficult experience with the law. But they could also be an unwanted limit on a more active queer life. Joseph Dillon and his brother Gerard, for example, grew up in a large family in west Belfast. In the postwar period they lived in an apartment block in London with their older sister Molly but found her overbearing and intrusive.[109] If sisters had their own children, however, queer men could become important family figures to a younger generation. Nephews even provided bail money on some occasions or memorialized their love for their queer uncle in newspaper notices and gravestones.[110]

Family support could take place across the whole life of those unfortunate men who were arrested. If we go beyond the religious or state rhetoric of the family in Ireland, we can find a diversity of these experiences that deviated from the traditional nuclear unit.[111] Families, north and south, were typically large, and several generations often lived within the same household; it was not until the 1960s and 1970s that smaller units started to become the norm. In this context, the existence of one bachelor brother or uncle was hardly a problem and could even be a social or economic benefit—as long as they stayed out of prison.[112]

Ignorance, Acceptance, and the Open Secret

If we look beyond the extreme experience of exposure, we can see the more banal ways that queer men could be visible parts of everyday family and neighborhood life in Belfast. Parents could know, on a rudimentary level at least, that their young sons were having relationships with other men. In 1917, for example, one participant-turned-state-witness, a medical student in his early twenties, described how he had been living with another man of a similar age in a hotel for several months. "My people knew . . . and allowed it," Hugh Sheehan explained to the court. "I told them. My father's house is two miles from the tram line. I spoke about the house being so far away but did not give that as an excuse." Sheehan had visited the family members of the accused in the Ulster countryside during their courtship. Whether these relatives understood that the friendship also involved anal sex is unlikely, but these lovers cannot have been overly concerned about the possibility of suspicion, and indeed their families supported them in the decades after the trial.[113] This sort of knowledge of sexual encounters may have been genuine ignorance, especially for those unfamiliar with the patterns of queer urban life, but it could also have been begrudging tolerance.[114]

There are examples of other young queer men who were so close to their sisters that they were happy to introduce them to their older partners. When the middle-class David Strain went to visit one lover in the hospital in the late 1930s, for example, the youth's sister delighted in telling him, "He was calling for you Mr. Strain, when he was coming out of the chloroform."[115] To understand why some working-class families accepted these relationships between their sons or brothers and older better-off men we must appreciate the assured power of the class hierarchy in Ulster well into the twentieth century. Middle-class queers could easily position their relationships with youths or young men as a type of benevolent mentorship, cloaking the romantic or sexual element with an assumption of respectability that came with their social status.[116] Parents may have been naïve about the reality, especially in a period where moral panics about sexual abuse were less common and the philanthropic role of the middle classes more assured.

John Boyd, who went on to become a BBC presenter and dramatist, remembered well the role that deference and ignorance could play in clandestine queer relationships. He described how one of his schoolteachers at the privileged Royal Academical Institution in Belfast—where he was on a scholarship—entertained a select few of the senior boys at his house on weekends and even took them on holidays abroad. Boyd's working-class father was first curious about the interest of this middle-aged man in his seventeen-year-old son, but that emotion was less significant than the mix of pride and anxiety when the schoolteacher visited their home. Boyd, writing in the mid-1980s, reflected that "nowadays parents would of course be much more knowledgeable and cautious." There was a greater visibility of child sexual abuse in Britain from the 1970s, emanating from both the tabloid press and feminist campaigning, if only uneven effects in terms of progress in government policy, social work and policing. Some of this visibility filtered down to Belfast, especially following a horrific scandal in a boys home in the 1980s. Contemporary mores about intergenerational encounters now hardened in an age of greater sexual awareness and more appreciation for the vulnerability of teenage boys.[117] Nonetheless, Boyd remained "glad" that his parents had not suspected he was "being exposed to moral danger" when his teacher took him to Cornwall and tried to kiss him. Even with this unwelcome if not aggressive advance, his memory was still of a man who was "generous and good, if sexually unhappy."[118] There was limited public discussion of sex of all types across Ireland, but there was still a gray area of knowingness that enabled certain types of intergenerational queer encounters to happen without censure.[119]

If there were some mothers or fathers who were unaware, there were others who were simply unbothered or those who even saw the benefits of queer relationships. The young working-class men that David Strain modestly supported sometimes introduced him to their parents. One of Strain's earliest and most intense infatuations was with a newspaper boy, Jack Murray, whom he met just before he reached his eighteenth birthday. This youth was never physically interested in Strain but endured his company for the financial and social benefits it brought, from gifts of clothes and money to driving lessons in the country. When Murray's father found out that his son had been truanting from technical college, he invited Strain into the family home so he could witness the then eighteen-year-old being reprimanded for taking advantage of his patron's generosity.[120] This performance from Murray's father suggests working-class deference and perhaps the hope that an older middle-class man would be a positive influence on his wayward son. But there were other motives at work too: the newspaper boy later relayed that his unemployed father hoped Strain would help him find a job, which he duly did.[121] On another occasion, one of Strain's occasional lovers tried to use him for housing and gifts, encouraged by his mother.[122] Amid the unemployment and instability of the Great Depression, these are examples of not just young men who accommodated middle-class queer desire for social or economic reasons but sometimes their families too.

Those queer men who remained bachelors faced their challenges, especially when they had an educated understanding of their desires as reflecting an engrained homosexuality they could do nothing to change.[123] Middle-class queers, who could not rely on the seemingly greater tolerance of working-class districts, had to negotiate their lives through the more ambiguous closet of the "open secret." David Strain's experiences in the 1930s best demonstrate this paradox. When he was still in his early thirties, his parents held out hope that he would marry—"Dear dear! What a pantomime," as he put it—and were enthusiastic when they found out he had been trying to court a local woman from a good family.[124] But it seems that his mother had a clue about why her son was still a bachelor. When she boldly asked him whether Oscar Wilde had been a "sodomite," he fiercely defended his idol and provocatively hinted in return that his father was a sexual hypocrite who seduced their own housemaids. She retaliated by expressing her disapproval of the "filthy" queer novels she had discovered in his personal library and threatened to throw them into the fire.[125] Strain's mother may have been a devout Reformed Presbyterian who strived for a pure and moral life, but her feigned innocence soon turned to anger when confronted with something she already suspected.

If David Strain's open admiration for Oscar Wilde had raised the suspicions of his parents, that did not stop him from entertaining a queer circle at the family home in south Belfast on Sunday evenings. After his stern father died in 1935, Strain—who did not take a break from his city center cruising in the period around the funeral—now brought home the poorest working-class youths he had met on the streets and introduced them to his widowed mother without fear (and she sometimes made them tea). He may have felt unable to talk about his queer life or simply uninterested in doing so, but that was not important: while his mother remained technically untold, she could maintain a performance of obliviousness about the reason for her son's bachelorhood.[126] Strain now used this tacit acceptance to live a more open existence while maintaining his duty of supporting the widowed matriarch. His brother, meanwhile, was much more aware of what was going on because they worked together daily in the family firm. When yet another youth turned up at the office to see Strain in late 1938, this brother quipped—seemingly without rancor—"there's a new one."[127]

Other middle-class bachelors got by in much the same way as David Strain, living with their mothers long after their other siblings had moved out, yet making no attempt to hide the close friendships they forged with working-class lads.[128] "Coming out" did not yet exist as a social or political act in the way it did after the birth of the gay liberation movement. But the open secret—if not without its drawbacks of internalized shame or fear of discovery—gave some queer men a way to exist not just in the anonymity of metropolitan capitals but in the more intimate circumstances of provincial cities too.[129]

In all the experiences or encounters I have so far described, religious fear is conspicuous by its absence. As we saw in chapter 3, the lack of an open debate about same-sex sins and contemporary Christianity could give some queer men a relative freedom or justification for their comradely love. Yet even when churches could not avoid the topic of sex between men, the response to a queer exposure could be quiet compassion rather than outright condemnation. The clearest example can be seen in the arrest of Sharman Stevenson, a postman in his mid-fifties, in the early 1930s. His Reformed Presbyterian community in the rural parish of Knockbracken quickly found out, and it became a topic of hushed conversation.[130] The newspaper had reported his crime euphemistically as "a serious charge," but some of the congregants knew full well it was an "act of gross indecency." Even so, the reverend led his flock in prayers for one of their own who was suffering in custody.[131] After Stevenson was released on a suspended sentence, he went back to live on his farm and even continued to worship at Knockbracken Church. When he died two decades after his arrest, he left money to the church that had supported him and was buried in its grounds.[132]

The kind of detail that survives about the response to Sharman Stevenson's arrest is rare—we are simply fortunate that he happened to worship in the same community as David Strain, who reflected on the event in his diary—but there are other examples of churches giving support rather than censure.[133] Queer men, even those who had served prison time, continued to be parts of their churches when released and donated money upon their deaths, and these are only examples revealed by the death notices of men well-off enough to leave documented bequests.[134] Small stories of compassion and the persistence of religious community are easily lost in the wellspring of homophobia that flowed in the later twentieth century, especially when biblical belief became the justification for very public bigotry in movements like Save Ulster from Sodomy in the late 1970s. But that only makes these echoes more important: families and neighborhoods of all classes and religions could accommodate the queer difference of their men.[135]

Eventually, a combination of developments both at home and abroad began to make it far harder for queer men to maintain their open secret. The United Kingdom was an anxious polity in the 1950s, still morally and physically reconstructing after a devastating global conflict and against the backdrop of the hyper-suspicion of the new Cold War. Two separate shifts now conspired to make queer men more visible than ever before: first, a growth of investigative social sciences in universities; and second, an increase in levels of everyday policing of sexual crimes. In the eyes of academics, constables, and soon the public too, homosexuals were no longer just individuals with a pathological problem but members of a broader social group with its own clandestine world.[136] British newspapers like the *News of the World* and the *Daily Mirror* reflected back this sense of a social crisis by reporting on the arrests of high-profile queer men, such as John Gielgud or Peter Wildeblood, though their increasingly sensational reporting was also a strategy to stimulate sales in response to the growing popularity of the television. At any rate, the public and private boundary was collapsing as the tabloids stimulated a range of sometimes conflicting stereotypes about homosexual men: depraved and disgusting, sick and sinful, emasculated and weak yet a danger to society.[137] In 1954, partly as an immediate response to how newspapers were exploiting homosexual scandals, the Wolfenden Committee was tasked by the British government with examining the laws that governed both female prostitutes and men who had sex with men.[138] Lord Wolfenden published his recommendations in 1957, including the decriminalization of consensual acts between men over twenty-one in private.[139] The unionist press in Belfast knew they had to cover the story: the British state, to which they remained steadfastly aligned, had legitimized public scrutiny. Homosexuality now became mainstream news in the north of Ireland for the first time, with discussion about its morality, causes, and solutions.[140]

If political developments in Westminster were shedding a new light on same-sex desire, there were also changes happening locally that were undermining the conservative social and cultural consensus of Ulster. The rise of the television, which at this point largely meant programs beamed in from Britain, was cutting a hole in the veil of silence that covered sexual discussion.[141] In late 1957, one local member of Parliament reported that there had been "indignation and disgust aroused among decent people of all religious beliefs" after they saw programs that were "pandering to the depraved tastes of a small section of the community in their morbid desire for details about various forms of sexual perversion." Another added that the result of such programs would be "to undermine the entire moral fibre of the community." Basil Brooke, Northern Ireland's prime minister, agreed. Their part of the United Kingdom "was probably clearer of perversion and sex crimes than most countries," Brooke insisted, so he promised to speak to the BBC about what could be done to limit the effects of unwanted sexual broadcasts.[142] Writing a few days later, the critic for the *Belfast Telegraph* supported this line of thinking. After the Wolfenden report was published, he lamented, there had been "a tendency to wallow" in the details. "I find it difficult to see what good was achieved by bringing a homosexual to the studio to discuss his problems," he admitted.[143] Just as in Britain, there were now signs of moral panic about the changing nature of society, heightened by the continued fragility of Northern Ireland's own constitutional identity, and a seed of the debates about permissiveness yet to come in the 1960s and 1970s.[144]

Families, and the neighborhoods in which they lived, shaped the experience of queerness in complex and often contradictory ways in pre–gay liberation

Belfast. What we might have assumed about responses to same-sex desire, given the more recent history of homophobia and intolerance in the region, was certainly true in some cases. Queer men who were exposed by the courts and then the press could find themselves emotionally and financially denied support at a moment of vulnerability, much like the women who also deviated from Ireland's moral code.[145] The number who were reported to the authorities may have remained relatively low, but we can only wonder how many more faced the violence, robbery, or blackmail that they knew it was unwise to disclose, or how many queer crimes were dealt with harshly in the home and neighborhood instead of the court.[146] For those who were convicted, the public shame could certainly be intense enough to encourage a move to another country; for the others who could not leave or did not want to, neighborhood life must surely have been made difficult by local gossip. Queer historians of Ireland, me included, must be careful of not falling into what the historian Jeffrey Weeks calls a "nostalgia for the ambivalences and fluidities of the pre-gay-liberation world," no matter how tempting. Queer life in Belfast was shaped in its own distinctive ways by repression and prejudice, with the intimate nature of its neighborhoods meaning that few sexual sins could be hidden forever.[147]

Even with all the dangers, a glimpse at the situation elsewhere suggests that a blind eye must have been turned to many a sexual encounter in Belfast. How else can we explain the rocketing of arrests in Dublin in the 1930s, when the rate stayed roughly the same just ninety miles north, or the virtual absence of prosecutions of sexual encounters that took place behind closed doors? And even if a public scandal did envelop a queer man, there could still be local support. From giving bail to providing a home after imprisonment, the intimate connections between families and neighborhoods held the key to the future direction of a man's life. In the most difficult of circumstances, they demonstrated a remarkable degree of "benevolent toleration" or "living and let live."[148] The family probably also protected itself from embarrassing accusations by hiding its queer men from potential sources of punishment such as the church, community and state.[149] Begrudging compassion or feelings of responsibility were not the same as enthusiasm for sexual liberty, of course, but that did not matter when families or neighbors were not forced to explicitly confront the mechanics of same-sex desire. Unfortunately, as we will see in the next chapter, the courts were not always as content to let queer men live their lives. If cases of men having sex with men finally reached the legal system, the more fundamental inequities of Ulster society then became apparent.

Chapter 6

Ulster's Manliness on Trial

Early one October evening in 1926, George Smyth of the Royal Ulster Constabulary was making his patrols in Belfast when he spotted two men in a urinal down Hamilton Court. Smyth had arrested two men in a toilet the year before so knew what might be happening inside this dimly lit public convenience just off the High Street.[1] He moved closer, peeping through the perforated side, and watched as one man masturbated the other. After two minutes of spying, the constable entered to make his arrest. Each man had a different response to being discovered. Thomas Carrick, married and in his late forties, chose frank denial. "I was doing nothing," he insisted, forgetting he should have been doing *something* in a public toilet. Samuel Ramsey, a retired schoolteacher approaching his eightieth birthday, was more contrite. Visibly shaking with nervousness, he tried to reason with the constable. "Don't keep me in [the cells] all night," he pleaded, "I have a weak heart." Constable Smyth was not swayed and charged both men with committing gross indecency. They appeared at the Belfast Commission Court the following month and pled not guilty. The jury rejected their defense, but the penalty from the judge was light: just a £20 fine for the prosecution costs.[2]

Lots of queer men had been dragged into the Belfast courts to defend themselves over the previous three decades, many of them discovered in the same or similar circumstances. Custodial sentences for the guilty were the norm, usually of at least six months and sometimes eighteen months, always with the added punishment of hard labor (unpicking rope, breaking rocks, and so on). So how can we explain the good fortune of these two men? What was said in court is now lost, but clues remain in the documentation of the judicial process. Thomas Carrick was bailed out by one of the owners of Kinkead Brothers, a large manufacturing firm. Robert Kinkead had some commercial and civic standing. Aged in his mid-sixties, he lived with his family in a mansion on a leafy street in south Belfast. He was also president of the Balmoral Golf Club; this institution, founded in 1914, drew its membership from the new bourgeoisie and brought them into contact with aristocratic and landowning unionist elites. Kinkead's golf captain, as an example of his connections, was Lieutenant-Commander Richard Milligen Harcourt: a lauded Royal Navy veteran, coal firm director, and municipal official who later served as high sheriff.[3]

It must have been Robert Kinkead or his friends who helped Thomas Carrick secure Thomas Joseph Campbell as legal representation for the trial. Campbell was a well-known barrister, journalist, and politician who later became the leader of the Nationalist Party in Northern Ireland.[4] In 1918 he had been appointed to the esteemed legal position of King's Counsel, which meant the governor of Northern Ireland had to be petitioned to grant the barrister the license to act against the Crown on behalf of an industrial foreman. Kinkead even appeared in court as the only witness for the defense, putting his reputation on the line. The result of powerful lawyers and character references was leniency and freedom for both the accused; the courts could hardly justify punishing one and not the other. Samuel Ramsay died a year later from the heart problems he had feared, but Thomas Carrick lived another twenty years, remaining married and living in the same house, and all the while working for Robert Kinkead, the man who had helped him escape punishment.[5]

In the trial of these two men, whether they had sex was never considered in terms of innate desires or identities. "Homosexuality" was never recorded in the documentation of Northern Ireland's legal system before the 1950s. Only a couple of cases of gross indecency or buggery came before the courts each year, sometimes even none, so judges and juries could be forgiven for not understanding the latest sexological models. There were two questions that the legal system asked instead. First, was a defendant who pled not guilty telling the truth, or was his morality so degenerated that he would have sex with another man and then lie about it? Second, if he did admit the offense or his protestations were not believed, could his sexual behavior be explained as atypical or the result of mitigating factors? Courtroom battles were accordingly centered more on the reputation, character, and social status of the accused than any strict medical understanding of sexuality. These factors shaped trials of sexual deviancy in other places too, but the difference in Belfast was how the ethnoreligious structures of the region also informed the deciding of guilt and responsibility.[6] As we will see in this chapter, not all queer men were equal before the law. The Protestant unionist establishment, like Thomas Carrick had found out to his benefit, tended to protect its own, even when the crime directly contravened the moral virtues of Ulster they claimed to uphold.

Character, Respectability, and Guilt

Most of the working-class and middle-class men who were arrested for same-sex crimes in Belfast were unable to depend on the grace and favor politics of the establishment to resist the full weight of the law. Instead, they had to use powers of persuasion and performances of virtue and remorse to shape an alternative narrative to that of the prosecution. Irish courtrooms were spaces of drama where defendants and their supporters appealed to the emotions and sensibilities of judge and jury to mitigate any natural disgust or condemnation they may have felt.[7]

Voluntary character references were one way that the accounts of the police or witnesses could be challenged. Personal status in Ireland mattered, from street and neighborhood to philanthropy and politics. Class hierarchies were determined by family background, education and wealth, and, as we will see, there were differences in what each rung of the social ladder prioritized to be a good man. But there was a common value system that brought all men together: a "hegemonic masculinity" that attempted to uphold the patriarchy by insisting on the fundamental gendered differences between men and women. There is academic debate about how hegemonic this masculinity could be, given the vulnerable realities of men's lives, but the discursive effects were clear: men were expected to at least publicly conform to ideals of manliness and so behave in a way that reflected well on their families, communities, and nation. In practice, this left no space for queer sex to be sanctioned from the legal or religious authorities, even if plenty of men ignored the official prohibition.[8]

In the courtroom, the defendant's task was to demonstrate how he *usually* satisfied the demands of being a man.[9] Working-class defendants aimed to show that they were economically productive members of society—reliable, strong, hardworking—and valued in their all-male associations.[10] In 1885, for example, when a mechanic in his mid-thirties was brought up on a charge of drunkenly importuning other men, the secretary of the Amalgamated Engineers' Society gave a reference to this effect, and the judge was convinced. "Hitherto you have maintained a very high character," he told Archibald Black. "I have the evidence of one who has known you for fifteen years, and his testimony is that you are highly respected in your trade . . . [and] have filled a variety of offices in the respectable organisation of which you are a member." Black was given a suspended sentence of twelve months, dependent on good behavior, and discharged with a final piece of advice: "let this be a warning to you."[11] There are other examples of employer support, and not just for men who held work prestige, from an apprentice stonecutter described in court by his master as "a very good boy always" to a young chemist shopworker deemed "trustworthy . . . upright at his work . . . courteous with customers . . . [and] always co-operative when called upon to perform any extra duties."[12] Juries were mostly male and petty bourgeoise, so appealing to a defendant's upstanding work—his breadwinning ability to support his family—was a way to distract them from the sexual sins under discussion.[13]

Witnesses who knew a working man through neighborhood life could also give evidence. Ministers sent letters to the police to stress the usually timid disposition of the accused or appeared in court to confirm that the defendant and his family were usually of good character. Religion was central to conceptions of respectability in Ireland, so such demonstrations of piety were important.[14] Close relatives—wives, mothers, brothers, uncles—gave character references for queer men too, though what they said has not often survived because of the reluctance of the press to say much at all about same-sex crimes. In trials of other offenses, though, such witnesses focused on the essential goodness of their men, especially if they were still young. They also gave excuses, from illness to marriage breakdown, or blamed a man's moral corruption on wayward friends.[15] Even the constable who made an arrest for gross indecency could speak up for his prisoner. These authority figures often lived near the neighborhoods they policed so could confirm in court that a man who had sex with another man was otherwise respectable and had never been in trouble before, did not take alcohol nor argue with his wife, or had a good record in the army.[16] All these witnesses suggested that a defendant was less interested in drinking and cavorting in public than he was in maintaining his home and family life, which were attributes of working-class respectability that had grown in importance over the nineteenth century.[17]

How a speaker in court acted was often as important as what they said. Newspapers sometimes commented on defendants and witnesses being well-dressed or if they turned up to court in military uniform. Manly bodily comportment—displaying defiance or confidence—suggested they were being honest about their sexual behavior or at least took the judiciary authority seriously.[18] On the other hand, some physical responses, like fainting or crying, betrayed a feminine-coded weakness. When one prominent queer man was on trial in 1893, the newspaper reported how "occasionally, on some stinging remark of counsel's, he contracted his brows as if in mental pain, closed his eyes, and passed his hand over his brow."[19]

In a few rare cases, a strong courtroom performance and glowing witness statements could convince the jury that it was impossible the defendant could have had sex with another man. Only middle- or upper-class defendants with long-standing reputations could use this tactic; the lowly working-class queer could not.[20] We can see this reasoning in the release of James Sinton, who, as we saw in the last chapter, fled the country after his ordeal. He was initially imprisoned for three months with hard labor—and three months more if he could not find bail—for his "indecent offence" in 1909.[21] Sinton was the image of an upstanding middle-class citizen: a married son of a grocer who, like his brother, had ascended to white-collar work in Belfast's city council. When his appeal reached the court, new witnesses were brought in to swear their friend could not be a guilty man. Reverends and the chief assistant superintendent of the city council described his excellent character. A brother-in-law, another municipal worker, gave an alibi for the time the crime had allegedly taken place. The judge now decided that James Sinton must have been mistaken for someone else. After all, with "the character he had been given by three clergymen, he ought to be incapable of such an act."[22]

In other cases where men accused each other of instigating a sexual encounter, whether consensual or not, the court's decision was shaped by their judgment of the moral fiber of each defendant. In 1940, for example, a middle-class man accused of sexual assault was publicly described as a "good Samaritan" and remained uncharged because the man who had violently resisted his probable advances had a longer history of criminal behavior.[23] That said, usually the defendant or his witness did not try to prove the prosecution was totally wrong about a same-sex encounter having taken place. Instead, the intent was to suggest that a defendant's previous morality meant that having sex with other men—whether for lust or money—was out of character. This defense certainly could work. Juries recommended mercy, and lenient judges passed suspended sentences for some while others were given long spells in prison for the same crime. On one occasion in 1924, a sympathetic judge even gave a short sentence of three months because the term would save the convicted man from losing his naval pension.[24]

What was said during the highest court trials does not often survive in the criminal archive, so we can only guess how many other cases ended because the defense of moral incapability was successful. But the earlier documentation of the criminal process shows how seeds of doubt about a man's guilt were sown before a case even reached the assizes. Witnesses first made statements at a petty sessions court, usually the day after an arrest. Written depositions went forward to the attorney general, who decided whether bringing a case was likely to result in prosecution. This meant that the petty sessions were the first opportunity for the accused and his solicitors, if he could afford them, to shape the evidence that would be used in the trial. Pointing out the untrustworthiness of the witness now became a tactic. An army deserter and a petty thief might have had questionable motives for reporting a former friend to the police. Uncouth youths, already in trouble for stealing, could be ignored in favor of the respectable man they accused. Fecklessly unemployed drunken men were even lower down the social hierarchy, so when they admitted they had often been in court and even prison, their evidence about a man from their neighborhood could be dismissed.[25]

Any suggestion that the prosecution was relying on witnesses who lacked good character was useful for the defense. We can see a successful example of this legal tactic in a case from 1902, after two young men were arrested in a brothel. They were reported to the police by the madam, after she realized they were not going to pay for her girls because they were more interested in each other.[26] In the eyes of the law and the churches, female prostitutes were a stain on the reputation of pure Ulster. Even so, it seems these women themselves believed that queer men were lower in the social-moral hierarchy and worthy of punishment, or at least had no qualms in taking revenge on them for fulfilling their disparaged desires. At any rate, three female sex workers gave statements at the petty sessions court. The solicitor for the defense began by having the arresting constable confirm it was a "low classed" establishment where he had often been called to quell disorder. The solicitor then turned to the women and had them describe the regular fighting that happened in the brothel, their excessive drinking, and their especial inebriation on the night in question. He then pointed out the contradictions of how the women had witnessed the men having sex in the brothel toilet: they could not even agree whether the door had been open. Faced with this inconsistency from disreputable "fallen women," and perhaps fearing the public interest that would accompany a trial where they turned up in court to give evidence, the Crown declined to prosecute.[27]

Carefully suggesting that a witness may have had immoral or criminal experience of his own was another useful ploy for the defense.[28] Already in the nineteenth century there was a concern that blackmailers were threatening the privileges of privacy, especially for leading men, and that they risked bringing knowledge about deviant desires into the light. The preoccupation with sexual blackmail only increased in the early twentieth century: social lines of class and gender were blurring, especially in large anonymous cities; there was a growing awareness of same-sex desire, even if loosely defined; and the centrality of family life meant middle-class queer men were more afraid than ever before about their desires being exposed.[29] In Belfast, the courts did not take kindly to witnesses they thought had lied about being victims of unwanted advances or who had maybe entrapped another man. In 1928, one witness told the petty sessions court that a cruiser had "accosted" and "pestered" him, grabbing at his crotch while he was minding his own business listening to an outdoor concert. So why, the defense solicitor wanted to know, had the witness not raised a row at the time instead of allowing the man to follow him? And why had he even paid for the cruiser's tram fare? The witness insisted that he was a married man, if living apart from his wife, but admitted he had been drinking most of the day. The grand jury decided that there was not enough evidence to prosecute.[30]

Other defendants were found not guilty or had their cases thrown out when the evidence came from just one witness who was spying or entrapping. For the court, the whiff of blackmail could be more alarming than a same-sex offense, and queer men could even be recast as victims.[31] An extreme example of this moral inversion was widely reported in 1932, when a blackmailed man died by suicide. Terence Moore left a note that explained how he had been entrapped and then threatened with exposure. His blackmailer had "stated he would get [Moore] tarred and feathered down the town," a humiliating punishment that became more well-known during the Troubles in the 1970s. "I bore with all, as long as I could, but now I am forced to commit suicide," Moore wrote in his final letter, ending, "God forgive him and me for my downfall." The shock and disgust from the judge and the public was notable, as was the sentence of three years passed down to the stunned blackmailer.[32]

If sexual encounters were between adults and seemingly consensual according to a public witness but the accused refused to admit the crime, the conviction rate was only about 15 percent, and even if another member of the public had seen the crime it climbed to only 40 percent.[33] The nature of urban life meant that most witnesses were from the working class and shared spaces with those they accused: rowdy pubs, insalubrious alleyways, and lawless dockside neighborhoods. In the "play of masculinity" that was the courtroom drama, the struggle over defining manly heroes and unmanly villains played an important role in deciding the result of the contest.[34]

The authority of police witnesses brought more success to court cases; roughly two-thirds of the encounters they had interrupted alone still resulted in convictions. But even they found their evidence challenged or discounted by suspicious Irish juries, many members of which resented the authorities prying into the privacy of male lives.[35] In February 1912, for example, the evidence of a constable was not enough to secure conviction. Christopher Moffett told the court that a member of the public had suggested he keep a watch on two men, whom he then saw "working in and out against each other" and "breathing heavily" with "flushed faces." When the jury acquitted both defendants, the judge could not hide his anger. Refusing to release them for the rest of the assizes, he exclaimed, "I never saw a clearer case in my life, and one in which guilt was more clearly proved." All the foreman could muster in response was "We had only the evidence of the policeman, and it was not very clear."[36] There are other cases where a constable found his evidence discounted by a higher power, and it was only when he also had support from members of the public that conviction was almost guaranteed.[37] In a legal system where guilt had to be proven beyond doubt, there were numerous ways that a mix of authority and respectability could be enough to absolve a queer man from acting on his desires.[38]

Sexuality and the Law

Britain shared in the wider European and North American anxieties about male sexuality that developed in the late nineteenth century but, as we have already seen, was slower to adopt scientific models of deviancy.[39] Courts in France and other places called upon doctors as respected experts, but the more adversarial Anglo-Saxon legal system instead subjected them to cross-examinations that were often harsh and humiliating.[40] Doctors were rightly wary about appearing in such an environment, which meant a legal-medicalization of homosexuality took longer to take root. Only in the 1930s was there a growing sense that homosexual men in Britain could and should be treated by psychiatric experts, and medical explanations consequently began to appear in the courtroom.[41] In Northern Ireland the legal system was essentially the same as in Britain, but progress toward using medical expertise was even slower. Psychiatry challenged local conservative religious authority and so was distrusted, and the dire economic conditions of the interwar decades meant there was little reform of the medical infrastructure anyway.[42]

In trials of same-sex offenses in Belfast in the first half of the twentieth century there was barely any reflection on the cause or treatment of homosexuality. In only one case, in 1913, was a doctor brought in to give evidence about a defendant's mental state. Even then it was an elderly man's dementia rather than his sexuality that was used as a justification for committing him to an asylum (the fact that the defendant was also longtime friends with his doctor may have helped him gain this excuse).[43] Even in 1947, by which time there had been a little development of psychiatric practice, one defendant could still demonstrate that his own knowledge went beyond that of the courts. He began his supposedly voluntary statement by saying, "I am according to the medical term," but the petty sessions clerk left a blank space where we might have expected to have seen *invert* or *homosexual*. Perhaps the clerk was temporarily embarrassed or simply unfamiliar with the concept the defendant had named.[44] When doctors did appear in court, and only rarely, it was simply to determine, after examining the bodies of usually younger men or boys, whether penetrative sex had taken place.[45] Only these sexual acts, and not identities, were easily defined and regulated by the old laws against gross indecency and sodomy, and even then relatively inconsistently.

Many Belfastmen swore in court it was their first and last time having queer sex: a momentary lapse of morality rather than the type of person they were. When there was so little policing, press reportage, or even strong self-understanding of homosexuality, the courts could accept that reasoning, or at least retained enough doubt to not assume a man was lying. In 1932, for example, two defendants were found guilty but given a suspended sentence of six months because the judge "believed it was an isolated transaction" despite both men being sober and mentally well.[46] But if the judge was aware that a man had been convicted before, harsher sentencing was assured. Archibald Black, who, as we saw earlier, escaped prison despite being found guilty, was not so lucky on his second time in court six years later. He admitted what he had done but was still given eighteen months in the Crumlin Road Gaol in comparison to his younger lover's sentence of six months. The judge was clear in his reasoning: the defendant already had a "very bad record against him for a similar class of offence."[47] Other men who had been arrested before faced similarly severe punishments.[48]

The age of a defendant also affected how the courts judged his behavior. Any sexual contact between males was illegal, so the law was a blunt tool for determining differing levels of culpability. Boys under sixteen were occasionally treated as responsible in the late nineteenth century, and even after the founding of the juvenile court in 1908 they could technically still be tried in the adult courts if they were charged alongside an older man.[49] In the early to mid-1930s there were two occasions where boys under the age of sixteen were charged or almost charged, though the assizes did not follow through with the prosecution after belatedly confirming each was a "minor."[50] In practice, even men into their early twenties could admit consent and receive more lenient sentences or remain uncharged and unpunished altogether.[51] If a boy or young man described consenting to sex with an older man, to punish both required a corroborating witness. In that sense, it was easier to simply treat boys or young men as witnesses for the prosecution and ensure that at least one person was convicted.[52] At any rate, in a time before a widespread understanding of homosexuality was innate, youths could be seen as victims, even if there was not yet a broad panic about how homosexuality was supposedly destroying childhood innocence.[53] These younger defendants were likely coached by the police and solicitors to give statements that supported a narrative of seduction or corruption.[54]

Power dynamics between males were also determined by the interaction of age with social hierarchies. In 1913, for example, a twenty-two-year-old rural laborer was surprised to find he was not in trouble for a sexual encounter with an older man in Belfast. "I thought the policeman was going to arrest me," William Cauldwell told the court, but the constable "afterwards said he did not want to do anything on me."[55] Before the 1930s, the courts could recognize that poor youths were engaging in sex for money rather than pleasure and usually—if not always—apportioned blame to the immoral man who paid.[56] It was only later in that decade, some time behind Britain, that the law began to shape a new legal approach for those who, as spoken in their own terms, had consented to sex with older men. Instead of being treated as just witnesses for the prosecution, boys as young as twelve but more often in their late adolescence were tried and placed on supervised probation for up to two years. The courts of Northern Ireland were finally catching up with those social scientists abroad who for at least half a century had been writing about how seduction and abuse imperiled children and adolescents. The system in Northern Ireland now became less interested in blame than in the personal difficulties of developing boys and the possibility of their reform through professional expertise.[57] Even so, inconsistency in legal practice remained: into the early 1950s there were still adult male prostitutes being treated only as witnesses, including those who hounded or blackmailed desperate queer men.[58]

Without sexological expertise, both judge and jury instead depended on social or religious models for understanding queer desires. By far the most common excuse given by an arrested man was that his rationality and restraint, a prized attribute of manliness from the Victorian era onward, had been dulled by alcohol.[59] Defendants claimed that any amount, from a few beers to a boozing session over several days—or a "spree" in local parlance—had led them into immoral behavior they often could not even remember.[60]

Today, such an explanation may seem fanciful, but it mirrored a broader public discussion in contemporary Ireland about the moral and criminal effects of inebriation. For women, sexual impurity and drink had long been seen as reinforcing evils that resulted in a "fall" into prostitution. As the Ulster Temperance Council put it simply, in an advert that appeared across the north of Ireland's newspapers in 1918, "Drink Is the Parent of Immorality. Immorality Is the Parent of Disease."[61] In a Christian culture that avoided a public debate about sexual desire, all were sinners, and anyone could be the victim of drunken temptation. Adding weight to this religious argument by the early twentieth century was an international eugenic influence in Ireland; alcohol could now be seen as not just a moral evil but a cause of physical and mental degeneration too.[62]

Juries drawn from broader society were persuaded by this link between the demon drink and immorality and believed that rehabilitation was possible for queer men. The result was a degree of empathy, as long as defendants were visibly remorseful about their offense.[63] We have a clear example of how strong this discourse of alcohol and responsibility could be in a case from 1935, when the police witnessed a man mutually masturbating and receiving oral sex from a schoolboy. John Ernest Ashfield was in his mid-thirties and worked as a joiner. He pled guilty and was given a suspended sentence of six months, and drunkenness was a major part of the defense. He told the court that he had now taken the pledge of Temperance, so the judge released him under the condition that he kept the peace and did not take another drop of alcohol for at least a year. Whether he stuck to his promise we will never know, but he was not arrested again in Belfast.[64] Equally, if a man could not persuade the courtroom of his drunkenness, the punishment could be severe. Policemen and witnesses often commented on a defendant's drinking, even without any official guidance from the state on defining a scale of inebriation. A witness might observe that a queer man had been drinking "but seemed to have all his senses" or that a couple were "under the influence of drink but both were able to know what they were doing."[65] The purpose of such testimony was to suggest that specific circumstances or a demoralizing environment could affect whether a man was in control of his desires. If he was, punishment was deserved; if he was not, then he was just another victim of the social scourge of alcohol.[66]

From the 1890s to the 1950s, just over half the men who pled not guilty to same-sex crimes were vindicated after trial or had their charge dismissed before it even reached the higher courts. There was little input from the medical profession, a lack of state guidance, and a general confusion about what led some men to have sex with men. Given the relatively low level of arrests, it would have been difficult to test any theory out in great depth anyway. The result was that a legal category of the homosexual never came into practice in the north of Ireland in the first half of the twentieth century, and there was an inconsistency in how the old, even medieval, laws were applied. Alcohol, age, and respectability were more useful for a jury trying to decide guilt than evidence of engrained sexual desires, let alone a modern homosexual identity.

Unionism, Nationalism, and Queerness

The evidentiary burden was high for most men accused of same-sex offenses, but there were some for whom it was even higher still. Elites were less likely than the working or even middle classes to have sexual encounters in public places because they had the wealth to take their partners to hotels or the privacy of their own secluded homes, and their neighbors were warier of the ramifications of reporting them to the police. Peter Montgomery, for example, lived a queer life almost certainly with the knowledge of others from high society throughout the mid-twentieth century. As the vice lord lieutenant of Tyrone and ensconced in a country house, he was physically and politically protected.[67] The linen merchant David Strain also picked up dozens of young men in Belfast in the 1930s and took them to his private office, his country hut, and even his suburban home and was seemingly never concerned about the police.[68] Yet if the risks of a queer life were lower for these men, the stakes were higher if exposure did happen. Defendants from the lower classes were unknown publicly beyond their families and immediate social networks, and there was little reason to give much newspaper coverage to their crimes. The same could not be said for men who were well-known in society. To lose honor they had to have it in the first place, which was mostly a privilege of being an upper-class man.[69]

More importantly for the Ulster establishment, elite queer men also risked bringing embarrassment and shame on them all. Public scandals on both sides of the Irish Sea, heavily reported through a sensational New Journalism and supported by feminist purity campaigners and evangelicals alike, created new anxieties about same-sex desire in the late nineteenth century.[70] There were growing alarmist fears more broadly, both in Europe and North America, about degeneration. Shrill commentators argued that physical and mental confusion had naturally accompanied the transition from a traditional rural society to a modern urban way of life. Part of this panic, including in Ireland, was the perception that masculine fitness was declining. Building a healthier and more virile manliness in response depended upon the categorizing of its obverse: the sexual deviants who seemed to gather in the great cities. Protecting vulnerable women and children, and so ensuring national survival, could happen only if such degenerated predatory men were castigated and controlled.[71] Even if a sexual science did not develop in Ireland in this era, this sense that sex between men was a social problem did have some currency.

The nearest moral outrage to Belfast, both literally and politically, was the Dublin Castle Scandal of 1884, which involved the discovery of a network of rent boys and the colonial elites who paid them. The local result of the extensive press coverage was the intensification of a long-established idea in Ireland: that sin, including the unnatural act of sex between men, was being brought into the country's pure and muscular Irish society by the immoral and effete British. In effect, this was a challenge to the usual gendered understanding of Britain's imperial dominance over Ireland, where the latter was positioned as feminized and in need of protection by the former because it was too emotional to govern itself. For Irish nationalists, a counter-discourse—and the weaponizing of queer desire as a central tactic—helped in their fight for Home Rule within the United Kingdom or full independence outside.[72]

Ulster-born unionists did not easily fit into this nationalist discourse of imported immorality. They had long genealogical roots in the region and were still constitutionally Irish yet opposed self-governance for Ireland and often stressed the Anglo-Saxon Englishness of Ulster Protestants.[73] In this context, there are hints that Ulster unionism could also weaponize same-sex desire in a counter-discourse to that of Irish nationalists. The public revelation that some of the young men of the Belfast Scandal in 1890 were members of an Emerald Troupe provides one example. The Emerald Minstrels had first formed in the 1860s as a diasporic project of John Denvir, a Fenian migrant to Liverpool who hoped to inspire more romantic Irish nationalist music, poetry, and drama.[74] Though his own troupe was defunct by the 1880s, others were stirred to operate under the same or similar name in Ireland and Britain. When the scandal hit the papers, it was the unionist establishment daily, the *Belfast News-Letter*, that first reported this hobby of the accused. The republican-leaning *Irish News*, meanwhile, chose not to comment on the trial at all.[75] Readers of both publications may have inferred, through these opposing approaches of publicity and silence, that there was some sort of link between unnatural desires and supporting the political project of Irish Home Rule.

A closer look at the prosecution of two men from the upper echelons of unionism at the turn of the twentieth century, and the very different legal and public responses to their crimes, further demonstrates how queer scandals played out in Belfast's complex context of imperial anxieties and growing challenges to Britain's grip on Ireland. The first notable figure to fall foul of the Criminal Law Amendment Act of 1885 was Edward Samuel Wesley de Cobain. Born in the County Down town of Newry in 1840 and the son of a reverend, by the 1880s he had risen to become a grand master of the Orange Order in Belfast and a Conservative MP for the east of the city. Whether he was guilty of gross indecency is difficult to say, even though reams of prosecution evidence survive in the criminal archive of Northern Ireland. The witness statements are compelling but alike to the point of suspicious replication, despite the offenses having taken place several years before a warrant was made for his arrest in 1890. De Cobain was almost certainly being blackmailed by a disreputable young man named George Heggie, and some of the other young witnesses he had allegedly propositioned inhabited the same societal underbelly.[76]

Even with this element of skepticism, most historians have agreed that there was more to Edward de Cobain's downfall than just extortion. Eighty years later, Montgomery Hyde—coincidentally another east Belfast unionist MP as well as an important supporter of homosexual law reform—reported there was "little doubt that de Cobain was a homosexual."[77] Though not noted since, there was evidence presented in the popular press after de Cobain's gross indecency trial that suggested he was not only active in Belfast's queer scene. An outgoing first detective-sergeant of Scotland Yard claimed in 1895 that a policeman friend had apparently helped the politician when a rent boy stole his watch in London, a procedural misstep that was then covered up by the force's higher-ups. When de Cobain was then arrested for his offenses in Belfast, according to this relatively reputable source, Scotland Yard made sure that the constable who had previously helped was "got rid of quietly"—presumably so he could not incriminate the Ulsterman further.[78]

When it came to Edward de Cobain's conviction, his actual guilt was less important than how he responded to the news of his public exposure. After he was tipped off by friends in Belfast that he was about to be arrested, he took the well-worn path of fleeing from England to the more sexually permissive parts of Europe. The question became not whether the defendant had indeed seduced young men. Instead, like in the case of James Sinton years later, it was if his character demonstrated a deficiency that suggested he was *capable* of unnatural offenses.[79] Edward de Cobain's trial now took place in the court of public opinion, long before it reached the Belfast assizes. *Truth* had the most scathing description of the accused's queerness. This radical London title served as the mouthpiece of Henry Labouchère, a Liberal politician, scandal exposer, and society gossip who is infamous for writing the gross indecency clause that was submitted late into the Criminal Law Amendment Act. In 1891, he was primed for the scandal, having relentlessly criticized the Home Office for letting upper-class elites implicated in the recent Cleveland Street Scandal escape arrest by fleeing Britain. The fact that Labouchère was also a supporter of Home Rule may have encouraged him to destroy the unionist politician. "Mr. De Cobain had, to use a French phrase, *la physionomie de son role*," Labouchère suggested. "He was a very florid person, over-dressed, with a flower in his button-hole, and smelling of musk like a civet cat—oily and unctuous."[80]

Other stories about Edward de Cobain circulated in the press: the suspicious all-male religious meetings held at his home; how it was "his philanthropic custom to address the Christian young men at Lambeth Baths"—a statement that coyly suggested male nudity and religious hypocrisy; and his admittance that he had taken handkerchiefs from George Heggie because he liked the perfume they still held.[81] By making ungenerous allusions to de Cobain's bodily manner and aesthetic dandyism (see fig. 6.1), *Truth* and other newspapers insinuated that he was the sort of man likely to have sex with other men. Oscar Wilde's spectacular downfall transformed various perceptions of effeminacy, aestheticism, and immorality into a clearer image of homosexuality, but Edward de Cobain's own encounter with the law had already begun firming up this association a few years before.[82]

An even darker mark against Edward de Cobain than his effeminacy was how quickly he sacrificed honor by refusing to come home and face justice. Over two years, he lived in France, was spotted in Spain, and spent time hiding in Brooklyn. Eyewitness reports made contradictory claims about how he was living, from quietly taking an assumed name to loudly practicing his evangelical preaching. De Cobain actually encouraged this media frenzy by sending public letters home that insisted on his innocence while weakly claiming he would return only when his health improved. Hundreds of newspapers in Britain and Ireland pointed out that this self-imposed exile was the behavior of not just a guilty man but one who was also a coward. The verdict was simple: Edward de Cobain's lack of character shamed the high station he held in public life. As Ulster's *Northern Whig* damningly put it, "Even men conscious of guilt have taken the more manly course."[83] At the least the newspaper meant coming back to Belfast to face his accusers, but such phrasing also hinted at the more drastic solution of suicide.

When Edward de Cobain finally faced trial at the Belfast assizes in early 1893, forced home after running out of money and friends, he managed to find some local people to support him. Sir James Haslett—a former mayor and Irish Conservative Party colleague—was the most notable of two wit-

FIGURE 6.1. Edward de Cobain with a characteristically flamboyant flower in his buttonhole. *The Penny Illustrated Paper* (February 25, 1893). Content provided by the British Library Board. All rights reserved. With thanks to The British Newspaper Archive (www.britishnewspaperarchive.co.uk).

nesses in court. He said he had known de Cobain for thirty years and had "never heard anything against his reputation, honour, or morality." Reverend Wesley Guard, who shared the Methodist faith of the defendant, was a less impressive civic figure. He insisted, more generically, that the devout MP "always bore the highest moral character." But the statements of these two men were not enough, as the nationalist *Irish News* reported with glee: the "Ex Orange Grand Master [Was] Convicted," sentenced to twelve months with hard labor, and banished from public life.[84]

It would be too easy to conclude that any figure of Edward de Cobain's public stature would have faced the same rough treatment if accused of gross indecency, but the unfortunate MP did have enemies who made the response harsher. His emotive populist criticism of the Royal Irish Constabulary's role in the Belfast Riots of 1886 had put him out of favor with the local police, and his standing up for the working man and the cause of Temperance marked him out among his Tory party colleagues too. For this reason, de Cobain claimed there was a conspiracy: the sin of unnatural desire weaponized to remove him from his office.[85] He was right in one respect: the ruining of his reputation was hastened at home by not just foes but former friends too. The nationalist press unsurprisingly found good copy in the hypocrisy of this Orangeman's refusal to return to face his accusers, though they were not as keen to expound on his behavior as they were with the more clearly Anglo-Irish elite occupying Dublin Castle. But some unionists were relentlessly critical too. De Cobain's few remaining supporters recognized how even the unionist newspapers of the province were holding de Cobain up "to the execration of the public . . . and goading on the Government to expel him."[86] The politician had simply lost the faith of the Ulster establishment. Evidence of good character and local connections was not enough to get him off a charge of gross indecency because he was so heavily disliked, and so the desire to evict him from public life overcame the usual regional tactic of remaining silent about local immorality.

A fresh scandal that erupted in 1904—one that, unlike Edward de Cobain's downfall, has been forgotten—is more representative of how the politics of sexual sin, exceptionalism, and masculinity usually worked in the north of Ireland. In the early hours of a September morning in 1904, Richard Lutton, a man in his mid-forties, was discovered having sex in a deep doorway in Belfast's center with a nineteen-year-old working-class lad.[87] In desperation, Lutton first tried to bribe Constable Normoyle with a promise of £5. For this twenty-four-year-old policeman that would have been a month's wages at a time when the Royal Irish Constabulary was losing new recruits over bitter pay disputes.[88] Maybe this approach had worked for Lutton on other occasions, but this time the policeman was stoic. Lutton next tried suggesting a promotion for Normoyle, intimating how this gift was in his power because he was Sir Daniel Dixon's private secretary. Dixon, a prominent businessman and unionist politician, was the first lord mayor of Belfast in 1893 and in 1904 only one year out of his second term.[89]

Richard Lutton had worked in Daniel Dixon's ship-owning empire since 1876, when he was just eighteen, and by 1901 had risen to managerial status in the timber trade part of the company. The two men were close friends. Lutton attended lavish civic events, such as a testimonial in 1894 where Ulster's businessmen and gentry gathered in the Municipal Buildings to witness the unveiling of two portraits of the outgoing lord mayor. Lutton was also present at private parties, like at Dixon's new estate at Glenville in 1903, where he was not just among the crowd of two hundred guests but identified by the newspapers as one of six who accompanied Dixon directly.[90] Daniel Dixon's name may not have been enough to stop the arrest of Richard Lutton, but the industrialist's family were loyal to their disgraced employee. Dixon's eldest son, Thomas, provided £100 bail for the accused, as did Joseph Shekelton Wright, a middle-aged city rate collector.[91]

When his day in court arrived, afterward described in a long report in the nationalist *Irish News*, Richard Lutton continued to draw on the support of men of his social and political class. His testimony was that excessive drinking that night had led to a total lapse of memory: he had no recollection of even meeting the young man in question. The tussle between defense and prosecution was now not whether Lutton had been penetrated in public by a man but if, as his solicitor Richard McGrath put it, "he knew what he was doing, and that he did it deliberately." Elite witnesses were called by the defense to emphasize Lutton's respectability, manliness, and reliability. Daniel McGonigal, a solicitor, said his friend was "always a manly, straightforward fellow, and one of the most popular men in the town." More evidence of character was given by Thomas Sinclair Kirk and Henry Hutton, respectively a prominent surgeon and the current high sheriff. But the most powerful courtroom moment was the appearance of Sir Daniel Dixon himself. The elderly statesman emphasized that Lutton "was always a very manly fellow," "one of his most trusted employees," and not usually a man who drank till he blacked out and dropped his trousers for a youth he had met in a disreputable oyster bar (see fig. 6.2).

The judge, summing up and addressing the jury, made his own opinion clear. It is so outrageous that it is worth quoting in full:

> If they did not know what they were doing, of course they could not be guilty. Suppose the prisoners were two lunatics, and acted in that way, they would not be guilty, because they would not be responsible. If drink put them into the same position, they would not be responsible for an act to which they were not consenting parties in the right senses. That was really the question before the jury . . . did they know what they were doing, did they do it deliberately? And if they did, they were guilty. If they did not know what they were doing, they were not responsible.

The jury took just twenty minutes to find both accused men not guilty, and Lutton was free to "go back into the world" with "the lesson he had learned

FIGURE 6.2. A typical oyster bar of the period, complete with working-class youths. A. R. Hogg, *West Side from City Oyster Rooms (Nos. 11–13) to Arthur Square* (c. 1900), BELUM.Y2805. Courtesy of National Museums NI, Ulster Museum Collection.

of the evil effects of drink . . . engraven upon his mind forever."[92] Richard Lutton had demonstrated his contribution to both business and civic life and the essential respectability of his character. In turn, the judge concluded that alcohol had made Lutton capable of buggery but not culpable.

But there was more to this case than just respectability and inebriation. *Truth*, not surprisingly given its previous interest in Irish and queer scandals, picked the story up from the Belfast-based *Irish News*. In his intimate and conversational Entre Nous columns, Henry Labouchère now described the "extraordinary example of justice as it is administered in Belfast." He emphasized the social dimensions—a middle-aged private secretary to a figure as powerful as an ex–lord mayor having sex with a working-class lad—and noted how the drunkenness excuse had been enough to prove innocence. "It was," Labouchère railed, "the most astounding performance of the kind

I have come across for a long time." He speculated that if both prisoners had been lower down the social hierarchy the result would have been very different.[93] *Reynold's News*, also England-based but with a bigger circulation than *Truth*, was similarly excised. This working-class radical newspaper embellished details from the original *Irish News* report and emphasized the aspects that fitted into their own popular societal critique. Lutton was "gentlemanly-looking [and] middle-aged . . . and a leading man in Belfast society" who brought "a poor orphan . . . a boy . . . aged 17" into "the awful predicament."[94]

Richard Lutton's behavior, viewed from London, was yet another case of upper-class degenerates corrupting the honest and powerless working class, just as had been the case in the Dublin Castle Scandal, the Cleveland Street Scandal, and the tastes of Oscar Wilde.[95] In reality, the "boy" was not exactly a victim. He was two years older than some reports claimed and had taken the active sexual role after a day of gambling and heavy drinking in rowdy bars. But for the press, this context did not matter. The form their stories took was instead a melodrama: a genre, as the historian Judith Walkowitz has powerfully shown, that followed scripts of upper-class sexual exploitation and was still popular with working-class audiences in the late nineteenth century.[96]

Belfast had briefly become tied up in a wider conversation about class, power, and sexual immorality that was emanating from the English capital and the influential social purity movement. But *Reynold's* also hinted at the peculiarly Irish aspects of the scandal, pointing out sardonically how it had taken place in the "superlatively moral" city of "Puritan Belfast." Poking fun at local debates about censorship, the newspaper observed how the Ulster elite wanted to ban newspaper accounts of horse racing but allowed themselves to have unnatural sex in public as long as they were drunk.[97] That missive could have been the end of *Reynold's* moral crusade: the behavior of Belfast's governors exposed as no better, and maybe even worse, than the hypocrisy of the English elite. But Belfast's guardians did not take kindly to being castigated from across the Irish Sea. A week later, *Reynold's* reported that their exposure of "the monumental hypocrisy and fraud" of Belfast's commercial and religious elites had led to the local police in the city tearing down their billboards. "How deeply the arrows of truth have penetrated into the canting hide of a town which always holds itself up to the rest of Ireland as a model of civic and religious virtue," they triumphantly concluded. *Reynold's* also noted how the Belfast press was "completely under the thumb of the creatures whom we have exposed" and suggested that—apart from the nationalist *Irish News* that first broke the story—no other outlet had "the courage to speak the truth."[98]

Eventually, the silence was broken by the *Mid-Ulster Mail*, a staunchly unionist newspaper imbued with a strict Presbyterian moral ethos. "If the charge by the Recorder of Belfast to a jury this week has been correctly reported," they gently suggested, "we imagine there will be a desire on the part of all wrongdoers to be tried in that court."[99] The *Donegal Independent*, two weeks after the court case, was far sharper in its criticism. It had become clear that "progressive English newspapers" were "astounded" at the operation of the law in Ireland, it detailed. As a nationalist title, the *Independent* also had an explanation: "Too often our law givers are but the puppets of the Orange and Masonic lodges and they think that it is old times in Ireland. When Parliament meets this travesty of justice will be exposed and Recorder Fitzgibbon should get his deserts [*sic*]. But he won't. The Chief Secretary will come to his rescue as he did with Sheridan and his ilk."[100]Gerald Fitzgibbon PC was a powerful figure in the Anglo-Irish establishment. He had served as both an advisor to the Dublin Castle and the solicitor general for Ireland in 1877–1878 and was promoted to lord justice of the Court of Appeal the following year. Fitzgibbon was also a freemason; he joined the Trinity College Dublin Lodge in 1876 and after 1899 was the Irish representative of the Grand Lodge of Canada.[101] The newspaper report was alluding to another recent scandal in which he was involved: the escape from justice of Sergeant Sheridan of the Royal Irish Constabulary, who allegedly burned farms, mutilated cattle, and framed others for his crimes. In evoking the corruption of that case, the newspaper positioned Lutton's trial as just another example of the British administration failing Ireland.[102]

A scandalous trial like this should have heralded the end of Richard Lutton's public standing. But Sir Daniel Dixon, even if personally embarrassed, stayed faithful to his friend and employee. During the trial, Dixon had promised Lutton his job if he cleared his name and never drank again. And the lord mayor was true to his word, even if his secretary had gotten off the charge only on a dubious technicality. Lutton carried on his lifetime of service in the family firm, first under the aging patriarch and then his son Thomas. When Daniel Dixon died in 1907, Lutton was one of two employees who was bequeathed a handsome £200.[103] Lutton also remained active in civic life. In 1912 he signed the Ulster Covenant and continued to act as the honorary treasurer for the Ballynafeigh and Newtownbreda Unionist Club; he also supported the Church of Ireland through his local congregation. When he died in 1935, he was still a bachelor and living in the same large house in south Belfast. The *Belfast News-Letter* described the funeral: "in addition to relatives, there were present many old friends and others who had been associated with Mr. Lutton at work and in private life."[104] It is difficult to know whether his drunken queer indiscretion had been forgotten or forgiven—or even repeated. But it had not spelled the end of Richard Lutton's public reputation.

In their reporting of the scandal, the Irish nationalist newspapers had made a convincing argument: Richard Lutton got away with an obscene sexual crime because he was imbricated in Ulster's power structure. Helpful to Lutton was not just what the elite were prepared to say in court but what they were not prepared to print. The *Belfast News-Letter*, the *Northern Whig*, and the *Belfast Telegraph*—the last the de facto "Orange organ," as the nationalist *United Irishman* dubbed it—were the standard bearers of unionism.[105] They all remained relatively quiet about Richard Lutton's disgrace.[106] In London, broadsheets similarly kept quiet about sexual crime of the country's leading men. To draw attention to the normal existence of queer men, they believed, could only damage the international reputation of Britain's manly virility.[107] In colonial Ireland, silence had that objective but another too: securing the legitimacy of the Protestant governing elite against the backdrop of challenges to their constitutional membership of the United Kingdom.

Avoiding Queer Scandal in an "Orange State"

In the decades after the Richard Lutton affair there were no more public queer outrages, but the power structures that helped one elite Protestant escape justice endured. It is true that most Catholic men arrested for same-sex crimes were treated roughly the same as the larger and more dominant community: character and respectability, rather than religious affiliation, informed how juries usually decided their guilt and punishment. But when religion intersected with class and politics, the dynamics remained in favor of rich Protestant unionists. Their cultural capital was far greater than working- and middle-class men of both faiths, and they could influence the legal procedure through their money and connections.[108] Even after the public backlash against Richard Lutton's acquittal, the establishment continued to intervene in the prosecution of some men who had sex with men. They had their own motives for doing so. Instability had reached a fresh climax in the region after the Third Home Rule Bill was passed by the Parliament of the United Kingdom in 1912, with unionists responding by creating the Ulster Volunteers to resist Ulster's coercion into a territory governed from Dublin.[109] When one of the key tenets of the construction of Ulster Protestant manliness was lawfulness, as distinguished from the revolutionary tactics of northern Catholic nationalists, it was not the time to again draw attention to the moral and illegal laxity of the unionist governing classes.[110]

When yet another elite was discovered intimately embracing a man in a city-center doorway, late one evening in January 1914, it was a problem for the authorities. Alexander Erskine was a Presbyterian merchant in his early sixties, almost a quarter of a century older than his working-class lover. He was linked to the Ulster establishment through his older brother, John Erskine, who had worked his way up over the previous fifty years from iron foundry apprentice to large-scale felt manufacturer. John Erskine had long held a prominent role in public life: he served on the Belfast Rural Council and Belfast Board of Guardians and was a justice of the peace and a member of the Lisburn and Belfast Regional Education Committee. When he died in 1934 the *Belfast News-Letter* described him as a "vigorous advocate of the Unionist cause."[111] Ulster's rapid economic and urban growth in the mid- to late nineteenth century had created a powerful class of Protestant industrialists who knew they shared at least some interests with the province's longer-established colonial landowners. The result was an alliance—if complex and riven with tensions—that continued to work in the favor of the union with Great Britain.[112]

The only witness in the case against Alexander Erskine was Constable William Edgeworth, who had discovered the two accused men *in flagrante*. After Edgeworth gave his evidence at the petty sessions court, the case was adjourned so he might produce a witness to verify his claim that the trousers of both men had been open when they arrived at the police barracks. "Have you been able to get that corroboration?" Erskine's solicitor asked at a second petty sessions hearing. "I have not," the constable replied. "The Head Constable or any of them in the Police Office couldn't corroborate that?" the solicitor pushed. "None of them noticed their trousers," Edgeworth admitted.[113]

When Erskine had been arrested it was his brother's sons who had provided the bail, and he was not disowned by the family after his trial.[114] Maybe John Erskine had directly intervened in the case too, given all his legal connections, or perhaps the head constable simply knew better than to cross such an influential figure. Either way, the attorney general for Ireland, John Moriarty QC, now had a decision to make.[115] He was an effective but unscrupulous political operator whose loyalties were swayed by the prospect of personal reward, maybe needed more than most because of a gambling habit. Though not a Protestant nor Ulsterman, even flirting with Nationalist allegiance, he was still what was pejoratively termed a "Castle Catholic"—someone who supported the British establishment for their own gain.[116] At any rate, he decided not to prosecute Alexander Erskine. The aging man was not arrested another time, though he lived for only a few years more. His former lover found himself in trouble for gross indecency again just over a decade later and, without the patronage of the elite on that occasion, was not so lucky in court.[117]

The Home Rule Crisis was interrupted by the First World War, the proposed Government of Ireland Act of 1914 was subsequently delayed, and unrest over the national question erupted again with the Easter Rising in 1916. While Irish men and women were taking to the streets of Dublin to fight the British, Edgar Milligen was cruising Belfast for rough trade. Milligen was well connected into the Ulster elite through his Orange Order–supporting father.[118] When he was eventually arrested in Liverpool for his various sexual offenses with boys aged fifteen or sixteen in Belfast, he was thus at risk of great exposure. One of the youths had made a complaint to a social worker, it seems, who informed the local police, who then put out the wire to England, where they must have known Milligen had business interests. Just before his trial in early 1917, Edgar Milligen's solicitor, John Graham, wrote to Dublin Castle and the lord lieutenant-general of Ireland asking for permission for James Chambers to serve as counsel against the Crown.[119] Chambers was an Ulster unionist MP and had just been appointed solicitor-general for Ireland, one of the most senior legal governmental roles.

When Edgar Milligen was arrested, he apparently told the detective he was "surprised that the boy's father did not come and see me instead of reporting it to the police." His admission suggests he knew that what he had done was illegal, but he expected to act with relative impunity.[120] He was right. In the opening petty sessions hearing, Milligen's solicitor had demolished the reputation of the criminal and untrustworthy newsboys, who did not then appear in court, and so a first charge against the defendant was thrown out.[121] It is unclear what happened in the trial for a second charge, but the most important witness was a poor orphan who later stole from Milligen—easy enough to discredit when faced with the weight of the defendant's philanthropic respectability. Milligen was found not guilty and released.[122] There was no newspaper mention of either the arrest or trial, in contrast to almost every other man tried in Belfast for the same crime in the previous three decades. The remarkable crossover between the Ulster political elite and unionist newspaper editors probably played its part in keeping the case hushed up.[123]

Into the interwar period and beyond, double standards were needed more than ever in the service of supporting the Ulster establishment. The new jurisdiction of Northern Ireland may have looked like a monolithic "Orange State," but its origins were rooted in palpable fears about the loss of regional Protestant hegemony. In the early years of partition in the 1920s, such anxieties were renewed by the prospect that the Irish Boundary Commission could redraw the border, with Northern Ireland being the territorial loser. Even after that danger passed in 1925, the prospect that the Irish Free State might assert a claim to the north remained a cause for unionist concern. A working-class loyalist power base, which had risen to resist Home Rule over the previous decade, now became a weakness. These potential voters were unlikely to convert to nationalism but could be tempted by the social benefits of the Labour Party. The political result would be a weakening of the dominant Unionist Party's control and, the apparatchiks feared, a justification for the British to sell Northern Ireland out to the newly independent government of the Irish Free State.[124]

Unionists imagined themselves as isolated and besieged from all directions and so placed their hopes for the endurance of Northern Ireland in the continued but fragile cross-class Protestant alliance. The most obvious way to achieve that goal was through "a moral economy of loyalty": the maintaining of the social and economic privileges that working-class Protestants received in return for supporting the state.[125] Shoring up the public image of Northern Ireland and the assuredness of its place within the United Kingdom was a priority that went hand in hand with this populism.[126] Bad press that revealed the vulnerability of the new jurisdiction or the hypocrisy of its governors was strictly to be avoided. Even historians who have been sympathetic to partition acknowledge that this political need led to a dual legal standard, especially when crimes threatened the legitimacy of the government. "The law was rigorously enforced against Catholics and nationalists," as Patrick Buckland put it in 1979, "but its application to Protestant and Unionist offenders was often tempered by discretion and political considerations." The attorney general and crown solicitor, he claimed, intervened in cases, especially when doing so was seen to secure better public relations.[127]

Unequal power dynamics were also embedded into the everyday infrastructure of the jurisdiction. On the eve of the Troubles in the late 1960s, Protestants outnumbered Catholics in the key offices at a rate far higher than simple demographics—six to one for High Court judges, for example, or nine to three for resident magistrates. Such positions were chosen by the governor of Northern Ireland, who reported in turn to the unionist minister of home affairs. By the early 1970s, fifteen of twenty High Court judges appointed since the jurisdiction was formed were openly associated with the Unionist Party. Even at the jury level there was a disparity. The requirement of jurors to be property taxpayers meant that fewer Catholics were eligible, given they were poorer on average and so more likely to live in rented or social housing. The Crown also had the right to stand by as many jurors as it pleased, which gave pro-unionist court officials the freedom to effectively select an all-Protestant jury.[128]

Given how effectively the legal system had stopped Alexander Erskine's case from reaching trial in 1914, how often were there similar interventions after Northern Ireland was formed? Policing could be lax or inconsistent, and the Royal Ulster Constabulary ultimately served its unionist masters. The British establishment restricted investigations or discussion of important public figures when they were caught in sex scandals, and the same appears to have been true in allied Northern Ireland.[129] Proving collusion or complicity is notoriously difficult, especially from the distance of the present, but the newspapers were certainly selective about the topics they would and would not cover. After all, the proprietors of the two major titles in Belfast, the *News-Letter* and the *Telegraph*, had been knighted in 1921 for their roles in the creation of the new jurisdiction. Not surprisingly, they maintained a consistently positive unionist editorial line.[130]

One suppressed case from 1952 offers the best queer evidence of how these power dynamics of Ulster unionist dominance intersected with anxieties about damaging Northern Ireland's public image. A criminal coverup began when a court-martial at the Palace Barracks in Holywood, a small town just outside Belfast, revealed that English national service soldiers were also selling sex. One young gunner described how he had been outside an amusement arcade in Belfast when a man in a luxurious car pulled up and offered him a lift back to base. Instead, they journeyed to a country house near Lisburn, where the soldier was given food, whiskey, and money for sexual favors. The gunner admitted that he had then gone back to the house several times and introduced a comrade to this elite man and his broader social circle. When the local newspapers reported the ensuing court martial of the soldiers for crimes of gross indecency, they neglected to name the "middle-aged civilians" who had done the seducing.[131]

Unfortunately for the Ulster elite, a journalist in Ireland must have tipped off the newspapers across the Irish Sea. There were the beginnings of a profitable explosion of tabloid journalism on homosexuality in the early postwar period in Britain and new narratives of corruption that encouraged the fears and fascinations of their readers.[132] In the *News of the World* article that followed a few days after the trial in Holywood, a lurid picture was painted of young and naïve men across the Irish Sea "ensnared" by highly educated yet morally bankrupt elites. Unconstrained by the still tight-lipped norms of the Belfast press, the London newspaper now named the most important man involved in the case: Patrick Barbour. He belonged, as they told their readers, to one of the richest families in Northern Ireland.[133]

A detective of the Royal Ulster Constabulary had also been present at the court-martial. The next day, he interviewed the two soldiers and gained the information he needed to make an arrest.[134] But when a one-off special trial was finally held in Lisburn almost eight months later, Patrick Barbour had been almost totally erased from the case. The soldiers still mentioned a man known as Patrick and his house in Lisburn but claimed now to not remember his surname. Barbour remained uncharged, and an English fashion supervisor named Cecil Robins—a friend and possibly lover—took the entirety of the blame. He eventually changed his plea to guilty and was sentenced to four months in prison.[135]

The different fates of Cecil Robins and Patrick Barbour were almost certainly the result of Ulster politicking. Harold Barbour, who was Patrick's father, had been the chairman of both Lisburn Urban District Council and Antrim County Council and a member of the new Northern Ireland senate from its inception in the early 1920s. Harold's brother, Sir John Milne Barbour, was even more powerful. Until 1947 he was the head of the family firm, which at one point was the largest thread-manufacturing combine in the world. For three decades he served as a unionist MP in the Northern Ireland parliament, including some of the more important minister positions, and he died just a few months before his nephew became embroiled in the scandal.[136] It is almost unfathomable that there had not been political interventions behind the scenes to ensure that Patrick—and his esteemed Barbour surname—stayed out of the mouth of the media.[137]

The archival survival of a glimpse into the subterfuge around Patrick Barbour's sexual behavior is rare evidence of political interference in crimes of same-sex desire in the north of Ireland. Technically, religious discrimination was forbidden under Article V of the Government of Ireland Act (1920). In his first speech to the new House of Commons in 1921, James Craig—the jurisdiction's first prime minister—thus declared "Every person inside our particular boundary may rest assured that there will be nothing meted out to them but the strictest justice."[138] But just over a decade later, in the more pessimistic context of economic depression, his language had become less conciliatory. "I have always said that I am an Orangeman first and a politician and a member of this parliament afterwards," Craig now claimed, adding, "All I boast is that we have a Protestant parliament and a Protestant state."[139] When it came to queer sex, there were some lucky Belfastmen who benefited from this promise that their leader had made.

The policing of male sexuality in Belfast was so slack that most queer men were unlikely to ever encounter the legal system in the first half of the twentieth century. Personal diaries and letters show little to no concern about being arrested, and never was there a public clamor for the sort of crackdown on sexual criminality that happened in other cities or countries, including the south of Ireland by the 1930s. Even the unfortunate few in the north who did find themselves in front of the courts had a strong chance of escaping without punishment. Juries could be convinced that a homosexual encounter—as disgusting as they saw it—was a one-off rather than indicative of a specific type of person. In this sense, they were still following an older "universalizing" rather than modern "minoritizing" view of same-sex desire: anyone was at risk, rather than such behaviors being the preserve of an identifiable subgroup of the population.[140] Marshaling a line of witnesses in court who could support that idea helped a defendant soften the legal judgment and, in a few cases, even persuaded the jury that the offense had not taken place at all. Trials of same-sex encounters were not different in this respect from any other crime: in a time before medical expertise was commonly used in Belfast's courts, respectability and good character could trump pathological or sociological explanations. Courtroom audiences were treated to familiar melodramatic narratives and moral lessons of "sin, redemption, and punishment" but learned little to nothing about homosexuality.[141]

Even when the behavior of men went against the moral purity that the region claimed to champion, those who were important to the image of the unionist regime were treated more leniently by the courts. We can only wonder how far this unfairness extended into everyday policing, both formal and informal. Elite men more likely acted with impunity, expecting a blind eye to be turned to their behavior if they remained relatively careful in public. Those who were challenged may have been successful in offering bribes when they were caught having sex with working-class men in the cruising sites of the city. Either way, the public silence and open secret of male same-sex relationships was ironically the greatest defense against exposure and punishment. Vagueness or imprecision about sexuality allowed both the legal system and high society to ignore that a queer subculture existed at all, a situation that lasted until at least the mid-1950s and the rise of a public debate about homosexuality in Northern Ireland.

Conclusion

I have traced the erotic and romantic lives of queer Belfastmen over a historical period of roughly seventy years. My book aimed to show how their same-sex encounters were intimately embedded into almost every part of the popular and public culture of the city. Using the spaces of anonymity and movement that came with modern urbanization, whether residential streets, busy toilets, or cheap hotels, they fulfilled their desires with only a relatively low chance of discovery. Using the familiarity of everyday urban patterns, they also learned to carefully and gradually forge relationships that existed mostly without causing alarm. By necessity, given the size of the city but perhaps out of a more open-minded tolerance too, many of these queer trysts were between men from across classed and religious divides. The general unacceptability in wider society of romantically mixing faiths was often ignored in the pursuit of queer sex, love, and friendship, though shared desires could not totally erase the power dynamics that underwrote the social and economic structures of Ulster.

The queer culture of Belfast was as much social as it was sexual. Men were not just having fleeting encounters but building networks of friends and fellow travelers. More knowledge about queerness had developed by the mid-twentieth century, helped along by daring pulp novels and sexological texts that were being imported from abroad. A shared understanding of sexual difference was now expressed in the clothes queer men wore, the poetry they read to each other, and the terminology they used to describe their friends (and enemies). But with a city of this size and its conservative religious culture, the kind of explicitly queer venues that were possible in bigger metropolises or smaller yet more permissive ports never really emerged before the late 1950s. On the one hand, this meant queer men had to be inventive, whether in how they cruised the city's streets or by subverting the newspapers through coded personal adverts. They also had to share social spaces with youths and men who were not open to queer encounters, even if they were not overly bothered by them either. Instead of a separate world, queer culture crossed over into otherwise normal cafés, churches, and stores.

This general visibility and even guarded tolerance of queerness in Belfast may be surprising for some readers who are familiar with the difficult recent past of Northern Ireland. But where we might have expected to find only shame and fear there was clearly pride and defiance. In scenarios that were sometimes oppressive and exclusionary, queer men still made a place for themselves and were often welcomed by others. Sometimes their friends and relatives showed ignorance about how and why they loved other men, and no doubt there were many who could express their desires only by living a double life outside of the family home. Yet a degree of knowingness and acceptance also characterized relationships between queer men and those around them. If they did fall foul of the law, families, neighbors, and colleagues could provide emotional and financial support. Violence and public disgust could certainly disrupt a queer life, but usually only if a man was found outraging public decency, especially if it was with a youth or much younger man.

Belfast's history demonstrates the continued pertinence of the generalized modern urban experience for understanding the development of queerness, if with a few caveats about intimacy that reflected its middling size. But there were divergences in the city's queer experience from even its near neighbors, which is yet more evidence of the regionality of queer historical cultures. Northern Ireland was really a continuation of a political regime rather than a clear break, unlike the Irish Free State. In the former, this meant anxious Protestant elites could tactfully ignore the existence of queerness whereas in the latter there was a more concerted effort to reframe sex between men as a pressing danger to a Catholic state. For Belfastmen, this meant their chances of being arrested for cruising the Entries was far lower than those who used the toilets of St. Stephen's Green in Dublin, which was just ninety miles away.

Being relatively distant from the imperial metropole of London meant there was little concern about the city's morality from British elites either.

Belfast was undeniably different from that totemic global city too, and not just in terms of size and vibrancy. The degree to which blatant feminine affectations were boldly used in London to emphasize the gendered nature of queerness was less apparent in Belfast's conservative context. Performative masculinity, which was so dominant in a paramilitarized culture, could certainly be oppressive of queer difference. In this way, Belfast seems to have had more in common with other workaday industrial towns and cities of the north of England. Yet at the same time, Belfast's dockside culture and expressive movement of its men between London and New York, as well as the seeming receptiveness to queer novels from all over the world, does suggest a cosmopolitan rather than just provincial experience. Acknowledging these regional complexities can only bring a greater depth to the New British (and now Irish) Queer History as it continues to expand its purview beyond London.[1]

This book has focused on experiences rather than societal structures, and desires instead of regulation, but it should be clear that toward the end of the period I covered, there were more governmental interventions being made into the lives of men who had sex with men. The belief that sexuality was something inherent to a person's being, and that it could be disordered in some way, was an idea that only began to grow in importance in the north of Ireland after the Second World War. This era saw the development of a prominent debate about same-sex desires among a range of individuals, institutions, and venues that had remained almost entirely silent before, from politicians and the press to medical professionals and the church. Spurred on by moral panics across the Irish Sea, these commentators now thought more carefully—and, most important, *publicly*—about what the response should be to a frightening new social problem called homosexuality. Though there were some lone voices of tolerance and compassion, or at least a begrudging separation between the ideas of sin and criminality, the overall shift in perspective was fundamental to queer men's lives. General arrest rates remained relatively low for now, but there were mass trials in 1958 and 1967 in small towns like Lurgan and Bangor, where local policemen went on moral crusades to round up circles of queer men. Those who were convicted were also given harsher prison sentences than before, and a convicted man could expect far more unpleasant attention to be given to his case in the local newspapers.[2]

The intimacy that had characterized the relative safety of Belfast's queer scene ironically contributed to the start of its demise in the postwar era. After the official veil of silence had been lifted, the open secret that had characterized the familiarity of a middling-sized city was almost impossible to maintain. Subtle signs of queer difference, even if they had always been evident to those in the know, would now have been far more obvious, as the oxygen of publicity was given to hysterical fears of contagion and moral decline. What could have been accepted in the 1930s as somewhat curious but acceptable relationships between older and younger men were rendered problematic in the 1950s, especially as understandings of adolescence as a separate stage of life took root. A man who never married was now suspicious rather than just another lonely Irish bachelor. Friends, colleagues, and family members who might not have been bothered about what queer men did in private would have found it harder to keep an open mind when tabloid newspapers from Britain—the circulation of which was growing significantly in the postwar era—were screaming about the dangers of "evil men."[3]

The results of this postwar shift for Belfast's queer men were grim. The scene was set for a more oppressive response to homosexuality at a time when most other European countries were gradually becoming more tolerant. Homophobia flourished especially in the final decades of the twentieth century, following the AIDS crisis, decriminalization in 1982, and a realization that LGBT people were now refusing to stay in the shadows.[4] In this difficult period, they now at least had the support of a fledging political movement, which had started organizing in 1972.[5] The deeper complexities of this later era of queer history will have to wait for another book, but it is worth insisting here that the society with which activists and communities were faced after the 1950s had fundamentally shifted from the one I have reconstructed. In an era when the people of Ulster were not being told by press nor pulpit that homosexuality was a societal danger, compassion and tolerance could be more common than fear and hatred. The lessons for today are simple. There is nothing essential about homophobia, even in a deeply religious society, and the level of tolerance can always change—both for the better and for the worse.

Acknowledgments

Belfastmen has been a long time coming. In 2009, living in Leicester, UK, I had just finished an MA degree and was locked into a PhD: a comparative study of shock cities in Britain and the United States. But I was already restless. I had recently come out of the closet at age twenty and developed an interest in queer history after writing about Manchester's gay village (the closest to my hometown of Buxton). My brilliant doctoral advisor, Simon Gunn, wisely told me that there would be a time when I could move on to this exciting topic, but firmly, it was *not now*.

Seven years later, I moved to Belfast—a city I had never even visited—for a lecturing job. Homesick in my first year, I made many journeys back to England. After one trip, I was waiting for a flight back and sat reading E. M. Forster's *Maurice* outside a Trattoria Milano. I felt a presence and looked up to see an older handsome Italian waiter. "Have you read *Brideshead Revisited*?" he asked. When I replied that I had, he smiled and whispered, "Look for the works of Derek Jarman" before sort of gliding away. My already growing desire for queer history was being divinely strengthened by moving to a strange city where I knew nobody. An opportunity—maybe a need—to search for a point of contact between its past and my present then started to emerge. I now need to thank those who helped me on this journey that began fifteen years ago.

The research and writing started and finished at Queen's University Belfast, where I have many wonderful colleagues. Special thanks to Kieran Connell and Keira Williams, my "midcareer" partners in crime; Sophie Cooper, who kept me right on Irish migration history; Elaine Farrell and Ciarán McCabe, for feedback on Irish families; Crawford Gribben, who told me about Arthur Greeves and has been a generous mentor; Andrew Holmes, a patient guide to Northern Ireland's religious history ("we both have an Ian Paisley problem"); Alex Murray, who made sure I did not say anything daft about literature; and Graham Walker, who showed keen early interest. Historians and activists have generously shared memories and knowledge, especially Mary Ellen Campbell, Jude Copeland, Jeff Dudgeon, Michael Fryar, Brian Gilmore, John Logan, Richard O'Leary, Anthony Malcomson, and Ciarán Wallace. My colleagues on a larger "Queer Northern Ireland" project—Maurice Casey, Charlie Lynch, and Leanne McCormick—have been invaluable, as were my PhD students Niall Herron, Michael Lawrence, Rhianne Morgan, Jamie Nugent, and Tom Ward; all have taught me much about both queer and Irish history.

Colleagues and friends elsewhere gave feedback when I needed it most. Two reading groups deserve special mention: in the United States, Averill Earls (a longtime queer Ireland coconspirator who also helped get me over the line in the final stages of revisions), Gil Engelstein, and Martha Robinson Rhodes (thank you for getting out of bed early so I could zoom in at a reasonable time!); and in Britain, Caitriona Beaumont, Matt Houlbrook (who also shared research materials, and has been a generous supporter for some time), Matthew Kelly, Laura King, Julia Laite, Lucy Noakes, and Michael Roper. Individually, Richard Butler, Lindsey Earner-Byrne, Craig Griffiths, Daryl Leeworthy, Seth Stein Lejacq, Joseph McBrinn, Michael Shaw, Charles Upchurch, and Chris Waters have been sounding boards for ideas or provided critical opinions on draft chapters. Leanne Calvert and Maeve O'Riordan commented on an earlier article as part of *ReCollecting the Irish Family Network*, as did Charlotte Wildman's *Challenging Domesticity: The Curative Home* group at the University of Manchester. Eric Cervini saved me a lot of money by kindly sharing his transcript of an oral history interview archived in New York.

Invitations to speak—at the Irish Modern Urban History Group (Limerick), Institute of Historical Research (London), University of Durham, Irish Historical Society (Dublin), Manchester Metropolitan University, Mary Immaculate College (Limerick), and University of Bristol, plus the Queer History Conference (San Francisco and Los Angeles), North American Conference on British Studies (Chicago, twice), Ireland Sexualities in History (Edinburgh), Love and War: 1914–2024 (Belfast), Urban History Group Conference (Belfast), and the Belfast LGBT History Club—were all opportunities to strengthen the work. Thank you also to the two anonymous reviewers for the press.

Funding and institutions made my book possible. The Arts and Humanities Research Council (AH/V008404/1), the Andrew W. Mellon Foundation, and Queen's University Belfast funded elements of the work. Archivists at the Public Record Office of Northern Ireland, especially Wesley Geddes, helped me navigate complex legal conditions for accessing and using criminal files. Laura Schmidt directed me toward information about Arthur Greeves at the Marion E. Wade Center (Wheaton College, Illinois). Elements of the research previously appeared in a different form in "Queer Belfast during the

First World War: Masculinity and Same-Sex Desire in the Irish City," *Irish Historical Studies* 45, no. 168 (Cambridge University Press, 2021);"Queering Family History and the Lives of Irish Men before Gay Liberation," *History of the Family* 29, no. 1 (Taylor & Francis, 2024); and, with Charlie Lynch, "Queer Men and Networks of Communication in Northern Ireland, c. 1921 to 1972," *Journal of History of Sexuality* 34, no. 3 (University of Texas Press, 2025). I am thankful for permission from journal editors and publishers to reuse this material in my book. Extracts and photographs from the David Strain archive (D2585) are reproduced with the kind permission of the deputy keeper of the records, Public Record Office of Northern Ireland (PRONI).

Finally, there are those who have been personally invested in my writing. I am grateful to the families of David Strain and Howard Aicken, who shared memories and photographs of their ancestors; I encourage anyone else who recognizes a relative in my writing to get in touch, especially if you have archives in your attic! At Cornell University Press, my editor Bethany Wasik has been a patient and enthusiastic guide—amazing from beginning to end. My parents, Howard and Susan Hulme, have remained a constant source of encouragement. But the foremost person to thank is my partner, Cormac McAteer, who has graciously shared me with the ghosts of queer men for around eight years. Finishing this book without his love, care, and support would have been a far lonelier journey, so it is to him that it is finally dedicated.

Notes

Note on Terminology

1. See Daly, "The Irish Free State / Éire / Republic of Ireland / Ireland."

2. For a more fun demonstration of the perils of contested language, see Fitzpatrick, "Words and Irish history."

3. Useful standard definitions in this vein are Halperin, *Saint Foucault*, 62, and, in my parent field of British queer history, Lewis "Introduction," 1–5. I reflect more on theoretical shifts in the introduction and chapter three.

Introduction

1. "House 2 Green Street (St Anne's, Antrim)," *Census of Ireland 1901*; "Archibald Gibney, Died December 2, 1878, Belfast."

2. Reconstructed from "Fearful Scandal in Belfast," *Ulster Echo*, February 3, 1890, 3; and "The Serious Charge against Young Men in Belfast," *Belfast News-Letter*, February 15, 1890, 3.

3. "County of Antrim Crown Book" (1890–95), 9–13.

4. "Assize Intelligence," *Northern Whig*, March 27, 1890, 6; "Thomas Gibney, Born October 24, 1868, Belfast."

5. "Elizabeth Gibney, Died August 2, 1906, Belfast"; "House 23 Edward Street (St Anne's Ward, Antrim)," *Census of Ireland 1911*; "Thomas Gibney, Died February 24, 1914, Belfast."

6. "Thomas Gibney, Died February 24, 1914, Belfast"; "House 2 Green Street (St Anne's, Antrim)," *Census of Ireland 1901*.

7. "Deaths," *Belfast Telegraph*, February 26, 1914, 7.

8. For how "telling tales" can work with queer theory insights, see Kaplan, *Sodom on the Thames*, 265–70.

9. Morris, "Intimacy in Modern British History," 796–97 outlines this distinction in intimate histories.

10. The exemplars were Rowse, *Homosexuals in History*, and the more nuanced Boswell, *Christianity, Social Tolerance and Homosexuality*, who disavowed the label of "essentialist." Hyde, *The Other Love*, is notable for its discussion of Irish scandals and figures (146–52, 156–58, 175–77). The longest-lasting advocate of essentialism is probably Norton, *The Myth of the Modern Homosexual*.

11. Plummer, ed., *The Making of the Modern Homosexual* captured the paradigm by outlining the charge and bringing together key proponents such as Jeffrey Weeks and reprinting the influential McIntosh, "The Homosexual Role." Duberman, Vicinus, and Chauncey, eds., *Hidden from History* housed "essentialists" and "social con-

structionists" in a way that more amiably demonstrated the theoretical shifts. For the radical social agenda then underpinning gay and lesbian histories, see Weeks, "Queer(y)ing the 'Modern Homosexual,'" 528–29.

12. Sedgwick, *Epistemology of the Closet*. Others—like Duggan, "The Discipline Problem"—attempted to demonstrate the continuities as well as the breaks.

13. Doan, *History, Sexuality, and Women's Experience of Modern War*, 58–66.

14. Lepore, "Historians Who Love Too Much."

15. Barclay, "Falling in Love with the Dead," 460.

16. Weeks, "Queer(y)ing the 'Modern Homosexual,'" 538–39; and Dinshaw, *Getting Medieval*, 21; see also Evans, *Queer Art of History*, 2–7. For a beautiful example of a queer connection through history in practice, see Bartlett, *Who Was That Man?*

17. The boldest attempt of recent years to account for the lasting of this "historical ordinariness" of relations between adults and children into the mid-twentieth century is Cleves, *Unspeakable*, who I have also followed in using the terminology of "encounters" to denote acts and relations that do not fall easily into the language of "consent." For a broader synthesis, see Syrett, "Introduction to 'Sex across the ages'."

18. Robertson, "What's Law Got to Do with It?"

19. Maynard, "Horrible Temptations."

20. Scott, "The Evidence of Experience."

21. Davis, *Fiction in the Archives*, 2–4. I was introduced to Davis, an early modernist, and this way of thinking about depositions through the rich work of Mansell, "Beyond the Home," 27–28.

22. Hartman, *Wayward Lives, Beautiful Experiments*, xii. See also the highly influential Trouillot, *Silencing the Past*, and, for broad queer discussions, two recent special issues: Murphy, Tortorici and Marshall, eds., "Queering Archives: Historical Unravellings" and "Queering Archives: Intimate Tracings."

23. For similar issues with a recovery history of prostitution, see Laite, "The Emmet's Inch."

24. Recent discussions: Farrell and McCormick, "Naming and Shaming?"; Meyer and Moncrieff, "Family Not to Be Informed?"; and Bengry, "Difficult Stories and Ethical Dilemmas" and "The Case of the Sultry Mountie."

25. The touchstone here is, of course, Thompson, *The Making of the English Working Class*.

26. For a useful critical overview of this digital revolution, see Hitchcock, "Confronting the Digital," and the discussion of other micro-biographical approaches below.

27. See recent conversations on creative historical writing—Twells et al., *Creative Histories*—and "rigorous speculation"—Pooley, "Show your Workings."

28. Still useful here is Raymond Williams's "structure of feeling"—the way that cultural contexts shaped both collective and individual responses to different historical experiences: Williams, *Cultural and Society*. More in practice, I have been inspired by a recent wave of creative approaches to micro-biography, especially Koven, *The Match Girl and the Heiress*; Laite, *The Disappearance of Lydia Harvey*; Rubenhold, *The Five*; Houlbrook, *Prince of Tricksters;* and Moran, "The Death of an Irishman." As Moran notes, "informed imagination" was a key approach of the foundational Davis, *The Return of Martin Guerre*.

29. "David Strain, born September 6, 1896, Lisburn"; House 3 in Galwally Park (Ormeau, Down), *Census of Ireland 1911*.

30. "April 27 1921," *PDDS*.

31. For diaries as a tool of both observation and self-making, and the possibilities and pitfalls for the historian, see Summerfield, *Histories of the Self*, chapter 3, and for brilliant practical examples, Feely, "From Dialectics to Dancing" and Clark, "Anne Lister's Construction of Lesbian Identity."

32. Blakeway, *The Last Dance 1936*, 153–57 for the queer content and quote from book blurb. The diaries cover 1920–43 and 1962–69. They are catalogued without a hint of the rare material they contain: "Personal Diary of David H Strain, Galwally Park, Belfast. It contains a detailed account of his everyday social activities, with some references to his father's business, W J Strain, linen merchant and manufacturer, in Bedford Street, Belfast," *PRONI Catalogue*. PRONI archivists told me in 2019 that most of the volumes had yet to be requested by researchers.

33. I have been deeply influenced here by Laite, "The Emmet's Inch." For an Irish example of this approach, see Herson, *Divergent Paths*, 22–26; and Crowson, "Tramps' Tales."

34. For useful overviews of this urban paradigm, see Potter, "A Queer Public Sphere: Urban History's Sexual Landscape," Hubbard, "Queering the City: Homosociality and Homosexuality in the Modern Metropolis," and Houlbrook, "Toward a Historical Geography of Sexuality." I draw on a multitude of specific urban studies in following chapters.

35. Douglas, *The Unpardonable Sin*.

36. Gillespie, "Making Belfast" 123, 125–30, 134, 148. See also Morris, "Urban Ulster since 1600."

37. Connolly, "Improving Town," 175–78.

38. Connolly and McIntosh, "Whose City?" 245–52. See also Doyle, *Fighting Like the Devil*, and Hirst, *Religion, Politics and Violence*.

39. For the Catholic population's structure and its experiences in the era this book covers, see Hepburn, *A Past Apart*, and, more broadly, Elliott, *The Catholics of Ulster*.

40. Connolly and McIntosh, "Whose City?" 252–53.

41. Boal, "Big Processes and Little People," 73.

42. Fernihough, Ó Gráda, and Walsh, "Intermarriage in a Divided Society," 5–6.

43. See discussion in Duggan, *Queering Conflict*, 65–67. For contrary opinions by those on the scene, see Mulholland, "Ghetto-Blasting," 133, and Paula, "Common Denominator." See also Herron, "Queer Experiences during the Troubles."

44. D'Emilio, "Capitalism and Gay Identity," 468. Other urban studies have also explicitly pushed back on this narrative. See Stein, *City of Sisterly and Brotherly Loves*, vii; and Chauncey, "The Trouble with Shame" and Chauncey, *Gay New York*.

45. Hanna, *Snapshot Stories*, 3–5.

46. Earls, "Queering Dublin," criticizes Ferriter, *Occasions of Sin*, for his briefer coverage of the interim period. Lacey, *Terrible Queer Creatures*, is also light on the mid-twentieth century, focusing mostly on famous figures, but was a pioneer in pulling together a broad general survey. For excellent books that nonetheless properly begin in the activist era, see Rose, *Diverse Communities*; McDonagh, *Gay and Lesbian Activ-*

ism; Kerrigan, *Reeling in the Queers*; and Kerrigan, *LGBTQ Visibility*. There is more written on queer Irish women in the south in the early to mid-twentieth century; see, for example, McAuliffe and Wheelock, eds., *The Diaries of Kathleen Lynn*; Tiernan, *Eva Gore-Booth*; and Foster, *Vivid Faces*, 133–42.

47. For the divergence in Ireland, see Tiernan, *The History of Marriage Equality*; Kerrigan, *LGBTQ Visibility*, chapters 5 and 6; and McGarry, "A Vision of Ireland." Scotland also had to wait until the early 1980s for decriminalization.

48. For these difficult decades, see Brady, "Sectarianism and Queer Lives"; Wallace, "Joy and Resilience"; Gilmore, "Gay Activism in Northern Ireland"; and Ferriter, *Occasions of Sin*, 475–81.

49. I read this BBC article in 2016 when looking for pragmatic information on the gay scene. Intriguingly, the article is no longer live, though there is a dead link to it on "Living Queer in Northern Ireland."

50. Nunn, "Against Anticipation."

51. D'Emilio, "Capitalism and Gay Identity." Contemporary sexologists, such as Edward Carpenter and Magnus Hirschfield, made much the same point—see Abraham, *Metropolitan Lovers*, 107–108. In both these cases, it is not hard to see the sort of thinking that was more broadly arising in the work of contemporary philosophers, psychologists and sociologists, most notably Simmel, "The Metropolis and the Mental Life."

52. For a similar take, see the "familiar strangers" of queer St. Petersburg in Petri, *Places of Tenderness and Heat*, chapter 1. For other reflections on how regionality shaped individual experiences, see Aldrich, "Homosexuality and the City," 1731; Smith, "Working-Class Ideas"; and the chapters on a range of British cities in Cook and Oram, *Queer beyond London*. For a comparative urban approach, see Tamagne, *A History of Homosexuality in Europe*.

53. See, for example, Kennedy and Davis, *Boots of Leather*; Beemyn, *A Queer Capital*, chapters 2 and 3; Howard, *Men Like That*; and Heap, *Slumming*, chapter 6.

54. Johnson, *Just Queer Folks*, 109, for "benevolent toleration." Ryan has also challenged the "modernization" narrative of "coming out" in Ireland, if for a different context; he argues that urban sexual experiences were less important for the development of sexual identities in Dublin in the 1960s and 1970s than the cultural sites of families, religious schooling, and sport. See Ryan, "Coming Out, Fitting In"; and Plummer, *Telling Sexual Stories*, chapter 6.

55. For an overview at the moment when the debate about empire was still relatively fierce, see Kenny, "Introduction," and for a useful explainer of why the debate rose and fell, see Tuathaigh, "Exemplar, Outlier, Impostor?" 36–37, 49. More recent developments in these terms are discussed in Bender, "Ireland and Empire." For balanced interpretations of modern Ulster's experience, see Jackson, "Irish Unionists and the Empire"; Ollerenshaw, "Businessmen in Northern Ireland"; and Howe, *Ireland and Empire*, chapter 10.

56. Howe, "Questioning the (Bad) Question."

57. See the various reflections in Dháibhéid et al., "Round Table."

58. Calculated from statistics for arrests between 1895 and 1915 in Cook, *London and the Culture of Homosexuality*, 151–52. Even these statistics must be approached with extreme caution; like in Belfast, incidences may have been sexual abuse and, as Cook notes, the figures for London included bestiality. The other law that regulated

male same-sex encounters—the Offences against the Person Act (1861)—was used only rarely in Belfast, probably because it required proof of anal penetration.

59. Cook, *London and the Culture of Homosexuality*, 43–44. Because the crimes defined under various vagrancy acts were not serious enough for the Assizes, there are no surviving depositions. My newspaper combing, however, has found little proof that men were being prosecuted under this act. Chapter 6 demonstrates the limited evidence in the case of James Sinton.

60. Luddy, *Prostitution and Irish Society*, chapter 5; Earls, "Unnatural Offenses of English Import." See also McDiarmid, *The Irish Art of Controversy*, which has a chapter on how Roger Casement's homosexuality was seen as an invention of English corruption but also looks more broadly at the discourse of the English enemy in Ireland.

61. Beatty, *Masculinity and Power*.

62. For other examples of this discourse in Africa and the Arabic world, see O'Murray and Roscoe, "Preface," xxix–xxx; Massad, *Desiring Arabs*, 5; and Bleys, *The Geography of Perversion*, 8–9.

63. Muldowney, "We Were Conscious," 403; McCormick, *Regulating Sexuality*, 27–28.

64. An excellent recent thesis, embargoed to researchers until I had essentially finished my book, similarly argues that Northern Ireland's sense of moral superiority and "half in half out" status in the UK led to a culture of silence and refusal to confront homosexuality: Fletcher, "From Partition to Decriminalisation."

65. The emergence of sexology has been a dominant theme in the history of sexuality, especially after Foucault, *The History of Sexuality, Volume I*, though important studies such as Weeks, *Coming Out*, were already tracing the contours in the British world before. For broad studies, see Birken, *Consuming Desire*; Porter and Teich, eds., *Sexual Knowledge*; Katz, *The Invention of Heterosexuality*; Bristow, *Sexuality*; and the essays in Bland and Doan, *Sexology in Culture*.

66. Inglis, "Foucault, Bourdieu," and Inglis, *Moral Monopoly*. It is worth noting, however, that there was engagement with understandings of sexual health (if not homosexuality) through several individuals and organizations—Houston, *Irish Modernism*.

67. William Lovell Northridge; see chapter 3.

68. McLoughlin, "Women and Sexuality," 266–67. See also Brozyna, *Labor, Love, and Prayer*.

69. For the north, McCormick, *Regulating Sexuality*, 100. The literature for the Irish Free State is extensive. For an introduction to the regulation of women's sexuality, see Smith, *Ireland's Magdalen Laundries*, esp. introduction and chapter 2; Earner-Byrne, "Reinforcing the Family"; Valiulis, "Virtuous Mothers and Dutiful Wives"; Crowley and Kitchin, "Producing 'Decent Girls.'"

70. Conrad, *Locked in the Family Cell*, 9. For a similar operation of a gendered double standard, see Kurimay, *Queer Budapest*, 156. It is worth noting, though, that Irish women negotiated instead of just passively accepting the moral dictates of the Church—Delay, *Irish Women*, 5–6.

71. Murray, "Twice Marginal and Twice Invisible."

72. The lives of queer women are a part of Queer Northern Ireland: Sexuality before Liberation, an Arts and Humanities Research Council project I run in collabo-

ration with Leanne McCormick, Maurice Casey, and Charlie Lynch. One publication in this area will be the first to look at lesbians in Belfast before the gay rights movement: Casey, "'Fairly Average'."

73. See, for example, "Henry Blair—Gross Indecency" (1939); "John Kingston and William Shaw—Gross Indecency" (1926); "Named individual—Gross Indecency and Buggery" (1947).

74. Ryder, *The RUC*, 84. For gossip, see David Strain's relating of how his being "a fruity individual" had become a topic of conversation at a city luncheon club: "November 19 1937," *PDDS*, discussed in more depth in chapter 4.

75. "John Sterling and William Gray—Gross Indecency" (1925); and "Thomas Carrick and Samuel Ramsey—Gross Indecency" (1926).

76. For stakeouts in Dublin, see Earls, "Queering Dublin," 152–56; and for a vice squad in Cork, see Ferriter, *Occasions of Sin*, 169.

77. Peniston, *Pederasts and Others*, chapters 2 and 3; Houlbrook, *Queer London*, chapter 1; Huneke, *States of Liberation*, chapter 2.

78. Farrell, "*'A Most Diabolical Deed,'*" 166. Other arrests for possibly consensual sex, like Muldoon and Smith (1912) or two men named in 1930, are in the (incomplete) prison registers: "General Register, Male Prisoners" (1912–14), 64; and "General Register, Male Prisoners" (1929–31), 120. These cases did not reach the court, so vital depositions do not usually survive.

79. Radford, *The Policing of Belfast*; Follis, *A State under Siege*; and Ellison and Smyth, *The Crowned Harp*, chapters 2 and 3. Financial and manpower constraints in the north of England similarly limited the reach and priorities of the police when compared to London—see Smith, *Masculinity, Class and Same-Sex Desire*, 52–58.

80. For discretion, see Finnane, "A Decline in Violence in Ireland?" 69; and in Britain, Klein, *Invisible Men*, 46. For men being warned and moved on, see Earls, "Queering Dublin," 106–107; and Meek, *Queer Voices*, 41.

81. Cocks, *Nameless Offences*, 1–5, drawing especially on Cohen, *Sex Scandal*, and Sedgwick, *Epistemology of the Closet*. For the role of the Catholic Church in enforcing silence, see Inglis, "Origins and Legacies"; Inglis sees the church as largely successful in containing rather than enabling divergent sexuality.

1. The Intimate Queer City

1. "Joseph Wilson McCullough, Born March 14, 1920, Belfast"; "House 14.1 in Brown Street (Wood Vale Ward, Antrim)," *Census of Ireland 1911*.

2. *Belfast Telegraph*, March 20, 1936, 4; *Belfast Telegraph*, June 21, 1935, 11; "July 25, 1938," *PDDS*.

3. "July 12, 1938," *PDDS*.

4. "July 18, 1938," *PDDS*.

5. "Charles O'Hara, Died June 30, 1907, Ballymena"; "House 18 in Pine Street (Cromac, Antrim)," *Census of Ireland 1911*.

6. "July 26, 1938," *PDDS*.

7. "April 2, 1939," *PDDS*.

8. Reconstructed from "8/9 Lancaster Gate, Paddington, London" (1947) and "12 Westbourne Grove Terrace, Paddington, London" (1954–1970) in *Westminster, London, Electoral Registers, 1902–1970* (McCullough was listed as living back in London

in 1954 and O'Hara had joined him by 1956); "*Empress of France*, Departing Liverpool, May 3, 1949, Destination Port of Montreal" in *UK and Ireland, Outward Passenger Lists, 1890–1960*; "*Washington* Arriving in Southampton from New York, August 24, 1949" in *UK and Ireland, Incoming Passenger Lists, 1878–1960* (the two men recorded that they were intending to permanently settle in another country of the British Empire, though it is not clear whether they meant Canada—after a London visit—or elsewhere); "Charles Henry Gibson O'Hara, Died November 5, 1972, Paddington, London"; and "Deaths," *Belfast News-Letter*, November 11, 1972, 2.

9. "Joseph Wilson McCullough," *Find a Grave*; "Joseph Wilson McCullough, Died December 8, 2012, Worthing (West Sussex, England)."

10. "September 1, 1938," *PDDS*.

11. I have been especially influenced here by three pioneering works of queer urban history: Houlbrook, *Queer London;* Cook, *London and the Culture of Homosexuality;* and Chauncey, *Gay New York*.

12. The term "shock city" was coined in Briggs, *Victorian Cities*, and developed in Platt, *Shock Cities*. For the fears these cities awoke, see Lees, *Cities Perceived*, Schlör, *Nights in the Big City*, and, for the specific concern about sex between men, discussion in chapter 6.

13. Daly, *Dublin, the Deposed Capital*; Dickson, "Town and City," 113–114, 123–124. For more on migration patterns, see chapter 2.

14. Connolly and McIntosh, "Imagining Belfast," 17, 22–27, 35–36; Royle, "Workshop of the Empire"; Dickson, "Town and City," 124.

15. See the discussion of D'Emilio, "Capitalism and Gay Identity," in the Introduction. As described in Halberstam's critique of "metronormativity," historians have become more attuned to the false dichotomy of the liberating city and the repressive rural—Halberstam, *In a Queer Time and Place*, 35–37. For a persuasive earlier articulation of this idea, see Weston, "Get Thee to a Big City."

16. I have not found Christie's birth certificate, but when arrested, he named Ballymena as his place of origin. The similarly aged Joseph Christie bailed William out of prison and recorded his occupation as farmer and address as rural Antrim; he was probably the accused's brother. See: "General Register, Male Prisoners" (1890–1891), 356; "House 13 in Downkillybegs (Clohogue, Antrim)," *Census of Ireland 1901*; and "House 20 in Nile Street (Dock Ward, Antrim)," *Census of Ireland 1901*. Christie placed an advert in the newspaper a few months before his arrest looking for work as a "boots" or waiter: *Belfast News-Letter* (December 1, 1891), 2.

17. "William Ayer Otherwise O'Neill Christie—Assault and Buggery" (1892).

18. See the life of George Davidson, reconstructed in Hulme, "Queering Family History"; the young man propositioned in "George Caldwell—Buggery" (1913); and a postman who lived on a family farm in Purdysburn: "David Purse and Sharman Stevenson—Gross Indecency" (1932); "House 52 in Mealough (Drumbo, Down)," *Census of Ireland 1911*.

19. Royle, *Portrait of an Industrial City*, 1.

20. The physical and cultural results of municipal and middle-class enterprise are detailed in Johnson, *Middle-Class Life*, chapters 2–3; Harron, "Big Vision City"; Bryan and Connolly with Nagle, *Civic Identity and Public Space*, chapter 3; Connolly and McIntosh, "Imagining Belfast," 42–47; and Irwin, "Belfast Corporation, 1874–1896."

21. Cathal O' Byrne and St. John Ervine quoted and discussed in Kirkland, *Cathal O'Byrne*, 13–15. See, more broadly, the literary overview in Craig, "The Place Had Character," and a firm pushing back on the ignorance and misunderstanding that sees Belfast as being cultureless in MacLoughlin, *City of Belfast*, 4.

22. "Belfast Saturday Nights," *Ireland's Saturday Night*, December 20, 1930, 1. For context on the newspaper, see Brodie, *The Tele*, 243–248.

23. Turner, *Backward Glances*, 9. See also the influential Bech, *When Men Meet*, for more on particular spaces and the modern city as the "natural" habitat of queer men.

24. "James O'Neill—Gross Indecency" (1928).

25. Reconstructed from entries between January 11, 1939, and February 10, 1939, *PDDS*.

26. Men at doorways or at lampposts: "David Straight—Gross Indecency" (1925) and "James Douglas—Assault and Attempted Buggery" (1894). Men catching a glance on the street or in windows: "November 16 1943" and "February 9 1939," *PDDS*. There are countless other such cruising encounters described throughout this book.

27. Owen, *History of Belfast*, 289–290; Dudgeon, "A Century and More."

28. The most vociferous skeptics of recent years are, for example, Hyde, *Anatomy of a Lie*, and Mitchell, *16 Lives*, chapter 13. The accusation was first publicly aired in Maloney, *The Forged Casement Diaries*. Some of the earlier doubters insisted that Casement had merely transcribed the writings of a contemporary colonial official, but the British forgery thesis has become more prominent. Cormack, *Roger Casement in Death*, followed the author's commissioning of forensic tests that he believed proved the authenticity of the diaries. Dudgeon, *Roger Casement*, written by another believer, presented new evidence to convincingly link Casement to a young lover, Millar Gordon. For homophobia, see Conrad, "Queer Treasons," and McDiarmid, *Irish Art of Controversy*, 167–210. For analysis of Casement's queer life, see Lewis, "The Queer Life"; Hyam, *Empire and Sexuality*, 35–38; and Lemmey and Miller, *Bad Gays*, 112–127.

29. Dudgeon, *Roger Casement*, 212.

30. For bars used in this area, see: a man who cruised another man on Rosemary Street and invited him to join him later at the Queen's Hotel—"David Straight—Gross Indecency" (1925); and Du Barry's Bar, discussed in depth in chapter 2. For sexual encounters outside: a doorway at the corner of Waring Street and Victoria Street—"Alexander Erskine and John Albert Kingston—Gross Indecency" (1914); an attempted encounter on Victoria Street by William Christie, discussed earlier in this chapter; and a boy picked up by an older a man in the vicinity—"Arthur Patterson—Indecency" (1939); Crown Files, Recorder's Court, *Belfast Crown and Peace*, BELF/1/2/2/49/43, PRONI.

31. O'Hanlon, *Walks among the Poor*, 44. For an overview of the development of the Entries, see Gillespie, *Early Belfast*, 147–148, and McNally, *Narrow Streets*.

32. MacCartan, *Glamour of Belfast*, 58.

33. For this process elsewhere, see Houlbrook, *Queer London*, 49, and, more broadly, Jerram, *Streetlife*, 260–263.

34. "Meeting of Police Committee" (March 27, 1924), 93–97, and "Meeting of Police Committee" (May 17, 1928), 200, in *Committee on Police Affairs*. More broadly, the minutes of this committee record the constant process of negotiation between

those who did not want public toilets near their workplaces or homes and the city council, which led to the Entries being one of the few ideal places to site them.

35. "David Purse and Sharman Stevenson—Gross Indecency" (1932). For this relationship between police surveillance of toilets and the creation of sexual knowledge, see Maynard, "Through a Hole." Though, as in my example, the police did understand how cruising worked, there was no consistent surveilling in Belfast.

36. For urinal touring, see "James Douglas—Assault and Attempted Buggery" (1894); and "Edward Summers—Gross Indecency" (1924).

37. For Great Victoria Street station: "Joseph Rea and Thomas Magee—Gross Indecency" (1913); and, for its continuing popularity into the 1960s, Weir, *Twenty Years A-Coming Out*. The York Street station was used, too—see "Arthur Patterson—indecency" (1939); and "May 11 1911" in Dudgeon, *Roger Casement*, 181. For the library toilets, "James Douglas—Assault and Attempted Buggery" (1894); and "John McCormick and Hugh Dunlop—Gross Indecency" (1909).

38. Others arrested in Hamilton's Court: "Edward Hull and William Johnston—Gross Indecency" (1900); "David Purse and Sharman Stevenson—Gross Indecency" (1932); and "Thomas Carrick and Samuel Ramsey—Gross Indecency" (1926). For Cave Entry, see "George Davidson—Gross Indecency" (1911). Winecellar Entry was also popular: "Edward Summers—Gross Indecency" (1924); "Samuel Magowan and Richard Morrison—Gross Indecency" (1927); "Named Individual and John Ernest Ashfield" (1935).

39. "Frederick McGlinchy—Gross Indecency" (1893).

40. "March 21 1942," "July 7 1937," "October 16 1937," "April 2 1939," *PDDS*.

41. See, for example, Howard Aicken, discussed in chapter 4.

42. Jones, "'The Lungs of the City.'"

43. Like London, St. Petersburg, Washington, Rio de Janeiro—see Houlbrook, *Queer London*, 47–67; Healey, *Homosexual Desire*, 32–33; Beemyn, *Queer Capital*, 20–24; Green, *Beyond Carnival*, chapter 1.

44. Liam Murphy is a pseudonym; I have not been able to ascertain if this man is still alive. "Named individual—Gross Indecency" (1937).

45. "Patrick Hughes—Gross Indecency" (1913); "James Dougan—Gross Indecency with a Minor" (1931); "May 27 1910" in Dudgeon, *Roger Casement*, 218–21; "September 25 1938," *PDDS*; Turner, *Backward Glances*, 61.

46. Thomas Gibney (Catholic, twenty-one), James Adair (Protestant, twenty-three), James Aylmer (Catholic, likely from the south of Ireland, eighteen), James Warnock (Protestant, twenty), Joseph Anderson (Protestant, twenty), Francis Ward (Catholic, seventeen)—"County of Antrim Crown Book" (1890–1895), 9–13.

47. "John Sterling and William Gray—Gross Indecency" (1925); "General Register, Male Prisoners" (1923–1925), 263. Gray's story is told more fully in the opening of the following chapter.

48. The men were Samuel Ramsey (Presbyterian, retired schoolteacher, unmarried, late seventies) and Thomas Carrick (Catholic, foreman, married, forties): "Thomas Carrick and Samuel Ramsay—Gross Indecency" (1926); "House 8, Ballygomartin Road (Woodvale, Antrim)" and "House 134 in Dover Street (Wood Vale Ward, Antrim)," *Census of Ireland 1911*. See also William Robin (Protestant, munitions worker, aged thirty-one) and Edward McLaughlin (Catholic baker, married,

aged fifty-six): "Edward McLaughlin and William Robin—Gross Indecency" (1927); "General Register, Male Prisoners" (1926–1929), 136; and James O'Neill (Catholic, laborer, aged twenty-nine) and Hugh Stitt (Protestant, plater, age unknown): "James O'Neill—Gross Indecency" (1928); "General Register, Male Prisoners" (1926–1929), 202—though it is worth noting the former only unsuccessfully cruised the latter (see chapter 5).

49. See, for example: a Church of Ireland man in his midthirties who was discovered in an entry urinal with a poor Catholic schoolboy—"Named individual and John Ernest Ashfield" (1935), "General Register, Male Prisoners" (1934–1937), 73, and "House 14 in Tyrone Street (Court, Antrim)," *Census of Ireland 1911*; the boys of the Belfast Scandal, discussed earlier; and Patrick O'Donnell, an orphan streetworker who sold sex to an older richer man—discussed in depth in Hulme, "Queer Belfast."

50. "County of Antrim Crown Book" (1890–1895), 9–13.

51. Lawrence, "'I Wished to See London,'" drawing on Amin, *Disturbing Attachments*.

52. See discussion in chapter 2.

53. "July 15 1937," *PDDS*; "April 14 1911" in Dudgeon, *Roger Casement*, 273–274; Lynch, "The Schoolteacher."

54. "October 23 1931," *PDDS*.

55. "February 1 1936," "March 28 1936," and "June 17 1936," *PDDS*. Strain was also open—to his diary, at least—about discounting a job applicant on account of a Catholic surname. "August 20 1936," *PDDS*.

56. "July 19 1941," "November 5 1941," "January 3 1943," and "January 18 1943," *PDDS*.

57. Desmond O'Callaghan, for example—a rare name, mostly Dublin-origin according to a search of the *Census of Ireland 1911*—"August 11 1938," *PDDS*.

58. For the lack of a vibrant avant-garde scene, see Kirkland, *Cathal O'Byrne*, 13–16. The classic work on Berlin is Beachy, *Gay Berlin*.

59. MacCartan, *Glamour of Belfast*, 1.

60. Pooley, "Cities, Spaces and Movement"; and Pooley, "Travelling through the City."

61. "October 12 1936," *PDDS*.

62. My understanding here is based on the countless examples described in David Strain's diaries, especially in the mid- to late 1930s.

63. Transport and stations have been commonly noted in many queer histories—see, for example, Cook, *London and the Culture of Homosexuality*, 26. For a thoughtful discussion of how such technologies of movement reshaped conceptions of personal space, intimacy, and touch, see Koole, "How We Came to Mind the Gap."

64. Smyth, "Return from Motown?" 105–109.

65. "James O'Neill—Gross Indecency" (1928). Casement met one man near the Albert Clock but traveled by tram to the privacy of the woods at the top of the Cregagh Road to have sex. "May 26 1910" in Dudgeon, *Roger Casement*, 212.

66. "Francis Wadman—Buggery" (1950).

67. "August 14 1936," "August 15 1936," "October 12 1936," "December 4 1937," *PDDS*.

68. "March 8 1940," *PDDS*.

69. "October 29 1934," *PDDS*.

70. "August 14 1936," "August 15 1936," "October 12 1936," *PDDS*.

71. "December 31 1937," *PDDS*.

72. For his "tour" or "prowl," see "July 29 1938" and "April 15 1939," *PDDS*. For examples of other men met on multiple occasions, see "February 23 1935," "October 23 1937," and "November 4 1937," *PDDS*. A thorough analysis of personal adverts is undertaken in chapter 4.

73. "March 20 1940" and "October 8 1940," *PDDS*.

74. For David Strain touring with his similarly middle-class friend Walter Smith: "November 12 1941" and "March 14 1942," *PDDS*. Other examples include Howard Aicken, Tommy McMeekin, and their friends, all of whom were working-class (and discussed more in chapter 4). "Down town wanderer" was a phrase used by David Strain—"March 20 1933," *PDDS*.

75. See, for example, Houlbrook, *Queer London*, chapter 1.

76. Reconstructed from "October 16 1937" and "October 18 1937," "August 20 1938" and "October 28 1938," "February 9 1939," and "July 9 1939," *PDDS*; "Dolcis Company open magnificent premises at Castle Place," *Belfast News-Letter*, July 23, 1932, 10.

77. Turner, *Backward Glances*, 10.

78. Connolly and McIntosh, "Imagining Belfast," 50–51; Larmour, "Bricks, Stone, Concrete and Steel," 39–40; and O'Connell, "Age of Conservative Modernity," 305–307.

79. Chauncey, *Gay New York*, 23.

80. "Big Fire in Belfast," *Frontier Sentinel* (December 22 1928), 2; Larmour, "Bricks, Stone, Concrete and Steel," 39–40.

81. "A Credit to Belfast," *Belfast Telegraph*, June 18, 1930, 10; Winkler, *Five and Ten*.

82. "Saturday—Oh, Boy," *Ireland's Saturday Night*, September 28, 1935, 10.

83. "Belfast Saturday Nights," *Ireland's Saturday Night*, December 20, 1930, 1.

84. "Saturday Night in Town," *Ireland's Saturday Night*, April 22, 1939, 5.

85. "December 21 1938," *PDDS*.

86. "July 23 1937," "September 29 1937," "April 14 1938," and "September 30 1938," *PDDS*. Woolworth's seemed to be particularly popular during the Second World War; see chapter 2.

87. Bardon, "Popular Culture," 277.

88. "Edward Summers—Gross Indecency" (1924); "Concert in Belfast," *Belfast News-Letter*, November 11, 1920, 7.

89. See, for example, the Hemisphere Bar, in Hamilton Court—"David Purse and Sharman Stevenson—Gross Indecency" (1932)—or the Rainbow Bar, in Wilson's Court—"John Reynolds (Alias Powell)—Gross Indecency" (1918).

90. "The de Cobain Case," *Cork Constitution*, September 18, 1891, 5; "Edgar Milligan [*sic*]—Gross Indecency" (1917); "James McKee and Richard Lutton—Assault and Buggery" (1904); "David Straight—Gross Indecency" (1925).

91. For rent boys: "Extraordinary Disclosures at Belfast," *Dundee Advertiser*, February 17, 1890, 7; "The Serious Charge against Young Men in Belfast," *Belfast News-Letter*, February 15, 1890, 3. For singing in bars: "James O'Neill—Gross Indecency" (1928). For theaters: George Davidson—Hulme, "Queering Family History;" Hugh Sheehan and Vincent Cassidy—Hulme, "Queer Belfast." For sharing drinks with female prostitutes, "Thomas O'Connor and David McDonald—Assault and Theft" (1902).

92. "Frank Kameny Interviewed by Barbara Gittings and Kay Tobin."

93. The first mention of the Royal Avenue Bar as an explicitly gay bar I've found is in the international gay guide produced by the Mattachine Society: Bard, *Le Guide Gris*, n.p. For early memories of the bar, see Jeff Dudgeon quoted in O'Doherty, *Fifty Years On*, 185–186.

94. An exception is Du Barry's, discussed in more depth in chapter 2.

95. "January 3 1942," *PDDS*. For other Second World War examples, see "March 2 1940," "October 8 1940," and "March 20 1940," *PDDS*.

96. "Edgar Milligan [*sic*]—Gross Indecency" (1917); "David Neill—Gross Indecency" (1949). Edward de Cobain may have had encounters at home, given the list of witnesses who said he propositioned them there—"Edward Samuel Wesley De Cobain—Buggery" (1893).

97. "164, York Street," *Belfast News-Letter*, August 17, 1921, 1; "Decision Affirmed," *Belfast News-Letter*, November 15, 1911, 3. McManus has demonstrated how such accommodation could be styled as "hotels" to avoid the reputational damage of being "common lodging houses" that were inciting panics about overcrowding and immorality. McManus, "Dublin's Lodger Phenomenon," 30.

98. "Edgar Milligan [*sic*]—Gross Indecency" (1917).

99. "May 28 1910" and "June 20 1910" in Dudgeon, *Roger Casement*, 215 and 220–221, underlining in the original text.

100. For sharing rooms at a similar age: George Davidson—Hulme, "Queering Family History"; Hugh Sheehan and Vincent Cassidy—Hulme, "Queer Belfast." For pretending to be father/uncle and son/nephew, see "Edgar Milligan [*sic*]—Gross Indecency" (1917); and Syrett, *Open Secret*, for an American couple who actually structured their relationship in this way.

101. Houlbrook, *Queer London*, 56–59. For cinemas more broadly as private spaces for courtship, away from family and neighborhood regulation, see Tebbutt, *Being Boys*, 28.

102. "James Dougan—Gross Indecency with a Minor" (1931).

103. Martin, "Being Irish Part Two—Trains."

104. "January 18 1943," *PDDS*.

105. Open, *Fading Lights*, 28–31; "Cinema to Seat 1,600," *Belfast Telegraph*, December 18, 1923, 6; "Belfast's New Cinema," *Northern Whig*, December 12, 1923, 8; "Classic Restaurant and Café Reopened," *Northern Whig*, August 31, 1926, 11.

106. "October 14 1937," "November 28 1936," "March 22 1933," *PDDS*.

107. "A New City Café," *Northern Whig*, November 22, 1927, 1; "Golden Dawn Café," *Belfast Telegraph*, January 7, 1939, 2.

108. "April 24 1936," *PDDS*. For more on queer novels, see chapter 3.

109. "Belfast's Leading Café," *Northern Whig*, August 9, 1932, 1. "Belfast v. Dublin," *Belfast News-Letter*, February 22, 1934, 3; "Ulster Sub-postmasters," *Belfast News-Letter*, February 9, 1934, 14.

110. "April 24 1936," *PDDS*.

111. "February 22 1935," "October 18 1936," "November 19 1936," "October 9 1937," *PDDS*.

112. For example, "January 18 1938," *PDDS*, where Strain related how Cecil Bond "hinted that he was going to a dance to-night! Strange doings for one who says he is 'queer.'" See Tebbutt, *Being Boys*, 219–220, 223, for how there was increasing suspi-

cion of men dancing together in British dance halls by the 1930s because of this fear of homosexuality.

113. For recent work on how youths co-opted spaces, see Harrison, *Dangerous Amusements*. For the rational recreation movement and youth more broadly: Snape, *Leisure, Voluntary Action*, chapters vi–xi; and Beaven, *Leisure, Citizenship*. For an important work that demonstrated how queer men co-opted religious associational settings, see Gustav-Wrathall, *Take the Young Stranger*, findings that were replicated in Boag, *Same-Sex Affairs*, 101–103, 162–168; Chauncey, *Gay New York*, 151–158; and Houlbrook, *Queer London*, 97–98, 124–125.

114. A Christian ethos was always at the fore, but actual clergy were unenthusiastic about supporting the society, seeing it as competition for their own parish activities. See McCready, "Influence on Corporate Life," "CIYMS: Report of Conference at Bishop's House, February 2, 1926."

115. McNeilly, *First Hundred Years*, n.p. The CIYMS reflected the broader shifts in youth associational cultural toward a loosely communitarian ethos—Hulme, *After the Shock City*, chapter 5. For the similarly enthusiastic and leisure-orientated YMCA in Belfast, see Fowler, *Youth Culture in Modern Britain*, 74–75, 78, 80–82.

116. "CIYMS Membership Register (1859–1946)," (A), 104 (A) and 109 (B), *Membership Registers: CIYMS (General)*.

117. See "Minutes of the General Committee and Some Sub-committees (December 1930–March 1948)" and "Minute Book of the Trustees of Hewitt Memorial House (June 1897–1956)"; *Syllabus 1935–1936*, 13; "A Meeting of the Trustees of Hewitt Memorial Hall, September 10, 1934." If the society were aware that queer men were cruising the reading room, it went unrecorded in their committee minutes. It is worth noting that "how little the [YMCA] Executive Committee in Belfast knew about what went on" in their branches—Fowler, *Youth Culture in Modern Britain*, 83—but also the possibility that ignorance was bliss—Beemyn, *Queer Capital*, 37–38.

118. For the Salvation Army Hostel, "Thomas Dazelle—Gross Indecency" (1923); for the Morning Star Hostel, "Further Achievements of Legion of Mary," *Irish Weekly and Ulster Examiner*, April 1, 1939, 14, and "Named Individuals—Gross Indecency" (1945).

119. "Francis Wadman—Buggery" (1950); there had been another case of gross indecency in a Waring Street hostel in 1923 (discussed more in chapter 2).

120. Whelan, "'A Real Revolution,'" 265–268. We know about these meetings because Bond took his friend, David Strain, with him—"March 15 1937," "September 18 1937," *PDDS*.

121. See Hilliard, "Some Find a Niche"; Howard, *Men Like That*, 51–56; and White, *Reforming Sodom*, 50–55. For more on theology and same-sex desire, see chapter 3.

122. In 1924, a cruising man suggested to his target that they could meet at the Ligoniel Baths the following week—"Edward Summers—Gross Indecency" (1924). I have sampled the extensive "Baths and Lodging Houses Committee Minute Books" and found no explicit concern about queer encounters in the sex-segregated baths. Attendants could sell sex in some cities—as described in Healey, *Homosexual Desire*, 26–30, 33–36, and Petri, *Places of Tenderness and Heat*, chapter 4—but Belfast's were explicitly employed and managed on behalf of the corporation rather than patrons.

2. The Queer Irish World

1. Assembled from "William Gray, Born July 29, 1877, Belfast"; "House 52 in Upper Newtownards Road," (Pottinger, Down, *Census of Ireland 1901*; "House 97 in Newtownards Road Upper," (Pottinger, Down), *Census of Ireland 1911*; and *Belfast News-Letter*, April 28, 1916, 1; "Death of Jane Gray, July 24, 1913, Belfast"; "Death of John Gray, April 7, 1920"; "Apartments," *Northern Whig*, February 12, 1927, 1; "General Register, Male Prisoners" (1923–1925), 263.

2. *Route Map and Guide to the Belfast City Tramways* (Belfast, c. 1920).

3. "John Sterling and William Gray—Gross Indecency" (1925).

4. "Must Go to Commission," *Belfast Telegraph* August 19, 1925, 3; and the judge in the case that followed at the Assizes was equally harsh—"Lord Justice's Regret," *Belfast Telegraph*, November 28, 1925, 4.

5. "Passenger list for SS *Calgaric* sailing from Liverpool to Boston, January 21, 1928."

6. *Fifteenth Census of the United States: 1930. Population, Volume III, Part I* (Washington, 1932), 1087; Edwards, *Historic Quincy Massachusetts*, 84–103.

7. "28 Cherry Avenue, Quincy Ward 1, Norfolk, MA, USA," *US Census 1910*; "Passenger list for SS *Cymric* sailing from Liverpool to Boston, April 8, 1913"; "21 Sea Avenue, Quincy District 0091, Norfolk, Massachusetts, USA," *US Census 1930*; "L.L.O.L. Lodge Is Sponsor of Party," *Patriot Ledger*, October 24, 1935, 2.

8. "Passenger list for SS *Calgaric* sailing from Liverpool to Boston January 21, 1928"; "William Gray Declaration of Intention, No. 257073, Massachusetts, 1935."

9. "City Briefs," *Patriot Ledger*, January 27, 1933, 12, and context in Chauncey, *Gay New York*, 86; and "Gray, Registration Card, Massachusetts, 1942."

10. "William Gray," *Patriot Ledger*, June 18, 1948, 13.

11. The beginnings of a transnational turn in queer studies were outlined by Povinelli and Chauncey, "Thinking Sexuality Transnationally." My thinking on queer movement and migration in a rapidly growing city has been influenced by Capó Jr., *Welcome to Fairyland*, 5, 7–8. For broader surveys: Canaday, "Thinking Sex in the Transnational Turn"; Meyerowitz, "Transnational Sex and U.S. History"; and Weeks, *What Is Sexual History?* chapter 6.

12. Fitzpatrick, *The Americanisation of Ireland*, prologue, chapters 1 and 2. Earlier, Fitzpatrick had vehemently rejected Delaney's characterizing of the "island story" as suggesting an "insularity" in Irish historiography and suggested that transnationalism was what Irish historians had been doing for decades. Delaney and McGarry countered by reaffirming the lack of communication between diasporic and domestic approaches. See Delaney, "Our Island Story?" 600–601; Fitzpatrick, "We Are All Transnationalists Now," 123; and Delaney and McGarry, "Introduction," 2.

13. Guinnane, *The Vanishing Irish*.

14. Fitzgerald and Lambkin, *Migration in Irish History*, figures at 172 and discussion in chapters 10–12.

15. For reflections on this colossal field, see Delaney, "The Irish Diaspora"; Delaney and MacRaild, "Introduction." For urban studies in particular: Belchem, *Irish, Catholic and Scouse*; Cooper, *Forging Identities*; Kelly, *The Shamrock and the Lily*; Kirkland, *Irish London*.

16. This argument is a major aspect of Houlbrook, *Queer London*, and Smith, *Masculinity, Class and Same-Sex Desire*.

17. Crisp, *The Naked Civil Servant*, 52–53.

18. See discussion in Houlbrook, *Queer London*, 189–190, and Lawrence, "Quare Fellows Abroad."

19. Lind, *Autobiography of an Androgyne*, 78–83, 86.

20. Historians have debated whether such stereotypes were fundamentally racialized (L.P. Curtis, M.A.G.Ó. Tuatigh, Mary J. Hickman) or a complex yet *un*racialized reflection of discourses of national character, class, and religion (Sheridan Gilley, Roy Foster). See, for an overview of these debates, MacRaild, *Irish Migrants*, 160–162 and the bibliography at 215. For "race" more as culturally encompassing than simply biological, I found Nie, *The Eternal Paddy*, 3–35, particularly useful. For a queer approach to Irish racialization, see Munt, *Queer Attachments*, 19–20.

21. Crisp, *The Naked Civil Servant*, 53.

22. Houlbrook, *Queer London*, 189–190, and Chauncey, *Gay New York*, 80–81.

23. McManus, "Dublin's Lodger Phenomenon," 28.

24. See Sargaison, *Growing Old*, 1–13; and Hepburn and Collins, "Industrial Society," 215.

25. "William Magill—Buggery" (1894), "James Doherty—Gross Indecency" (1894), "James Patterson—Assault and Attempted Buggery" (1894), "William Harrison Alias Burns, Alias Havelin—Assault and Buggery" (1891).

26. Flanagan, *Constructing the Patriarchal City*, chapter 3.

27. See Sargaison, *Growing Old*, 1–5; McCormick, *Regulating Sexuality*, 21.

28. For more on these scandals, see chapter 6.

29. Examples: "John Small—Assault with Intent to Commit Buggery" (1930); "Named Individuals—Gross Indecency" (1945); "Thomas Dazelle—Gross Indecency" (1923).

30. For more on masculinity and queerness, see chapters 4 and 5.

31. "Edward Graham—Buggery" (1935) and "Samuel Currie—Buggery" (1935).

32. "Joseph Fitzsimons and William Erskine—Attempt to Procure an Act of Gross Indecency" (1938).

33. Syrett, focusing on middle-class businessmen, describes such movement as "a queer epistolary network"—Syrett, "A Busman's Holiday," 125.

34. Tommy McMeekin and his visits to Blackpool, likely via the Lancashire seaport of Fleetwood, are described by David Strain: "June 28 1937," "August 7 1937," "October 23 1937," *PDDS*. See also a laborer in his twenties arrested with a Blackpool man: "Belfast Man Fined at Blackpool," *Belfast News-Letter*, September 29, 1955, 6.

35. For a full exploration of Smyth's life, see Hulme and Lynch, "Queer Men and Networks of Communication."

36. "August 11 1937," *PDDS*.

37. For the (trans)gender implications of this culture, see chapters 3 and 4. For more on Knox, see Hulme, "Queering Family History." I am indebted to Matt Houlbrook, who alerted me to the anonymized presence of William in his own research and shared his archival notes. See Houlbrook, *Queer London*, 48, 149; "Defendant: Knox, William. Charge: Importuning for Immoral Purposes, October 11, 1938"; "One of a Gang: Whipping for Despicable Character Next Time," *News of the World*,

October 3, 1926, 3; "Tower Bridge: Waterloo Road Pests Sentenced," *Illustrated Police News*, April 30, 1925, 7.

38. McNeill, *Irish Passenger Steamship Services: Vol 1*, 13–16, 19–95.

39. "Interview with John Keyes."

40. The Belfast-born artist Gerard Dillon and his singer brother moved to London as soon as they could in the interwar period, as did the young author Kenneth Martin from Bangor in the 1950s. See Dillon, *Crossing the Line*, chapter 3; Martin, *Aubade*, "Introduction."

41. "Interview with John Keyes."

42. Jones, "Late Victorian Belfast," 110; and figures in Owen, *A Short History*. See also Glasscock, "The Growth of the Port," 100–102, 108.

43. Beaven, Bell, and James, "Introduction." The sailortown, as Milne puts it, was "where the maritime and urban worlds collided." Milne, *People, Place and Power*, 1.

44. See O'Connell, "The Troubles with a Lower-Case T," 226.

45. See Smyth, *Days of Unity*; Smyth, *Sailortown*; and Campbell, *Once There Was a Community Here*.

46. See, for example, "Work Amongst the Sailors," *Belfast News-Letter*, January 26, 1906, 5. For broader context: Milne, *People, Place and Power*, chapter 5; and Beaven, "Foreign Sailors."

47. For the sharing of queer knowledge among friends, see chapter 4. The docks area was one of several "synonymous with immoral behaviour" at this time—McCormick, *Regulating Sexuality*, 21. For a similar dock queer scene in Cardiff, see Leeworthy, *A Little Gay History of Wales*, chapter 2.

48. Other examples of cruising and socializing in Sailortown: the discovery of the male brothel described in the prologue and the cheap hotel used as a brothel discussed in chapter 1.

49. See "House 152 Shear Brow (St John's, Blackburn)," *Census for England 1891*; "Mr. James Douglas," *Blackburn Standard*, June 15, 1889, 2; "James Douglas, Died December 7, 1894, Blackburn."

50. "James Douglas—Assault and Attempted Buggery" (1894).

51. Archibald Andrews's father ran the oyster house until he died in 1876, aged thirty-three, when his son was four; he had often been in trouble with the police. See "Disorderly," *Belfast Telegraph*, June 26, 1871, 3; "Alfred Andrews, died August 13, 1876, Belfast"; "Mr. F. Curley's New Premises in High Street," *Northern Whig*, November 1, 1889, 5.

52. In France, *Germinism* was a similarly short-lived neologism following the exposure of the Count de Germiny. See Peniston, "A Public Offense against Decency."

53. See discussion of this area in chapter 1.

54. Patton, *Central Belfast*, 290.

55. "Helen's Bay Contractor Fined for Assaulting Head-Constable," *Northern Whig*, November 6, 1940, 6.

56. "Royal Cinema," *Belfast Telegraph*, January 19, 1935, 4.

57. Slater, "Pimps, Police and Filles de Joie."

58. "Xmas Holidays," *Northern Whig*, December 24, 1938, 1; "Do You Need a Change of Outlook?," *Belfast Telegraph*, May 19, 1944, 3.

59. "Personals," *Belfast Telegraph*, August 3, 1939, 1; "Personals," *Belfast Telegraph*, August 1, 1939, 1; "Personals," *Belfast Telegraph*, August 7, 1939, 2; "Personals," *Belfast Telegraph*, July 28, 1939, 1.

60. Law, *Historic Pubs of Belfast*, 32.

61. Dudgeon, "A Century and More of Belfast Gay Life."

62. "February 14 1942," *PDDS*.

63. White, *Gerard Dillon*, 42; and Dillon, *Crossing the Line*, chapter 2.

64. "Interview with Peter McVea."

65. See, for similar dynamics, pubs in London, discussed by Houlbrook, *Queer London*, 88, 121, 156; the "mutual reliance" that observers noted in Paris, discussed by Ross, *Public City/Public Sex*, chapter 4, quote at 144; dockland bars in Stanley and Baker, *Hello Sailor!*, 150; and similar in Welsh towns and cities, Leeworthy, *A Little Gay History of Wales*, 69–70.

66. See William Christie, discussed in more depth in chapter 1.

67. Stanley and Baker, *Hello Sailor!*, 11–13. For the masculine construction of sailors, Downing, Thayer, and Begiato, eds., *Negotiating Masculinities*.

68. Harbinson, *The Protégé*, 206. My thanks to Charlie Lynch for alerting me to this passage. For a more overt English example, see the memoir by Ackerley, *My Father and Myself*.

69. The phrase was apparently first used by Winston Churchill, but the stereotypes have a longer genesis: Gilbert, "Buggery and the British Navy."

70. Lyons, "Mapping an Atlantic Sexual Culture"; and LeJacq, "Buggery's Travels." Both focus on the eighteenth century, but their arguments about same-sex desire and eroticism moving from ship to shore stand true for pre–gay liberation Belfast.

71. Luddy, *Prostitution and Irish Society*, 198–199.

72. Many Royal Navy ships had been christened HMS *Flying Fish*; there is a series of imperialistic novels for boys by Harry Collingwood, such as Collingwood, *The Log of the "Flying Fish"*; and the term also denoted sailors who served in Asiatic seas, where flying fish originated—see Spectre, *A Mariner's Miscellany*, 104. Chauncey, *Gay New York*, is particularly useful on the variety of nonscientific terms queer men used to describe themselves.

73. A bob was equal to one shilling—just a couple of pounds today. The term was also used to denote a contextually dependent sum ("He has a bob or two," referring to a well-off person, for example).

74. "March 22 1934," *PDDS*.

75. Hugh Dunlop was another young married laborer and former sailor who was accused of selling sex in a urinal in 1909. See "John McCormick and Hugh Dunlop—Gross Indecency" (1909); and "General Register, Male Prisoners" (1909–1910), 51.

76. See Chauncey Jr., "Christian Brotherhood," for a deconstruction of these various identities and understandings in one American seaport.

77. "March 22 1934," "March 28 1934," "May 21 1934," "March 14 1942," *PDDS*.

78. Titman, "The Drift of Desire," 172. Allan Bérubé suggests sailors were preferred by queer men in the United States because they were seen as gentler than other branches of the military, such as marines. Bérubé, *Coming Out under Fire*, 110–111. Prison registers, which describe in depth the tattoos of arrested men, have enabled me to identify the commonality of former sailors.

79. Houlbrook, "Soldier Heroes and Rent Boys;" Cook, *London and the Culture of Homosexuality*, 137–138.

80. McCormick, *Regulating Sexuality*, chapter 4. See also Chauncey, *Gay New York*, 85; Stanley and Baker, *Hello Sailor!*, 37; Healey, *Homosexual Desire*, 48. Syrett notes that

in Italy, prohibition on sex before marriage made men more likely to have sex with each other—Syrett, *An Open Secret*, 75.

81. Mayne, *The Intersexes*, 184–185; Crisp, *The Naked Civil Servant*, 98–99.

82. Stanley and Baker, *Hello Sailor!*, chapter 2. See also transcripts of American sailor interviews by an ardent admirer of military eroticism: Zeeland, *Sailors and Sexual Identity*.

83. See John Sterling, arrested in 1925 with another adult man in a urinal—"General Register, Male Prisoners" (1923–1925), 263; James O'Neill, arrested in 1928 after cruising another adult man—"General Register, Male Prisoners" (1926–1928), 202; William Shaw, arrested 1926 with another adult man in a field—"General Register, Male Prisoners" (1926–1928), 54; Joseph Smith, arrested 1912 after having sex with an older man—"General Register, Male Prisoners" (1911–1912), 232; Patrick Meehan—arrested 1924 after trying to suggest sex to a fifteen-year-old boy in the docks area—"General Register, Male Prisoners" (1923–1925), 181; "Jones Thomas—Buggery" (1926), arrested after making strange propositions to newsboys in the city center.

84. "William McMullen—Buggery" (1924).

85. Conley, "Epilogue," 304.

86. Alexander Smith is a pseudonym; I have not managed to ascertain whether this man is still alive.

87. "Letter to A. Smith on H.M.S. Loch Fyne from W.L. Nelson at Famagusta (October 5, 1958)" in "William Nelson and Named Individual—Buggery" (1959).

88. "Letter to A. Smith, at R.M. Barracks, Plymouth from W.L. Nelson, HMS Bulwark, Portsmouth, November 28, 1958" in "William Nelson and Named Individual—Buggery" (1959). For the Criterion: Williams, *A Queer A-Z of Hampshire*, 25.

89. "Former Marine Is Jailed for 5 Years," *Belfast Telegraph*, April 14, 1959, 6. Nelson's mother may have regretted what she had done; she paid for her son's bail.

90. "William La Coste Nelson, probate October 18, 2021."

91. See, for example, Ellis and Symonds, *Sexual Inversion*, 9–11, with a discussion of Marc-André Raffalovich, Karl Heinrich Ulrichs, and John Addington Symonds.

92. Mayne, *The Intersexes*, 220. Born in 1868 in New Jersey, Prime-Stevenson lived in Europe in the 1890s, settling eventually in Italy, to escape the sexual laws of the United States. Lauritsen, "Edward Irenaeus Prime-Stevenson (Xavier Mayne)," 35–36.

93. Hulme, "Queer Belfast."

94. Robb, *British Culture*, 82; Cook with Mills, Trumbach, and Cocks, *A Gay History of Britain*, chapter 5; and Crouthamel, *An Intimate History of the Front*, 128–134. Oral histories recorded in the 1970s with queer former British servicemen testify to this culture of intimacy and opportunity: see Porter and Weeks, eds., *Between the Acts*, 5–8, 15–16, 25–26. See also Frederick McGlinchy, a soldier-chef who was arrested in 1893—discussed briefly in chapter 1 for propositioning a police officer.

95. Bérubé, *Coming Out under Fire*; Vickers, *Queen and Country*; and Smaal, *Sex, Soldiers and the South Pacific*. Prison registers are sketchy for the war period, but at least two men were court-martialed for buggery in Belfast. See "General Register, Male Prisoners" (1926–1953), 18, 19.

96. Ollerenshaw, *Northern Ireland*.

97. Barton, *Northern Ireland*, 84.

98. "Named Individual—Gross Indecency and Buggery" (1947); and "8 sentenced at Down Assizes in Indecency Case," *Belfast Telegraph*, October 14, 1964, 8.

99. McVea, *Fruitz*.

100. See Houlbrook, "Soldier Heroes and Rent Boys" for the practicalities of relationships; and for an eroticizer of soldiers, Butler, *The Passions of John Addington Symonds*, chapter 7.

101. Blair lived in Hopefield House, a former Antrim Road mansion converted into flats—*Belfast News-Letter*, September 15, 1925, 7.

102. The private maintained that he had been an unwilling participant, but either way, Blair was found not guilty and discharged. See "Henry Blair—Gross Indecency" (1939); and "Crown Book, Indictment and Pleas, Belfast City Commission" (1937–1940).

103. See David, *On Queer Street*, 146–150; Beemyn, *A Queer Capital*, chapter 3.

104. Ollerenshaw, *Northern Ireland*; and Barton, *Northern Ireland*, 7.

105. See McCormick, "'One Yank and They're Off.'" More broadly, see Rose, "Sex, Citizenship, and the Nation."

106. Dudgeon, "A Century and More of Belfast Gay Life." Northern men echoed the reminiscences of eager participants on the scene in British cities. See Cook et al., *A Gay History of Britain*, 149–150.

107. See Ollerenshaw, *Northern Ireland*, 140–144, 149–152, 161–166.

108. Nevill Johnson quoted in Woodward, *Culture, Northern Ireland, and the Second World War*, 36.

109. Johnson later lived in London with a gay couple, and when he was living in Belfast during the war, he knew John Luke and Gerard Dillon. See Hall, "New Visions of Belfast"; and Johnson, *The Other Side of Six*, 69.

110. See Dudgeon, "A Century and More of Belfast Gay Life." For this paradox of war and sexual desire, see Herzog, "Introduction," 5–6.

111. For encounters between servicemen and civilians, see "Named Individuals—buggery" (1941) and "Named Individual—Gross Indecency" (1942).

112. "Named Individual—Gross Indecency and Assault" (1940). John Hughes is a pseudonym; I have not managed to ascertain whether this man is still alive.

113. Beemyn, *A Queer Capital*, 107–108, notes how common it has been to see the war as purely positive in creating urban queer opportunities but found that in Washington the increased conspicuousness of cruising and gay bars, plus the unfamiliar military visitors, could lead to unwelcome and violent encounters.

114. "April 25 1942," *PDDS*.

115. One such soldier was Douglas Free, who—judging by his name—was likely American.

116. "January 31 1942," *PDDS*.

117. For more detail on this scandal, see chapter 6.

118. "The Christian Sunday," *Belfast News-Letter*, October 28, 1940, 3.

119. McCormick, "'One Yank and They're Off.'"

120. Crisp, *The Naked Civil Servant*, 149.

3. Sexology, Religion, and Reading Queer in Ulster

1. See Folders 1–4, covering January 1917 to April 1918, in *Arthur Greeves Diaries Collection [AGDC]*.

2. Carpenter, *Towards Democracy*, 410. For the placing of Carpenter's writings on sexuality within his socialist politics, Weeks and Rowbotham, *Socialism and the New Life*.

3. "Memo, w/c March 16 1918," Folder 4, *AGDC*.

4. Carpenter, *The Intermediate Sex*.

5. "March 18 1918," Folder 4, *AGDC*.

6. Edward Carpenter "ransack[ed] world literature" to create a guide to "homosexually themed reading." Mitchell and Leavitt, *Pages Passed from Hand to Hand*, xiii. The editions of Symonds's *A Problem in Modern Ethics* and Ellis's *Studies in the Psychology of Sex: Vol II: Sexual Inversion* used by Greeves are not recorded in his diary, but it seems unlikely he managed to obtain the earliest privately printed versions because of how rare they were. See "Memoranda [w/c December 31 1918]," Folder 6, *AGDC*.

7. "March 19, 1918," "March 27, 1918," Folder 4, *AGDC*.

8. "Saturday July 13, 1918." Greeves also used the term "urning." See Bauer, *English Literary Sexology*, 73–79; and Pretsell, *Urning*, chapter 8, for the movement of these terminologies between German and English authors.

9. "June 30, 1922," "July 1, 1922," "July 30, 1922," "August 8, 1922," "August 11, 1922," Folder 7, *AGDC*.

10. A critical point made by Bristow, "Remapping the Sites," echoing the spirited defense of Halperin, *Saint Foucault*, and Halperin, *How to Do the History of Homosexuality*, chapter 1. For the original quote, see Foucault, *The History of Sexuality, Volume I*, 43.

11. The queer theory turn in the 1990s heralded this fresh challenge to both "essentialists" and "constructionists," with the work of the literary scholar Eve Sedgwick being especially influential—see Sedgwick, *Epistemology of the Closet*, 44–48. The shift is evident in the work of the New British Queer History, to which my own work is indebted. See, for an overview, Lewis, "Introduction"; and Waters, "Distance and Desire." For the uneven reception of sexology in other different geographic contexts, though Ireland is not among them, see Bauer, *Sexology and Translation*; and Fuechtner et al., *A Global History of Sexual Science*.

12. Brady, *Masculinity and Male Homosexuality*, 6, has made the most forceful case for how the "medico-legal analysis of homosexual identity formations" was less evident in Britain.

13. Brady, *John Addington Symonds and Homosexuality*, 20; Hall, "Heroes or Villains?" 7–8; and Sigel, *Making Modern Love*, 39–40.

14. The Society stayed wedded to the ideas of Carpenter and Ellis, who were prominent figures in the organization (though Ellis never officially joined). See Waters, "Havelock Ellis, Sigmund Freud and the State," 169; Hall, "'Disinterested Enthusiasm for Sexual Misconduct'"; and Weeks, *Coming Out*, 128–137. More broadly, Mort argues that the dominance of social hygiene—and its prioritizing of physiological processes over the subconscious—also hindered the spread of psychoanalysis. Mort, *Dangerous Sexualities*, 148–149.

15. Prior, *Mental Health and Politics*," 39–51; Lucey, "On the Brink of Universalism."

16. Government of Northern Ireland, *The Protection and Welfare of the Young*, 19, 21; and Lothian, "From the Case-Book of a Medical Psychologist."

17. References were to events abroad, historical (Napoleonic and Ancient) or contemporary (propaganda against Nazi Germany or the infamous case of Charles Barataud in France in 1928).

18. See Oosterhuis, *Stepchildren of Nature*, 11–12.

19. "Archibald Black and Alfred Shaw—Assault" (1891).

20. "Joseph Smith and George Caldwell—Gross Indecency" (1912); and the recording of an anchor tattoo on his body, proving he was a sailor, in "General Register, Male Prisoners" (1911–1912), 232.

21. "The Serious Charge against Young Men in Belfast," *Belfast News-Letter*, February 25, 1890, 3.

22. Such as the Manchester Drag Ball in 1880 and Ireland's own Dublin Castle Scandal in 1884, where camp characters used feminine names. The most infamous example however was the London trial in 1870 of Frederick William Park and Thomas Ernest Boulton, better known as Fanny and Stella. Upchurch argues that this case especially made more concrete the link between cross-dressing and sodomitic desire: Upchurch, "Forgetting the Unthinkable." For the other queer meanings historians and literary scholars have read into the case, see Joyce, "Two Women Walk into a Theatre Bathroom." Queer trials in Belfast are analyzed in chapter 6.

23. "John Kingston and William Shaw—Gross Indecency" (1926).

24. See, as examples, "Post-War Croakers," *Northern Whig*, December 1, 1928, 11; and "Prohibition—a Working Man's Appeal," *Northern Whig*, December 14, 1922, 7. For these fears and debates more broadly in the British press, some of which could be accessed in Belfast, see Bingham, *Gender, Modernity, and the Popular Press*, 229–236.

25. In rethinking my own approach and blind spots, I have found particularly useful Stryker, "Transgender History"; LaFleur, Raskolnikov, and Klosowska, "Introduction"; Heyam, *Before We Were Trans*.

26. "The Constable and the Militiaman," *Northern Whig*, September 1, 1908, 9.

27. Nunn, "Trans Liminality and the Nazi State"; Boyd, *Wide-Open Town*, chapter 1.

28. For the interwar gender anxieties that were emanating from Britain into Ireland, see Bourke, *Dismembering the Male*; Roper, "Between Manliness and Masculinity"; and Tebbutt, *Being Boys*, 87–88, 91–93, 107–113.

29. For the growth of this industry, see Deslandes, *Culture of Male Beauty*, 167–186; and for cosmetics, Houlbrook, "'The Man with the Powder Puff.'" For the construction of Ulster Protestant masculinity in this era, see McGaughey, *Ulster's Men*.

30. "August 31 1932," *PDDS*. In this sense there are echoes of the much older definition of effeminacy—see Cohen, "Manliness, Effeminacy and the French." For the effeminizing of such commercial culture in Britain, see Tebbutt, *Being Boys*, 117.

31. "John Sterling and William Gray—Gross Indecency" (1925). For these complexities of masculinity and desire in queer relationships, see chapter 4.

32. "Edward McLaughlin and William Robin—Gross Indecency" (1927); "General Register, Male Prisoners" (1926–1929), 136.

33. "Assize Intelligence," *Northern Whig*, March 27, 1912, 10; "Summons Court," *Belfast News-Letter*, May 24, 1912, 4; and "George Caldwell—Buggery" (1913). Finnane, drawing on the work of Brian Griffin, has noted that the general decline in conflict in Ireland between the police and the policed—the "domestication" of the force—was at its weakest in Belfast and Dublin. See Finnane, "A Decline in Violence in Ireland?" 62; and Griffin, "The Irish Police." For masculinity and the challenging of authority, see Archer, "'Men Behaving Badly'?"

34. Houlbrook, *Queer London*, 244–245.

35. "Named Individual—Gross Indecency and Buggery" (1947); I have not cited the newspaper here because it will identify the man, and I am not sure if he is still

alive. For the interpretation of heat and homosexuality, see Burton, "Terminal Essay"; and Kennedy, "'Captain Burton's Oriental Muck Heap,'" 333–338.

36. "Francis Wadman—Buggery" (1950). For Robinson's career: MacC, "Obituary: Charles Booth Robinson."

37. "Charles McCarte—Attempting to Procure Commission of Act of Gross Indecency" (1950).

38. In the case of Billy Nelson and his lover in 1958, discussed in chapter 2, the judge also recommended psychiatric treatment—"Former Marine Is Jailed for 5 Years," *Belfast Telegraph*, April 14, 1959, 6. For the growth of conversion therapy, see Lynch, "Between Sickness and Sin."

39. Waters, "Havelock Ellis, Sigmund Freud and the State," 165–166.

40. "The Borders of Sanity," *Belfast Telegraph*, November 28, 1958, 4.

41. "Assize intelligence," *Northern Whig*, March 27, 1890, 6.

42. See, as examples, "Thomas O'Connor and David McDonald—Assault and Theft" (1902); "Indecency," *Northern Whig*, July 26, 1927, 8; and "Antrim Assizes," *Belfast News-Letter*, July 9, 1942, 2.

43. See Trumbach, "London's Sodomites; and, for discussion, Upchurch, "Liberal Exclusions."

44. For examples of uses of "unnatural" outside of sex between men, see: incest—"Assaulting His Mother," *Belfast News-Letter*, September 24, 1907, 3; sexual assaults on girls—"Assize Intelligence," *Belfast News-Letter*, March 20, 1909, 5; and bestiality—"Petty Sessions," *Belfast News-Letter*, June 25, 1904, 8. For a usefully broad discussion of how Sodom represented not just "sins against nature" but also "sins against faith" and "sins against charity" and their overlap, see Dellamora, *Friendships' Bonds*, 6–11.

45. White, *Reforming Sodom*, introduction, chapter 1; and for the discursive origins, Jordan, *The Invention of Sodomy*.

46. Thatcher, "Theological Amnesia and Same-Sex Love," 17.

47. For Save Ulster from Sodomy: Brady, "Sectarianism and Queer Lives," 55–57. Other Protestant churches did not join Paisley but had conservative sexual beliefs; for more discussion, see Lynch, "Between Sickness and Sin."

48. Coleman, *Christian Attitudes to Homosexuality*, 153–157. Jones has argued the White Cross Society shows how male same-sex acts were regulated as part of the Christian and feminist social purity movement in England, but I have not found explicit evidence of this in Belfast—Jones, "Moral Welfare and Social Well-Being," 199–202. For the suggestion of a Belfast branch: "Church of England White Cross League," *Belfast News-Letter*, November 28, 1903.

49. See Hall, *Muscular Christianity*; and Vance, *The Sinews of the Spirit*. For the Church of Ireland Young Men's Society promotion of these ideals, see McNeilly, *The First Hundred Years*.

50. "Executive Committee in Clarence Place on January 28, 1943," 68–70.

51. Hime, "The Grave Social Problem," 175–176; Hime, *Morality*; and Hime, "Immorality among School Boys," 614–617; Church of Ireland Moral Welfare Association, *Occasional Bulletin No. 1*. For similar silence in the south of Ireland, see McDonagh, "Homosexuality," 455–456.

52. For context, Hunt, "The Great Masturbation Panic," 605–607; Mort, *Dangerous Sexualities*, 137–138; and, more broadly, the late nineteenth and early twentieth

century decline—if uneven—of masturbation public health panics under the pressure of psychological explanations for deviance (less apparent in Northern Ireland, as we have seen)—Laqueur, *Solitary Sex*, 363–376 esp. See similar discussions of (the lack of) policy on venereal disease in McCormick, *Regulating Sexuality*, 101–102.

53. See Earner-Byrne, "Religion, Gender, and Sexuality," 285; McCormick, *Regulating Sexuality*, 27–28; Urquhart, *Irish Divorce*, 149.

54. The classic work is Brown, *The Death of Christian Britain*, which revised the modern secularization thesis but dated a significant decline to the 1960s. For Belfast's resistance, see Holmes, "Protestant Religion in Northern Ireland to 1980," 238–239.

55. For overviews of the churches in everyday life: Megahey, *The Irish Protestant Church*, chapters 3, 5, 6; and Hepburn, *A Past Apart*, chapter 7.

56. "Methodist Who Pioneered Use of Psychology for Churches," *Belfast Telegraph*, December 10, 1966, 2.

57. Northridge, *Psychology and Pastoral Practice*, 61.

58. Northridge's ideas are more evidence of the interwar relationship between sexual science and religion, described in Morgan, *"Sex and Common-Sense."* See also Thomson, "Psychology and the 'Consciousness of Modernity.'"

59. Mondimore, *A Natural History of Homosexuality*, 75–76.

60. Northridge, *Psychology and Pastoral Practice*, 58. Privately, the Church of England was coming to a similar understanding in the 1940s. See Jones, "Moral Welfare and Social Well-Being," 203.

61. Northridge, *Psychology and Pastoral Practice*, 65.

62. Northridge, *Psychology and Pastoral Practice*, 12.

63. "PROFILE: WL Northridge," *Belfast Telegraph*, June 10, 1960, 10.

64. "New Book," *Witness*, November 25, 1938, 8.

65. A first-edition copy of this book, held in my own university (Queen's, Belfast) library, was originally gifted to the Reverend Robert Allen of the Townsend Presbyterian Church (Belfast) from his Bible class students.

66. "Moderator Pays Tribute to Dr Northridge," *Belfast Telegraph*, December 12, 1966, 2. Northridge left behind a series of treatises on the importance of psychology in pastoral practice and clear evidence of an impact on popular thinking—especially in the United States. *Psychology and Pastoral Practice* went through at least five editions (1938 to 1953) and was influential in liberally minded American Protestant circles—White, *Reforming Sodom*, 28.

67. Northridge, *Psychology and Pastoral Practice*, 61, 139.

68. This distinction lasted well into the twentieth century and even the present day. See Lynch, "Between Sickness and Sin."

69. Inglis, *Moral Monopoly*, 218. There was more support for—and greater availability of—contraception for family planning within marriage from the Protestant churches than Catholic, especially after the Anglican Lambeth Conference of 1958 affirmed a change in policy. See McCormick, *Regulating Sexuality*, chapter 6. For Catholic distrust of Freud, see Kelly, "Ego, Id, and Ireland," 281.

70. Cronon, *Impure Thoughts*, 55–57; and Davis, *Moral and Pastoral Theology*, 207–224.

71. Northridge, *Psychology and Pastoral Practice*, 129, 155.

72. Fuller, "Irish Catholic Culture," 181.

73. See Inglis, *Moral Monopoly*; Fuller, "Irish Catholic Culture"; Kennedy, "The Suppression of the Carrigan Report"; and Finnane, "The Carrigan Committee of 1930–1931."

74. Kelly, "Ego, Id, and Ireland," 281.

75. Inglis, *Moral Monopoly*, 139–145; Earls, "Queering Dublin," 70–71, 190–193; Fuller, "Irish Catholic Culture," 181. Delay, "'Language Which Will Move Their Hearts,'" 440–441, discusses how priests publicly denounced the sins of those who shamefully failed to measure up to Irish standards of morality, but I have not yet found any evidence that this happened to the few queer Catholic men arrested.

76. Janes suggests that both Anglo and Roman Catholic clergy "could participate in certain aspects of camp performance, but the price they had to pay, entailing on occasion much suffering, was the renunciation of open sexual self-expression"—Janes, *Visions of Queer Martyrdom*, 20. The queer Irish clergy are beyond the scope of this book but deserve further attention.

77. Dillon, *Crossing the Line*, 22–33; White, *Gerard Dillon*, 23. We can see elements of Dillon's queer longing in his art—Coulter, "Gerard Dillon."

78. For the beginnings of change in attitudes toward homosexuality in the south of Ireland, see Fuller, *Irish Catholicism since 1950*; Ryan, *Asking Angela Macnamara*, chapter 6 on "same sex intimacies"; and Earner-Byrne, "Religion, Gender, and Sexuality."

79. Jones, "The Stained-Glass Closet"; White, *Reforming Sodom*, 46; and Doan, "Sappho's Apotheosis?"

80. Holmes, "Protestant Religion in Northern Ireland to 1980," 240.

81. For the "biblical authorizations of the homoerotic" see Frontain, "The Bible"; Harding, *The Love of David and Jonathan*, 329–350; and Janes, *Visions of Queer Martyrdom*, chapter 6. The story is also featured in the influential Carpenter, *Ioläus*.

82. "August 14 1932," *PDDS*.

83. "December 31 1932," *PDDS*. It is Anglo-Catholicism that has been seen to have the most potential for the expression of this sort of belief, but David Strain—who could be actively *anti*-Catholic—does not fit that model. See Hilliard, "UnEnglish and Unmanly"; and Roden, *Same-Sex Desire in Victorian Religious Culture*.

84. "July 15 1937," "August 26 1937," *PDDS*; and, describing a visit to Kilmood church, "March 24 1938," *PDDS*.

85. Yacovone, "'Surpassing the Love of Women'"; Cocks, "Religion and Spirituality," 169. Wilde had pioneered—if unsuccessfully—this defense in his 1895 trial.

86. "November 30 1933," "March 9 1940," *PDDS*.

87. "February 21 1917," "March 1 1917," "April 23 1917," Folder 1, *AGDC*; "July 8 1917," Folder 2; "Memo w/c. January 26 1918," "March 4 1918," Folder 4, *AGDC*; "July 5 1918," Folder 5, *AGDC*.

88. "July 19–27 1918," Folder 5, *AGDC*. The unrequited love was with Arthur Goodbody, who likely knew Greeves's cousin—Lucius Frederick O'Brien—through their interests in the laundry trade and Quakerism. The sympathetic Friend is described as "Standing"; he was probably a son of William Standing, a middle-class Quaker from Rathmines (like the Goodbodys). See "House 418 in Temple Gardens (Rathmines & Rathgar East, Dublin)," *Census of Ireland 1901*; "House 14 in Myrtlefield Park," *Census of Ireland 1911*; and "Marriage between Arthur Brand Goodbody and Kathleen Frood McNally, December 18, 1920."

89. Hooper, *They Stand Together*, 28–29.

90. Jones, "The Stained-Glass Closet." For religion and gay rights in Ireland see Norris, "Homosexual People"; O'Leary, "Christians and Gays in Northern Ireland," 126–128; and Earner-Byrne, "Religion, Gender, and Sexuality," 299.

91. Frank, Moreton, and White, "Introduction—More than Missionary." For similar religious compromise in Scotland, see Meek, *Queer Voices in Post-War Scotland*, chapter 7.

92. Janes, *Visions of Queer Martyrdom*, 23–24.

93. Cocks, "Religion and Spirituality," 175–176.

94. Grimley, "Law, Morality and Secularisation"; Jones, "Moral Welfare and Social Well-Being." For an early example of this distinction between sin and crime in reference to same-sex desires, see Anomaly, *The Invert and his Social Adjustment*, chapter 7.

95. "Sanity at Last," *Church of Ireland Gazette*, no. 3877, CII, October 18, 1957.

96. Anon., "The Wolfenden Report." The United Council of Christian Churches and Religious Communities in Ireland—an interfaith organization representing the Moravians, Presbyterians (both subscribing and nonsubscribing), Church of Ireland, Methodists, Congregationalists, and Quakers—apparently surveyed the Wolfenden Report, but I have not managed to locate the results. See Barkley, *The Irish Council of Churches*, 11.

97. Representatives of the Catholic Church in Britain did submit a report to Wolfenden, even recommending the separation of sin and crime, though this did not signal a liberal approach more broadly in the religion—Harris, "'Pope Norman'." In Ireland, one of the new and more progressive Irish Catholic journals briefly mentioned the scientific analysis of homosexuality in 1954—Lennon, "New books," *The Furrow* 5, no. 1 (1954)—and there was some (negative) discussion of homosexuality in reference to a BBC documentary—Conway, "Ireland and Television," *The Furrow* 9, no. 1 (1958). A more open conversation in the Irish Catholic Church then seems to have begun, tentatively, in the 1960s: see O'Doherty, "Sexual Deviations," following a conference in 1960 organized by the Archbishop of Dublin. There was similar ambivalence in the Scottish ecclesiastical circles, but the Catholic Church was far more engaged than in Ireland—see Meek, *Queer Voices in Post-War Scotland*.

98. My thinking on how literature and reading was a method of discovering and forming a sense of queer self, especially in a period where sexology disseminated slowly and unevenly, has been informed by Sigel, *Making Modern Love*, 3–6, and chapter 1; Houlbrook, *Queer London*, 207–208; Mitchell and Leavitt, *Pages Passed from Hand to Hand*; Chauncey, *Gay New York*, 283–286; Marhoefer, "'The Book Was a Revelation'"; Hurley, "The Queer Traffic in Literature"; and Rose, "Introduction."

99. Fisher and Langlands, "General Introduction," 6–8.

100. "June 11 1931," *PDDS*.

101. For details on the scandal that brought Smyth to the attention of the police, see van den Berg, "The *Link* Trial (1921)"; and Cocks, *Classified*, 3–15.

102. "Criminal Investigation Department, March 20, 1921." A few women in Ireland had been writing to Carpenter in England since the late nineteenth century, though the extent to which it was his wisdom on sexuality they wanted is unclear; some Irishmen may have also encountered the sage of Sheffield, whether directly or through the passing around of his books. See Casey, "'I Want to Be to Ireland,'"

and, more broadly, Hall, "Heroes or Villains," 10–11, and Houlbrook, *Queer London*, 200–201, 207.

103. Raitt, "Sex, Love and the Homosexual Body," 158.

104. "Letter from Ernest Smyth to Walter Birks, October 21, 1920."

105. The transnational influence of Oscar Wilde in shaping modern queer categories is well known, if contested. See Cohen, *Talk on the Wilde Side*; Sinfield, *The Wilde Century*; and Walshe, *Oscar's Shadow*.

106. For a deeper history of Ernie Smyth, see Hulme and Lynch, "Queer Men and Networks of Communication."

107. Syrett, *An Open Secret*, 29–31. See, more broadly, Potvin, *Bachelors of a Different Sort*, and Cook, *Queer Domesticities*.

108. Nealon, *Foundlings*, 8, 13.

109. For similar men in London, see Cook, *London and the Culture of Homosexuality*, 122–132.

110. "Letter from Walter Smith [unnamed] (September 10, 1937)" in "Bundle of c.200 letters to D H Strain," *Correspondence and Accounts of D H Strain, Senior and Junior*.

111. "Letter from C. S. Lewis to Arthur Greeves, May 23, 1918" in Hooper, ed., *They Stand Together*, 215. He did not know Greek himself, however—see "Letter from C. S. Lewis to Arthur Greeves, c. June 1914" in Hooper, ed., *They Stand Together*, 47. David Strain also noted how Oscar Wilde "was only following the ways of the early Dorian Greeks who had boy lovers"—a point he gleaned from Finger, *The Tragic Story of Oscar Wilde's Life*—"June 11, 1931," *PDDS*.

112. For his literary output, see Cruise, "Error and Eros," and Barr, "Forrest Reid's Queer Ulster Pastoral."

113. James broke off all contact with Reid after reading *The Garden God*, which had even been dedicated to him, seemingly because of the pederastic themes. See Sherbo, "Henry James and Forrest Reid." For this genre of writing more broadly, see Aldrich, *The Seduction of the Mediterranean*, chapter 1, and Kaylor, *Secreted Desires*. For the edited manuscript, "Youth, Gods, Beasts, Earth," *Forrest Reid Collection*.

114. See Dowling, *Hellenism and Homosexuality*, 33, and Dellamora, *Masculine Desire*, chapter 10.

115. James Leslie quoted in Martin, *Censorship in the Two Irelands*, 57.

116. One book was banned in the Irish Free State in 1941 solely because of a sentence that referenced two men during intimacy: "She saw *Etienne* and her father, in the embrace of love." See Fischerova, "The Banning and Unbanning of Kate O'Brien's *The Land of Spices*." Other banned works included those on sexology by Havelock Ellis, and Hall, *The Well of Loneliness*.

117. There was still a focus on censorship to ensure security and a belief that promoting virtue was more effective than controlling literature. See Martin, *Censorship in the Two Irelands*, 76, 93–97. For the intensification of censorship in Britain in the 1920s before a thaw in the 1930s, see Hilliard, *A Matter of Obscenity*, 34–60.

118. Kirkland, *Cathal O'Byrne*. John Hewitt was critical of Ulster's provincialism in art and literature in the 1930s and 1940s and attempted to promote a modern regional movement—Coulter, "John Hewitt."

119. "September 21 1930," "December 20 1933," "December 25 1933, *PDDS*.

120. For the realities of the slumming world these Harlem Renaissance novels depicted, see Heap, *Slumming*, chapter 6.

121. Forster, *Maurice*, 254. Slide, *Lost Gay Novels*, 1–2. Woods traces the ascendancy of tragedy narratives to the late nineteenth century and Wilde's trial in particular but notes they were often more complex than just "unhappy endings"; they also involved "fatedness which casts the queer as an inglorious version of the tragic hero." Woods, *A History of Gay Literature*, 217–218. See also Marshik, "History's 'Abrupt Revents.'"

122. "Thomas Henry Ritchie, Born December 6, 1916, Belfast"; *Belfast Street Directory* (1932); "House 54 in Thorndyke (Pottinger, Down)," *Census for Ireland (1911)*. Ritchie's story is told more fully in Hulme and Lynch, "Queer Men and Networks of Communication."

123. "August 12 1936," *PDDS*; "James Dougan—Gross Indecency with a Minor" (1931).

124. "April 24 1936," *PDDS*.

125. "July 12 1937," *PDDS*. For the popularity of *Strange Brother* in its own urban context, see Mumford, "Homosex Changes," 395–396.

126. Jeffrey Escoffier has written about this process in the 1960s and 1970s from both a personal and scholarly perspective—Escoffier, *American Homo*, chapter 3, and see also Bartlett, *Who Was That Man?*

127. "April 12 1934," *PDDS*.

128. "Heredity," *Hull Daily Mail*, February 20, 1933, 4; "Undergraduate's Novel," *Birmingham Mail*, June 12, 1933, 5; "Novelist Banned by Vatican," *Belfast Telegraph*, September 28, 1933), 5.

129. "Cermak Transferred to Oxygen Room," *Northern Whig*, March 2, 1933, 8.

130. "March 7 1933," *PDDS*.

131. For more on literature and reading as a form of queer bonding, see chapter 4.

132. As is clear from David Strain's diaries. See, for example, "April 28 1934," "February 28 1932," *PDDS*.

133. The biggest bookshops traded on their respectability and longevity and so probably erred on the side of caution when it came to books that were obviously indecent. Sigel, *Making Modern Love*, 20–23.

134. Hilliard, "The Literary Underground of 1920s London," 166–169.

135. "There Is Only One Bookshop In Belfast," *Belfast Telegraph*, November 19, 1927, 1.

136. Longley, "Progressive Bookmen," and Gray, "A Shop Steward Remembers." John Hewitt, "Sonnet for the Progressive Bookshop" (1929), quoted in Smith, "On 'The Edge of a Crumbling Continent,'" 45.

137. "June 11 1931," *PDDS*.

138. It was published in the frank Little Blue Books series, run from Kansas by the socialist reformer Emanuel Haldeman-Julius. See "Finding Aid for 'Haldeman-Julius "Little Blue Book" Collection 1919–1947.'"

139. Craig, "The Liberal Imagination in Northern Irish Prose."

140. See Denny's—"March 13 1918," "March 14 1918," "March 18 1918," Folder 4, *AGDC*; Harrods—"July 17 1933," *PDDS*; and John Grant's "December 7 1934," *PDDS*. The BSSSP refused to send their most provocative work—*The Social Problem of Sexual Inversion*, an abridged translation of a German treatise from 1903—limiting

it to members only but did send a Walt Whitman pamphlet; see "Letter from A T. McNeilly c. March 1925" in "Incoming—Ma-Mai."

141. "July 17 1933," "August 2 1933," *PDDS*.

142. Forster's *Maurice* remained unpublished until his death in the 1970s but was read in manuscript by his Belfast friend Forrest Reid (who disapproved of its depiction of sexual desire).

143. Gifford states that "networking must have been more common than we realize, for even books of limited circulation found their way into appreciative hands" in Gifford, *Glances Backward*, xxiii. See also Colligan, "Teleny."

144. "English-Banned Book," *Belfast Telegraph*, April 13, 1929, 9. "July 17 1933," "August 2 1933," *PDDS*.

145. Prior, *Mental Health and Politics*, 56–95.

146. Sigel, *Making Modern Love*, 18.

147. Cocks, *Religion and Spirituality*, 157.

4. Boys, Friends, and Lovers

1. "Frederick Aicken, Born September 24, 1919, Newtownards"; "David Aicken and Eva Howard, Married September 8, 1909"; "House 4 in Victoria Avenue (Newtownards Urban, Down)," *Census of Ireland 1911*; Abbott, "Memories of Frederick Howard Aicken." For the daughter's death: "Winifred Aicken, Died October 3, 1926, Newtownards."

2. "Situations Vacant," *Belfast Telegraph*, September 22, 1936, 1.

3. "September 28 1936," "September 30 1936," *PDDS*.

4. This relationship is reconstructed from "May 28 1937," "June 11 1937," "July 20 1937," "August 4 1937," "September 24 1937," "October 18 1937," "June 1 1937," "June 19 1937," "June 21 1937," *PDDS*.

5. "December 31 1938," *PDDS*.

6. Abbott, "Memories of Frederick Howard Aicken."

7. "December 14 1936," "June 19 1937," "July 20 1937," "July 7 1937," "January 9 1938," *PDDS*.

8. Katz, *Love Stories*, is a vivid charting of these shifts. See, for a broader overview, Peel, "New Worlds of Friendship," 281, 303–304, 309–310.

9. See discussion of Eve Sedgwick and the New British Queer History in chapter 3.

10. As Jeff Meeks notes, queer male prostitution is ubiquitous in the historiography though there has not been an attempt to construct a general theory—Meek, *Queer Trades, Sex and Society*, 1–4.

11. For more on this Belfast Scandal, see especially the introduction and chapter 6.

12. Dudgeon, *Roger Casement*, 275.

13. Lewis, "The Queer Life and Afterlife of Roger Casement," 381–382.

14. By the late 1930s, the Belfast courts were developing a sense of culpability in age-differentiated same-sex encounters, though not one that was entirely consistent—see chapter 6.

15. Akenson, *Education and Enmity*, 13–16, 89, 91–92. The school-leaving age was raised to fifteen in 1957, two decades after England and Wales and almost four decades later than Scotland.

16. Daly, "The Emergence of an Irish Adolescence," 199, 203, 205; Laragy, "'For Those Whose Benefit These Burdens Must Be Taken'"; Fowler, *Youth Culture in Modern Britain*, 84–85; and, for a concise discussion of defining adolescence and youth, Tebbutt, *Being Boys*, 16–17.

17. Smyth, "Obituary: Joseph Tomelty."

18. Tomelty, *The Apprentice*, 158. A similar sexual learning is evident in the account of a boy sent away from Donegal to apprentice in Scotland in Macgill, *The Dead End*, 190–191.

19. Prominent members of the Ulster Group Theatre included two queer civil servants, Alfred Arnold and Ritchie McKee, and Jimmie Young too—as described in "Interview with John Keyes." Tomelty was close to the locally famous Young, whom he cast as a sympathetic effeminate character in the radio sitcom *The McCooeys* (1949)—see Pettitt, "Queering Broadcast Boundaries."

20. "February 2 1939," *PDDS*.

21. Because the same laws were used to prosecute all sexual crimes between males, distressing abuse cases are archivally catalogued the same as encounters between adults. See, for example, the rape of a five-year-old boy by a lodger in his mother's home—"John Tyrell (Alias Kelly)—Gross Indecency" (1913); a man who sexually assaulted both his nephew (eleven) and niece (six)—"Named Individual—Unlawful Carnal Knowledge and Buggery" (1925); a drill instructor for a youth organization who assaulted a ten-year-old boy—"James Stevenson—Gross Indecency" (1928); and a man accused of abuse in a Barnardo's Home—"Named Individual—Buggery with a Minor" (1941).

22. Ambiguous cases include a fourteen-year-old machinist in an entry with a thirty-two-year-old man at eleven o'clock p.m., who said he was forced into sex—"John Reynolds (Alias Powell)—Gross Indecency" (1918); and two seventeen-year-old boys in a docklands urinal who blamed each other—"Sidney Day—Attempted Buggery and Gross Indecency" (1926).

23. "Arthur Patterson—Indecency" (1939). The fifteen-year-old shopworker witness said the older man "did not force him."

24. See: a seventeen-year-old boy mutually masturbating an older man in a park, whom he had met several times before—"Named Individual—Gross Indecency" (1937); and, for bartering—"John Wilson (Alias Dornan)—Gross Indecency" (1910).

25. McIntosh, "Children, Street Trading"; Rains, "City Streets and the City Edition." For the romantic interpretation, see "The Belfast Newsboy," *Northern Whig*, August 6, 1924, 4, and for the negative, "Juvenile Rowdyism at Castle Junction," *Northern Whig*, August 21, 1916, 7. For the complexities of corner boys, "In Defence of Corner Boys," *Ireland's Saturday Night*, August 13, 1938, 10.

26. Hindmarch-Watson, "Male Prostitution and the London GPO," 598–599, 606.

27. See: a twelve-year-old who, when propositioned on the street, reported a middle-aged man—"John O'Neill—Attempted Gross Indecency with a Minor" (1930); a boy (unknown age) who reported a man who tried to pay him for sex in a Salvation Army Home—"Thomas Dazelle—Gross Indecency" (1923); a man reported after asking a sixteen-year-old suggestive questions—"Jones Thomas—Buggery" (1926); a twelve-year-old boy who reported a man who tried to pay him—"Robert Brown—attempted gross indecency" (1932); and the boy propositioned by Arthur Patterson, described above.

28. *Report of the Inter-Departmental Committee on the Employment of Children during School Age*, vi.

29. "Edgar Milligan [*sic*]—Gross Indecency" (1917). Newsboys were prominent in queer scenes all over the Western world. See, for example, Smaal, "Boys and Homosex"; and Boag, *Same-Sex Affairs*, 76–79.

30. "Edgar Milligen—Gross Indecency" (1917); "House 160 in Matilda Street (St George's, Antrim)," *Census of Ireland 1911*. For more detail on the other boys, see Hulme, "Queer Belfast," 251.

31. "Urban passport" is a term used by Jerram, *Streetlife*, 268.

32. "'Ensnared' after Visit to Luxury House," *News of the World*, May 4, 1952. For more on this case, see the discussion of Patrick Barbour in chapter 6.

33. Examples: a fifteen-year-old orphan bought expensive clothing and taken to the theater and country home of a rich industrialist—"Edgar Milligan [*sic*]—Gross Indecency" (1917); a thirteen-year-old boy given money and trips to the cinema and local cafés with a twenty-year-old he met in a billiard hall, "Named Individual—Gross Indecency and Buggery" (1947); and the relationship between David Strain and Jack Murray, which involved countless small gifts of money and clothing, despite Murray not allowing anything more than affectionate embraces—a constant feature of 1931–32, *PDDS*.

34. "John Wilson (Alias Dornan)—Gross Indecency" (1910); "House 81 in Agincourt Avenue (Cromac, Antrim)" and "House 36 in Damascus Street (Cromac, Antrim)," *Census of Ireland 1911*. See also a boy just shy of his thirteenth birthday who was enlisted by his eighteen-year-old friend to sell sex in public toilets in the well-known cruising site of Ormeau Park—"Named Individuals—Gross Indecency" (1937).

35. Tebbutt, *Being Boys*, chapter 7.

36. "November 26 1937," "February 2 1938," *PDDS*.

37. "March 25 1939" and also "November 12 1938," *PDDS*.

38. "Queer kinship networks" described as "street families" by Plaster, *Kids on the Street*, 4–6.

39. "Francis Wadman—Buggery" (1950).

40. Under cross-examination, a young man in 1949 admitted that he'd been told to "clear off" by a customer but had kept on coming back and bringing his friend too, "Samuel Stewart—Buggery" (1949).

41. "Edgar Milligan [*sic*]—Gross Indecency" (1917).

42. Houlbrook, "Soldier Heroes and Rent Boys," 360–361, demonstrates the most intense form of this relationship in the Brigades, but it was evident more broadly.

43. See "James Doherty—Gross Indecency" (1894); "James McKee and Richard Lutton—Assault and Buggery" (1904); and "Sidney Day—Attempted Buggery and Gross Indecency" (1926).

44. "August 26 1937," "September 9 1937," "April 1 1939," "June 6 1939," "May 26 1933," *PDDS*. See also a youth who responded to Strain's apology for kissing him by saying "It's alright, but I don't like that." "December 16 1938," *PDDS*.

45. For the construction of masculinity in Belfast, see McGaughey, *Ulster's Men*, and further discussion in chapter 6.

46. "December 23 1938," "February 20 1940," *PDDS*. For other young men who "did not object to mild fooling," though they expected payment, see "June 6 1939," *PDDS*.

47. The *Report of the Inter-Departmental Committee on the Employment of Children During School Age*, which included witness testimony from Belfast, was most concerned with how street trading would lead to gambling, intemperance, fighting, and general rowdy behavior.

48. See the deconstruction of "the charmed circle vs. the outer limits" of the "sex hierarchy" in Rubin, "Thinking Sex," 280–281. For recent critical deconstructions of the reclamation urge: Amin, *Disturbing Attachments*, and Evans, *The Queer Art of History*, chapter 2.

49. Maynard, "'Horrible Temptations,'" 196.

50. "James Dougan—Gross Indecency with a Minor" (1931).

51. Francis Wadman told the police, "I am not going to have the boys blamed, it is not their fault at all" when arrested in 1949, and David Neill claimed to be helping a boy avoid legal trouble. "Francis Wadman—Buggery" (1950) and "David Neill—Gross Indecency" (1949).

52. See chapter 3.

53. Houlbrook, "Soldier Heroes and Rent Boys," 360. For an Irish example, see Earls, "Solicitor Brown and His Boy."

54. "February 10 1939," "April 1 1938," *PDDS*. See also the end with another youth: "at back of all there is a girl, so I shall drop the acquaintance quietly." "December 21 1941," *PDDS*.

55. For masculinity as process, see Houlbrook, Jones, and Mechen, "Introduction" in Houlbrook, Jones, and Mechen, eds., *Men and Masculinities in Modern Britain: A History for the Present*, which is, more broadly, an exemplary overview of the field. For a critical interpretation of the relative lack of focus on Irish masculinities—as resulting from a dominance of deeply traditional political and empirical narratives and also the tendency to treat gender and women's histories as indivisible—see Barr, Brady, and McGaughey, *Ireland and Masculinities in History*.

56. For a useful examination of this stage of life from the perspective of opposite-gender relationships, see Charnock, "'How Far Should We Go?'" Even before adolescence became a defined concept in the social sciences, intimate and romantic male friendships were expected to end when marriage with a woman fulfilled the same purposes—see Rotundo, "Romantic Friendship," 14–18 esp.

57. "April 24, 1938," "May 8, 1938," and "September 12, 1938," *PDDS*.

58. "On Active Service," *Northern Whig*, July 9, 1943, 2.

59. The first man is Alfred Shaw: "Archibald Black and Alfred Shaw—Assault" (1891); "Wellington Barracks, St George Hanover Square, London," *Census of England 1901*; and "House 10.1 in Shandon Street (Dock Ward, Antrim)," *Census of Ireland 1911*. The second man: "Named Individuals—Gross Indecency" (1937); I have found this man's marriage certificate in GRONI but cannot confirm if he is no longer alive so will not cite it here.

60. I have shied away from the terminology of "situational homosexuality" because, as queer historians have pointed out, *all* expressions of same-sex desire or acts were shaped by the environment in which they took place. See Kunzel, "Situating Sex," 253–256.

61. These figures include men arrested for gross indecency or buggery, including unwanted sexual advances in public, but exclude sex between men and solely boys below sixteen plus clear cases of child abuse in familial/institutional settings.

62. Murphy, "'I Conformed; I Got Married,'" 167–168.

63. See, for example: Conrad, *Locked in the Family Cell*, 15–22; Valiulis, "Virtuous Mothers and Dutiful Wives," 100–114; and McCormick, *Regulating Sexuality*, 27–28.

64. Harry Ritchie—discussed in chapter 3—married not long after being arrested, while Vincent Cassidy married a decade or so after his conviction (see Hulme, "Queer Belfast").

65. Greeves's friend had seen H. G. Wells's *Island of Dr. Moreau* in Paris and mused that "it must have been pretty horrible"—perhaps because of the queer subtext. "July 24, 1922," Folder 8, *AGDC*. For context, Canadas, "Going Wilde."

66. Northridge, *Psychology and Pastoral Practice*, 62, 64–65.

67. "Named Individual—Gross Indecency and Buggery" (1947). I found this individual's marriage record through www.ancestry.co.uk but do not know if he is alive, so have not cited it here.

68. For novels and films providing knowledge about sex and romance models, see Sigel, *Making Modern Love*, and Brooke, "'A Certain Amount of Mush.'" More broadly, see Langhamer, *The English in Love*, though, as I discuss later in this chapter, these trends were somewhat slower to take hold in Ireland.

69. "Ethel Norwood, Born August 25, 1915, Lisburn." For diary entries describing this relationship, see especially "November 22, 1933," "November 25, 1933," "December 2, 1933," "December 9, 1933," "December 30, 1933," "March 15 1934," and "September 5, 1934," *PDDS*.

70. John Kingston, for example, lived in Belfast for decades—where he was arrested in 1914 and 1926—while his wife and child remained in England: "House 108 Madrid Street (Pottinger, Down)," *Census of Ireland 1911*; and "John Albert Kingston, died October 18, 1954, Belfast."

71. "Archibald Black and Alfred Shaw—Assault" (1891); Black then went to live in his niece's boarding home after his release—"House 41 Moscow Street (Shankill, Antrim)," *Census of Ireland 1901*. See also Joseph Rea, who asked for word to be sent to his wife while he was in the cells—"Joseph Rea and Thomas Magee—Gross Indecency" (1913).

72. For more on shame, families, and emigration, see chapter 5.

73. Cook, *Queer Domesticities*, 92; Smith, *Masculinity, Class and Same-Sex Desire in Industrial England*, chapter 4.

74. For more on the classed implications of this statement, see Hulme, "Queer Belfast."

75. "Hugh P. Sheehan and Rachel McKinney, married January 25, 1923, Belfast"; "*Adriatic* leaving Belfast, September 20, 1930."

76. "Samuel Magowan and Richard Morrison—Gross Indecency" (1927); and "General Register, Male Prisoners" (1926–1929), 141; "Indecency," *Northern Whig*, July 26, 1927, 8; and "Crown Book, Indictment and Pleas, Belfast City Commission" (July 1927), 29.

77. "Washed," *Belfast Telegraph*, August 1, 1964, 4.

78. See, as examples, "Character," *Belfast Telegraph*, November 4, 1961, 5; "Encounter," *Belfast Telegraph*, July 28, 1962, 4; and "Perfection," *Belfast Telegraph*, May 11, 1963, 4. For the memorials: "Deaths," *Belfast Telegraph*, June 26, 1968, 2.

79. For this recalling of memories of love late in the life cycle, see Greenhalgh, "Love in Later Life." For more examples from Belfast, see Edward McLaughlin, a middle-aged baker given six months in prison and exposed in the press, who returned to live

with his wife and children for decades after. "Edward McLaughlin and William Robin—Gross Indecency" (1927); "Mr. E. McLaughlin," *Ballymena Weekly Telegraph*, May 22, 1958, 2.

80. Urquhart, *Irish Divorce*, 22.

81. Luddy, "Marriage, Sexuality and the Law in Ireland."

82. See discussion in chapter 5.

83. The transformation of love and courtship in mid-twentieth century Britain is a vibrant field, and so the literature is extensive; a useful summary and critique can be found in Jones and Harris, "Introduction," 1–7, 14–15. I have found especially useful Langhamer, "Love, Selfhood and Authenticity in Post-war Britain," and King, *Family Men*. For the effects of these shifts on male queerness, see Houlbrook, *Queer London*, 190–194, and Smith, *Masculinity, Class and Same-Sex Desire in Industrial England*, 85–86, 189–190, 193–195.

84. Bardon, *Belfast*, chapter 10; Urquhart, "Gender, Family, and Sexuality," 246; Earner-Byrne, "Religion, Gender, and Sexuality," 648; O'Connell, "An Age of Conservative Modernity," 311–312; and Barritt and Carter, *The Northern Ireland Problem*, 146. Relatedly, Laura Doan has shown how marital advice literature in Britain carved out social and sexual norms between men and women rather than a fixed "heterosexual" identity—Doan, "'A Peculiarly Obscure Subject,'" 91–92. The key figure being Marie Stopes—Cook, *The Long Sexual Revolution*, chapter 8—but she had less influence in sexually unprogressive Northern Ireland, as demonstrated by the short-lived nature of the Mother's Clinic—Jones, "Marie Stopes in Ireland," which means the development of companionate marriage ideas arguably happened later. The same can be said for the south of Ireland: the "emotional revolution" was happening, just later and more gradually. See Clear, *Women's Voices in Ireland*, 99–104, and Ryan, *Asking Angela Macnamara*, chapters 4–6.

85. Bauer and Cook, "Introduction," 2.

86. Meeker, *Contacts Desired*, "Introduction."

87. See discussion in chapters 2 and 3 and Hulme and Lynch, "Queer Men and Networks of Communication in Northern Ireland before the 1970s."

88. "Personals," *Belfast Telegraph*, June 3, 1914, 1. For another early advert: "Young Man (26) Wants Another as Companion for Evenings" in "Personals," *Belfast Telegraph*, June 2, 1919, 1.

89. "Advertising Rates," *Belfast Telegraph*, January 18, 1935, 1. See *National Archives Currency Converter*, £2.53 in 2017, to be precise.

90. See Riddell, *Music and the Queer Body in English Literature*, chapter 1.

91. "Personals," *Belfast Telegraph*, May 19, 1921, 1; "Personals," *Belfast Telegraph*, May 9, 1933, 1; "Personals," *Northern Whig*, December 5, 1940, 6; "Personals," *Belfast Telegraph*, April 7, 1936, 2; "Personals," *Belfast Telegraph*, July 5, 1938, 1; "Personals," *Belfast Telegraph*, July 8, 1936, 2; "Personals," *Belfast Telegraph*, May 9, 1933, 1; "Personals," *Belfast Telegraph*, July 18, 1939, 1; "Personals," *Belfast Telegraph*, July 22, 1940, 1; "Personals," *Belfast Telegraph*, December 29, 1942, 1; "Personals," *Belfast Telegraph*, December 8, 1939, 1; "Personals," *Belfast Telegraph*, March 1, 1940, 1; "Personals," *Belfast Telegraph*, May 9, 1933, 1; "Personals," *Belfast Telegraph*, May 1, 1934, 2; "Personals," *Belfast Telegraph*, February 17, 1938, 2.

92. "Personals," *Belfast Telegraph*, October 16, 1937, 2. The author of this advert was Cecil Bond—discussed more later in this chapter.

93. "Personals," *Belfast Telegraph*, February 26, 1921, 1. The responses to Strain's advert—and some of the dates that followed—are detailed in "March 20 1933," "April 27 1933," "April 28, 1933," "April 29, 1933," "April 30, 1933," "May 1, 1933," "May 3, 1933," "May 5, 1933," and "May 10, 1933," *PDDS*.

94. "Belfast Saturday Nights," *Ireland's Saturday Night*, December 20, 1930, 1.

95. "Walter Smith, Born May 3, 1898, Belfast"; "House 48 Old Park (Clifton Ward, Belfast, Antrim)," *Census of Ireland 1901*; "House 45 in Dunluce Avenue (Windsor, Antrim)," *Census of Ireland 1911*.

96. "Leslie Cecil Bond, Born October 17, 1900, Nelson, New Zealand"; "Passenger List for *Persie*, Travelling from Sydney to London (January 1904)"; "House 4 in Kilrush (Hollymount, Mayo)," *Census of Ireland 1911*.

97. "September 18, 1937," *PDDS*. For networks between Dublin and Belfast, see Walter Smith—"September 14 1938," *PDDS*; and Arthur Greeves, discussed in more depth in chapter 3.

98. "August 24, 1935," *PDDS*.

99. "June 24, 1936," "May 10, 1936," "May 7, 1937," *PDDS*.

100. "November 19, 1937," "March 14, 1942," *PDDS*.

101. "November 19, 1937," *PDDS*.

102. "May 8, 1937," *PDDS*. These walks are a frequent facet of Strain's diaries in the late 1930s.

103. "July 24, 1938," *PDDS*.

104. Chauncey, *Gay New York*, 3.

105. "July 24, 1934," *PDDS*.

106. "September 6, 1937," *PDDS*.

107. See William Knox, as described in "Defendant: Knox, William"; and Harry Ritchie, as described in "The Information of the Director of Public Prosecutions," 2, and "Central Criminal Court, January 18 sessions, 1937," 35.

108. For the "Dilly Boys," see Houlbrook, *Queer London*, 140–163; for the *Tetki*, see Healey, *Homosexual Desire in Revolutionary Russia*, 39–41.

109. For the classic analysis of the same culture in London, see Weeks, "Inverts, Perverts, and Mary-Annes." For the Dublin Scandal, see further discussion in chapter 6.

110. "March 14, 1942," *PDDS*.

111. "September 29, 1937," "March 13, 1937," "October 12, 1934," *PDDS*.

112. For more on movement between urban scenes, see chapter 2. For reflections on camp and its relationship to homosexual self-presentation, see Sontag, "Notes on Camp," and Bergman, *Camp Grounds*.

113. See discussion in previous chapter.

114. Chauncey, *Gay New York*, chapter 2. For husbands, see "May 28, 1937," "October 18 1937," *PDDS*.

115. Valocchi, "'Where Did Gender Go?'" 454.

116. "December 19, 1938," "20 February 1939," *PDDS*.

117. "April 24, 1936," *PDDS*.

118. See Houlbrook, *Queer London*, chapters 8 and 10; Mort, "Mapping Sexual London"; and Waters, "Disorders of the Mind." Similar discourses were evident in the United States; Chauncey, *Gay New York*, chapter 4. For the lasting influence of respectability politics in Northern Ireland's gay rights movement in the 1970s: Gilmore, "Gay Activism in Northern Ireland." For the broader use of nationalism,

masculinity, and respectability in sexological discourse, see Mosse, *Nationalism and Sexuality*, 41–43.

119. "February 10, 1939," "February 13, 1943," *PDDS*.

120. Houlbrook, *Queer London*, 266, 5–6.

121. Cook et al., *A Gay History of Britain*, 163–164.

122. Doan, *History, Sexuality, and Women's Experience of Modern War*, 58–66; Brickell, "Sexology, the Homo/Hetero Binary," 427; and the interactions and contradictions between medical-psychological "inversion" models and more recent "ethnic" understandings of homosexuals as a specific group, in Nealon, *Foundlings*, 1–13.

123. The bachelor farmer was seen as symbolizing the ill health of the nation in the mid-twentieth century, as captured in Guinnane, *The Vanishing Irish* and, controversially, the anthropological work Scheper-Hughes, *Saints, Scholars and Schizophrenics*. At the same time, they can also be read "as a cultural figure that may mobilise non-hegemonic if not counter-hegemonic masculinities, despite the way it may seem to reinforce gender norms" as argued by Madden, "Bachelor trouble, *Troubled Bachelors*." See, more broadly, Earner-Byrne, "The family in Ireland," 650–653, and more discussion of bachelors in the following chapter.

124. Jerram, *Streetlife*, 254–255. For examples of historians: Smith with Kuefler and Wiesner-Hanks, "Class in the History of Sexuality," 208–209; Terry, *An American Obsession*, 19–20; Chauncy, *Gay New York*, chapter 4.

5. Families, Neighborhoods, and the Public

1. "George Hogg, born September 10 1889, Lisburn."

2. "House 6 Well Street (Ormeau, Down), *Census of Ireland 1901*; "House 11 Ship Street (Dock Ward, Antrim)," *Census of Ireland 1901*.

3. "House 1 Ettrick Street (Cromac, Antrim)," *Census of Ireland 1911*. The enumerator classed the house as just meeting second-class status (on a scale of fourth to first). His mother was listed as a widow but also as having been married for twenty-eight years, but George Hogg senior was alive and living in Island Magee: "House 13.1 Castletown and Chester Avenue (Island Magee, Antrim)," *Census of Ireland 1911*.

4. *Belfast and Province of Ulster Directory* (Belfast, 1918).

5. "George Hogg and Mary McCleery, married August 5, 1919, Belfast." Jones, *A Social Geography of Belfast*, noted that the standard of housing was high for a working-class area and that the area's provision of indoor toilets was a rarity for this time.

6. "George Hogg—Buggery" (1925).

7. The McCleery family were from Donaghanie (rural Co. Tyrone). By 1925, George, Margaret, Mary, John, Albert, Charlotte, and Rebecca had moved to Belfast; two other siblings and the parents remained behind. See George McCleery's obituary: *Belfast Telegraph*, February 25, 1925, 9. Lyon, *British Wages*, 60.

8. Another McCleery brother, Albert, also lived on Palestine Street. See *Belfast and Providence of Ulster Directory* (1925).

9. "Nine Months for Assault," *Belfast News-Letter*, December 3, 1925, 12.

10. *Belfast and Ulster Directory* (1943); "George Hogg, Died October 27 1947, Belfast."

11. "Deaths," *Northern Whig*, October 29, 1947, 2; "A Serious Charge," *Northern Whig*, December 3, 1925, 9.

12. Defining consensual and nonconsensual when there was no age of consent between males in law or understanding makes tallying cases problematic. I have excluded males under sixteen, regardless of their motivations or legal treatment, but discuss intergenerational sex in chapter 4. I have not included aggressive sexual assaults, even if they were prosecuted as "gross indecency" or "buggery."

13. For more on censorship and queer literature, see chapter 3.

14. See, for example, two men arrested after a night watchman saw them "wandering about" in a field near a workplace he was guarding—"Archibald Black and Alfred Shaw—Assault" (1891); and two men who raised suspicions by idling on vacant ground between houses, "Robert Smith and John Reid—Gross Indecency" (1927).

15. For toilets, money, suspicion, see James Magee and Joseph Rea, discussed later in this chapter; and "Edward McLaughlin and William Robin—Gross Indecency" (1927).

16. See Alexander Gibson, wearing women's clothing and hinted to be soliciting men, "The Constable and the Militiaman," *Northern Whig*, September 1, 1908, 9; a young man who raised suspicions because he "spoke very like a girl," "David Straight—Gross Indecency" (1925); and a man suspected "owing to his movement," "John Sterling and William Gray—Gross Indecency" (1925).

17. See "Edward Samuel Wesley De Cobain—Buggery" (1893); and "Named Individual—Gross Indecency and Assault with Intent to Commit Buggery" (1940). Patrick Meehan was arrested after propositioning a fifteen-year-old boy in the docks by suggesting he had given his own father and uncle sexual relief, "Patrick Meehan—Indecent Assault on a Male Person" (1924).

18. See "William Ritchie and Samuel Coulter—Gross Indecency" (1932). For context: Fitzpatrick and Gellately, "Introduction to the Practices of Denunciation in Modern European History," 751. Examples of extortion are uncommon in Belfast records, but David Strain knew that "little blackmailer[s]" existed—"July 18 1938," *PDDS*; and a schoolmaster was hounded for money by rent boys—"Francis Wadman—Buggery" (1950)—discussed in chapter 4.

19. Ferriter, *Occasions of Sin*, 15. "[The] expression of sexuality was less inhibited than historians believed" is now commonly argued for sex between men and women. Luddy, "Marriage, Sexuality and the Law in Ireland," 359. Ferriter was reacting to sociologist Inglis, "Origins and Legacies of Irish Prudery."

20. John Ferrer called William Ritchie (fifty-two, customs officer) "dirty names" and punched him for seducing a "boy" he knew, a twenty-three-year-old milkman, in the Ardoyne area, "William Ritchie and Samuel Coulter—Gross Indecency"' (1932); and one witness was unemployed but refused a bribe from a man who seduced his vulnerable friend (an eighteen-year-old former inmate of an industrial school)—"Edward Summers—Gross Indecency" (1924), and "House 2 Ballygammon (Ballygomartin, Antrim)," *Census of Ireland 1911*. For "honorable" violence and the policing of manliness, see D'Cruze, "Introduction: Unguarded Passions." See also Earner-Byrne, "Religion, Gender, and Sexuality," 288–289, and Tosh, "Masculinities in an Industrializing Society," 335.

21. We know Dunlop was a sailor because of his tattoos, described in "General Register, Male Prisoners" (1909–1910), 51.

22. "House 90 Great Georges Street (St. Anne's Ward, Antrim)" and "House 28 North Queen Street (Duncairn Ward, Antrim)," *Census of Ireland 1901*.

23. "John McCormick and Hugh Dunlop—Gross Indecency" (1909).

24. Croll, "Street Disorder, Surveillance and Shame," 254.

25. Earls, "Queering Dublin," 109–110, and Smith, *Masculinity, Class and Same-Sex Desire*, chapter 4.

26. McGaughey, *Ulster's Men*; McKane, "'No Idle Sightseers.'"

27. Ellison and Smyth, *The Crowned Harp*, 20. More broadly, see Parkinson, *Belfast's Unholy War*.

28. Brady, "Why Examine Men, Masculinities and Religion in Northern Ireland?" 224, 231; and Beatty, *Masculinity and Power in Irish Nationalism*. See also the special issue Redmond, "Revolutionary Masculinities."

29. "David Straight—Gross Indecency" (1925).

30. See Archibald Andrews entrapping James Douglas in 1894—discussed in chapter 2; a cruising man led into a police station (again, the witness claimed because "we met no constable on the way")—"James O'Neill—Gross Indecency" (1928); men in a boardinghouse who joined together—whether as decoys or watchers—to entrap an older man who offered money for sex—"Thomas Dazelle—Gross Indecency" (1923); and a schoolmaster who found the police waiting in the bushes when he was trying to meet a youth—"Francis Wadman—Buggery" (1950).

31. Earls, "Queering Dublin," 152–156; Keating, "Sexual Crime in the Irish Free State 1922–33," 137–138.

32. Micheler, "Homophobic Propaganda"; Huneke, *States of Liberation*.

33. See the discussion of intergenerational sex in chapter 4.

34. "House 76 University Street (Cromac, Antrim)," *Census of Ireland 1911*; "The Crescent Church," *Northern Whig*, November 26, 1903, 12; and "The Lagan from Source to Fall," *Belfast News-Letter*, April 7, 1897, 6.

35. "Joseph Rea and Thomas Magee—Gross Indecency" (1913), and "Joseph Rea—Gross Indecency" (1913).

36. "House 26 Henry Street (Dock Ward, Antrim)," *Census of Ireland 1901*; "Hooliganism in Belfast," *Northern Whig*, October 10, 1902, 2; "An Extraordinary Case," *Irish News and Belfast Morning News*, October 10, 1902, 6.

37. See "Bible Temperance Association," *Belfast News-Letter*, April 25, 1892, 3; and "Belfast Family Grocers' and Spirit Dealers Association," *Northern Whig*, June 8, 1899, 8.

38. See: For drugged and assaulted, "Thomas Kirk—Gross Indecency" (1914); the soldier and sailor assaults discussed in chapter 2; and a man who had been drinking in Du Barry's (one of the accused aggressors, Denis Dorrian, had a "story" he had "kept" for the court but the press did not elaborate, which suggests there may have been a more scandalous element to the case)—"Like 'Highway Robbery,'" *Belfast Telegraph*, December 5, 1949, 5.

39. "Robert Smith and John Reid—Gross Indecency" (1927).

40. Conley, *Melancholy Accidents*; O'Donnell, "Killing in Ireland at the Turn of the Centuries"; O'Connell, "Violence and Social Memory in Twentieth-Century Belfast." Each caveated the highly influential Elias, *The Civilizing Process*.

41. Doyle, *Fighting Like the Devil for the Sake of God*, 1–13.

42. For more on the nuances of masculinity and queerness, see chapters 3 and 4.

43. Houlbrook, *Queer London*, 177–179.

44. Upchurch, *Before Wilde*, 47–48, and chapter 1 more broadly is a rich treatment of the family and queerness in working-class families.

45. "106 West Acre (Harrow, Middlesex)," *Census of England and Wales 1901*. Milligen's father was heavily involved in local unionist culture: "Death of Mr. John M Milligen," *Northern Whig*, September 19, 1947, 3. For Milligen's philanthropy, see "Belgian Refugee Relief Fund," *Northern Whig*, March 8, 1915, 8; and "Lambeg National School," *Northern Whig*, May 13, 1916, 3.

46. "Edgar Milligen—Gross Indecency" (1917).

47. "Belfast Commission of April 8 1930," Crown Book; and "General Register, Male Prisoners" (1929–1941), 90. Unfortunately, no depositions from the case survive.

48. "Kaiser-I-Hind Leaving London (November 21 1930)"—the National Archives (London).

49. Aldrich, *Cultural Encounters and Homoeroticism in Sri Lanka*, chapters 1, 2, and 4. For the allure of the colonies for queer opportunity more broadly, see Aldrich, *Colonialism and Homosexuality*.

50. The house was sold in 1921—*Belfast News-Letter*, June 13, 1919, 10; "Edgar Milligen, Died January 17 1939."

51. "The De Cobain Scandal," *Cardiff Times*, September 26, 1891, 4. For more on de Cobain and also Richard Lutton, a middle-aged private secretary of Lord Mayor Daniel Dixon who told the police, "You are taking my life . . . I'll be ruined," see chapter 6. "James McKee and Richard Lutton—Assault and Buggery" (1904).

52. "Thomas O'Connor and David McDonald—Assault and Theft" (1902).

53. "Alleged Indecent Offence," *Northern Whig*, June 5, 1902, 2.

54. The Dublin Castle Scandal was reported in depth in Belfast's dailies: see "The Dublin Scandals," *Belfast News-Letter*, November 1, 1884. For context: Earls, "Unnatural Offenses of English Import"; Cocks, *Nameless Offences*, 135–154; Steele and de Nie, "Introduction"; Larkin, "'Green Shoots' of the New Journalism in the *Freeman's Journal*." Chapter 6 analyzes the cultural politics of these scandals.

55. "James Magee and William Seaton—Assault and Attempted Buggery" (1898).

56. Attempted bribe—"Named Individual—Buggery" (1953); clinging to streetlamp to resist arrest—"James McKee and Richard Lutton—Assault and Buggery" (1904); and countless examples of trying to run away, such as "James Magee and William Seaton—Assault and Attempted Buggery" (1898).

57. See discussion in the introduction. For the censorship culture in the 1920s and 1930s, see Martin, *Censorship in the Two Irelands*, 62–63. There was a similar silence in the Scottish press—see Meek, *Queer Voices in Post-War Scotland*, 23–24, 37.

58. See, for example, cases from England: "Clergyman Sent to Hard Labour," *Northern Whig*, November 13, 1905, 9; and "Serious Charges against Country Gentleman," *Northern Whig*, November 13, 1924, 7. More broadly, Lawless and Breathnach, "Homosexuality and Lesbianism in Irish Newspapers," 182–184. For fears about lurid British papers, Martin, *Censorship in the Two Irelands*, 31–32.

59. See Bingham, *Family Newspapers?* 173–180. See "Missioner on Trial in Belfast," *Belfast Telegraph*, November 28, 1925, 4. *News of the World*, which was by far the most explicit British newspaper on homosexuality in the interwar era, had a special

weekly edition (the national edition being banned) imported into Northern Ireland by Eason's, but in the 1930s there were only one to two thousand copies in circulation—Rafter, "The Irish Edition," 183.

60. Patrick O'Donoghue, "New R.M. for Belfast," *Northern Whig*, April 27, 1925, 12; and, for his comments, "Must Go to Commission," *Belfast Telegraph*, August 19, 1925, 3. In the Irish Free State there was also an "official cognitive dissonance" emanating from a desire to dampen fears that purity was widely at risk, which led judges to profess shock about the existence of same-sex encounters despite frequently presiding over such cases. See Earls, "Queering Dublin," 57.

61. Lord Justice William Moore—"Belfast City Commission," *Belfast News-Letter*, November 28, 1925, 13; "Lord Justice's Regret," *Belfast Telegraph*, November 28, 1925, 4.

62. McCormick, *Regulating Sexuality*, 27–28.

63. Nash and Kilday, *Cultures of Shame*, 9. In another challenge to Elias's "civilizing process," Nash and Kilday emphasize that practices of "shame" (usually deemed premodern, communally sanctioned, and internalized) were not always replaced by "guilt" cultures (modern, individualized, and possible to overcome through self-growth) and remained a tool of shaping behavior into the twentieth century. Work on Irish female sexuality has certainly demonstrated this longevity: Fischer, "Gender, Nation, and the Politics of Shame."

64. Erber and Robb, "Introduction," 7. See especially "Serious Charge at the Recorder's Court," *Irish News and Belfast Morning News*, September 23, 1904, 8, following the arrest of Richard Lutton—discussed in more detail in chapter 6.

65. McLaverty, *Lost Fields*, 27, 39; McLaverty, *The Three Brothers*, 18–19, 117.

66. King, *The Silken Twine*; O'Connell, "An Age of Conservative Modernity;" Boyd, *Out of My Class*, 17–18, 31, 69; Blood, *Watch My Lips, I'm Speaking!*, 26–27.

67. Pled for "mercy" because he was a widow's son—"George Davidson—Gross Indecency" (1911); cried "it will break my sister's heart"—"Robert Smith and John Reid—Gross Indecency" (1927); and so afraid of a brother finding out that he tried bribing the man who caught him—"William Ritchie and Samuel Coulter—Gross Indecency" (1932).

68. Cohen, *Family Secrets*, 157.

69. "Named Individual—Buggery" (1953). In 1927, after convicting a man for gross indecency, a judge similarly stated that "the tragedy of the affair was the respectability of the younger prisoner's parents." "Indecency," *Northern Whig*, July 26, 1927, 8.

70. Conrad, *Locked in the Family Cell*, 3–4, building on Backus, *The Gothic Family Romance*.

71. "Acquitted of a Serious Charge," *Irish News and Belfast Morning News*, September 10, 1909, 7.

72. "Nutshell News," *Wicklow News-Letter and County Advertiser*, July 10, 1909, 3.

73. "SS Lake Erie, Departing Belfast September 30 1909 Bound for Quebec & Montreal," and "196 Worthington, North Bay City (Nipissing, Ontario)," and "153 Northcliffe Boulevard, York Township (Ontario)," *Census of Canada 1911*.

74. Alexander Gibson was humiliated in extensive press coverage of his cross-dressing and less than three months later emigrated to the United States, where he married and had children: "The Constable and the Militiaman," *Northern Whig*,

September 1, 1908, 9; and "*SS Caledonia*, Departing Londonderry December 26 1908 Bound for New York," and "359 Hubbard Street, Chicago (Cook County, Illinois)," *US Census 1940*. See also William Gray, discussed at the opening of chapter 2, who emigrated to live with his sister in 1926 after being released from prison following a heavily reported trial; they lived together for the rest of his life. For context: Earner-Byrne, "The Family in Ireland," 648; Murphy, "The Fionnuala Factor," 99; and Clear, *Social Change and Everyday Life in Ireland*, 63–69.

75. Davidoff, *Thicker Than Water*, 16; Morgan, *Family Connections*.

76. Upchurch, *Before Wilde*, 22. For theorizing communal support more broadly, see Bourke, *Working Class Cultures in Britain*, 123; Jones, *The Working Class in Mid Twentieth-Century England*, 154.

77. Siblings "share[d] the old while experiencing the new" in times of social change, acting as "shock absorbers," Hemphill, *Siblings*,108–109.

78. Of those charged in Belfast between 1890 and 1958, fifty-eight were broadly working class and twenty were middle class or higher (I have excluded cases recorded only in prison registers; encounters that involved under-sixteens; and two assault cases where the charge of same-sex desire was a defendant's counterclaim). Men could bail themselves by the early 1950s.

79. "Belfast City Commission," *Belfast News-Letter*, November 28, 1925, 13. I have found one case of bail-skipping: Hull, a porter, who apparently disappeared to the United States, in "Edward Hull and William Johnston—Gross Indecency" (1900).

80. See, as examples: McCormick, from a grocer and well-off draper close by in "John McCormick and Hugh Dunlop—Gross Indecency" (1909); and from a publican of his boyhood neighborhood, "Henry Blair—Gross Indecency" (1939).

81. Excluding four cases where the bailer is unrecorded, and it is not always possible to ascertain kinship connections when men had married into the accused's family (and so had a different surname).

82. "James Dougan—Gross Indecency with a Minor" (1931). When Dougan's mother died twelve years later, he was still unmarried and living in the family home, "Letitia Dougan, died September 30 1943." Married women could not act as sureties because their "recognisance cannot be estreated." See Atteridge, *Royal Ulster Constabulary Constables' Guide*, 65.

83. The charge was eventually withdrawn: "Named Individual and John Ernest Ashfield–Gross Indecency" (1935). Because of his age, I have not included this case in my statistics above. The only adult son bailed out, by his middle-class father, is "Named Individual—Buggery" (1953).

84. Frost, "'I Am Master Here'"; Purvis, "Irish Fatherhood in the Twentieth Century," 209–210; Upchurch, *Before Wilde*, 25–26; and, for the tensions and changes in fatherhood, King, *Family Men*, chapter 5.

85. Alexander Gibson, discussed in endnotes above; and "John Riddell—Gross Indecency" (1925).

86. For brothers-in-law see George Caldwell, who, after the second time he was arrested, was bailed by Isaac Todd (with whom he also lived alongside his sister): "George Caldwell—Buggery" (1913). For uncles as a "precious resource," see Davidoff, *Thicker Than Water*, chapter 7; examples of money given from rural uncles: "William Ayer Otherwise O'Neill Christie—Assault and Buggery" (1892); and George Davidson, Hulme, "Queering Family History." There was a man bailed out by his

brother in 1947, but because this was an encounter between an adult man and a thirteen-year-old schoolboy I have not included him in the statistics here, "Named Individual—Gross Indecency and Buggery" (1947).

87. For "mutual aid" and rural kinship, see Gray, "The Circulation of Children in Rural Ireland"; and social studies of Arensberg and Kimball, *Family and Community in Ireland*, and Leyton, *The One Blood*.

88. For theorizing "mutual support" see Kidd, *State, Society and the Poor in Nineteenth-Century England*, chapter 4. Examples from Belfast: O'Connell, "Conservative Modernity," 272; Blood, *Watch My Lips, I'm Speaking!*, 26–27; and Simms, *Farewell to the Hammer*, 128. For notes on communal protection of queer men in Dublin, see Earls, "Queering Dublin," 111–112.

89. Smith, from the Shankill, received bail from a next-door neighbor in his father's trade and a barman across the road, "Joseph Smith and George Caldwell—Gross Indecency" (1912); *Belfast and Ulster Directory* (Belfast, 1910).

90. See "William Ritchie and Samuel Coulter—Gross Indecency" (1932); and "Edward Hull and William Johnston—Gross Indecency" (1900).

91. See, for example, a foreman given £20, "Thomas Carrick and Samuel Ramsey—Gross Indecency" (1926), discussed in depth in the following chapter.

92. Bourke, *Working Class Cultures in Britain*, was the most critical and was tempered by Jones, *The Working Class in Mid Twentieth-Century England*, which unpacked the complexities of working-class memory. For Belfast and community, see O'Connell, "The Troubles with a Lower-Case t," 224–225; and Hepburn, *A Past Apart*, for segregation/community.

93. For O'Neill and McDonald—"House 1 and House 3 in Ludlow Street (Dock Ward, Antrim)," *Census of Ireland 1911*; for Mary Ann O'Neill (nee McDonald), "House 3 in Hardinge Street (Dock Ward, Antrim)," *Census of Ireland 1911*; "Alexander McDonald and Sarah O'Neill, married December 3 1913, Belfast"; and "General Register, Male Prisoners" (1926–1929), 202.

94. "James O'Neill—Gross Indecency" (1928).

95. Sailortown especially was a microcosm of the tentatively accepting queer scenes of dockside districts in London. See Houlbrook, *Queer London*, 160, and chapter 2.

96. Galway, *An Autobiography*, 17–18.

97. Simms, *Farewell to the Hammer*, 127. See memories of a relative, Joseph Dillon, who "minced rather than walked" around the Falls with his dachshund in the 1950s, Dillon, *Crossing the Line*, 25. For context, Davidoff, *Thicker Than Water*, 8. There is similar evidence in the tough working-class Valleys of Wales, though other queer men found the masculine atmosphere oppressive—see Leeworthy, *A Little Gay History of Wales*, 6–12, 52–53.

98. For workplaces: Smith, *Masculinity, Class and Same-Sex Desire in Industrial England*, chapter 4; for respectability, Weeks, *The World We Have Won*, chapter 2. "George Hogg—Buggery" (1925). For the importance of toughness to masculinity for working-class men, see Davies, "Youth Gangs, Masculinity and Violence in Late-Victorian Manchester and Salford."

99. For similar accommodation of queerness, see working-class Sheffield in Wells, "Male-to-Female Cross-Dressing in Yorkshire," 71–72; and trans men in rural or small-town America, Skidmore, *True Sex*.

100. Murphy, "Gender and the Irish Family," 12; and Earner-Byrne and Urquhart, "Gender Roles in Ireland Since 1740," 315.

101. "House 43 in Convention (Victoria, Down)" and "House 47 in Central Street (Victoria Down)," *Census of Ireland 1901*; "House 28 in Cuba Street (Victoria, Down)," *Census of Ireland* 1911; "Mary Spence, died February 1 1910, Belfast," "James Spence, died July 8 1905, Belfast." Their other children were living with paternal grandparents. See "House 5 in Central Street (Victoria, Down)," *Census of Ireland 1911*.

102. See, for example, a middle-aged mechanic who lived with his widowed niece, her children, and boarders after his conviction in the 1890s; when he died, she was present at the death. "Archibald Black and Alfred Shaw—Assault" (1891); "House 41 in Moscow Street (Shankill, Antrim)," *Census of Ireland 1901*; "Archibald Black, died January 28 1903, Belfast."

103. Fries, "Two Hundred Years of English Death Notices," 57, 70.

104. See Hulme, "Queering Family History."

105. "David Purse and Sharman Stevenson—Gross Indecency" (1932). Bail money also came from another local neighborhood man.

106. "Deaths," *Belfast Telegraph*, March 28, 1938, 13. See "Deaths," *Belfast Telegraph*, August 24, 1923, 9, for evidence of the Purse family in the Orange Order, and *Belfast and Ulster Directory* (Belfast, 1931).

107. "Thanks," *Belfast Telegraph*, April 4, 1938, 13.

108. See Guinnane, *The Vanishing Irish*, and Clear, *Social Change and Everyday Life in Ireland*, 81–82.

109. Davidoff, *Thicker Than Water*, 138. See William Gray, George Davidson, and George Caldwell—who appear throughout this book—who all lived with their sisters. For the Dillon siblings, see Dillon, *Crossing the Line*, 28; and for a British example, Joe Ackerley and his sister's influence—described in Cook, *Queer Domesticities*, 123.

110. Erskine's nephews provided bail in 1914 when he was arrested aged sixty-three, and one was present at his death five years later, "Alexander Erskine and John Albert Kingston—Gross Indecency" (1914), and "Alexander Erskine, died February 22 1919, Belfast." William Shaw, who lived with his mother and then sister/brother-in-law for decades after a conviction, died with his nephew present in 1967; his nephew maintained a gravestone that listed his uncle alongside his mother and father: "John Kingston and William Shaw—Gross Indecency" (1926); "Margaret Power, died April 29 1929, Belfast"; "William Shaw, died January 17 1967, Belfast"; "Plot U1792," Find a Grave Memorial ID: 225195833.

111. Calvert and O'Riordan, "Introduction," 4. This has been an important argument of sociologically based work; see Connolly, "Locating the Irish Family," and Ryan-Flood, "Staying Connected."

112. Kennedy, *Cottage to Creche*, 2–3, and Urquhart, "Gender, Family, and Sexuality," 246.

113. "Vincent Cassidy—Buggery" (1917), and Hulme, "Queer Belfast." See also: an adolescent boy removed from a bed in the boardinghouse his mother ran after an older man made a complaint, only to be reported to the police a few months later for again making a move on a laborer occupying a different bed, "William Magill—Buggery" (1894). Roger Casement also socialized with his boyfriend's mother at their home, as mentioned in chapter 1.

114. See Karczewski, "'Call Me by My Name,'" 648.

115. "August 11 1937," *PDDS*. This young man, Frederick Howard Aicken (discussed more in chap. 4), remained close to his sister Louie throughout his life. He would bring different male friends when visiting her, after both had relocated to England, though his homosexuality remained tactfully unspoken. These memories were kindly provided via email by his nephew, Basil Abbott.

116. Koven, *Slumming*, chapters 2 and 5.

117. Delap, "'Disgusting Details Which Are Best Forgotten,'" 98–104; Backus, "'Things That Have the Potential to Go Horribly Wrong.'"

118. Boyd, *Out of My Class*, 82–94.

119. McCormick, *Regulating Sexuality*, 102. For memories of no sexual discussion within families: Blood, *Watch My Lips, I'm Speaking!*, 32, and Simms, *Farewell to the Hammer*, 66–68.

120. "December 9 1932," *PDDS*.

121. John Murray was a baker in Co. Armagh before migrating to Belfast to work as an industrial painter after Jack was born; Strain found him work as a builder. "House 18 Corporation (Armagh Rural, Armagh)," *Census of Ireland 1911*; "January 4 1933," "April 28 1933," *PDDS*.

122. See Billy McBride, an eighteen-year-old, whose mother had seen that David Strain was selling a garage and "thought it would do" for her son. "July 29 1939," *PDDS*. See also economic motivations discussed in chapter 4.

123. See chapter 3 for more on the development of these knowledges and identities.

124. "June 6 1929," "January 16 1934," *PDDS*. The woman was Ethel Norwood, as discussed in chapter 4.

125. "November 30 1933," *PDDS*.

126. Cohen, *Family Secrets*, 157. See, for the American equivalent, Syrett, *An Open Secret*. There are brief memories of the "open secret" in the 1940s in Pettitt, "Queering Broadcast Boundaries," 207–208.

127. "October 10 1938," *PDDS*.

128. Walter Smith—discussed in chapter 4—lived with his mother until her death in 1938 and stayed there until his own passing several decades later. "House 45 in Dunluce Avenue (Windsor, Antrim)," *Census of Ireland 1911*; "November 10 1935," *PDDS*; "Walter Edward Ferguson Smith, died November 22 1962, Belfast." For an elite who benefited from the open secret, see Peter Montgomery in Hulme and Lynch, "Queer Men and Networks of Communication." For more focus on the subjectivities of bachelors, see the emerging work of Piers Haslam, such as Haslam, "Debating the Bachelor Tax."

129. Plummer, *Telling Sexual Stories*, chapter 6.

130. "David Purse and Sharman Stevenson—Gross Indecency" (1932).

131. "Recorded Sentences," *Belfast Telegraph*, February 25, 1932, 13; "November 29 1931," *PDDS*.

132. "Deaths," *Northern Whig*, April 1, 1950, 4; "Belfast Postman Leaves Farm to 'Faithful Friend,'" *Belfast Telegraph*, September 6, 1950, 7. That the *Telegraph* framed their story like this suggests something queer about Stevenson's decision to leave everything to a male friend rather than a relative.

133. See the discussion of character references in chapter 6.

134. Richard Lutton left a substantial £2,000 to All Saints' Church, University Street, "Notice of Charitable Bequests," *Belfast News-Letter*, February 28, 1936, 1. Samuel Ramsey, a teacher, gave a more modest £50 to the Presbyterian Church in Ireland's Orphan Society and his local Woodvale Presbyterian Church—"Notice of Charitable Bequests," *Northern Whig*, October 11, 1927, 1.

135. Cook, *Queer Domesticities*, 89, has stressed the "malleability" of the British family in this sense in late nineteenth to mid-twentieth centuries, and Upchurch, *Before Wilde*, chapter 1, has found many similar expressions of support/compassion in Britain in the early nineteenth century.

136. Waters, "The Homosexual as a Social Being in Britain." The British capital was at the center of the panics—Houlbrook, *Queer London*, 236–239.

137. Bingham, *Family Newspapers?*, 180–188; Waters, "Disorders of the Mind, Disorders of the Body Social," 139–140; and Bengry, "Profit (f)or the Public Good?"

138. Bengry, "Queer Profits."

139. Lewis, *Wolfenden's Witnesses*, 3–10.

140. See, for example, the expansive reporting in "Homosexuality Discussed by House of Lords," *Belfast News-Letter*, May 20, 1954, 6. Meek notes how the Wolfenden Report led to similar public debate for the first time in the Scottish press—Meek, *Queer Voices in Post-War Scotland*, 43.

141. Savage, *A Loss of Innocence?* chapter 1.

142. "Premier to Approach B.B.C. on Sex Broadcasts," *Belfast Telegraph*, December 4, 1957, 11.

143. "Our M.P.s Were Right to Protest," *Belfast Telegraph*, December 9, 1957, 3.

144. Ferriter, *Occasions of Sin*, 327–323. Mort, *Capital Affairs*, explicitly traces the birth of the permissive society to these shifts in the 1950s, including scandals and new understandings of homosexuality. Pettitt, "Queering Broadcast Boundaries," demonstrates how the axing of a queer character in a Northern Irish sitcom in the 1950s reflected this cultural instability.

145. Urquhart, "Gender, Family, and Sexuality," 245.

146. Upchurch, *Before Wilde*, 45, 48.

147. Weeks, "Queer(y)ing the 'Modern Homosexual,'" 526–527.

148. Johnson, *Just Queer Folks*, 109, for benevolent toleration; and Hoggart, *The Uses of Literacy*, as discussed in Smith, *Masculinity, Class and Same-Sex Desire in Industrial England*, 89–90, for "living and let live."

149. Conrad, *Locked in the Family Cell*, 9. See also Crowley and Kitchin, "Producing 'decent girls.'" For workplaces: Smith, *Masculinity, Class and Same-Sex Desire in Industrial England*, chapter 4.

6. Ulster's Manliness on Trial

1. "John Sterling and William Gray—Gross Indecency" (1925).

2. "Thomas Carrick and Samuel Ramsey—Gross Indecency" (1926).

3. "Order for the Completion of the Back Street between Dunluce Avenue and Ulsterville Avenue," *Northern Whig*, May 9, 1924, 5; "What Firms Have Done," *Belfast Telegraph*, August 29, 1940, 3; "Balmoral Club's Annual Meeting," *Northern Whig*, March 31, 1927, 4; "House 7 in Osborne Park (Windsor Ward, Antrim)", *Cen-*

sus of Ireland 1911; "Vote for Harcourt," *Northern Whig*, March 13, 1925, 1; "Death of Comm. Harcourt," *Belfast Telegraph*, November 16, 1943, 3. For golf and unionism, see Dooley, "The Big House, Aristocracy, and Golf in Ireland," 114.

4. See Phoenix, *Northern Nationalism*.

5. "Samuel Ramsay, died June 25 1927, Belfast." For Carrick: "Deeply Regretted," *Northern Whig*, December 1, 1948, 2; "What Firms Have Done," *Belfast Telegraph*, August 29, 1940, 3; "Deeply Regretted," *Northern Whig*, December 1, 1948, 2.

6. Cocks, "Trials of Character," and Upchurch, *Before Wilde*, chapter 1. More broadly, Donovan, *Respectability on Trial*.

7. Barclay, *Men on Trial*; Steinbach, "The Melodramatic Contract."

8. John Tosh, drawing on sociologist R. W. Connell, popularized "hegemonic masculinity" in historical research—Tosh, *Manliness and Masculinities in Nineteenth-Century Britain*, 43–44 especially; and critique by Bristow, "Remapping the Sites of Modern Gay History," 129–130. Scott, "Gender," was foundational for encouraging historians to think about the power dynamics of gender as a relational category. For British respectability culture more broadly see Thompson, *The Rise of Respectable Society*; Collini, *Public Moralists*; Roper and Tosh, *Manful Assertions*; Johnson, *Middle-Class Life in Victorian Belfast*, 197–201, demonstrates these ideas in the north of Ireland. For women's respectability in relation to men, see Cronin, "'You'd Be Disgraced!'"

9. Cocks, *Nameless Offences*, made this point for middle-class men, and Brady, *Masculinity and Male Homosexuality in Britain*, 21, extended the analysis to working-class witnesses and defendants. The same logic was apparent for other crimes in Ireland—see Doyle and O'Callaghan, *Capital Punishment in Independent Ireland*, 139–141, and Black, *Gender and Punishment in Ireland*, 50.

10. Tosh, *Manliness and Masculinities in Nineteenth-Century Britain*, 37–38. Smith has shown how these attributes were more important than sexual desires when it came to incorporating queer men into industrial working-class communities. See Smith, *Masculinity, Class and Same-Sex Desire in Industrial England*, chapter 4.

11. "Criminal Business," *Belfast News-Letter*, October 29, 1885, 3; "Criminal Business," *Northern Whig*, October 31, 1885, 7.

12. "Serious Charge at the Recorder's Court," *Irish News and Belfast Morning News*, September 23, 1904, 8; "Named Individual—Buggery" (1953). See also a representative of United States Shipping Board giving a character reference for an American sailor: "Sidney Day—Attempted Buggery and Gross Indecency" (1926); "The Balsam's Steering Gear," *North Down Herald and County Down Independent*, June 9, 1923, 3.

13. Ferriter, *Occasions of Sin*, 41. For working-class "breadwinning" masculinity, see McClelland, "Masculinity and the 'Representative Artisan' in Britain."

14. See Rev. Herbert Clements speaking for Samuel Coulter—"Crown Book, Indictment and Pleas, Belfast City Commission" (1930–1932); Rev. John McIlveen for Joseph Rea—"Crown Book, Indictment and Pleas, Belfast Assizes" (Summer 1913); and a reverend (whom I will leave unnamed for reasons of privacy) who sent a letter on behalf of a young man—"Named Individual—Buggery" (1953). For religion and respectability, see Johnson, *Middle-Class Life in Victorian Belfast*, 197–201.

15. A mother for her son: "James McKee and Richard Lutton—Assault and Buggery" (1904). Other family members served as character references, such as mothers,

fathers, sisters, and brothers-in-law, during the Belfast Scandal: "County of Antrim Crown Book" (1890–1895), 9–13. For illness as an excuse for theft, "Northern Law Courts," *Belfast News-Letter*, December 16, 1932, 3; for good character despite theft, "The City Commission," *Belfast News-Letter*, July 25, 1925, 10; and for a mother saying her "good boy" was corrupted by friends, "Youth's Savings Frauds," *Belfast Telegraph*, October 27, 1948, 2.

16. See "Joseph Smith and George Caldwell—Gross Indecency" (1912); "Nine Months for Assault," *Belfast News-Letter*, December 3, 1925, 12; "Ulster Assizes," *Belfast News-Letter*, December 9, 1937, 11; and "William Nelson and Named Individual—Buggery" (1959).

17. See Tosh, "Masculinities in an Industrializing Society," 331, drawing on Clark, *The Struggle for the Breeches*, and McClelland, "England's Greatness, the Working Man."

18. "Criminal Business," *Belfast News-Letter*, October 29, 1885, 3; "Criminal Business," *Northern Whig*, October 31, 1885, 7; "Charge against a Belfast Constable," *Belfast Weekly News*, September 3, 1908, 5.

19. "Trial of de Cobain," *Irish News and Belfast Morning News*, March 22, 1893, 6.

20. Cocks, "Trials of Character," 37; Cocks, *Nameless Offences*, 118–119.

21. "The Charge against a Corporation Official," *Northern Whig*, September 10, 1909, 2. The newspaper description was euphemistic; Sinton was charged under the Vagrancy Act (1824), which made provisions for public genital exposure, but he was reported to the police by another man, which suggests importuning. The Vagrancy Act (1898) had clauses for male importuning but was not extended to Ireland until 1912, though Vagrancy Acts were generally methods of policing hard-to-define crimes (if rarely in Belfast, from what I have found). See Cook, *London and the Culture of Homosexuality*, 43–44.

22. "A Successful Appeal," *Belfast News-Letter*, September 10, 1909, 5; "Acquitted of a Serious Charge," *Irish News and Belfast Morning News*, September 10, 1909, 7.

23. "Soldier Sentenced for Assault," *Northern Whig*, January 12, 1940, 7.

24. "William McMullan—Buggery" (1924). For a man recommended to mercy for a boardinghouse proposition: "James Patterson—Assault and Attempted Buggery" (1894). For inconsistency in leniency, see three similar cases prosecuted by Justice Best with starkly different punishments: "The City Commission," *Belfast News-Letter*, July 26, 1927, 9.

25. For the deserter, see "Vincent Cassidy—Buggery" (1917)—though Cassidy was still convicted, likely because of the additional testimony from a more respectable witness. For the uncouth youths, see the newsboy witnesses described in Hulme, "Queer Belfast." For drunken unemployed criminals, "John McCormick and Hugh Dunlop—Gross Indecency" (1909).

26. "Thomas O'Connor and David McDonald—Assault and Theft" (1902). Frequent court cases demonstrate that there were also illegally operated drinking establishments and drunken violence in this street, and a danger of theft for visiting sailors. See, for example, "Life in Clarke's Lane," *Belfast Telegraph*, August 25, 1905, 4; "Assault on a Woman," *Belfast News-Letter*, April 7, 1910, 4; and "Belfast Police Courts," *Northern Whig*, March 23, 1909, 3.

27. "Crown Book, Recorder's Court" (1901–1904), 110; "Thomas O'Connor and David McDonald—Assault and Theft" (1902).

28. Cocks, "Trials of Character," 41–43.

29. For the nineteenth century, Cocks, *Nameless Offences*, 115–116, and for the interwar period, McLaren, *Sexual Blackmail*, 4–6.

30. "James O'Neill—Gross Indecency" (1928); "Crown Book, Indictment and Pleas, Belfast City Commission" (July 21, 1928). For a useful investigation of how judges and others in the legal system contested or resisted arrests through entrapment, see Lvovsky, *Vice Patrol*.

31. "David Straight—Gross Indecency" (1925), the effeminate mill worker discussed further in chapter 5; "William Ritchie and Samuel Coulter—Gross Indecency" (1932); and "James Douglas—Assault and Attempted Buggery" (1894).

32. "The Tyrone Blackmailer," *Belfast Telegraph*, December 22, 1933, 3; "Coalisland Blackmail Charge," *Mid-Ulster Mail*, May 27, 1933, 5.

33. My statistics do not include the cases mentioned only in prison registers (where ascertaining witnesses is not possible), encounters that involved boys under sixteen, or clearly violent sexual assaults.

34. McLaren, *The Trials of Masculinity*, 37–38.

35. Conley, *Melancholy Accidents*, 6; Earls, "Queering Dublin," 109–110. For similar concerns about perjuring policemen in England, see Allen, *The Law of Evidence in Victorian England*, 163–164.

36. "Joseph Smith and George Caldwell—Gross Indecency" (1912). "Assize Intelligence," *Northern Whig*, March 27, 1912, 10. Judges were appalled when juries refused to convict. Conley, *Melancholy Accidents*, 38.

37. The only case where conviction did not follow when both the police and someone else witnessed the crime was due to said witness not turning up to court, leading to a declination to prosecute. "George Caldwell—Buggery" (1913).

38. Shapiro, *Beyond Reasonable Doubt and Probable Cause*.

39. For more on this lag, see chapter 3.

40. McLaren, *The Trials of Masculinity*, 135.

41. See Waters, "Havelock Ellis, Sigmund Freud and the State," and Dickinson, *"Curing Queers,"* 22–23.

42. The same was true in the Irish Free State—Kelly, *Hearing Voices*, 155–158. The Irish Psycho-Analytical Association, established 1942, still had only five practicing members in the early 1960s—Kelly, "Ego, Id, and Ireland," 281. Recent work, however, has suggested "hundreds" of people still encountered Freudian psychoanalysis through practitioners in Dublin after 1928—Campbell, "Freud in Dublin?" 127.

43. "Joseph Rea and Thomas Magee—Gross Indecency" (1913). Rea's doctor told the court he had known Rea "practically" all his life but probably neglected to mention they were also in the same cricket club or that he had treated Rea on the previous occasions he had been suspiciously assaulted by working-class men—"Cricket," *Belfast News-Letter*, March 24, 1909, 3, and "An Extraordinary Case," *Irish News and Belfast Morning News*, October 10 1902, 6. The lack of more "insanity pleas" for adult same-sex offenses is striking, given how asylum committal marked out the boundaries of normal behavior in post-famine Ireland—Finnane, *Insanity and the Insane in Post-Famine Ireland*. Future work on the sketchy institutional records of asylums may reveal answers.

44. "Named Individual—Gross Indecency and Buggery" (1947).

45. See, for example, "Samuel Stewart—Buggery" (1949), and "Edward Graham and Samuel Curry—Buggery" (1935). For medical evidence and its origins in venere-

ology, and the lack of certainty it involved, see Crozier, "The Medical Construction of Homosexuality," 66–73.

46. "Recorded Sentences," *Belfast Telegraph*, February 25, 1932, 13.

47. "An Unnatural Crime," *Northern Whig*, July 14, 1891, 3; "Archibald Black and Alfred Shaw—Assault" (1891).

48. Other men who received stronger sentences upon a second arrest include: George Davidson—see Hulme, "Queering Family History"; John Kingston, the lover of Alexander Erskine, and Edgar Milligen, both discussed later in this chapter; and John O'Neill, a middle-aged man who received twelve months for trying to procure an act of gross indecency with a twelve-year-old newsboy (the judge lamented his "fearful" record)—"Mis-Directed Skill," *Northern Whig*, April 10, 1930, 11, and "John O'Neill—Attempted Gross Indecency with a Minor" (1930). For context: Cocks, "Trials of Character," 45–46.

49. In 1894, a fifteen-year-old pled guilty to attempting buggery with older men and was sentenced to six months in prison with hard labor: "William Magill—Buggery" (1894), and "Crown Book, Recorder's Court" (1888–1894), 330. The law stipulated that under-sixteens be tried in the juvenile court unless they were charged alongside someone older than sixteen. Whether boys were frequently sentenced through the juvenile court with lesser sentences for having relations with each other is difficult to know because comprehensive records survive for only the 1950s onward. See Government of Northern Ireland, *The Protection and Welfare of the Young*, 31, 40–42.

50. See "Named Individual and John Ernest Ashfield—Gross Indecency" (1935); "Crown Book Indictment and Pleas, Belfast City Commission" (1933–1936); "Took Money But Did Not Steal It," *Belfast News-Letter*, April 11, 1935, 13; and "James Dougan—Gross Indecency with a Minor" (1931).

51. Hugh Sheehan, for example, in his early twenties and only a couple of years younger than his lover, described the mutuality of their relationship but was still treated as a witness—see Hulme, "Queer Belfast." Conley suggests that in comparison to Victorian England, the Irish courts were not often swayed by the defense claiming provocation for rape or sexual assault. Conley, *Melancholy Accidents*, 90–105.

52. Cocks, "Trials of Character," 28.

53. This discursive formation, emanating first from late-Victorian British scandals such as W. T. Stead's Maiden Tribute of Modern Babylon, was powerful in Ireland in the first half of the twentieth century, in the Irish Free State in particular, though the silence around homosexuality limited interventions (and covered up abuses in Catholic institutions). See Valente and Backus, *The Child Sex Scandal and Modern Irish Literature*.

54. For coaching, see Maynard, "Horrible Temptations." For young males as victims in contemporary discourse, see Egan and Hawkes, "Imperiled and Perilous," 355–367, and Bates, *Sexual Forensics in Victorian and Edwardian England*, 159–167.

55. "George Caldwell—Buggery" (1913). For more on these boys, see chapter 4.

56. An exception: Hugh Dunlop claimed to have been paid but was still punished: "John McCormick and Hugh Dunlop—Gross Indecency" (1909).

57. See: the twelve-year-old and his eighteen-year-old friend who sold sex in public toilets—"Named individuals—Gross Indecency" (1937); and a seventeen-year-old discovered having sex with an older man, seemingly unpaid, "Named individual—Gross Indecency" (1937). For the social scientific debate, see Fisher and Funke,

"The Age of Attraction," 267–269. For the late-Victorian shift in the use of the law and its effects on treatment of juvenile offenders, see Wiener, *Reconstructing the Criminal*, 202, 285–294, and, for its effects into the twentieth century, 358–365, 380. For the shift in Britain in the 1920s in relation to treating boys as incapable of consent, see Houlbrook, *Queer London*, 234–236. Northern Ireland naturally lagged behind, especially after legal change in Britain in the 1920s, see *The Protection and Welfare of the Young and the Treatment of Young Offenders*, 38.

58. "Francis Wadman—Buggery" (1950); "Samuel Stewart—Buggery" (1949).

59. Tosh, *Manliness and Masculinities in Nineteenth-Century Britain*, 75; Wiener, *Reconstructing the Criminal*, 38–40.

60. "John Sterling and William Gray—Gross Indecency" (1925); "William Ritchie and Samuel Coulter—Gross Indecency" (1932); "Archibald Black and Alfred Shaw—Assault" (1891).

61. "Drink Is the Parent of Immorality," *Witness*, November 8, 1918, 1. See McCormick, *Regulating Sexuality*, 53–54.

62. Chauncey, "Christian Brotherhood or Sexual Perversion?" 202; Mauger, "From 'Pledge' to 'Public Health,'" 526–527. More broadly, Reidy, *Criminal Irish Drunkards*, and Malcolm, *"Ireland Sober, Ireland Free."* The eugenics influence did not result in a strong professional following—Jones, "Eugenics in Ireland," 81–95.

63. Ferriter, *Occasions of Sin*, 9; Kilcommins et al., *Crime, Punishment and the Search for Order in Ireland*, 24; McAuley, "The Intoxication Defence in Criminal Law," 249–253; Conley, *Melancholy Accidents*, 29.

64. "Crown Book Indictment and Pleas, Belfast City Commission" (1933–1936); "Commission Cases," *Northern Whig*, April 11, 1935, 11. This happened in other cases too, such as a convicted thief; "Promise to Take Pledge," *Belfast Telegraph*, April 9, 1932, 3. See also a middle-aged former championship boxer who received a recorded sentence, despite being found guilty of aggressively trying to pay a twelve-year-old boy for sex; his solicitor convinced the judge that his life went downhill after he "took to drink, and his friends disowned him." "Recorded Sentences," *Belfast Telegraph*, February 25, 1932, 13.

65. "Sidney Day—Attempted Buggery and Gross Indecency" (1926); "Archibald Black and Alfred Shaw—Assault" (1891). For the lack of guidance on inebriation, Conley, *Melancholy Accidents*, 28–29.

66. For the late-Victorian origins of social policy that respected circumstances as well as character, and the movement of this discourse of "causalism" into criminal policy in the early twentieth century, see Wiener, *Reconstructing the Criminal*, 201–214, 224–244, chapter 9.

67. Hulme and Lynch, "Queer Men and Networks of Communication in Northern Ireland."

68. See: 1931–1943, *PDDS*. For the perils and possibilities of urban residential space, see chapter 1 and Houlbrook, *Queer London*, 125–133.

69. Upchurch, *Before Wilde*, 48.

70. Weber, "Henry Labouchère, *Truth* and the New Journalism of late Victorian Britain," and, for Irish response, Steele and de Nie, "Introduction," and Backus, *Scandal Work*, chapters 1 and 2.

71. McLaren, *The Trials of Masculinity*, 13–36; Mosse, *Nationalism and Sexuality*, 23–37; Cohen, *Sex Scandal*, chapter 3. More broadly, Pick, *Faces of Degeneration*; Mort,

Dangerous Sexualities, 133–141; and Weeks, *Sex, Politics, and Society*, chapter 5. For the translating of these British ideas in Irish debates about cities and fitness, see Heffernan, "Physical Degeneracy and Racial Fitness in Prewar Ireland," 229–237.

72. Valente, *The Myth of Manliness in Irish National Culture*, 12. See Earls, "Unnatural Offenses of English Import"; Zanghellini, *The Sexual Constitution of Political Authority*, chapter 4; Cocks, *Nameless Offences*, 139–144; and Heffernan, "Physical Degeneracy and Racial Fitness in Prewar Ireland," 245–251.

73. Howe, *Ireland and Empire*, 195.

74. Denvir, *The Life Story of an Old Rebel*.

75. "The Serious Charge against Young Men in Belfast," *Belfast News-Letter*, February 15, 1890, 3.

76. "Edward Samuel Wesley De Cobain—Buggery" (1893). Another trial resulted after a witness against de Cobain was accused of showing indecent images in public: "The de Cobain Case," *Cork Constitution*, September 18, 1891, 5.

77. Hyde, *The Other Love*, 138. For doubt of de Cobain's guilt, see "Was Orangeman Edward de Cobain Jailed for a Crime He Didn't Commit?"

78. "Scotland Yard," *Reynold's*, May 26, 1895, 3. A local newspaper in Ulster provocatively reprinted the article: *Ballymena Observer*, May 31, 1895, 7.

79. A point cogently argued by Murgu, "'Innocence Is as Innocence Does.'"

80. "Mr. De Cobain," *Truth*, May 7, 1891, 15; Kaplan, *Sodom on the Thames*, 170.

81. "Pen and Ink Sketches," *Hartlepool Northern Daily Mail*, April 15, 1891, 3; "Trial of de Cobain," *Irish News and Belfast Morning News*, March 22, 1893, 6.

82. Sinfield, *The Wilde Century*, 118.

83. "The Case of Mr. de Cobain," *Northern Whig*, June 6, 1891, 7. The *Northern Whig* had also reprinted *Truth's* excoriating caricature: "*Truth* on Mr. De Cobain," *Northern Whig*, May 7, 1891), 5.

84. "Trial of de Cobain," *Irish News and Belfast Morning News*, March 22, 1893, 6.

85. For De Cobain's reasoning, see his widely reprinted letter, sent to the Press Association: "Mr. De Cobain, M.P.," *London Evening Standard*, May 2, 1891, 3. Cocks notes that "Even the respectable press and the government itself were not beyond employing the services of notorious blackmailers to slander their opponents." Cocks, *Nameless Offences*, 117.

86. For Irish nationalist press, "The De Cobain Case," *People's Advocate and Monaghan, Fermanagh, and Tyrone News*, September 26, 1891, 5; for criticism of the *Northern Whig*, "To the Editor," *Northern Whig*, June 9, 1891, 3.

87. "James McKee and Richard Lutton—Assault and Buggery" (1904).

88. Thomas Normoyle joined the Royal Irish Constabulary in 1899, aged nineteen—"Normoyle, Thos," *Ireland, the Royal Irish Constabulary 1816–1921*. In 1904, he would have earned approximately £57 a year. For pay rates, and officers "continually brooding" over the paltry amount, see Radford, *The Policing of Belfast*, 125–126.

89. Froggatt, "Sir Daniel Dixon (1844–1907)."

90. See "House 19 Knockbreda Road (Ormeau, Down)," *Census of Ireland 1901*; "The Dixon Testimonial," *Northern Whig*, October 3, 1894, 6; "Tenantry of Glenville Estate," *Northern Whig*, September 7, 1903, 9.

91. "House 33 Hopefield Avenue (Clifton Ward, Belfast, Antrim)," *Census of Ireland 1901*.

92. "Serious Charge at the Recorder's Court," *Irish News and Belfast Morning News*, September 23, 1904, 8.

93. "The Summing Up of the Recorder," *Truth*, September 29, 1904, 13.

94. "Sensational Scandal in Belfast," *Reynold's*, September 25, 1904, 1.

95. For the British-Irish connections and trope of upper-class corruption, see Kaplan, *Sodom on the Thames*, 166–186, 205–206, 232–241. For the similar discourse in 1870s–1900s France, see Peniston, "A Public Offense against Decency," and Erber, "Queer Follies." For the Social Purity movement, see Mort, *Dangerous Sexualities*, 79–118.

96. As apparent in the far bigger Maiden Tribute child prostitution scandal of 1885. *Reynold's* played a part that scandal too, and, as Walkowitz notes, "openly addressed the homosexual subtext that provided a shadow discourse to female outrage." See Walkowitz, *City of Dreadful Delight*, chapter 3 and 278 (n. 123).

97. "A Belfast Scandal," *Reynold's*, October 2, 1904, 7.

98. "Secret History of To-Day," *Reynold's*, October 9, 1904, 6.

99. "Cookstown," *Mid-Ulster Mail* September 24, 1904, 5; Doughan, *The Voice of the Provinces*, 216.

100. "'Truth,' 'Reynolds,' and Other English Newspapers," *Donegal Independent*, October 7, 1904, 4—the Letterkenny edition of the *Donegal Vindicator*, edited by the Irish-Scottish John McAdam, "noted for his wholehearted Catholicism." Doughan, *The Voice of the Provinces*, 214.

101. Fitzgerald, "Fitzgibbon, Gerald (1837–1909)," 30–31.

102. "The Sheridan Scandal," *Irish Independent*, July 12, 1902, 4; and the United Irish League of Great Britain, *Who Is Sheridan?*

103. "Diary," *Portadown Times*, November 8, 1935, 7; "Late Sir Daniel Dixon," *Newry Reporter*, May 16 1907, 7.

104. "R. Lutton, Ormiston, Rosetta Park," *Ulster's Solemn League and Covenant* (1912); "Funeral of Mr. SB Quin," *Belfast News-Letter*, April 12, 1921, 6; "The Late Mr. Richard Lutton," *Belfast News-Letter*, November 6, 1935, 5.

105. "The Posters Torn Down By the Constabulary," *United Irishman*, September 24, 1904, 4.

106. Only one reported the crime, using the euphemistic "offense." "Criminal Business," *Belfast News-Letter*, September 23, 1904, 8.

107. Brady, *Masculinity and Male Homosexuality in Britain*, 53, 82.

108. Cocks, *Nameless Offences*, 119–121.

109. See Jackson, *Home Rule*, chapters 5–9; and, for UVF's establishment, Bowman, *Carson's Army, the Ulster Volunteer Force.*

110. McGaughey, *Ulster's Men*, 8.

111. "Mr. John Erskine, JP," *Belfast News-Letter*, January 30, 1934, 9.

112. Ruane and Todd, "The Changing Role of the Middle Classes in Twentieth Century Ireland," 179; Bilenberg, "The Industrial Elite in Ireland"; Gibbon, *The Origins of Ulster Unionism.*

113. "Alexander Erskine and John Albert Kingston—Gross Indecency" (1914).

114. Alexander Erskine died in 1919 aged sixty-eight, living in the same house; a nephew was present, "Alexander Erskine, died February 22 1919, Belfast."

115. "Crown Book, Indictment and Pleas, Belfast Assizes" (Spring 1914).

116. Healy, *The Old Munster Circuit*, 85–93; Sullivan, *Old Ireland*, 81–82, 86–88, 93–95. For a definition of Castle Catholic, see Hepburn, *A Past Apart*, 6.

117. "John Kingston and William Shaw—Gross Indecency" (1926).

118. Milligen's father entertained the "Orangemen of the district" each July 12—"Death of Mr. John M Milligen," *Northern Whig*, September 19, 1947, 3. For Edgar's activities, see "Lambeg National School," *Northern Whig*, May 13, 1916, 3, and "Lambeg Village School," *Northern Whig*, May 3, 1915, 2. For the Orange Order's growing power during the Home Rule Crisis, see Govan, "Towards a Religious Understanding of the Orange Order," 502–504.

119. "Edgar Milligen—Gross Indecency" (1917).

120. "Edgar Milligen—Gross Indecency" (1917), and, for men acting with impunity, Smith, *Masculinity, Class and Same-Sex Desire in Industrial England*, 44. Conley notes that the accused in Victorian sexual assault cases sometimes expressed "doubt that there would be repercussions and surprise that a sexual assault should be considered criminal." Conley, *Melancholy Accidents*, 107.

121. For the moral panics about newsboys and how Milligen's solicitor led them to incriminate themselves, see Hulme, "Queer Belfast," 254–256.

122. "Crown Book, Indictment and Pleas, Belfast Assizes" (Spring 1917).

123. Kennedy, *The Widening Gulf*, 11–24.

124. For the revealing of these fissures in "pan-Protestant and cross-class unity" in the postwar period, see Patterson and Kaufmann, *Unionism and Orangeism in Northern Ireland since 1945*, 1. See also Follis, *A State under Siege*, 181–193; Walker, *A History of the Ulster Unionist Party*, 70; and, more broadly, Walker, *The Politics of Frustration*; Mulholland, *The Longest War*, 38–40; Bew, Gibbon, and Patterson, *Northern Ireland 1921–1994*, 17–75.

125. Loughlin, "The Moral Economy of Loyalty." After the start of the Troubles and the release of cabinet and departmental papers since the late 1970s, debates have raged about the extent of Catholic discrimination. There is agreement that exaggerating discrimination was a nationalist political tool, but there was undeniably unequal treatment. For the historiographical and political positions, see Whyte, "How Much Discrimination Was There under the Unionist Regime," and O'Brien, *Discrimination in Northern Ireland*.

126. Loughlin, "Consolidating 'Ulster,'" 162, and Loughlin, *Ulster Unionism and British National Identity Since 1885*.

127. Buckland, *The Factory of Grievances*, 206, 219. Examples in the early 1920s include special treatment given to lawless sectarian gangs and rougher treatment of Catholic and nationalist men imprisoned for sectarian rioting.

128. Campaign for Social Justice in Northern Ireland, *Northern Ireland*, 10; Hadden and Hillyard, *Justice in Northern Ireland*, 11, 58. For these dynamics within a colonial framework, see McGloin, "A Historical Consideration of the Police and Prosecution/Courts in Northern Ireland," 83.

129. Murgu, "Innocence Is as Innocence Does," 318. For examples from Britain in the interwar period, see McLaren, *Sexual Blackmail*, 121. On collusion and cooperation between the state and police in Northern Ireland, see Ellison and Smyth, *The Crowned Harp*, chapters 2 and 3.

130. Moroney and O'Neill, "Continuity and Change in the Belfast Press," 382.

131. "Gunners Sentenced at Holywood," *Belfast Telegraph*, May 1, 1952, 7.

132. Waters, "Disorders of the Mind, Disorders of the Body Social," 139–140; Houlbrook, *Queer London*, 238; and Bengry, "Profit (f)or the Public Good?"

133. "'Ensnared' after Visit to Luxury House."

134. "Cecil R. Robins—Gross Indecency" (1953).

135. "Lagan-Side (and Other) Echoes," *Lisburn Herald and Antrim and Down Advertiser*, January 24, 1953, 3.

136. Hawkins, "Barbour, Sir John Milne" and Woods, "Barbour, Harold Adrian Milne."

137. Charlie Lynch and I had both heard Belfast rumors of a Barbour family member and a 1950s homosexual scandal, but he made the vital connection in the court depositions: the mention of a "Patrick" who lived at "Windy Brow," a house belonging to the family. See Lynch, "Dirty Linen."

138. Buckland, *The Factory of Grievances*, 179.

139. Farrell, *Northern Ireland*, 92. This double standard was less overt sectarian discrimination and more a product of a politics that saw Catholics as potentially disloyal—Loughlin, "The Moral Economy of Loyalty."

140. As in the influential formulation of Sedgwick, *Epistemology of the Closet*, 82–86.

141. Erber and Robb, "Introduction," 7.

Conclusion

1. Lewis, *British Queer History*. For key regional works in Britain and Ireland covering my period, see Leeworthy, *A Little Gay History of Wales*; Smith, *Masculinity, Class and Same-Sex Desire in Industrial England*; Meek, *Queer Voices in Post-War Scotland;* and Earls, *Love in the Lav.*

2. Nineteen men were initially put on trial in Lurgan in 1958, and eleven in Bangor in 1967. See "19 Men Appear at Special Court," *Belfast Telegraph*, October 23, 1958, 20; and "Homosexual Case: Man (66) Sent to Jail," *Belfast Telegraph*, October 13, 1967, 4.

3. Bengry, "Queer Profits."

4. See Duggan, *Queering Conflict*; Kitchin and Lysaght, "Heterosexism and the Geographies of Everyday Life in Belfast"; Brady, "Sectarianism and Queer Lives in Northern Ireland Since the 1970s" 50–51, 56–57; and Ferriter, *Occasions of Sin*, 475–81.

5. The Elmwood Association was set up in 1969, following a visit to Belfast by campaigner Anthony Grey, but, being dominated by heterosexual legal and medical professionals rather than gay people, it was a lame duck and already ceased activity in 1971; the Gay Liberation Society, based out of Queen's University Belfast, was thus the first proper organization. See Hulme, "Out of the Shadows."

Bibliography

Unpublished Primary Sources

Public Record Office of Northern Ireland (Belfast)

Belfast Crown and Peace

Crown Books, Assizes and Commission

"Crown Book, Indictment and Pleas, Belfast Assizes," (1900–1921), BELF/1/1/1/1–41.

"Crown Book, Indictment and Pleas, Belfast City Commission," (1922–1960), BELF/1/1/1/42–85.

Crown Files, Assizes and Commission

"James Patterson—Assault and Attempted Buggery" (1894), BELF/1/2/2/4/42.

"William Magill—Buggery" (1894), BELF/1/2/2/4/16–17.

"John McCormick and Hugh Dunlop—Gross Indecency" (1909), BELF/1/1/2/30/15.

"John Wilson (Alias Dornan)—Gross Indecency" (1910), BELF/1/1/2/32/30.

"George Davidson—Gross Indecency" (1911), BELF/1/1/2/35/31.

"Joseph Smith and George Caldwell—Gross Indecency" (1912), BELF/1/1/2/37/16.

"George Caldwell—Buggery" (1913), BELF/1/1/2/41/32.

"John Tyrell (Alias Kelly)—Gross Indecency" (1913), BELF/1/1/2/40/12.

"Joseph Rea and Thomas Magee—Gross Indecency" (1913), BELF 1/1/2/41/33.

"Joseph Rea—Buggery" (1913), BELF 1/1/2/41/45.

"Patrick Hughes—Gross Indecency" (1913), BELF/1/1/2/41/22.

"Alexander Erskine and John Albert Kingston—Gross Indecency" (1914), BELF/1/1/2/45/12.

"Thomas Kirk—Gross Indecency" (1914), BELF/1/1/2/44/13–14.

"Edgar Milligan [*sic*]—Gross Indecency" (1917), BELF/1/1/2/52/19–20.

"Vincent Cassidy—Buggery" (1917), BELF/1/1/2/54/25–6.

"John Reynolds (Alias Powell)—Gross Indecency" (1918), BELF/1/1/2/57/14.

"Thomas Dazelle—Gross Indecency" (1923), BELF/1/1/2/70/24.

"Edward Summers—Gross Indecency" (1924), BELF/1/1/2/74/49.

"William McMullan—Buggery" (1924), BELF/1/1/2/74/53.

"David Straight—Gross Indecency"; (1925), BELF/1/1/2/77/30.

"George Hogg—Buggery" (1925), BELF/1/1/2/78/30.

"John Sterling and William Gray—Gross Indecency" (1925), BELF/1/1/2/78/21.

"Named Individual—Unlawful Carnal Knowledge and Buggery" (1925), BELF/1/1/2/78/22.

"Jones Thomas—Buggery" (1926), BELF/1/1/2/80/51.
"Thomas Carrick and Samuel Ramsey—Gross Indecency" (1926), BELF/1/1/2/83/18.
"Edward McLaughlin and William Robin—Gross Indecency" (1927), BELF/1/1/2/85/42.
"Robert Smith and John Reid—Gross Indecency" (1927), BELF/1/1/2/84/40.
"Samuel Magowan and Richard Morrison—Gross Indecency" (1927), BELF/1/1/2/85/45.
"James O'Neill—Gross Indecency" (1928), BELF/1/1/2/86/64.
"James Stevenson—Gross Indecency" (1928), BELF/1/1/2/86/20.
"John O'Neill—Attempted Gross Indecency with a Minor" (1930), BELF/1/1/2/92/66.
"John Small—Assault with Intent to Commit Buggery" (1930), BELF/1/1/2/93/29.
"James Dougan—Gross Indecency with a Minor" (1931), BELF/1/1/2/95/16.
"David Purse and Sharman Stevenson—Gross Indecency" (1932), BELF/1/1/2/98/8.
"Robert Brown—Attempted Gross Indecency" (1932), BELF/1/1/2/98/39.
"William Ritchie and Samuel Coulter—Gross Indecency" (1932), BELF/1/1/2/98/58.
"Edward Graham—Buggery" (1935), BELF/1/1/2/108/34.
"Edward Graham and Samuel Curry—Buggery" (1935), BELF/1/1/2/108/35.
"Named Individual and John Ernest Ashfield—Gross Indecency" (1935), BELF/1/1/2/107/62.
"Samuel Currie—Buggery" (1935), BELF/1/1/2/108/35.
"Joseph Fitzsimons and William Erskine—Attempt to Procure an Act of Gross Indecency" (1938), BELF/1/1/2/116/37.
"Named Individual—Gross Indecency" (1937), BELF/1/1/2/114/35.
"Named Individuals—Gross Indecency" (1937), BELF/1/1/2/114/45.
"Henry Blair—Gross Indecency" (1939), BELF/1/1/2/119/35.
"Named Individuals—Buggery" (1941), BELF/1/1/2/124/34.
"Named Individual—Buggery with a Minor" (1941), BELF/1/1/2/124/12.
"Named Individuals—Gross Indecency" (1945), BELF/1/1/2/137/7.
"Francis Wadman—Buggery" (1950), BELF/1/1/2/153/23.
"William Nelson and Named Individual—Buggery" (1959), BELF/1/1/2/187/32.
Crown Books, Recorder's Court
"Crown Book, Recorder's Court," (1888–1953), BELF/1/2/1–32.
Crown Files, Recorder's Court
"James Douglas—Assault and Attempted Buggery" (1894), BELF/1/2/2/4/72.
"James Magee and William Seaton—Assault and Attempted Buggery" (1898), BELF/1/2/2/8/93.
"Edward Hull and William Johnston—Gross Indecency" (1900), BELF/1/2/2/10/10.
"Thomas O'Connor and David McDonald—Assault and Theft" (1902), BELF/1/2/2/12/67.
"James McKee and Richard Lutton—Assault and Buggery" (1904), BELF/1/2/2/14/130.
"Patrick Meehan—Indecent Assault on a Male Person" (1924), BELF/1/2/2/34/117.

"John Riddell—Gross Indecency" (1925), BELF/1/2/2/35/21.
"Sidney Day—Attempted Buggery and Gross Indecency" (1926), BELF/1/2/2/36/102.
"Arthur Patterson—Indecency" (1939), BELF/1/2/2/49/43.
"Named Individual—Gross Indecency and Assault with Intent to Commit Buggery" (1940), BELF/1/2/2/50/14.
"Named Individual—Gross Indecency" (1942), BELF/1/2/2/52/7.
"Named Individual—Gross Indecency and Buggery" (1947), BELF/1/2/2/57/16.
"George Davidson—Gross Indecency" (1952), BELF/1/2/2/62/161.
"Walter Rennie—Gross Indecency" (1952), BELF/1/2/2/62/162.
"Named Individual—Buggery" (1953), BELF/1/2/2/63/2/100–101.

Antrim, County, Crown and Peace

Crown Books, General Assizes
"County of Antrim Crown Book," (1890–95), ANT/1/2/A/5.
Crown Files, Quarter Sessions
"William Harrison Alias Burns, Alias Havelin—Assault and Buggery" (1891).
"William Ayer Otherwise O'Neill Christie—Assault and Buggery" (1892), ANT/1/1/B/1/3/15.
"Frederick McGlinchy—Gross Indecency" (1893), ANT/1/1/B/1/4/8.
Crown Files, General Assizes Including Winter Assizes
"Archibald Black and Alfred Shaw—Assault" (1891), ANT/1/2/C/1/39.
"Edward Samuel Wesley De Cobain—Buggery" (1893), ANT/1/2/C/3/30.
"James Doherty—Gross Indecency" (1894), ANT/1/2/C/4/16.
"Samuel Stewart—Buggery" (1949), ANT/1/2/C/59/31–2.
Quarter Sessions, Crown Files
"Cecil R. Robins—Gross Indecency" (1953), ANT/1/1/B/1/64/8.

Down, County, Crown and Peace

Crown Files, General and Winter Assizes
"John Kingston and William Shaw—Gross Indecency" (1926), DOW/1/2/B/33/30/44.
"David Neill—Gross Indecency" (1949), DOW/1/2/B/56.
"Named Individual—Procure Commission of Act of Gross Indecency" (1952), DOW/1/2/B/58.
"Charles McCarte—Attempting to Procure an Act of Gross Indecency" (1951), DOW/1/2/B/58.

Records of the Church of Ireland Young Men's Society. (C.I.Y.M.S.).

"CIYMS Membership Register (1859–1946)," *Membership Registers: CIYMS (General)*, D3936/D/1/1.
"CIYMS: Report of Conference at Bishop's House, February 2 1926," *Miscellaneous Booklets*, D3936/H/1.

Norman McNeilly, *The First Hundred Years: A History of the Development of the Church of Ireland Young Men's Society* (unpublished manuscript, c. 1982), n.p., D3936/H/5, PRONI.

"Minutes of the General Committee and Some Sub-committees (December 1930–March 1948)," *Minute Books: Committee and General Meeting of the CIYMS*, D3936/A/1/12.

"Minute Book of the Trustees of Hewitt Memorial House (June 1897–1956)," *Minute Books: Trustees of Hewitt Memorial House*, D3936/A/4.

Syllabus 1935–1936 (Belfast, 1935), 13, *Printed and Typescript Annual Reports of the CIYMS*, D/3936/B/1/16.

Records Relating to the Strain Family, Ouley, Co Down and Belfast

"Bundle of c.200 letters to D H Strain," *Correspondence and Accounts of D H Strain, Senior and Junior*, D2585/10/4.

"Personal Diary of David H. Strain," (1920–1943), *Personal Diaries of D. H. Strain, Junior and Mrs W. J. Strain, Senior*, D/2585/3/1–20.

"Photograph Album Containing Photographs of Members of the Strain Family, of Their Residences at Ouley, Carryduff, and 5 Galwally Park, Belfast . . . ," *Photograph Albums of the Strain Family and Related Families*, D/2585/4/1.

Belfast Corporation/County Borough Council

"Baths and Lodging Houses Committee Minute Books," *Baths and Lodging Houses*, LA/7/32/AA/1–7.

"Minute Book of the Police Committee," *Police Committee*, LA/7/10/AB/1/9–24.

Records of Her Majesty's Prisons

"General Register, Male Prisoners" (1890–1961), *Belfast Prison*, HMP/2/1/1/3–21.

Records of Her Majesty's Prisons (Uncatalogued)

Ulster's Solemn League and Covenant (1912), 5055, Sheet 102—available at https://apps.proni.gov.uk/ulstercovenant/image.aspx?image=M0050550102.

General Register Office of Northern Ireland—Accessed Online at https://www.nidirect.gov.uk/services/go-groni-online

"Alexander Erskine, Died February 22 1919, Belfast," D/1919/48/1007/82/34.

"Alexander McDonald and Sarah O'Neill, Married December 3 1913, Belfast," M/1914/B1/2326/23/73.

"Alfred Andrews, Died August 13 1876, Belfast," D/1876/47/1007/11/58.

"Archibald Black, Died January 28 1903, Belfast," D/1903/50/1007/109/446.

"Archibald Gibney, Died December 2 1878, Belfast," D/1878/48/1007/16/31.

"Charles O'Hara, Died June 30 1907, Ballymena," D/1907/21/1004/8/432.
"Charles Henry Gibson O'Hara, Born June 23 1903, Belfast," U/1903/55/1007/32/356.
"David Aicken and Eva Howard, Married September 8 1909, Belfast," M/1909/B1/416/2/26.
"David Strain, Born September 6 1896, Lisburn," U/1896/140/1018/9/449.
"Edgar Milligen, Died January 17 1939," D/1939/48/1007/104/54).
"Elizabeth Gibney, Died August 2 1906, Belfast," D/1906/47/1007/33/28.
"Ethel Norwood, Born August 25 1915, Lisburn," U/1915/150/1018/12/167.
"Frederick Aicken, Born September 24 1919, Newtownards," U/1919/201/1024/43/119.
"George Hogg, Died October 27 1947, Belfast," D/1947/52/1007/105/154.
"George Hogg, Born September 10 1880, Lisburn," U/1889/148/1018/24/447.
"Hugh P. Sheehan and Rachel McKinney, Married January 25 1923, Belfast," M/1923/B1/2333/12/155.
"George Hogg and Mary McCleery, Married August 5 1919, Belfast," M/1919/B1/662/3/4.
"James Spence, Died July 8 1905, Belfast," D/1905/50/1007/118/406.
"John Albert Kingston, Died October 18 1954, Belfast," D/1954/48/1007/115/64.
"Joseph Wilson McCullough, Born March 14 1920, Belfast," U/1920/51/1007/75/426.
"Letitia Dougan, Died September 30 1943, Belfast," D/1943/56/1007/39/81.
"Margaret Power, Died April 29 1929, Belfast," D/1929/58/1007/39/68.
"Mary Spence, Died February 1 1910, Belfast," D/1910/50/1007/136/79.
"Samuel Ramsay, Died June 25 1927, Belfast," D/1927/56/1007/29/393.
"Thomas Gibney, Born October 24 1868, Belfast," U/1868/47/1007/6/206.
"Thomas Henry Ritchie, Born December 6 1916, Belfast," U/1916/49/1007/152/194.
"Walter Edward Ferguson Smith, Died November 22 1962, Belfast," D/1962/90/1007/3/116.
"William Shaw, Died January 17 1967, Belfast," D/1967/43/1007/21/221.
"Winifred Aicken, Died October 3 1926, Newtownards," D/1926/201/1024/40/65.
"Walter Smith, Born May 3 1898, Belfast," U/1898/49/1007/100/15.

The National Archives (London)

"Criminal Investigation Department, March 20 1921" in *"The Link" Publication; Conspiracy to Corrupt Public Morals—Reports and Correspondence*, MEPO/3/283.
"The Information of the Director of Public Prosecutions" in *"The Link" Publication; Conspiracy to Corrupt Public Morals—Reports and Correspondence*, MEPO/3/283.
"Central Criminal Court, January 18 Sessions, 1937" in *"The Link" Publication; Conspiracy to Corrupt Public Morals—Reports and Correspondence*, MEPO/3/283.
"Letter From Ernest Smyth to Walter Birks, October 21, 1920" in *"The Link" Publication; "Conspiracy to Corrupt Public Morals—Reports and Correspondence*, MEPO/3/283.
"Defendant: Knox, William. Charge: Importuning for Immoral Purposes" (October 11, 1938), *Central Criminal Court*, CRIM/1/1041.

Representative Church Library (Dublin)

Records of the Church of Ireland Moral Welfare Association, MS1130.

"Executive Committee in Clarence Place on January 28 1943" in Church of Ireland Moral Welfare Association, *Occasional Bulletin No. 1* (Belfast, c. 1943).

General Register Office (England)

"Charles Henry Gibson O'Hara, Died November 5 1972, Paddington, London," 5D, 1258.

Probate Records (England)

"William La Coste Nelson, probate October 18 2021," Registry Office: Liverpool, 1631693387585026.

Records Accessed through www.ancestry.com

"Kaiser-I-Hind Leaving London (November 21 1930)"—the National Archives (London), Board of Trade: Commercial and Statistical Department and Successors: Outwards Passenger Lists. BT27.

"Normoyle, Thos," *Ireland, the Royal Irish Constabulary 1816–1921*, Provo, UT, USA.

"Passenger list for *Persie*, travelling from Sydney to London (January 1904)"

"Joseph Wilson McCullough, Died December 8 2012, Worthing (West Sussex, England)" in *England and Wales, Death Index, 1989–2022*.

Adriatic leaving Belfast, September 20 1930, T.N.A., Board of Trade: Commercial and Statistical Department and Successors: Outwards Passenger Lists, BT27).

"William Gray, Naturalization Record," National Archives at Boston; Waltham, Massachusetts; Petitions and Records of Naturalization, 8/1845—12/1911; NAI Number: 3000057; Record Group Title: Records of District Courts of the United States, 1685–2009; Record Group Number: RG 21.

"*SS Caledonia*, Departing Londonderry December 26 1908 Bound for New York," in *New York, U.S., Arriving Passenger and Crew Lists, 1820–1957*.

"*SS Lake Erie*, Departing Belfast September 30 1909 Bound for Quebec & Montreal," in *UK and Ireland, Outward Passenger Lists, 1890–1960*.

"Washington Arriving in Southampton from New York, August 24 1949," in *UK and Ireland, Incoming Passenger Lists, 1878–1960*.

"Empress of France, Departing Liverpool, May 3 1949, Destination Port of Montreal" in *UK and Ireland, Outward Passenger Lists, 1890–1960*.

"8/9 Lancaster Gate, Paddington, London" (1947) and "12 Westbourne Grove Terrace, Paddington, London" (1954–1970) in *Westminster, London, Electoral Registers, 1902–1970*.

"196 Worthington, North Bay City (Nipissing, Ontario)" and "153 Northcliffe Boulevard, York Township (Ontario)," *1911 Census of Canada*.

"James Douglas, Died December 7 1894, Blackburn." *General Register Office of England*.

Harry Ransom Center (Austin, TX)

"Incoming—Ma-Mai," Container 8.10, *British Sexological Society Records*.

"Youth, Gods, Beasts, Earth: Poems from Greek Anthology, Chosen and Done into English by Forrest Reid, Typescript with Handwritten Emendations and Additions," Container 4.1, *Forrest Reid Collection*.

Marion E. Wade Center, Wheaton College (Wheaton, IL)

Box 1, *Arthur Greeves Diaries Collection* (1917–1922), WADE-A-5.

Bishopsgate Institute (London)

"'Ensnared' after Visit to Luxury House," *News of the World*, May 4, 1952, in *LAGNA: Lesbian and Gay Newsmedia Archive*, LAGNAPC/CHR/1952/8,

New York Public Library

"Frank Kameny Interviewed by Barbara Gittings and Kay Tobin" (1971), in *Barbara Gittings and Kay Tobin Lahusen Gay History Papers and Photographs*, New York Public Library—transcribed by Eric Cervini and kindly shared with me via email (2023).

Birth, Marriage and Death Records (New Zealand)—https://www.bdmhistoricalrecords.dia.govt.nz

"Leslie Cecil Bond, Born October 17 1900, Nelson, New Zealand," 1900/4027.

Census Data

Census of Ireland 1901 and Census of Ireland 1911—accessed online at *The National Archives of Ireland*—https://www.census.nationalarchives.ie.

Census of England and Wales 1891, 1901, 1911—accessed online at https://www.ancestry.com.

Irish Genealogy.ie Records

"Marriage between Arthur Brand Goodbody and Kathleen Frood McNally, December 18 1920, Dublin," Group Registration ID: 1219386.

Official Documents and Publications

Government of Northern Ireland, *The Protection and Welfare of the Young and the Treatment of Young Offenders*. Belfast: H. M. Stationery Office, 1938.

Report of the Inter-Departmental Committee on the Employment of Children During School Age, Especially In Street Trading in the Large Centres of Population in Ireland. Dublin: H. M. Stationery Office, 1902.

Newspapers

Ballymena Observer
Ballymena Weekly Telegraph
Belfast News-Letter
Belfast Telegraph
Belfast Weekly News
Birmingham Daily Post
Birmingham Mail
Blackburn Standard
Bulletin of the Royal College of Psychiatrists
Cardiff Times
Cork Constitution
Donegal Independent
Dundee Advertiser
Globe
Hartlepool Northern Daily Mail
Hull Daily Mail
Illustrated London News
Ireland's Saturday Night
Irish Independent
Irish News and Belfast Morning News
Irish Weekly and Ulster Examiner
Lisburn Herald and Antrim and Down Advertiser
Mid-Ulster Mail
Newry Reporter
News of the World
North Down Herald and County Down Independent
Northern Whig
Penny Illustrated News
People's Advocate and Monaghan, Fermanagh, and Tyrone News
Portadown Times
Reynold's Newspaper
The Times
Truth
Ulster Echo
United Irishman
Wicklow News-Letter and County Advertiser
Witness

Unarchived Oral Histories

"Interview with John Keyes" (2006), the Rainbow Project, Belfast, transcribed by Benjamin Boswell (2022).

"Interview with Peter McVea" (2006), the Rainbow Project, Belfast, transcribed by Benjamin Boswell (2022).

Contemporary Books and Articles

Anomaly. *The Invert and His Social Adjustment*. Bailliere, Tindall, & Cox, 1927.
Anon. "Sanity at Last." *Church of Ireland Gazette*, no. 3877, CII (October 18, 1957), 2.
Anon. "The Wolfenden Report." *Biblical Theology* 8, no. 2 (1958), 43–47.
Arensberg, Conrad M., and Solon Kimball. *Family and Community in Ireland*, Harvard University Press, 1940.
Atteridge, W. M. *Royal Ulster Constabulary Constables' Guide*. Alex Thom & Co., 1936.
Bard, Brice. *Le Guide Gris*, 3rd edition. Mattachine Society, 1962.
Barritt, Denis, and Charles Carter. *The Northern Ireland Problem: A Study in Group Relations*. Oxford University Press, 1962.
Belfast Street Directory/Belfast and Province of Ulster Directory. Belfast News-Letter, 1890–1960.
Benson, E. F. *The Inheritor*. Hutchinson, 1930.
British Society of the Study of Sex Psychology. *The Social Problem of Sexual Inversion*. BSSSP, 1913.
Burton, Richard Francis. "Terminal Essay." In *The Book of the Thousand Nights and a Night*, trans. Richard Francis Burton. H. S. Nichols, 1885.
Campaign for Social Justice in Northern Ireland. *Northern Ireland: The Plain Truth*. Campaign for Social Justice in Northern Ireland, 1969.
Carpenter, Edward. *The Intermediate Sex: A Study of Some Transitional Types of Men and Women*. George Allen and Unwin, 1912 [1908].
Carpenter, Edward. *Ioläus: An Anthology of Friendship*. W. Swan Sonnenschein & Co., 1902.
Carpenter, Edward. *Towards Democracy*. George Allen and Unwin Ltd., 1917 [1883].
Collingwood, Harry. *The Log of the "Flying Fish": A Story of Aerial and Submarine Peril and Adventure*. Blackie and Son, 1887.
Conway, Ethna. "Ireland and Television." *Furrow* 9, no. 1 (1958), 33–38.
Davis, Henry. *Moral and Pastoral Theology*, vol. 2. Sheed and Ward, 1936.
Denvir, John. *The Life Story of an Old Rebel*. Sealy, Bryers and Walker, 1910.
Douglas, James. *The Unpardonable Sin*. E. Grant Richards, 1907.
Ellis, Havelock, and John Addington Symonds. *Sexual Inversion*. Wilson & MacMillan, 1897.
Ellis, Havelock. *Studies in the Psychology of Sex: Vol II: Sexual Inversion*. Wilson and Macmillan, 1897.
Fielding, William J. *Homo-Sexual Life*. Haldeman-Julius Co., 1925.
Finger, Charles Joseph. *The Tragic Story of Oscar Wilde's Life*. Haldeman-Julius Co., 1923.
Fitzgerald, David. "Fitzgibbon, Gerald (1837–1909)." In *Dictionary of National Biography: Second Supplement*, vol. II, edited by Sidney Lee. Smith, Elder, & Co., 1912.
Forster, E. M. *Maurice*. Hodder Arnold, 1971.

Glaeser, Ernst. *Class 1902*. Martin Secker Ltd., 1929.

Hadden, Tom, and Paddy Hillyard. *Justice in Northern Ireland: A Study in Social Confidence*. Cobden Trust, 1973.

Hall, Radclyffe. *The Well of Loneliness*. Jonathan Cape, 1928.

Harbinson, Robin. *The Protégé*. Blackstaff, 1963.

Hime, Maurice C. "Immorality among School Boys." *Lancet*, September 4, 1897, 614–617.

Hime, Maurice C. *Morality: An Essay on Some Points Thereof Addressed to Young Men*. J. and A. Churchill, 1884.

Hime, Maurice C. "The Grave Social Problem." *British Medical Journal* 1, no. 1101 (February 4, 1882), 175–176.

Jeunesse, Ernest La, André Gide, and Franz Blei. *Recollections of Oscar Wilde*. Translated by Percival Pollard. John W. Luce and Co., 1906.

Lennon, Patrick. "New Books." *Furrow* 5, no. 1 (1954), 58–59.

Leyton, Elliott. *The One Blood: Kinship and Class in an Irish Village*. Institute of Social and Economic Research, Memorial University of Newfoundland, 1975.

Lind, Earl. *Autobiography of an Androgyne*. Medico-Legal Journal, 1918.

Lothian, Douglas B. M. "From the Case-Book of a Medical Psychologist." *Ulster Medical Journal* 8, no. 1 (1939), 29–46.

MacC, W. A. G. "Obituary: Charles Booth Robinson." *Bulletin of the Royal College of Psychiatrists* 8, no. 9 (1984), 181–182.

MacCartan, Hugh A. *The Glamour of Belfast*. Talbot, 1921.

Macgill, Patrick. *The Dead End: The Autobiography of an Irish Navvy*. Herbert Jenkins, 1914.

Martin, Kenneth. *Aubade*. Valancourt, 2013 [1957].

Matthews, Kenneth. *Aleko*. Peter Davies, 1934.

Mayne, Xavier. *The Intersexes: A History of Similisexualism as a Problem in Social Life*. Arno, 1975 [1908].

McLaverty, Michael. *Call My Brother Back*. Blackstaff, 2003 [1939].

McLaverty, Michael. *Lost Fields*. Blackstaff, 2004 [1941].

McLaverty, Michael. *The Three Brothers*. Poolbeg, 1982 [1948].

Moore, Brian. *The Emperor of Ice Cream*. Viking, 1965.

Niles, Blair. *Strange Brother*. Horace Liveright, 1931.

Norris, David. "Homosexual People and the Christian Churches in Ireland: A Minority and Its Oppressors." *Crane Bag* 5, no. 1 (1981), 31–37.

Northridge, William Lovell. *Psychology and Pastoral Practice*. Epworth, 1938.

O'Doherty, E. F. "Sexual Deviations." In *The Priest and Mental Health*, edited by E.F. O'Doherty and S. Desmond McGrath. Clonmore and Reynolds, 1962.

O'Hanlon, W. M. *Walks among the Poor of Belfast, and Suggestions for Their Improvement*. Belfast, 1852.

Owen, D. J. *A Short History of the Port of Belfast*. Mayne, Boyd & Son, 1917.

Owen, D. J. *History of Belfast*. W. & G. Baird, 1921.

Potter, La Forrest. *Strange Loves: A Study in Sexual Abnormalities*. National Library Press, 1933.

Reid, Forrest. *The Garden God: A Tale of Two Boys*. Valancourt, 2007 [1905].

Rumbold, Richard. *Little Victims*. Fortune, 1933.
Sargaison, E. Miriam. *Growing Old in Common Lodgings: A Survey of Elderly Men and Their Living Conditions in Belfast Common Lodging Houses*. Nuffield Provincial Hospitals Trust, 1954.
Simmel, Georg. "The Metropolis and Mental Life" (1903), in *On Individuality and Social Forms: Selected Writings of Georg Simmel*, edited by Donald N. Levine. University of Chicago Press, 1971.
Smith, Derek Walker. *Out of Step*. Victor Gollancz, 1930.
Symonds, J. A. *A Problem in Modern Ethics, Being an Inquiry into the Phenomenon of Sexual Inversion*. London, 1896 [1891].
Tellier, André. *Twilight Men*. Greenberg, 1931.
Tomelty, Joseph. *The Apprentice*. Blackstaff, 1983 [1953].
Underwood, Reginald. *The Flame of Freedom*. Fortune, 1936.
United Irish League of Great Britain. *Who Is Sheridan?* United Irish League of Great Britain, 1902.
Wilde, Oscar. *The Picture of Dorian Gray*. Penguin, 2003 [1891].
Winkler, John K. *Five and Ten: The Fabulous Life of F. W. Woolworth*. Robert M. McBride and Co., 1940.

Memoir and Autobiography

Abbott, Basil. "Memories of Frederick Howard Aicken." Kindly provided via email (2024).
Ackerley, J. R., *My Father and Myself*. Review of Books, 1999 [1968].
Blood, Baroness May. *Watch My Lips, I'm Speaking!* Gill & Macmillan, 2007.
Boyd, John. *Out of My Class*. Blackstaff, 1985.
Campbell, John. *Once There Was a Community Here: A Sailortown Miscellany*. Lagan, 2001.
Crisp, Quentin. *The Naked Civil Servant*. Harper Perennial, 2007 [1968].
Dillon, Martin. *Crossing the Line: My Life on the Edge*. Merrion, 2017.
Galway, James. *An Autobiography*. Chappell and Co., 1978.
Healy, Maurice. *The Old Munster Circuit: A Book of Memories and Traditions*. Michael Joseph, 1939.
Johnson, Nevill. *The Other Side of Six: An Autobiography*. Academy, 1984.
McVea, Peter. *Fruitz: A Tale of How a Young Boy Survived Stalking by a Rogue RUC Police Officer*. Self-published, 2020.
Mulholland, Marie. "Ghetto-Blasting." In *Lesbian and Gay Visions of Ireland: Towards the 21st Century*, edited by Ide O'Carroll and Eoin Collins. Continuum, 1995.
Paula. "Common Denominator." In *Threads: Stories of Lesbian Life in Northern Ireland in the 1970's and 1980's*. Nova, 2013.
Simms, John Young. *Farewell to the Hammer: A Shankill Boyhood*. White Row, 1992.
Sullivan, A. M. *Old Ireland: Reminiscences of an Irish K.C.* Butterworth, 1928.
Porter, Kevin, and Jeffrey Weeks, eds. *Between the Acts: Lives of Homosexual Men 1885–1967*. Routledge, 1991.

Secondary Published Sources

Abraham, Julie. *Metropolitan Lovers: The Homosexuality of Cities*. University of Minnesota Press, 2009.

Akenson, Donald Harman. *Education and Enmity: The Control of Schooling in Northern Ireland, 1920–1950*. Routledge, 2012 [1973].

Aldrich, Robert. *Colonialism and Homosexuality*. Routledge, 2003.

Aldrich, Robert. *Cultural Encounters and Homoeroticism in Sri Lanka: Sex and Serendipity*. Routledge, 2014.

Aldrich, Robert. "Homosexuality and the City: An Historical Overview." *Urban Studies* 41, no. 9 (2004), 1719–1737.

Aldrich, Robert. *The Seduction of the Mediterranean: Writing, Art and Homosexual Fantasy*. Routledge, 1993.

Allen, Christopher. *The Law of Evidence in Victorian England*. Cambridge University Press, 1997.

Amin, Kadji. *Disturbing Attachments: Genet, Modern Pederasty, and Queer History*. Duke University Press, 2017.

Archer, John E. "'Men Behaving Badly'? Masculinity and the Uses of Violence, 1850–1900." In *Everyday Violence in Britain, 1850–1950*, edited by Shani D'Cruze. Routledge, 2000.

Backus, Margot. "'Things That Have the Potential to Go Horribly Wrong:' Homosexuality, Paedophilia and the Kincora Boys' Home Scandal." In *The Ashgate Research Companion to Queer Theory*, edited by Noreen Giffney and Michael O'Rourke, Ashgate, 2009.

Backus, Margot. *Scandal Work: James Joyce, the New Journalism, and the Home Rule Newspaper*. University of Notre Dame Press, 2013.

Backus, Margot. *The Gothic Family Romance: Heterosexuality, Child Sacrifice, and the Anglo-Irish Colonial Order*. Duke University Press, 1999.

Barclay, Katie. "Falling in Love with the Dead." *Rethinking History* 22, no. 4 (2018), 459–473.

Barclay, Katie. *Men on Trial: Performing Emotion, Embodiment and Identity in Ireland, 1800–1845*. Manchester University Press, 2018.

Bardon, Jonathan. *Belfast: An Illustrated History*. Blackstaff, 1982.

Bardon, Jonathan. "Popular Culture." In *Enduring City: Belfast in the Twentieth Century*, edited by Frederick W. Boal and Stephen A. Royle. Blackstaff, 2006.

Barkley, John M. *The Irish Council of Churches 1923–1983*. Ulster Services, 1983.

Barr, Rebecca Anne. "Forrest Reid's Queer Ulster Pastoral." In *Engendering Ireland: New Reflections on Modern History and Literature*, edited by Rebecca Anne Barr, Sarah-Anne Buckley, and Laura Kelly. Cambridge Scholars Publishing, 2015.

Barr, Rebecca Anne, Sean Brady, and Jane McGaughey. "Ireland and Masculinities in History: An Introduction." In *Ireland and Masculinities in History*, edited by Rebecca Anne Barr, Sean Brady, and Jane G. V. McGaughey. Palgrave Macmillan, 2019.

Bartlett, Neil. *Who Was That Man? A Present for Mr Oscar Wilde*. Serpent's Tail, 1988.

Barton, Brian. *Northern Ireland in the Second World War*. Ulster Historical Foundation, 1995.

Bates, Victoria. *Sexual Forensics in Victorian and Edwardian England: Age, Crime and Consent in the Courts*. Palgrave Macmillan, 2016.

Bauer, Heike. *English Literary Sexology: Translations of Inversion, 1860–1930*. Palgrave Macmillan, 2009.

Bauer, Heike, ed. *Sexology and Translation: Cultural and Scientific Encounters across the Modern World*. Temple University Press, 2015.

Bauer, Heike, and Matt Cook. "Introduction." In *Queer 1950s: Rethinking Sexuality in the Postwar Years*, edited by Heike Bauer and Matt Cook. Palgrave Macmillan, 2012.

Beachy, Robert. *Gay Berlin: Birthplace of a Modern Identity*. Alfred A. Knopf, 2014.

Beatty, Aidan. *Masculinity and Power in Irish Nationalism, 1884–1938*. Palgrave Macmillan, 2016.

Beaven, Brad. "Foreign Sailors and Working-Class Communities: Race, Crime, and Moral Panics in London's Sailortown." In *Migrants and the Making of the Urban-Maritime World*, edited by Christina Reimann and Martin Öhman. Routledge, 2021.

Beaven, Brad. *Leisure, Citizenship and Working-Class Men, 1850–1945*. Manchester University Press, 2005.

Beaven, Brad, Karl Bell, and Robert James. "Introduction." In *Port Towns and Urban Cultures: International Histories of the Waterfront, c. 1700–2000*, edited by Brad Beaven, Karl Bell, and Robert James. Palgrave Macmillan, 2016.

Bech, Henning. *When Men Meet: Homosexuality and Modernity*. University of Chicago Press, 1997.

Belchem, John. *Irish, Catholic and Scouse: The History of the Liverpool Irish, 1800–1939*. Liverpool University Press, 2007.

Beemyn, Genny. *A Queer Capital: A History of Gay Life in Washington, D.C.* Routledge, 2015.

Bender, Jill C. "Ireland and Empire." In *The Princeton History of Modern Ireland*, edited by Richard Bourke and Ian McBride. Princeton University Press, 2016.

Bengry, Justin. "Profit (f)or the Public Good? Sensationalism, Homosexuality, and the Postwar Popular Press." *Media History* 20, no. 2 (2014), 146–166.

Bengry, Justin. "Queer Profits: Homosexual Scandal and the Origins of Legal Reform in Britain." In *Queer 1950s: Rethinking Sexuality in the Postwar Years*, edited by Heike Bauer and Matt Cook. Palgrave Macmillan, 2012.

Bergman, David, ed. *Camp Grounds: Style and Homosexuality*. Amherst, 1993.

Bérubé, Allan. *Coming Out under Fire: The History of Gay Men and Women in World War II*. University of North Carolina Press, 2010 [1990].

Bew, Paul, Peter Gibbon, and Henry Patterson. *Northern Ireland 1921–1994: Political Forces and Social Classes*. Serif, 1995.

Bilenberg, Andy. "The Industrial Elite in Ireland from the Industrial Revolution to the First World War." In *Politics, Society and the Middle Class in Modern Ireland*, edited by Fintan Lane. Palgrave Macmillan, 2010.

Bingham, Adrian. *Family Newspapers? Sex, Private Life and the British Popular Press, 1918–1978*. Oxford University Press, 2009.

Bingham, Adrian. *Gender, Modernity, and the Popular Press in Inter-War Britain*. Oxford University Press, 2004.

Birken, Lawrence. *Consuming Desire: Sexual Science and the Emergence of a Culture of Abundance, 1871–1914*. Cornell University Press, 1988.

Black, Lyndsey. *Gender and Punishment in Ireland: Women, Murder and the Death Penalty, 1922–1964*. Manchester University Press, 2022.

Blakeway, Denys. *The Last Dance 1936: The Year Our Lives Changed*. John Murray, 2010.

Bleys, Rudi C. *The Geography of Perversion: Male-to-Male Sexual Behavior outside the West and the Ethnographic Imagination, 1750–1918*. New York University Press, 1995.

Boag, Peter. *Same-Sex Affairs: Constructing and Controlling Homosexuality in the Pacific Northwest*. University of California Press, 2003.

Boal, Frederick W. "Big Processes and Little People: The Population of Metropolitan Belfast, 1891–2001." In *Enduring City: Belfast in the Twentieth Century*, edited by Frederick W. Boal and Stephen A. Royle. Blackstaff, 2006.

Boswell, John. *Christianity, Social Tolerance and Homosexuality: Gay People in Western Europe from the Beginning of the Christian Era to the Fourteenth Century*. University of Chicago Press, 1980.

Bourke, Joanna. *Dismembering the Male: Men's Bodies, Britain and the Great War*. Reaktion, 1996.

Bourke, Joanna. *Working Class Cultures in Britain, 1890–1960: Gender, Class, and Ethnicity*. Routledge, 1994.

Bowman, Timothy. *Carson's Army, the Ulster Volunteer Force 1910–1922*. Manchester University Press, 2007.

Boyd, Nan Alamilla. *Wide Open Town: A History of Queer San Francisco to 1965*. University of California Press, 2003.

Brady, Sean. *John Addington Symonds and Homosexuality: A Critical Edition of Sources*. Palgrave Macmillan, 2012.

Brady, Sean. *Masculinity and Male Homosexuality in Britain, 1861–1913*. Palgrave Macmillan, 2005.

Brady, Sean. "Sectarianism and Queer Lives in Northern Ireland Since the 1970s." In *Locating Queer Histories: Places and Traces Across the UK*, edited by Matt Cook, Alison Oram, and Justin Bengry. Bloomsbury, 2022.

Brady, Sean. "Why Examine Men, Masculinities and Religion in Northern Ireland?" In *Men, Masculinities and Religious Change in Twentieth-Century Britain*, edited by Lucy Delap and Sue Morgan. Palgrave Macmillan, 2013.

Brickell, Chris. "Sexology, the Homo/Hetero binary, and the Complexities of Male Sexual History." *Sexualities* 9, no. 4 (2006), 423–447.

Briggs, Asa. *Victorian Cities*. Penguin, 1990 [1963].

Bristow, Joseph. "Remapping the Sites of Modern Gay History: Legal Reform, Medico-legal Thought, Homosexual Scandal, Erotic Geography." *Journal of British Studies* 46, no. 1 (2007), 116–142.

Bristow, Joseph. *Sexuality*. Routledge, 1997.

Brodie, Malcolm. *The Tele: A History of the Belfast Telegraph*. Blackstaff, 1995.

Brooke, Stephen. "'A Certain Amount of Mush:' Love, Romance, Celluloid and Wax in the Mid-twentieth Century." In *Love and Romance in Britain, 1918–1970*, edited by Alana Harris and Timothy Willem Jones. Palgrave Macmillan, 2015.

Brown, Callum G. *The Death of Christian Britain: Understanding Secularisation, 1800–2000*. Cambridge University Press, 2000.

Brozyna, Andrea Ebel. *Labor, Love, and Prayer: Female Piety in Ulster Religious Literature, 1850–1914*. McGill-Queen's University Press, 1999.

Bryan, Dominic, and S. J. Connolly, with John Nagle. *Civic Identity and Public Space: Belfast Since 1780*. Manchester University Press, 2019.

Buckland, Patrick. *The Factory of Grievances: Devolved Government in Northern Ireland 1921–1939*. Gill and Macmillan, 1979.

Butler, Shane. *The Passions of John Addington Symonds*. Oxford University Press, 2023.

Calvert, Leanne, and Maeve O'Riordan. "Introduction: Women and the Family in Ireland. New Directions and Perspectives 1550–1950." *Women's History* 2, no. 15 (2020), 3–5.

Campbell, Fergus. "Freud in Dublin? The Formation of Psychoanalysis in Ireland, c. 1928–1993." *History Workshop Journal* 95 (Spring 2023), 101–130.

Canadas, Ivan. "Going Wilde: Prendick, Montgomery and Late-Victorian Homosexuality in *The Island of Doctor Moreau*." *JELL: Journal of the English Language and Literature Association of Korea* 56, no. 3 (2010), 461–485.

Canaday, Margot. "Thinking Sex in the Transnational Turn: An Introduction." *American Historical Review* 114, no. 5 (2009), 1250–1257.

Capó Jr., Julio. *Welcome to Fairyland: Queer Miami before 1940*. University of North Carolina Press, 2017.

Casey, Maurice. "'A Fairly Average "White Middle-Class" Species of Lesbian': Lorna Gulston, Ireland and the Early Anglophone Lesbian Press, 1965–1980." Under review in *Gender & History*.

Casey, Maurice. "'I Want to Be to Ireland What Walt Whitman Was to America:' Esotericism and Queer Sexuality in an Irish Social Circle, 1890s-1920s." *History Workshop Journal*, 99 (2025), 52–72.

Charnock, Hannah. "'How Far Should We Go?': Adolescent Sexual Activity and Understandings of the Sexual Life Cycle in Postwar Britain." *Journal of the History of Sexuality* 32, no. 3 (2023), 245–268.

Chauncey, George. *Gay New York: Gender, Urban Culture, and the Makings of the Gay Male World, 1890–1940*. Basic Books, 1994.

Chauncey, George. "The Trouble with Shame." In *Gay Shame*, edited by David M. Halperin and Valerie Traub. University of Chicago Press, 2009.

Chauncey, George. "Christian Brotherhood or Sexual Perversion? Homosexual Identities and the Construction of Sexual Boundaries in World War One Era." *Journal of Social History* 19, no. 2 (1985), 189–211.

Clark, Anna. "Anne Lister's Construction of Lesbian Identity." *Journal of the History of Sexuality* 7, no. 1 (1996), 23–50.

Clark, Anna. *The Struggle for the Breeches*. University of California Press, 1995.

Clear, Caitriona. *Social Change and Everyday Life in Ireland, 1850–1922*. Manchester University Press, 2007.

Clear, Caitriona. *Women's Voices in Ireland: Women's Magazines in the 1950s and 60s*. Bloomsbury, 2016.

Cleves, Rachel H. *Unspeakable: A Life Beyond Sexual Morality*. University of Chicago Press, 2020.

Cocks, H. G. *Nameless Offences: Homosexual Desire in the Nineteenth Century*. IB Tauris, 2003.

Cocks, H. G. "Religion and Spirituality." In *Palgrave Advances in the Modern History of Sexuality*, edited by H. G. Cocks and Matt Houlbrook. Palgrave Macmillan, 2016.

Cocks, H. G. "Trials of Character: The Use of Character Evidence in Victorian Sodomy Trials." In R. A. Melkian. *The Trial in History, 2, Domestic and International Trials, 1700–2000*. Manchester University Press, 2003.

Cocks, Harry. *Classified: The Secret History of the Personal Column*. Random House, 2009.

Cohen, Deborah. *Family Secrets: Shame and Privacy in Modern Britain*. Oxford University Press, 2013.

Cohen, Ed. *Talk on the Wilde Side*. Routledge, 1993.

Cohen, Michelle. "Manliness, Effeminacy and the French: Gender and the Construction of National Character in Eighteenth-Century England." In *English Masculinities, 1660–1800*, edited by Tim Hitchcock and Michelle Cohen. Routledge, 1999.

Cohen, William. *Sex Scandal: The Private Parts of Victorian Fiction*. Duke University Press, 1996.

Coleman, Peter. *Christian Attitudes to Homosexuality*. Society for Promoting Christian Knowledge, 1980.

Colin, Pooley. "Cities, Spaces and Movement: Everyday Experiences of Urban Travel in England c. 1840–1940." *Urban History* 44, no. 1 (2017), 91–109.

Colin, Pooley. "Travelling through the City: Using Life Writing to Explore Individual Experiences of Urban Travel c. 1840–1940." *Mobilities* 12, no. 4 (2017), 598–609.

Colligan, Colette. "Teleny, the Secret Touch, and the Media Geography of the Clandestine Book Trade (1880–1900)." In *Media, Technology, and Literature in the Nineteenth Century: Image, Sound, Touch*, edited by Margaret Linley and Colette Colligan. Ashgate, 2011.

Collini, Stefan. *Public Moralists: Political Thought and Intellectual Life in Britain, 1850–1930*. Oxford University Press, 1991.

Conley, Carolyn. *Melancholy Accidents: The Meaning of Violence in Post-Famine Ireland*. Lexington, 1999.

Conley, Mary. "Epilogue: Manhood Found and Lost at Sea." In *Negotiating Masculinities and Modernity in the Maritime World, 1815–1940: A Sailor's Progress?* edited by Karen Downing, Jonathan Thayer, and Joanne Begiato. Palgrave Macmillan, 2021.

Connolly, Linda. "Locating the Irish Family: Towards a Plurality of Family Forms?" In *The 'Irish' Family*, edited by Linda Connolly. Routledge, 2015.

Connolly, S. J. "Improving Town, 1750–1820." In *Belfast 400: People, Place and History*, edited by S. J. Connolly. Liverpool University Press, 2012.

Connolly, S. J., and Gillian McIntosh. "Imagining Belfast." In *Belfast 400: People, Place and History*, edited by S. J. Connolly. Liverpool University Press, 2012.

Connolly, S. J., and Gillian McIntosh. "Whose City? Belonging and Exclusion in the Nineteenth-Century Urban World." In *Belfast 400: People, Place and History*, edited by S. J. Connolly. Liverpool University Press, 2012.

Conrad, Kathryn. *Locked in the Family Cell: Gender, Sexuality, and Political Agency in Irish National Discourse*. University of Wisconsin Press, 2004.

Conrad, Kathryn. "Queer Treasons: Homosexuality and Irish National Identity." *Cultural Studies* 15, no. 1 (2001), 124–137.

Cook, Hera. *The Long Sexual Revolution: English Women, Sex, and Contraception 1800–1975*. Oxford University Press, 2004.

Cook, Matt. *London and the Culture of Homosexuality, 1885–1914*. Cambridge University Press, 2003.

Cook, Matt. *Queer Domesticities: Homosexuality and Home Life in Twentieth-Century London*. Palgrave Macmillan, 2014.

Cook, Matt, and Alison Oram. *Queer Beyond London*. Manchester University Press, 2022.

Cook, Matt, with Robert Mills, Randoph Trumbach, and H. G. Cocks. *A Gay History of Britain: Love and Sex Between Men Since the Middle Ages*. Bloomsbury, 2007.

Cooper, Sophie. *Forging Identities in the Irish World: Melbourne and Chicago, 1830–1922*. Edinburgh University Press, 2022.

Cormack, W. J. *Roger Casement in Death: Or Haunting the Free State*. University College Dublin Press, 2002.

Coulter, Riann. "Gerard Dillon: Nationalism, Homosexuality, and the Modern Irish Artist." *Eire-Ireland* 45, no. 3 (2010), 63–94.

Coulter, Riann. "John Hewitt: Creating a Canon of Ulster Art." *Journal of Art Historiography* no. 8 (2013), 1–18.

Craig, Patricia. "The Liberal Imagination in Northern Irish Prose." In *Returning to Ourselves: Second Volume of Papers from the John Hewitt International Summer School*, edited by Eve Patten. Lagan, 1995.

Craig, Patricia. "The Place Had Character." In *Enduring City: Belfast in the Twentieth Century*, edited by Frederick W. Boal and Stephen A. Royle. Blackstaff, 2006.

Croll, Andy. "Street Disorder, Surveillance and Shame: Regulating Behaviour in the Public Spaces of the Late Victorian British Town." *Social History* 24 no. 3 (1999), 250–268.

Cronin, Maura. "'You'd Be Disgraced!' Middle-Class Women and Respectability in Post-famine Ireland." In *Politics, Society and the Middle Class in Modern Ireland*, edited by Fintan Lane. Palgrave Macmillan, 2010.

Cronon, Michael G. *Impure Thoughts: Sexuality, Catholicism and Literature in Twentieth-Century Ireland*. Manchester University Press, 2012.

Crouthamel, Jason. *An Intimate History of the Front: Masculinity, Sexuality, and German Soldiers in the First World War*. Palgrave, 2014.

Crowley, Una, and Rob Kitchin. "Producing 'Decent Girls:' Governmentality and the Moral Geographies of Sexual Conduct in Ireland (1922–1937)." *Gender, Place, Culture* 15, no. 4 (2008), 355–372.

Crowson, N. J. "Tramps' Tales: Discovering the Life-Stories of Late Victorian and Edwardian Vagrants." *English Historical Review* 135, no. 577 (2020), 1488–1526.

Crozier, Ivan Dalley. "The Medical Construction of Homosexuality and Its Relation to the Law in Nineteenth-Century England." *Medical History* 45, no. 1 (2001), 61–82.

Cruise, Colin. "Error and Eros: The Fiction of Forrest Reid as a Defense of Homosexuality." In *Sex, Nation, and Dissent in Irish Writing*, edited by Eibhear Walshe. St. Martin's, 1997.

D'Cruze, Shani. "Introduction: Unguarded Passions: Violence, History and the Everyday." In *Everyday Violence in Britain, 1850–1950*, edited by Shani D'Cruze. Routledge, 2000.

D'Emilio, John. "Capitalism and Gay Identity." In *Powers of Desire: the Politics of Sexuality*, edited by Ann Snitow, Christine Stansell, and Sharon Thompson. New York University Press, 1983.

Daly, Mary E. "An Alien Institution? Attitudes towards the City in Nineteenth and Twentieth Century Irish Society." *Études Irlandaises* 10 (1985), 181–194.

Daly, Mary E. *Dublin, the Deposed Capital: A Social and Economic History, 1860–1914*. Cork University Press, 1984.

Daly, Mary E. "The Emergence of an Irish Adolescence: 1920s to 1970s." In *Adolescence in Modern Irish History*, edited by Catherine Cox and Susannah Riordan. Palgrave Macmillan, 2015.

Daly, Mary E. "The Irish Free State / Éire / Republic of Ireland / Ireland: 'A Country by Any Other Name'?" *Journal of British Studies* 46, no. 1 (2007), 72–90.

David, Hugh. *On Queer Street: A Social History of British Homosexuality, 1895–1995*. Harper Collins, 1997.

Davidoff, Leonore. *Thicker Than Water: Siblings and Their Relations, 1780–1920*. Oxford University Press, 2011.

Davies, Andrew. "Youth Gangs, Masculinity and Violence in Late-Victorian Manchester and Salford." *Journal of Social History* 32, no. 2 (1998), 349–369.

Davis, Natalie Zemon. *Fiction in the Archives: Pardon Tales and their Tellers in Sixteenth-Century France*. Cambridge University Press, 1987.

Davis, Natalie Zemon. *The Return of Martin Guerre*. Harvard University Press, 1983.

Delaney, Enda. "Our Island Story? Towards a Transnational History of Late Modern Ireland." *Irish Historical Studies* 37, no. 148 (2011), 599–621.

Delaney, Enda. "The Irish Diaspora." *Irish Economic and Social History* 33 (2006), 35–45.

Delaney, Enda, and Donald M. MacRaild. "Introduction." In *Irish Migration, Networks and Ethnic Identities Since 1750*, edited by Enda Delaney and Donald M. MacRaild. Routledge, 2007.

Delaney, Enda, and Fearghal McGarry. "Introduction: A Global History of the Irish Revolution." *Irish Historical Studies* 44, no. 165 (2020), 1–10.

Delap, Lucy. "'Disgusting Details Which Are Best Forgotten': Disclosures of Child Sexual Abuse in Twentieth-Century Britain." *Journal of British Studies* 57, no. 1 (2018), 79–107.

Delay, Cara. "'Language Which Will Move Their Hearts': Speaking Power, Performance, and the Lay-Clerical Relationship in Modern Catholic Ireland." *Journal of British Studies* 53 (2014), 426–452.

Delay, Cara. *Irish Women and the Creation of Modern Catholicism, 1850–1950*. Manchester University Press, 2019.

Dellamora, Richard. *Friendships' Bonds: Democracy and the Novel in Victorian England*. University of Pennsylvania Press, 2004.

Dellamora, Richard. *Masculine Desire: The Sexual Politics of Victorian Aestheticism*. University of North Carolina Press, 1990.

Deslandes, Paul, *The Culture of Male Beauty in Britain: From the First Photographs to David Beckham* (University of Chicago Press, 2021).

Dháibhéid, Caoimhe Nic, Shahmima Akhtar, Dónal Hassett, Kevin Kenny, Laura McAtackney, Ian McBride, Timothy G. McMahon, and Jane Ohlmeyer. "Round Table: Decolonising Irish History? Possibilities, Challenges, Practices." *Irish Historical Studies* 45, no. 168 (2021), 303–332.

Dickinson, Tommy. *"Curing Queers:" Mental Nurses and their Patients, 1935–1974*. Manchester University Press, 2015.

Dickson, David. "Town and City." In *The Cambridge Social History of Modern Ireland*, edited by Eugenio F. Biagini and Mary E. Daly. Cambridge University Press, 2017.

Dinshaw, Carolyn. *Getting Medieval: Sexualities and Communities, Pre- and Postmodern*. Duke University Press, 1999.

Doan, Laura. "'A Peculiarly Obscure Subject': The Missing 'Case' of the Heterosexual." In *British Queer History: New Approaches and Perspectives*, edited by Brian Lewis. Manchester University Press, 2013.

Doan, Laura. *History, Sexuality, and Women's Experience of Modern War*. Chicago, 2013.

Doan, Laura. "Sappho's Apotheosis? Radclyffe Hall's Queer Kinship with the Watchdogs of the Lord." *Sexuality and Culture* 8, no. 2 (2004), 80–106.

Donovan, Brian. *Respectability on Trial: Sex Crimes in New York City, 1900–1918*. SUNY Press, 2016.

Dooley, Terence. "The Big House, Aristocracy, and Golf in Ireland, c.1890–1921." In *Sport and Leisure in the Irish and British Country House*, edited by Terence Dooley and Christopher Ridgway. Four Courts, 2019.

Doughan, Christopher. *The Voice of the Provinces: The Regional Press in Revolutionary Ireland, 1914–1921*. Liverpool University Press, 2019.

Dowling, Linda. *Hellenism and Homosexuality in Victorian Oxford*. Cornell University Press, 1994.

Downing, Karen, Jonathan Thayer, and Joanne Begiato, eds. *Negotiating Masculinities and Modernity in the Maritime World, 1815–1940: A Sailor's Progress?* Palgrave Macmillan, 2021.

Doyle, David M., and Liam O'Callaghan. *Capital Punishment in Independent Ireland: A Social, Legal and Political History*. Liverpool University Press, 2019.

Doyle, Mark. *Fighting Like the Devil for the Sake of God: Protestants, Catholics and the Origins of Violence in Victorian Belfast*. Manchester University Press, 2009.

Duberman, Martin Bauml, Martha Vicinus, and George Chauncey, eds. *Hidden from History: Reclaiming the Gay and Lesbian Past*. Meridian, 1989.

Dudgeon, Jeffrey. *Roger Casement: The Black Diaries—with a Study of his Background, Sexuality and Irish Political Life*. Belfast Press, 2002.

Duggan, Lisa. "The Discipline Problem: Queer Theory Meets Lesbian and Gay History." *GLQ: A Journal of Lesbian and Gay History* 2, no. 3 (1995), 179–191.

Duggan, Marian. *Queering Conflict: Examining Lesbian and Gay Experiences of Homophobia in Northern Ireland*. Routledge, 2012.

Earls, Averill. *Love in the Lav: A Social Biography of Same-Sex Desire in Ireland, 1922–1972*. Temple University Press, 2025.

Earls, Averill. "Solicitor Brown and His Boy: Love, Sex, and Scandal in Twentieth-Century Ireland." *Historical Reflections* 46, no. 1 (2020), 79–94.

Earls, Averill. "Unnatural Offenses of English Import: The Political Association of Englishness and Same-Sex Desire in Nineteenth-Century Irish Nationalist Media." *Journal of the History of Sexuality* 28, no. 3 (2019), 396–424.

Earner-Byrne, Lindsey, and Diane Urquhart. "Gender Roles in Ireland Since 1740." In *Cambridge Social History of Modern Ireland*, edited by Mary Daly and Eugenio Biagini. Cambridge University Press, 2017.

Earner-Byrne, Lindsey. "Reinforcing the Family: The Role of Gender, Morality and Sexuality in Irish Welfare Policy, 1922–1944." *History of the Family* 13, no. 4 (2008), 360–369.

Earner-Byrne, Lindsey. "Religion, Gender, and Sexuality, 1922–1968." In *The Oxford Handbook of Religion in Modern Ireland*, edited by Gladys Ganiel and Andrew R. Holmes. Oxford University Press, 2024.

Earner-Byrne, Lindsey. "The Family in Ireland, 1880–2015." In *The Cambridge History of Ireland, Vol. IV: 1880 to the Present*, edited by Thomas Bartlett. Cambridge University Press, 2018.

Edwards, William Churchill. *Historic Quincy Massachusetts*. City of Quincy, 1945.

Egan, R. Danielle, and Gail L. Hawkes. "Imperiled and Perilous: Exploring the History of Childhood Sexuality." *Journal of Historical Sociology* 21, no. 4 (2008), 355–367.

Elias, Norbert. *The Civilizing Process*. Blackwell, 1994.

Elliott, Marianne. *The Catholics of Ulster*. Basic, 2002.

Ellison, Graham, and Jim Smyth. *The Crowned Harp: Policing Northern Ireland*. Pluto, 2000.

Erber, Nancy, and George Robb. "Introduction." In *Disorder in the Court: Trials and Sexual Conflict at the Turn of the Century*, edited by George Robb and Nancy Erber. Palgrave Macmillan, 1999.

Erber, Nancy. "Queer Follies: Effeminacy and Aestheticism in *Fin-de-siecle* France, the Case of Baron d'Adelsward Fersen and Count de Warren." In *Disorder in the Court: Trials and Sexual Conflict at the Turn of the Century*, edited by George Robb and Nancy Erber. Palgrave Macmillan, 1999.

Escoffier, Jeffrey. *American Homo: Community and Perversity*. University of California Press, 1998.

Evans, Jennifer F. *The Queer Art of History: Queer Kinship After Fascism*. Duke University Press, 2023.

Farrell, Elaine. *"A Most Diabolical Deed": Infanticide and Irish Society, 1850–1900*. Manchester University Press, 2013.

Farrell, Elaine, and Leanne McCormick. "Naming and Shaming? Telling Bad Bridget® Stories." *Transactions of the Royal Historical Society*, 2 (2024), 413–432.

Farrell, Michael. *Northern Ireland: The Orange State*. Pluto, 1976.

Feely, Catherine. "From Dialectics to Dancing: Reading, Writing and the Experience of Everyday Life in the Diaries of Frank P. Forster." *History Workshop Journal* 69, no. 1 (2010), 90–110.

Fernihough, Alan, Cormac Ó Gráda, and Brendan M. Walsh. "Intermarriage in a Divided Society: Ireland a Century Ago." *Explorations in Economic History* 56 (2015), 1–14.

Ferriter, Diarmaid. *Occasions of Sin: Sex and Society in Modern Ireland*. Profile, 2009.

Finnane, Mark. "A Decline in Violence in Ireland? Crime, Policing, and Social Relations, 1860–1914." *Crime, History & Societies* 1, no. 1 (1997), 51–70.

Finnane, Mark. *Insanity and the Insane in Post-Famine Ireland*. Croom Helm, 1981.

Finnane, Mark. "The Carrigan Committee of 1930–31 and the 'Moral Condition of the Saorstát.'" *Irish Historical Studies* 32, no. 128 (2001), 519–536.

Fischer, Clara. "Gender, Nation, and the Politics of Shame: Magdalen Laundries and the Institutionalization of Feminine Transgression in Modern Ireland." *Signs: Journal of Women in Culture and Society* 41, no. 4 (2016), 821–843.

Fischerova, Jana. "The Banning and Unbanning of Kate O'Brien's *The Land of Spices*." *Irish University Review* 48, no. 1 (2018), 69–83.

Fisher, Kate, and Jana Funke. "The Age of Attraction: Age, Gender and the History of Modern Male Homosexuality." *Gender and History* 31, no. 2 (2019), 266–283.

Fisher, Kate, and Rebecca Langlands. "General Introduction." In *Sex, Knowledge, and Receptions of the Past*, edited by Kate Fisher and Rebecca Langlands. Oxford University Press, 2015.

Fitzgerald, Patrick, and Brian Lambkin. *Migration in Irish History, 1607–2007*. Palgrave Macmillan, 2008.

Fitzpatrick, David. *The Americanisation of Ireland: Migration and Settlement, 1841–1925*. Cambridge University Press, 2019.

Fitzpatrick, David. "We Are All Transnationalists Now." *Irish Historical Studies* 41, no. 159 (2017).

Fitzpatrick, David. "Words and Irish History: An Experiment." In *Uncertain Futures: Essays about the Irish Past for Roy Foster*, edited by Senia Paseta. Oxford University Press, 2016.

Fitzpatrick, Sheila, and Robert Gellately. "Introduction to the Practices of Denunciation in Modern European History." *Journal of Modern History* 68, no. 4 (1996), 747–767.

Flanagan, Maureen. *Constructing the Patriarchal City: Gender and the Built Environments of London, Dublin, Toronto, and Chicago, 1870s into the 1940s*. Temple University Press, 2018.

Follis, Bryan. *A State Under Siege: The Establishment of Northern Ireland, 1921–1925*. Oxford University Press, 1995.

Foster, Roy. *Vivid Faces: The Revolutionary Generation in Ireland, 1890–1923*. Penguin, 2014.

Foucault, Michel. *The History of Sexuality, Volume I: An Introduction*. Translated by Robert Hurley. Vintage, 1978.

Fowler, David. *Youth Culture in Modern Britain, C. 1920–C. 1970: From Ivory Tower to Global Movement—a New History*. Bloomsbury, 2008.

Frank, Gillian, Bethany Moreton, and Heather R. White. "Introduction—More than Missionary: Doing the Histories of Religion and Sexuality Together." In *Devotions and Desires: Histories of Sexuality and Religion in the Twentieth-Century United States*, edited by Gillian Frank, Bethany Moreton, and Heather R. White. University of North Carolina Press, 2018.

Fries, Udo. "Two Hundred Years of English Death Notices." In *On Strangeness*, edited by Margaret Bridges. Narr, 1990.

Frontain, Raymond-Jean. "The Bible." In *Gay and Lesbian Literary Heritage*, edited by Claude J. Summers. Routledge, 2013.

Frost, Ginger. "'I Am Master Here': Illegitimacy, Masculinity, and Violence in Victorian England." In *The Politics of Domestic Authority in Britain since 1800*, edited by Lucy Delap, Ben Griffin, and Abigail Wills. Palgrave Macmillan, 2009.

Fuechtner, Veronika, Douglas E. Haynes, and Ryan M. Jones, eds. *A Global History of Sexual Science, 1880–1960*. University of California Press, 2017.

Fuller, Louise. "Irish Catholic Culture before and after Vatican II." In *The Oxford Handbook of Religion in Modern Ireland*, edited by Gladys Ganiel and Andrew R. Holmes. Oxford University Press, 2024.

Fuller, Louise, *Irish Catholicism Since 1950: The Undoing of a Culture*. Gill and Macmillan, 2004.

Gibbon, Peter. *The Origins of Ulster Unionism: The Formation of Popular Protestant Politics and Ideology in Nineteenth-Century Ireland*. Manchester University Press, 1975.

Gifford, James, ed. *Glances Backward: An Anthology of American Homosexual Writing 1830–1920*. Broadview, 2007.

Gilbert, Arthur N. "Buggery and the British Navy, 1700–1861." *Journal of Social History* 10, no. 1 (1976), 72–98.

Gillespie, Raymond. *Early Belfast: The Origins and Growth of an Ulster Town to 1750*. Ulster Historical Foundation, 2007.

Gillespie, Raymond. "Making Belfast, 1600–1750." In *Belfast 400: People, Place and History*, edited by S. J. Connolly. Liverpool University Press, 2012.

Glasscock, R. E. "The Growth of the Port.' In *Belfast: The Origin and Growth of an Industrial City*, edited by J. C. Beckett and R. E. Glasscock. BBC Books, 1967.

Govan, D. H. "Towards a Religious Understanding of the Orange Order: Belfast 1910 to 1914." *Irish Studies Review* 29, no. 4 (2021), 501–514.

Gray, Jane. "The Circulation of Children in Rural Ireland during the First Half of the Twentieth Century." *Continuity and Change* 29, no. 3 (2014), 399–421.

Gray, Malachy. "A Shop Steward Remembers." *Saothar* 11 (1986), 109–115.

Green, James N. *Beyond Carnival: Male Homosexuality in Twentieth-Century Brazil*. University of Chicago Press, 1999.

Greenhalgh, Charlotte. "Love in Later Life: Old Age, Marriage and Social Research in Mid-twentieth Century Britain." In *Love and Romance in Britain, 1918–1970*, edited by Alana Harris and Timothy Willem Jones. Palgrave Macmillan, 2015.

Grimley, Matthew. "Law, Morality and Secularisation: The Church of England and the Wolfenden Report, 1954–1967." *Journal of Ecclesiastical History* 60, no. 4 (2009), 725–741.

Guinnane, Timothy. *The Vanishing Irish: Households, Migration, and the Rural Economy in Ireland, 1850–1915*. Princeton University Press, 2007.

Gustav-Wrathall, John Donald. *Take the Young Stranger by the Hand: Same-Sex Relations and the YMCA*. University of Chicago Press, 1998.

Halberstam, Judith. *In a Queer Time and Place: Transgender Bodies, Subcultural Lives*. NYU Press, 2005.

Hall, Donald. *Muscular Christianity: Embodying the Victorian Age*. Cambridge, 1994.

Hall, Lesley. "Heroes or Villains? Reconsidering British Fin de Siècle Sexology and Its Impact." In *New Sexual Agendas*, edited by Lynne Segal. Palgrave Macmillan, 1997.

Hall, Leslie. "'Disinterested Enthusiasm for Sexual Misconduct': The British Society for the Study of Sex Psychology, 1913–1947." *Journal of Contemporary History* 30, no. 4 (1995), 665–686.

Halperin, David. *How to Do the History of Homosexuality*. University of Chicago Press, 2002.

Halperin, David. *Saint Foucault: Towards a Gay Hagiography*. Oxford University Press, 1997.

Hanna, Erika. *Snapshot Stories: Visuality, Photography, and the Social History of Ireland, 1922–2000*. Oxford University Press, 2020.

Harding, James E. *The Love of David and Jonathan: Ideology, Text, Reception*. Routledge, 2014.

Harris, Alana. "'Pope Norman,' Griffin's Report and Roman Catholic Reactions to Homosexual Law Reform in England and Wales, 1954–1971." In Mark D. Chapman and Dominic Janes, *New Approaches to History and Theology to Same-Sex Love and Desire*. Palgrave Macmillan, 2018.

Harrison, Laura. *Dangerous Amusements: Leisure, the Young Working-Class and Urban Space in Britain, c. 1870–1939*. Manchester University Press, 2022.

Harron, Paul. "Big Vision City: The Physical Transformation of Belfast by Provincial Architects, 1870–1910." In *Belfast: The Emerging City 1850–1914*, edited by Olwen Purdue. Irish Academic Press, 2012.

Hartman, Saidya. *Wayward Lives, Beautiful Experiments: Intimate Histories of Social Upheaval*. W. W. Norton & Co., 2019.

Haslam, Piers. "Debating the Bachelor Tax: Masculinity and the Politics of Taxation in Britain, 1894–1920." *Modern British History* (forthcoming).

Hawkins, Richard. "Barbour, Sir John Milne." In *Dictionary of Irish Biography*, edited by James McGuire and James Quinn. Cambridge University Press, 2009.

Healey, Dan. *Homosexual Desire in Revolutionary Russia: The Regulation of Sexual and Gender Dissent*. University of Chicago Press, 2001.

Heap, Chad. *Slumming: Sexual and Racial Encounters in American Nightlife, 1885–1940*. Chicago, 2009.

Heffernan, Conor. "Physical Degeneracy and Racial Fitness in Prewar Ireland." *Éire-Ireland* 57, no. 3 & 4 (2022), 225–253.

Hemphill, C. Dallett. *Siblings: Brothers and Sisters in American History*. Oxford University Press, 2011.

Hepburn, A. C. *A Past Apart: Studies in the History of Catholic Belfast, 1850–1950*. Ulster Historical Foundation, 1996.

Hepburn, A. C., and B. Collins. "Industrial Society: The Structure of Belfast, 1901." In *Plantation to Partition: Essays in Honour of J. L. McCracken*, edited by Peter Roebuck. Blackstaff, 1981.

Herson, John. *Divergent Paths: Family Histories of Irish Emigrants in Britain 1820–1920*. Manchester University Press, 2015.

Herzog, Dagmar. "Introduction." In *Brutality and Desire: War and Sexuality in Europe's Twentieth Century*, edited by Dagmar Herzog. Palgrave Macmillan, 2009.

Heyam, Kit. *Before We Were Trans: A New History of Gender*. Basic, 2022.
Higgins, Patrick. *Heterosexual Dictatorship: Male Homosexuality in Postwar Britain*. Fourth Estate, 1996.
Hilliard, Christopher. *A Matter of Obscenity: The Politics of Censorship in Modern England*. Princeton University Press, 2021.
Hilliard, Christopher. "The Literary Underground of 1920s London." *Social History* 33, no. 2 (2008), 164–182.
Hilliard, David. "Some Find a Niche: Same-Sex Attracted People in Australian Anglicanism." In Mark D. Chapman and Dominic Janes, *New Approaches to History and Theology to Same-Sex Love and Desire*. Palgrave Macmillan, 2018.
Hilliard, David. "UnEnglish and Unmanly: Anglo-Catholicism and Homosexuality." *Victorian Studies* 25, no. 2 (1982), 181–210.
Hindmarch-Watson, Katie. "Male Prostitution and the London GPO: Telegraph Boys' 'Immorality' from Nationalization to the Cleveland Street Scandal." *Journal of British Studies* 51, no. 3 (2012), 594–617.
Hirst, Catherine. *Religion, Politics and Violence in Nineteenth-Century Belfast: The Pound and Sandy Row*. Four Courts, 2001.
Hitchcock, Tim. "Confronting the Digital: Or How Academic History Writing Lost the Plot." *Cultural and Social History* 10, no. 1 (2013), 9–23.
Hoggart, Richard. *The Uses of Literacy*. Transaction, 2004 [1957].
Holmes, Andrew R. "Protestant Religion in Northern Ireland to 1980." In *The Oxford Handbook of Religion in Modern Ireland*, edited by Gladys Ganiel and Andrew R. Holmes. Oxford University Press, 2024.
Hooper, Walter, ed. *They Stand Together: The Letters of CS Lewis to Arthur Greeves (1914–1963)*. William Collins & Sons, 1979.
Houlbrook, Matt. *Prince of Tricksters: The Incredible True Story of Netley Lucas, Gentleman Crook*. University of Chicago Press, 2016.
Houlbrook, Matt. "Soldier Heroes and Rent Boys: Homosex, Masculinities, and Britishness in the Brigade of Guards, Circa 1900–1960." *Journal of British Studies* xlii, no. 3 (2003), 351–388.
Houlbrook, Matt. "'The Man with the Powder Puff' in Interwar London." *Historical Journal* 50, no. 1 (2007), 145–171.
Houlbrook, Matt. "Toward a Historical Geography of Sexuality." *Journal of Urban History* 27, no. 4 (2001), 497–504.
Houlbrook, Matt, Katie Jones, and Ben Mechen. "Introduction." In *Men and Masculinities in Modern Britain: A History for the Present*, edited by Matt Houlbrook, Katie Jones, and Ben Mechen. Manchester University Press, 2024.
Houlbrook, Matt. *Queer London: Perils and Possibilities in the Sexual Metropolis, 1918–1957*. University of Chicago Press, 2005.
Houston, Lloyd (Meadhbh). *Irish Modernism and the Politics of Sexual Health*. Oxford University Press, 2023.
Howard, John. *Men Like That: A Southern Queer History*. University of Chicago Press, 2001.
Howe, Stephen. *Ireland and Empire: Colonial Legacies in Irish History and Culture*. Oxford University Press, 2000.
Howe, Stephen. "Questioning the (Bad) Question: 'Was Ireland a Colony?'" *Irish Historical Studies* 36, no. 142 (2008), 138–152.

Hubbard, Phil. "Queering the City: Homosociality and Homosexuality in the Modern Metropolis." *Journal of Urban History* 33, no. 2 (2007), 310–319.

Hulme, Tom, and Charlie Lynch. "Queer Men and Networks of Communication in Northern Ireland before the 1970s." *Journal of the History of Sexuality* (forthcoming).

Hulme, Tom. *After the Shock City: Urban Culture and the Making of Modern Citizenship*. Boydell, 2019.

Hulme, Tom. "Out of the Shadows: 100 Years of LGBT Life in Northern Ireland." In *Northern Ireland 1921–2021: Centenary Historical Perspectives*, edited by Paul Bew, Marie Coleman, and Caoimhe Nic Dháibhéid. Ulster Historical Foundation, 2022.

Hulme, Tom. "Queer Belfast during the First World War: Masculinity and Same-Sex Desire in the Irish City." *Irish Historical Studies* 45, no. 168 (2021), 239–261.

Hulme, Tom. "Queering Family History and the Lives of Irish Men before Gay Liberation." *History of the Family* 29, no. 1 (2024), 62–83.

Huneke, Samuel Clowes. *States of Liberation: Gay Men between Dictatorship and Democracy in Cold War Germany*. University of Toronto Press, 2022.

Hunt, Alan. "The Great Masturbation Panic and the Discourses of Moral Regulation in Nineteenth- and Early Twentieth-Century Britain." *Journal of the History of Sexuality* 8, no. 4 (1998), 575–615.

Hurley, Nat. "The Queer Traffic in Literature; or, Reading Anthologically." *ESC: English Studies in Canada* 36, no. 1 (2010), 81–108.

Hyam, Ronald. *Empire and Sexuality: The British Experience*. Manchester University Press, 1990.

Hyde, H. Montgomery. *The Other Love: An Historical and Contemporary Survey of Homosexuality in Britain*. Harper Collins, 1970.

Hyde, Paul. *Anatomy of a Lie: Decoding Casement*. Wordwell, 2019.

Inglis, Tom. "Foucault, Bourdieu and the Field of Irish Sexuality." *Irish Journal of Sociology* 7, no. 1 (1997), 5–28.

Inglis, Tom. *Moral Monopoly: The Rise and Fall of the Catholic Church in Modern Ireland*. University College Dublin Press, 1998.

Inglis, Tom. "Origins and Legacies of Irish Prudery: Sexuality and Social Control in Modern Ireland." *Éire-Ireland* 40, no. 3 & 4 (2005), 9–37.

Israel Ross, Andrew. *Public City/Public Sex: Homosexuality, Prostitution, and Urban Culture in Nineteenth-Century Paris*. Temple University Press, 2019.

Jackson, Alvin. *Home Rule: an Irish History, 1800–2000*. Oxford University Press, 2003.

Jackson, Alvin. "Irish Unionists and the Empire, 1880–1920." In *"An Irish Empire"? Aspects of Ireland and the British Empire*, edited by Keith Jeffery. Manchester University Press, 1996.

Janes, Dominic. *Visions of Queer Martyrdom from John Henry Newman to Derek Jarman*. University of Chicago Press, 2015.

Jerram, Leif. *Streetlife: The Untold History of Europe's Twentieth Century*. Oxford University Press, 2011.

Johnson, Alice. *Middle-Class Life in Victorian Belfast*. Liverpool University Press, 2020.

Johnson, Colin R. *Just Queer Folks: Gender and Sexuality in Rural America*. Temple University Press, 2013.

Jones, Ben. *The Working Class in Mid Twentieth-Century England: Community, Identity and Social Memory*. Manchester University Press, 2012.

Jones, Emrys. *A Social Geography of Belfast* (London, 1960).

Jones, Emrys. "Late Victorian Belfast: 1850–1900." In *Belfast: The Origin and Growth of an Industrial City*, edited by J. C. Beckett and R.E. Glasscock. BBC Books, 1967.

Jones, Greta. "Eugenics in Ireland: The Belfast Eugenics Society, 1911–1915." *Irish Historical Studies* 28, no. 109 (1992), 81–95.

Jones, Greta. "Marie Stopes in Ireland—The Mother's Clinic in Belfast, 1936–47." *Social History of Medicine* 5, no. 2 (1992), 255–277.

Jones, Karen R. "'The Lungs of the City:' Green Space, Public Health and Bodily Metaphor in the Landscape of Urban Park History." *Environment and History* 24, no. 1 (2018), 39–58.

Jones, Timothy Willem. "Moral Welfare and Social Well-Being: The Church of England and the Emergence of Modern Homosexuality." In *Men, Masculinities and Religious Change in Twentieth-Century Britain*, edited by Lucy Delap and Sue Morgan. Palgrave Macmillan, 2013.

Jones, Timothy Willem. "The Stained-Glass Closet: Celibacy and Homosexuality in the Church of England to 1955." *Journal of the History of Sexuality* 20, no. 1 (2011), 132–152.

Jones, Timothy Willem, and Alana Harris. "Introduction: Historicizing 'Modern' Love and Romance." In *Love and Romance in Britain, 1918–1970*, edited Alana Harris and Timothy Willem Jones. Palgrave Macmillan, 2015.

Jordan, Mark D. *The Invention of Sodomy in Christian Theology*. University of Chicago press, 1998.

Joyce, Simon. "Two Women Walk into a Theatre Bathroom: The Fanny and Stella Trials as Trans Narrative." *Victorian Review* 44, no.1 (2018), 83–98.

Kaplan, Morris. *Sodom on the Thames: Sex, Love, and Scandal in Wilde Times*. Cornell University Press, 2005.

Karczewski, Kamil. "'Call Me by My Name': A 'Strange and Incomprehensible' Passion in the Polish Kresy of the 1920s," *Slavic Review* 81, no. 3 (2022), 631–652.

Katz, Jonathan Ned. *Love Stories: Sex between Men before Homosexuality*. University of Chicago Press, 2003.

Katz, Jonathan Ned. *The Invention of Heterosexuality*. University of Chicago Press, 1995.

Kaylor, M. M. *Secreted Desires: The Major Uranians—Hopkins, Pater and Wilde*. Masaryk University Press, 2006.

Keating, Anthony. "Sexual Crime in the Irish Free State 1922–1933: Its Nature, Extent and Reporting." *Irish Studies Review* 20, no. 2 (2012), 137–158.

Kelly, Brendan D. "Ego, Id, and Ireland." *Lancet* 4, no. 4 (2017), 281–282.

Kelly, Brendan. *Hearing Voices: The History of Psychiatry in Ireland*. Irish Academic Press, 2016.

Kelly, Mary C. *The Shamrock and the Lily: The New York Irish and the Creation of a Transatlantic Identity, 1845–1921*. Peter Lang, 2007.

Kennedy, Dane. "'Captain Burton's Oriental Muck Heap': *The Book of the Thousand Nights* and the Uses of Orientalism." *Journal of British Studies* 39, no. 3 (2000), 317–339.

Kennedy, Dennis. *The Widening Gulf: Northern Attitudes to the Independent Irish State, 1919–1949*. Blackstaff, 1988.

Kennedy, Elizabeth L., and Madeline Davis. *Boots of Leather, Slippers of Gold: The History of a Lesbian Community*. Routledge, 1993.

Kennedy, Finola. *Cottage to Creche: Family Change in Ireland*. Institute of Public Administration, 2001.

Kennedy, Finola. "The Suppression of the Carrigan Report: A Historical Perspective on Child Abuse." *Studies: An Irish Quarterly Review* 8, no. 356 (2000), 354–363.

Kenny, Kevin. "Introduction." In *Ireland and the British Empire*, edited by Kevin Kenny. Oxford University Press, 2004.

Kerrigan, Páraic. *LGBTQ Visibility, Media and Sexuality in Ireland*. Routledge, 2020.

Kerrigan, Páraic. *Reeling in the Queers: Tales of Ireland's LGBTQ Past*. New Island, 2024.

Kidd, Alan. *State, Society and the Poor in Nineteenth-Century England*. Basingstoke, 1999.

Kilcommins, Shane, Ian O'Donnell, Eoin O'Sullivan, and Barry Vaughan. *Crime, Punishment and the Search for Order in Ireland*. Institute of Public Administration, 2005.

King, Laura. *Family Men: Fatherhood and Masculinity in Britain, c. 1914–1960*. Oxford University Press, 2015.

King, Sophia Hillan. *The Silken Twine: A Study of the Works of Michael McLaverty*. Dufour Editions, 1992.

Kirkland, Richard. *Cathal O'Byrne and the Northern Revival in Ireland, 1890–1960*. Liverpool University Press, 2006.

Kirkland, Richard. *Irish London: A Cultural History 1850–1916*. Bloomsbury, 2021.

Kitchin, Rob, and Karen Lysaght. "Heterosexism and the Geographies of Everyday Life in Belfast, Northern Ireland." *Environment and Planning* 34, no. 3 (2003), 489–510.

Klein, Joanne. *Invisible Men: The Secret Lives of Police Constables in Liverpool, Manchester, and Birmingham 1900–1939*. Liverpool University Press, 2010.

Koole, Simeon. "How We Came to Mind the Gap: Time, Tactility, and the Tube." *Twentieth Century British History* 27, no. 4 (2016), 524–554.

Koven, Seth. *Slumming: Sexual and Social Politics in Victorian London*. Princeton University Press, 2004.

Koven, Seth. *The Match Girl and the Heiress*. Princeton University Press, 2014.

Kunzel, Regina G. "Situating Sex: Prison Sexual Culture in the Mid-twentieth Century United States." *GLQ: A Journal of Lesbian and Gay Studies* 8, no. 3 (2002), 253–270.

Kurimay, Anita. *Queer Budapest, 1873–1961*. University of Chicago Press, 2020.

Lacey, Brian. *Terrible Queer Creatures: Homosexuality in Irish History*. Wordwell, 2009.

LaFleur, Greta, Masha Raskolnikov, and Anna Klosowska. "Introduction: The Benefits of Being Trans Historical." In *Trans Historical: Gender Plurality before the Modern*, edited by Greta LaFleur, Masha Raskolnikov, and Anna Klosowska. Cornell University Press, 2021.

Laite, Julia. *The Disappearance of Lydia Harvey: A True Story of Sex, Crime and the Meaning of Justice*. Profile, 2021.

Laite, Julia. "The Emmet's Inch: 'Small' History in a Digital Age." *Journal of Social History* 53, no. 4 (2020), 963–989.

Langhamer, Claire. "Love, Selfhood and Authenticity in Post-war Britain." *Cultural and Social History* 9, no. 2 (2012), 277–297.

Langhamer, Claire. *The English in Love: The Intimate Story of a Sexual Revolution*. Oxford University Press, 2013.

Laqueur, Thomas. *Solitary Sex: A Cultural History of Masturbation*. Princeton University Press, 2004.

Laragy, Georgina. "'For Those Whose Benefit These Burdens Must Be Taken': Children, Employment, and Training in Northern Ireland, 1921–1939." *Journal of the History of Childhood and Youth* 9, no. 2 (2016), 277–293.

Larkin, Felix M. "'Green Shoots' of the New Journalism in the *Freeman's Journal*, 1877–1890." In *Ireland and the New Journalism*, edited by Karen Steele and Michael de Nie. Palgrave Macmillan, 2014.

Larmour, Paul. "Bricks, Stone, Concrete and Steel: The Built Fabric of Twentieth-Century Belfast." In *Enduring City: Belfast in the Twentieth Century*, edited by Frederick W. Boal and Stephen A. Royle. Blackstaff, 2006.

Lauritsen, John. "Edward Irenaeus Prime-Stevenson (Xavier Mayne) (1868–1942)." In *Before Stonewall: Activists for Gay and Lesbian Rights in Historical Context*, edited by Vern L. Bullough. Routledge, 2002.

Law, Gary. *Historic Pubs of Belfast*. Appletree, 2002.

Lawless, Catherine, and Ciara Breathnach. "Homosexuality and Lesbianism in Irish Newspapers, 1861–1922." In Catherline Lawless and Ciara Breathnach, *Gender and History*. Routledge, 2022.

Lawrence, Michael. "'I Wished to See London': Transnational Irish Sexualities and the Dublin Castle Scandal of 1883–1884." Article in draft.

Lees, Andrew. *Cities Perceived: Urban Society in European and American Thought, 1820–1940*. Manchester University Press, 1985.

Leeworthy, Daryl. *A Little Gay History of Wales*. Cardiff, 2019.

LeJacq, Seth Stein. "Buggery's Travels: Royal Navy Sodomy on Ship and Shore in the Long Eighteenth Century." *Journal for Maritime Research* 17, no. 2 (2015), 103–116.

Lemmey, Huw, and Ben Miller. *Bad Gays: A Homosexual History*. Verso, 2022.

Lepore, Jill. "Historians Who Love Too Much: Reflections on Microhistory and Biography." *Journal of American History* 88, no. 1 (2001).

Lewis, Brian. "Introduction: British Queer History." In *British Queer History: New Approaches and Perspectives*, edited by Brian Lewis. Manchester University Press, 2013.

Lewis, Brian. "The Queer Life and Afterlife of Roger Casement." *Journal of the History of Sexuality* 14, no. 4 (2005), 363–382.

Lewis, Brian. *Wolfenden's Witnesses: Homosexuality in Postwar Britian*. Palgrave Macmillan, 2016.

Longley, Edna. "Progressive Bookmen: Politics and Northern Protestant Writers Since the 1930s." *Irish Review* 1 (1986), 50–57.

Loughlin, Christopher. "The Moral Economy of Loyalty: Labour, Law, and the State in Northern Ireland, 1921–1939." *Labour History Review* 82, no. 1 (2017), 1–22.

Loughlin, James. "Consolidating 'Ulster': Regime Propaganda and Architecture in the Inter-war Period." *National Identities* 1, no. 2 (1999), 161–177.

Loughlin, James. *Ulster Unionism and British National Identity Since 1885*. Frances Pinter, 1995.

Love, Heather. *Feeling Backward: Loss and the Politics of Queer History*. Harvard University Press, 2007.

Lucey, Seán. "On the Brink of Universalism: The Emergency Hospital Services in Second World War Northern Ireland." In *Medicine, Health and Irish Experiences of Conflict, 1914–1945*, edited by David Durnin and Ian Miller. Manchester University Press, 2016.

Luddy, Maria. "Marriage, Sexuality and the Law in Ireland." In *The Cambridge Social History of Modern Ireland*, edited by Eugenio F. Biagini and Mary E. Daly. Cambridge University Press, 2017.

Luddy, Maria. *Prostitution and Irish Society, 1800–1940*. Cambridge University Press, 2007.

Lvovsky, Anna. *Vice Patrol: Cops, Courts, and the Struggle over Urban Gay Life before Stonewall*. University of Chicago Press, 2021.

Lynch, Charlie. "Between Sickness and Sin: Models of Male Homosexuality in Northern Ireland c. 1960–1990." *Irish Historical Studies* (forthcoming).

Lynch, Charlie. "Dirty Linen." *History Today* 74, no. 4 (2024), 68–75.

Lyon, Charles E. *British Wages*. Government Printing Office, 1926.

Lyons, Clare A. "Mapping an Atlantic Sexual Culture: Homoeroticism in Eighteenth-Century Philadelphia." In *Long before Stonewall: Histories of Same-Sex Sexuality in Early America*, edited by Thomas A. Foster. NYU Press, 2007.

MacLoughlin, Adrian. *The City of Belfast*. Dublin, 1982.

MacRaild, Donald M. *Irish Migrants in Modern Britain, 1750–1922*. Palgrave Macmillan, 1999.

Madden, Ed. "Bachelor Trouble, *Troubled Bachelors:* The Cultural Figure of the Bachelor in Ballbunnion and Mullingar." In *Ireland and Masculinities in History*, edited by Rebecca Anne Barr, Sean Brady, and Jane G.V. McGaughey. Palgrave Macmillan, 2019.

Malcolm, Elizabeth. *"Ireland Sober, Ireland Free:" Drink and Temperance in Nineteenth-Century Ireland*. Gill and Macmillan, 1986.

Maloney, William J. *The Forged Casement Diaries*. Talbot, 1936.

Mansell, Charmain. "Beyond the Home: Space and Agency in the Experiences of Female Service in Early Modern England." *Gender & History* 33, no. 1 (2021), 24–49.

Marhoefer, Laurie. "'The Book Was a Revelation, I Recognized Myself in It': Lesbian Sexuality, Censorship, and the Queer Press in Weimar-Era Germany." *Journal of Women's History* 27, no. 2 (2015), 62–86.

Marshik, Celia. "History's 'Abrupt Revents:' Censoring War's Perversions in *The Well of Loneliness* and *Sleeveless Errand*." *Journal of Modern Literature* 26, no. 2 (2002), 145–159.

Martin, Peter. *Censorship in the Two Irelands, 1922–1939*. Irish Academic Press, 2006.

Massad, Joseph A. *Desiring Arabs*. University of Chicago Press, 2007.

Mauger, Alice. "From 'Pledge' to 'Public Health': Medical Responses to Ireland's Drinking Culture, c. 1890–2018." In *Routledge Handbook of Intoxicants and Intoxication*, edited by Geoffrey Hunt, Tamar Antin, Vibeke Asmussen Frank. Routledge, 2023.

Maynard, Steven. "'Horrible Temptations': Sex, Men, and Working-Class Male Youth in Urban Ontario, 1890–1935." *Canadian Historical Review* 78, no. 2 (1997), 191–235.

Maynard, Steven. "Through a Hole in the Lavatory Wall: Homosexual Subcultures, Police Surveillance, and the Dialectics of Discovery, Toronto, 1890–1930." *Journal of the History of Sexuality* 5, no. 2 (1994), 207–242.

McAuley, Finbarr. "The Intoxication Defence in Criminal Law." *Irish Jurist* 32 (1997).

McAuliffe, Mary, and Harriet Wheelock, eds. *The Diaries of Kathleen Lynn: A Life Revealed Through Personal Writing*. University College Dublin Press, 2023.

McClelland, Keith. "England's Greatness, the Working Man." In *Defining the Victorian Nation: Class, Race, Gender and the British Reform Act of 1867*, edited by Catherine Hall, Keith McClelland and Jane Rendall. Cambridge University Press, 2000.

McClelland, Keith. "Masculinity and the 'Representative Artisan' in Britain, 1850–1880." In *Manful Assertions: Masculinities in Britain Since 1800*, edited by Michael Roper and John Tosh. Routledge, 1991.

McCormick, Leanne. "'One Yank and They're Off': Interaction between U.S. Troops and Northern Irish Women, 1942–1945." *Journal of the History of Sexuality* 15, no. 2 (2006), 228–257.

McCormick, Leanne. *Regulating Sexuality: Women in Twentieth-Century Northern Ireland*. Manchester University Press, 2013.

McDiarmid, Lucy. *The Irish Art of Controversy*. Lilliput, 2005.

McDonagh, Enda. "Homosexuality: Sorrowful Mystery, Joyful Mystery—a Straight View and Its Origins." *The Furrow* 54, no. 9 (2003), 455–464.

McDonagh, Patrick. *Gay and Lesbian Activism in the Republic of Ireland, 1973–1993*. Bloomsbury, 2021.

McGarry, Fearghal. "A Vision of Ireland: Remembering the Struggle for Self-Determination." In *Art and Self-Determination: A Reader*, edited by Lisa Moran and Stephen O'Neill. Irish Museum of Modern Art, 2023.

McGaughey, Jane G. V. *Ulster's Men: Protestant Unionist Masculinities and Militarization in the North of Ireland, 1912–1923*. McGill-Queen's University Press, 2012.

McGloin, Jean Marie. "A Historical Consideration of the Police and Prosecution/Courts in Northern Ireland." *International Criminal Justice Review* 16, no. 2 (2006), 77–98.

McIntosh, Gillian. "Children, Street Trading and the Representation of Public Space in Edwardian Ireland." In *Children, Childhood and Irish Society: 1500 to the Present*, edited by Maria Luddy and James Smith. Four Courts, 2014.

McIntosh, Mary. "The Homosexual Role." *Social Problems* 16, no. 2 (1968), 182–192.

McKane, Pamela. "'No Idle Sightseers': The Ulster Women's Unionist Council and the Masculine World of Politics during the Ulster Crisis, 1912–1914." In *Ireland and Masculinities in History*, edited by Rebecca Anne Barr, Sean Brady, and Jane G. V. McGaughey. Palgrave Macmillan, 2019.

McLaren, Angus. *Sexual Blackmail: A Modern History*. Harvard University Press, 2002.

McLaren, Angus. *The Trials of Masculinity: Policing Sexual Boundaries, 1870–1930*. University of Chicago Press, 1997.

McLaughlin, Noel, and Joanna Braniff. *How Belfast Got the Blues: A Cultural History of Popular Music in the 1960s*. Intellect, 2020.

McLoughlin, Dympna. "Women and Sexuality in Nineteenth Century Ireland." *Irish Journal of Psychology* 15, no. 2–3 (1994), 266–275.

McManus, Ruth. "Dublin's Lodger Phenomenon in the Early Twentieth century." *Irish Economic and Social History* 45, no. 1 (2018), 23–46.

McNally, Kenneth. *The Narrow Streets*. Blackstaff, 1972.

McNeill, D. B. *Irish Passenger Steamship Services: Vol 1. North of Ireland*. David & Charles, 1969.

Meek, Jeff. *Queer Trades, Sex and Society: Male Prostitution and the War on Homosexuality in Interwar Scotland*. Routledge, 2023.

Meek, Jeff. *Queer Voices in Post-War Scotland: Male Homosexuality, Religion and Society*. Palgrave, 2015.

Meeker, Martin. *Contacts Desired: Gay and Lesbian Communications and Community, 1940s-1970s*. University of Chicago Press, 2006.

Megahey, Alan. *The Irish Protestant Church in the Twentieth Century*. Palgrave Macmillan, 2000.

Meyer, Jessica, and Alexia Moncrieff. "Family Not to Be Informed? The Ethical Use of Historical Medical Documentation." In *Patient Voices in Britain, 1840–1948*, edited by Jessia Meyer and Anne Hanley. Manchester University Press, 2021.

Meyerowitz, Joanne. "Transnational Sex and U.S. History." *American Historical Review* 114, no. 5 (2009), 1273–1286.

Micheler, Stefan. "Homophobic Propaganda and the Denunciation of Same-Sex Desiring Men under National Socialism." *Journal of the History of Sexuality* 11, no. 1/2 (2002), 95–130.

Milne, Graeme. *People, Place and Power on the Nineteenth-Century Waterfront: Sailortown*. Palgrave Macmillan, 2016.

Mitchell, Angus. *16 Lives: Roger Casement*. O'Brien, 2013.

Mitchell, Mark, and David Leavitt. *Pages Passed from Hand to Hand: The Hidden Tradition of Homosexual Literature in English from 1748 to 1914*. Chatto & Windus, 1998.

Mondimore, Francis Mark. *A Natural History of Homosexuality*. John Hopkins University Press, 1996.

Moran, Joe. "The Death of an Irishman: A Speculative Biography." *History Workshop Journal* 98 (2024), 209–233.

Morgan, David H. J. *Family Connections: An Introduction to Family Studies*. Cambridge University Press, 1996.

Morgan, Sue. "*Sex and Common-Sense:* Maude Royden, Religion, and Modern Sexuality." *Journal of British Studies* 52, no. 1 (2013), 153–178.

Moroney, Nora, and Stephen O'Neill. "Continuity and Change in the Belfast Press, 1900–1994." In *The Edinburgh History of the British and Irish Press. Vol 3: Competition and Disruption, 1900–2017*, edited by Martin Conboy and Adrian Bingham. Edinburgh University Press, 2000.

Morris, George. "Intimacy in Modern British History." *Historical Journal* 64, no. 3 (2021), 796–811.

Morris, R. J. "Urban Ulster Since 1600." In *Ulster Since 1600: Politics, Economy, and Society*, edited by Liam Kennedy and Philip Ollerenshaw. Oxford University Press, 2013.

Mort, Frank. *Capital Affairs: London and the Making of the Permissive Society*. Yale University Press, 2010.

Mort, Frank. *Dangerous Sexualities: Medico-Moral Politics in England Since 1830*. Routledge, 2000 [1987].

Mort, Frank. "Mapping Sexual London: The Wolfenden Committee on Homosexual Offences and Prostitution, 1954–1957." *New Formations* 37 (1999), 92–113.

Mosse, George. *Nationalism and Sexuality: Middle-Class Morality and Sexual Norms in Modern Europe*. University of Wisconsin Press, 1985.

Muldowney, Mary. "We Were Conscious of the Sort of People We Mixed with: The State, Social Attitudes and the Family in Mid Twentieth Century Ireland." *History of the Family* 13 (2008), 402–415.

Mulholland, Marc. *The Longest War: Northern Ireland's Troubled History*. Oxford University Press, 2002.

Mumford, Kevin J. "Homosex Changes: Race, Cultural Geography, and the Emergence of the Gay." *American Quarterly* 48, no. 3 (1996), 395–414.

Munt, Sally. *Queer Attachments: The Cultural Politics of Shame*. Routledge, 2007.

Murgu, Cal. "'Innocence Is as Innocence Does': Anglo-Irish Politics, Masculinity and the de Cobain Gross Indecency Scandal of 1891–1893." *Gender and History* 29, no. 2 (2017), 309–328.

Murphy, Amy Tooth. "'I Conformed; I Got Married. It Seemed Like a Good Idea at the Time': Domesticity in Postwar Lesbian Oral History." In *British Queer History: New Approaches and Perspectives*, edited by Brian Lewis. Manchester University Press, 2013.

Murphy, Kevin P., Zeb Tortorici, and Daniel Marshall, eds. "Queering Archives: Intimate Tracings." *Radical History Review* no. 122 (2015).

Murphy, Kevin P., Zeb Tortorici, and Daniel Marshall, eds. "Queering Archives: Historical Unravellings." *Radical History Review* no. 120 (2014).

Murphy, Maureen. "The Fionnuala Factor: Irish Sibling Emigration at the Turn of the Century." In *Gender and Sexuality in Modern Ireland*, edited by Anthony Bradley and Maryann Gialanella Valiulis. University of Massachusetts Press, 1997.

Murphy, Rachel. "Gender and the Irish Family." In Catherline Lawless and Ciara Breathnach, *Gender and History*. Routledge, 2022.

Murray, Jacqueline. "Twice Marginal and Twice Invisible: Lesbians in the Middle Ages." In *Handbook of Medieval Sexuality*, edited by Vern L. Bullough and James A. Brundage. Routledge, 1996.

Nash, David, and Anne-Marie Kilday. *Cultures of Shame: Exploring Crime and Morality in Britain 1600–1900*. Palgrave Macmillan, 2010.

Nealon, Christopher. *Foundlings: Lesbian and Gay Historical Emotion before Stonewall*. Duke University Press, 2001.

Nie, Michael de. *The Eternal Paddy: Irish Identity and the British Press, 1798–1882*. University of Wisconsin Press, 2004.

Norton, Rictor. *The Myth of the Modern Homosexual: Queer History and the Search for Cultural Unity*. Bloomsbury, 2016.

Nunn, Zavier. "Against Anticipation, or, Camp Reading as Reparative to the Trans Feminine Past: A Microhistory in Nazi-Era Vienna." *Gender and History* 36, no. 1 (2024), 191–207.

Nunn, Zavier. "Trans Liminality and the Nazi State." *Past and Present* 260, no. 1 (2023), 123–157.

O'Brien, John. *Discrimination in Northern Ireland, 1920–1939: Myth or Reality?* Cambridge University Press, 2010.

O'Connell, Sean. "An Age of Conservative Modernity, 1914–1968." In S. J. Connolly, *Belfast 400: People, Place and History*. Liverpool University Press, 2012.

O'Connell, Sean. "The Troubles with a Lower-Case T: Undergraduates and Belfast's Difficult History." *Transactions of the Royal Historical Society* 28 (2018), 219–239.

O'Connell, Sean. "Violence and Social Memory in Twentieth-Century Belfast: Stories of Buck Alec Robinson." *Journal of British Studies* 53, no. 3 (2014), 734–756.

O'Doherty, Malachi. *Fifty Years On: The Troubles and the Struggle for Change in Northern Ireland*. Atlantic, 2020.

O'Donnell, Ian. "Killing in Ireland at the Turn of the Centuries." *Irish Economic and Social History* 37 (2010), 53–74.

O'Leary, Richard. "Christians and Gays in Northern Ireland: How the Ethnoreligious Context Has Shaped Christian Anti-gay and Pro-gay Activism." In *Contemporary Christianity and LGBT Sexualities*, edited by Stephen Hunt. Ashgate, 2009.

Ollerenshaw, Philip. *Northern Ireland in the Second World War: Politics, Economic Mobilisation and Society, 1939–1945*. Manchester University Press, 2013.

Ollerenshaw, Philip. "Businessmen in Northern Ireland and the Imperial Connection, 1886–1939." In *"An Irish Empire"? Aspects of Ireland and the British Empire*, edited by Keith Jeffery. Manchester University Press, 1996.

O'Murray, Stephen, and Will Roscoe. "Preface." In *Boy-Wives and Female Husbands: Studies in African Homosexualities*, edited by Stephen O'Murray and Will Roscoe. Routledge, 1998.

Oosterhuis, Harry. *Stepchildren of Nature: Krafft-Ebing, Psychiatry and Making of Sexual Identity*. University of Chicago Press, 2000.

Open, Michael. *Fading Lights, Silver Screens: A History of Belfast's Cinemas*. Greystone, 1985.

Parkinson, Alan F. *Belfast's Unholy War: The Troubles of the 1920s*. Four Courts, 2004.

Patterson, Henry, and Eric P. Kaufmann. *Unionism and Orangeism in Northern Ireland Since 1945: The Decline of the Loyal Family*. Manchester University Press, 2007.

Patton, Marcus. *Central Belfast: A Historical Gazetteer*, 2nd edition. Ulster Architectural Society, 2015 [1993].

Peel, Mark. "New Worlds of Friendship: The Early Twentieth Century." In *Friendship: A History*, edited by Barbara Caine. Routledge, 2009.

Peniston, William A. *Pederasts and Others: Urban Culture and Sexual Identity in Nineteenth-Century Paris*. Routledge, 2004.

Peniston, William. "A Public Offense against Decency: The Trial of the Count de Germiny and the 'Moral Order' of the Third Republic." In *Disorder in the*

Court: Trials and Sexual Conflict at the Turn of the Century, edited by George Robb and Nancy Erber. Palgrave Macmillan, 1999.

Petri, Olga. *Places of Tenderness and Heat: The Queer Milieu of Fin-de-Siècle St. Petersburg*. Cornell University Press, 2022.

Pettitt, Lance. "Queering Broadcast Boundaries: An Episode in Northern Ireland's Radio History." *Media History* 11, no. 3 (2005), 207–224.

Phoenix, Eamon. *Northern Nationalism: Nationalist Politics, Partition and the Catholic Minority in Northern Ireland, 1890–1940*. Ulster Historical Foundation, 1994.

Pick, Daniel. *Faces of Degeneration: A European Disorder, c. 1848–1918*. Cambridge University Press, 1989.

Plaster, Joseph. *Kids on the Street: Queer Kinship and Religion in San Francisco's Tenderloin*. Duke University Press, 2023.

Platt, Harold L. *Shock Cities: The Environmental Transformation and Reform of Manchester and Chicago*. University of Chicago Press, 2005.

Plummer, Kenneth, ed. *The Making of the Modern Homosexual*. Barnes and Noble, 1981.

Plummer, Kenneth. *Telling Sexual Stories: Power, Change and Social Worlds*. Routledge, 1995.

Pooley, William G. "Show Your Workings: Towards a Creative Historical Toolkit." In *Speculative Biography: Experiments, Opportunities and Provocations*, edited by Donna Lee Brien and Keira Lindsey. Routledge, 2022.

Porter, Roy, and Mikuláš Teich, eds. *Sexual Knowledge, Sexual Science: The History of Attitudes to Sexuality*. Cambridge University Press, 1994.

Potter, Claire. "A Queer Public Sphere: Urban History's Sexual Landscape." *Journal of Urban History* 40, no. 4 (2014), 812–822.

Potvin, John. *Bachelors of a Different Sort: Queer Aesthetics, Material Culture, and the Modern Interior in Britain*. Manchester University Press, 2014.

Povinelli, Elizabeth A., and George Chauncey. "Thinking Sexuality Transnationally." *GLQ: A Journal of Lesbian and Gay Studies* 5, no. 4 (1999), 439–449.

Pretsell, Douglas. *Urning: Queer Identity in the German Nineteenth Century*. University of Toronto Press, 2024.

Prior, Pauline. *Mental Health and Politics in Northern Ireland: A History of Service Development*. Avebury, 1993.

Purvis, Dara E. "Irish Fatherhood in the Twentieth Century." In *Ireland and Masculinities in History*, edited by Rebecca Anne Barr, Sean Brady, and Jane G.V. McGaughey. Palgrave Macmillan, 2019.

Radford, Mark. *The Policing of Belfast 1870–1914*. Bloomsbury, 2015.

Rafter, Kevin. "The Irish Edition—from 'Filthy Scandal Sheet' to 'Old Friend' of the Taoiseach." In *The* News of the World *and the British Press, 1843–2011: Journalism for the Rich, Journalism for the Poor*, edited by Laurel Brake, Chandrika Kaul, and Mark W. Turner. Palgrave Macmillan, 2016.

Rains, Stephanie. "City Streets and the City Edition: Newsboys and Newspapers in Early Twentieth-Century Ireland." *Irish Studies Review* 24, no. 2 (2016), 142–158.

Raitt, Suzanne. "Sex, Love and the Homosexual Body in Early Sexology." In Lucy Bland and Laura Doan, *Sexology in Culture: Labelling Bodies and Desires*. University of Chicago Press, 1998.

Redmond, Jennifer, ed., "Revolutionary Masculinities." *Irish Studies Review* 29, no. 2 (2021).

Reidy, Conor. *Criminal Irish Drunkards: The Inebriate Reformatory System 1900–1920*. History Press, 2014.

Riddell, Fraser. *Music and the Queer Body in English Literature*. Cambridge University Press, 2022.

Robb, George. *British Culture and the First World War*. Bloomsbury, 2002.

Robertson, Stephen. "What's Law Got to Do with It? Legal Records and Sexual Histories." *Journal of the History of Sexuality* 14, no. 1/2 (2005), 161–185.

Roden, Frederick S. *Same-Sex Desire in Victorian Religious Culture*. Palgrave Macmillan, 1998.

Roper, Michael. "Between Manliness and Masculinity: The 'War Generation' and the Psychology of Fear in Britain, 1914–1950." *Journal of British Studies* 44, no. 2 (2005), 343–362.

Rose, Jonathan. "Introduction." In The *Edinburgh History of Reading: Subversive Readers*, edited by Jonathan Rose. Edinburgh University Press, 2020.

Rose, Kieran. *Diverse Communities: The Evolution of Lesbian and Gay Politics in Ireland*. Cork University Press, 1994.

Rose, Sonya. "Sex, Citizenship, and the Nation in World War II Britain." *American Historical Review* 103, no. 4 (1998), 1147–1176.

Rotundo, E. Anthony. "Romantic Friendship: Male Intimacy and Middle-Class Youth in the Northern United States, 1800–1900." *Journal of Social History* 2, no. 1 (1989), 1–25.

Rowse, A. L. *Homosexuals in History: A Study of Ambivalence in Society, Literature and the Arts*. Dorset Press, 1977.

Royle, Stephen A. *Portrait of an Industrial City: "Clanging Belfast," 1750–1914*. Belfast Natural History and Philosophical Society, 2011.

Royle, Stephen A. "Workshop of the Empire, 1820–1914." In *Belfast 400: People, Place and History*, edited by S. J. Connolly. Liverpool University Press, 2012.

Ruane, Joseph, and Jennifer Todd. "The Changing Role of the Middle Classes in Twentieth Century Ireland." In *The Cambridge Social History of Modern Ireland*, edited by Eugenio F. Biagini and Mary E. Daly. Cambridge University Press, 2017.

Rubenhold, Hallie. *The Five: the Untold Lives of the Women Killed by Jack the Ripper*. Doubleday, 2019.

Rubin, Gayle S. "Thinking Sex: Notes for a Radical Theory of the Politics of Sexuality." In *Pleasure and Danger: Exploring Female Sexuality*, edited by Carole S. Vance. Kegan Paul, 1984.

Ryan-Flood, Róisín. "Staying Connected: Irish Lesbian and Gay Narratives of Family." In *The "Irish" Family*, edited by Linda Connolly. Routledge, 2015.

Ryan, Paul. *Asking Angela Macnamara: An Intimate History of Irish Lives*. Irish Academic Press, 2013.

Ryan, Paul. "Coming Out, Fitting In: The Personal Narratives of Some Irish Gay Men." *Irish Journal of Sociology* 12, no. 2 (2003), 68–85.

Ryder, Chris. *The RUC: A Force under Fire*. Mandarin, 1989.

Savage, Robert J. *A Loss of Innocence? Television and Irish Society, 1960–1972*. Manchester University Press, 2010.

Scheper-Hughes, Nancy. *Saints, Scholars and Schizophrenics: Mental Illness in Rural Ireland*. University of California Press, 1979.

Schlör, Joachin. *Nights in the Big City: Paris, Berlin, London, 1840–1930*. Reaktion, 1998.

Scott, Joan W. "Gender: A Useful Category of Historical Analysis." *American Historical Review* 91, no. 5 (1986), 1053–1075.

Scott, Joan W. "The Evidence of Experience." *Critical Inquiry* 17 (1991), 773–797.

Sedgwick, Eve Kosofsky. *Epistemology of the Closet*. University of California Press, 1990.

Shapiro, Barbara. *Beyond Reasonable Doubt and Probable Cause: Historical Perspectives on the Anglo-American Law of Evidence*. University of California Press, 1991.

Sherbo, Arthur. "Henry James and Forrest Reid." *Henry James Review* 13, no. 1 (1992), 82–87.

Sigel, Lisa. *Making Modern Love: Sexual Narratives and Identities in Interwar Britain*. Temple University Press, 2012.

Sinfield, Alan. *The Wilde Century: Effeminacy, Oscar Wilde and the Queer Moment*. Columbia University Press, 1994.

Skidmore, Emily. *True Sex: The Lives of Trans Men at the Turn of the Twentieth Century*. NYU Press, 2017.

Slater, Stefan. "Pimps, Police and Filles de Joie: Foreign Prostitution in Interwar London." *London Journal* 32, no. 1 (2007), 53–74.

Slide, Anthony. *Lost Gay Novels: A Reference Guide to Fifty Works from the First Half of the Twentieth Century*. Routledge, 2011.

Smaal, Yorick. "Boys and Homosex: Danger and Possibility in Queensland, 1890–1914." In *Children, Childhood and Youth in the British World*, edited by Shirleene Robinson and Simon Sleight. Palgrave Macmillan, 2016.

Smaal, Yorick. *Sex, Soldiers and the South Pacific, 1939–1945: Queer Identities in Australia in the Second World War*. Palgrave Macmillan, 2005.

Smith, Helen. *Masculinity, Class and Same-Sex Desire in Industrial England, 1895–1957*. Palgrave Macmillan, 2015.

Smith, Helen, with Mathew Kuefler and Merry E. Wiesner-Hanks. "Class in the History of Sexuality." In *The Cambridge World History of Sexualities: Vol I, General Overviews*, edited by Merry E. Wiesner-Hanks and Mathew Kuefler. Cambridge University Press, 2024.

Smith, Helen, "Working-Class Ideas & Experiences of Sexuality in 20th C. Britain: Regionalism as a Category of Analysis." *Twentieth Century British History* 29, no. 1 (2018), 58–78.

Smith, James M. *Ireland's Magdalen Laundries and the Nation's Architecture of Containment*. Indiana University Press, 2007.

Smyth, Austin. "Return from Motown?" In *Enduring City: Belfast in the Twentieth Century*, edited by Frederick W. Boal and Stephen A. Royle. Blackstaff, 2006.

Smyth, Denis. *Days of Unity in the Docklands of Sailortown, 1907–1969*. Portlight, 1986.

Smyth, Denis. *Sailortown: The Story of a Dockside Community*. North Belfast History Workshop, 1991.

Snape, Robert. *Leisure, Voluntary Action and Social Change in Britain, 1880–1939*. Bloomsbury, 2018.

Sontag, Susan. "Notes on Camp." In *A Susan Sontag Reader*, edited by Elizabeth Hardwick, Farrar, Straus and Giroux, 1982.

Spectre, Peter H. *A Mariner's Miscellany*. Seafarer, 2005.

Stanley, Jo, and Paul Baker. *Hello Sailor! The Hidden History of Gay Life at Sea*. Routledge, 2003.

Steele, Karen, and Michael de Nie. "Introduction." In *Ireland and the New Journalism*, edited by Karen Steele and Michael de Nie. Palgrave Macmillan, 2014.

Stein, Marc. *City of Sisterly and Brotherly Loves: Lesbian and Gay Philadelphia, 1945–1972*. University of Chicago Press, 2004.

Steinbach, Susie L. "The Melodramatic Contract: Breach of Promise and the Performance of Virtue." *Nineteenth Century Studies* 14, no. 1 (2000), 1–34.

Stryker, Susan. "Transgender History, Homonormativity, and Disciplinarity." *Radical History Review* no. 100 (2008), 145–157.

Summerfield, Penny. *Histories of the Self: Personal Narratives and Historical Practice*. Routledge, 2019.

Syrett, Nicholas. "Introduction to 'Sex across the Ages: Restoring Intergenerational Dynamics to Queer History.'" *Historical Reflections/Réflexions Historiques* 46, no. 1 (2020), 1–12.

Syrett, Nicholas. "A Busman's Holiday in the Not-So-Lonely-Crowd: Business Culture, Epistolary Networks, and Itinerant Homosexuality in Mid-twentieth-century America." *Journal of the History of Sexuality* 21, no. 1 (2012), 121–140.

Syrett, Nicholas. *An Open Secret: The Family Story of Robert and John Gregg Allerton*. University of Chicago Press, 2021.

Tamagne, Florence. *A History of Homosexuality in Europe: Berlin, London, Paris 1919–1939*, vol. I and II. Algora, 2004.

Tebbutt, Melanie. *Being Boys: Youth, Leisure and Identity in the Inter-War Years*. Manchester University Press, 2012.

Terry, Jennifer. *An American Obsession: Science, Medicine, and Homosexuality in Modern Society*. University of Chicago Press, 1999.

Thatcher, Adrian. "Theological Amnesia and Same-Sex Love." In Mark D. Chapman and Dominic Janes, *New Approaches to History and Theology to Same-Sex Love and Desire*. Palgrave Macmillan, 2018.

Thompson, E. P. *The Making of the English Working Class*. Victor Gollancz, 1963.

Thompson, F. M. L. *The Rise of Respectable Society: A Social History of Victorian Britain, 1830–1900*. Harvard University Press, 1988.

Thomson, Mathew. "Psychology and the 'Consciousness of Modernity' in Early Twentieth-Century Britain." In *Meanings of Modernity: Britain from the Late-Victorian Era to World War II*, edited by Martin Daunton and Bernhard Reiger. Oxford University Press, 2001.

Tiernan, Sonja. *Eva Gore-Booth: An Image of Such Politics*. Manchester University Press, 2012.

Tiernan, Sonja. *The History of Marriage Equality in Ireland: A Social Revolution Begins*. Manchester University Press, 2020.

Tosh, John. *Manliness and Masculinities in Nineteenth-Century Britain*. Routledge, 2016 [1993].

Tosh, John. "Masculinities in an Industrializing Society: Britain, 1800–1914." *Journal of British Studies* 44, no. 2 (2005), 330–342.

Trouillot, Michel-Rolph. *Silencing the Past: Power and the Production of History.* Beacon, 1995.

Trumbach, Randolph. "London's Sodomites: Homosexuality Behavior and Western Culture in the 18th Century." *Journal of Social History* 11, no. 1 (1977), 1–33.

Tuathaigh, Gearóid Ó. "Exemplar, Outlier, Impostor? A Reflection on Ireland and the Discourses of Colonialism." In *The Shadow of Colonialism on Europe's Modern Past*, edited by Róisín Healy and Enrico Dal Lago. Palgrave Macmillan, 2014.

Turner, Mark W. *Backward Glances: Cruising the Queer Streets of London and New York.* Reaktion, 2003.

Twells, Alison, Matt Houlbrook, William G. Pooley, and Helen Rogers, eds. *Creative Histories: Reflections on Research and Practice*. UCL Press, 2021.

Upchurch, Charles. *Before Wilde: Sex between Men in Britain's Age of Reform*. University of California Press, 2009.

Upchurch, Charles. "Forgetting the Unthinkable: Cross-Dressers and British Society in the Case of the Queen vs. Boulton and Others." *Gender and History* 12, no. 1 (2000), 127–157.

Upchurch, Charles. "Liberal Exclusions and Sex between Men in the Modern Era: Speculations on a Framework." *Journal of the History of Sexuality* 19, no. 3 (2010), 409–431.

Urquhart, Diane. "Gender, Family, and Sexuality, 1800–2000." In *Ulster Since 1600: Politics, Economy, and Society*, edited by Liam Kennedy and Philip Ollerenshaw. Oxford University Press, 2012.

Urquhart, Diane. *Irish Divorce: A History*. Cambridge University Press, 2020.

Valente, Joseph, and Margot Gayle Backus. *The Child Sex Scandal and Modern Irish Literature: Writing the Unspeakable*. Indiana University Press, 2020.

Valente, Joseph. *The Myth of Manliness in Irish National Culture, 1880–1922*. University of Illinois Press, 2011.

Valiulis, Maryann Gialanella. "Virtuous Mothers and Dutiful Wives: The Politics of Sexuality in the Irish Free State." In *Gender and Power in Irish History*, edited by Maryann Gialanella Valiulis. Irish Academic Press, 2008.

Valocchi, Stephen. "'Where Did Gender Go?' Same-Sex Desire and the Persistence of Gender in Gay Male Historiography." *GLQ: A Journal of Lesbian and Gay Studies* 18, no. 4 (2012), 453–479.

Vance, Norman. *The Sinews of the Spirit: The Ideal of Christian Manliness in Victorian Literature and Religious Thought*. Cambridge University Press, 1985.

Vickers, Emma. *Queen and Country: Same-Sex Desire in the British Armed Forces, 1939–1945*. Manchester University Press, 2015.

Walker, Graham. *A History of the Ulster Unionist Party: Protest, Pragmatism and Pessimism*. Manchester University Press, 2004.

Walker, Graham. *The Politics of Frustration: Harry Midgley and the Failure of the Labour Party in Northern Ireland*. Manchester University Press, 1986.

Walkowitz, Judith. *City of Dreadful Delight: Narratives of Sexual Danger in Late-Victorian London*. University of Chicago Press, 1992.

Wallace, Rachel. "Joy and Resilience: Oral Histories of Finding a Gay Community amid the Troubles in Belfast, 1968–1982." *Oral History* 51, no. 1 (2023), 70–80.

Walshe, Eibhear. *Oscar's Shadow: Wilde, Homosexuality and Modern Ireland*. Cork University Press, 2011.

Waters, Chris. "Disorders of the Mind, Disorders of the Body Social: Peter Wildeblood and the Making of the Modern Homosexual." In *Moments of Modernity: Rethinking Britain, 1945–1964*, edited by Becky Conekin, Frank Mort, and Chris Waters. Rivers Oram, 1999.

Waters, Chris. "Distance and Desire in the New British Queer History." *GLQ: A Journal of Lesbian and Gay Studies* 14, no. 1 (2008), 139–155.

Waters, Chris. "Havelock Ellis, Sigmund Freud and the State: Discourses of Homosexual Identity in Interwar Britain." In Lucy Bland and Laura Doan, *Sexology in Culture: Labelling Bodies and Desires*. University of Chicago press, 1998.

Waters, Chris. "The Homosexual as a Social Being in Britain, 1945–1968." *Journal of British Studies* 51, no. 3 (2012), 685–710.

Weber, Gary. "Henry Labouchère, *Truth* and the New Journalism of late Victorian Britain." *Victorian Periodicals Review* 26, no. 1 (1993), 36–43.

Weeks, Jeffrey, and Sheila Rowbotham. *Socialism and the New Life: The Personal and Sexual Politics of Edward Carpenter and Havelock Ellis*. Quartet, 1977.

Weeks, Jeffrey. *Coming Out: Homosexual Politics in Britain, from the Nineteenth Century to the Present*. Quartet, 1977.

Weeks, Jeffrey. "Inverts, Perverts, and Mary-Annes: Male Prostitution and the Regulation of Homosexuality in England in the Nineteenth and Early Twentieth Centuries." *Journal of Homosexuality* 6, no. 1–2 (1981), 113–134.

Weeks, Jeffrey. "Queer(y)ing the 'Modern Homosexual.'" *Journal of British Studies* 51, no. 3 (2012), 523–539.

Weeks, Jeffrey. *Sex, Politics, and Society: The Regulation of Sexuality Since 1800*. Longman, 1981.

Weeks, Jeffrey. *The World We Have Won: The Remaking of Erotic and Intimate Life*. Routledge, 2007.

Weeks, Jeffrey. *What Is Sexual History?* Polity, 2016.

Weston, Kath. "Get Thee to a Big City: Sexual Imaginary and the Great Gay Migration." *GLQ: A Journal of Lesbian and Gay Studies* 2, no. 3 (1995), 253–277.

Whelan, Bernadette. "'A Real Revolution': Ireland and the Oxford Group / Moral Re-Armament Movement, 1933–2001." *Irish Historical Studies* 45, no. 168 (2022), 262–281.

White, Heather R. *Reforming Sodom: Protestants and the Rise of Gay Rights*. University of North Carolina Press, 2015.

White, James. *Gerard Dillon: An Illustrated Biography*. Merlin, 1993.

Whyte, John. "How Much Discrimination Was There under the Unionist Regime, 1921–1968." In *Contemporary Irish Studies*, edited by Tom Gallagher and James O'Connell. Manchester University Press, 1983.

Wiener, Martin J. *Reconstructing the Criminal: Culture, Law, and Policy in England, 1830–1914*. Cambridge University Press, 1990.

Williams, Clifford. *A Queer A-Z of Hampshire: Aspects of LGBT+ History in the County of Hampshire*. Publisher unknown, 2019.

Williams, Raymond. *Culture and Society: 1780–1950*. Chatto and Windus, 1958.

Woods, C. J. "Barbour, Harold Adrian Milne." In *Dictionary of Irish Biography*, edited by James McGuire and James Quinn. Cambridge University Press, 2009.

Woods, Gregory. *A History of Gay Literature: The Male Tradition*. Yale University Press 1998.

Woodward, Guy. *Culture, Northern Ireland, and the Second World War*. Oxford University Press, 2015.

Yacovone, Donald. "'Surpassing the Love of Women': Victorian Manhood and the Language of Fraternal Love." In *A Shared Experience: Men, Women and the History of Gender*, edited by Laura McCall and Donald Yacovone. NYU Press, 1998.

Zanghellini, Aleardo. *The Sexual Constitution of Political Authority: The "Trials" of Same-Sex Desire*. Routledge, 2015.

Zeeland, Steven. *Sailors and Sexual Identity: Crossing the Line between "Straight" and "Gay" in the U.S. Navy*. Routledge, 1995.

Unpublished Dissertations

Berg, Suus van den. "The *Link* Trial (1921) and the Formation of Queer Networks in Early Twentieth Century Britain." MA thesis submitted to Goldsmiths, University of London (2021).

Earls, Averill. "Queering Dublin: Same-Sex Desire and Masculinities in Ireland, 1884–1964." PhD thesis submitted to University at Buffalo (2016).

Fletcher, Abigail. "'From Partition to Decriminalisation': Homosexuality in Northern Ireland, 1921–1982." PhD thesis submitted to the University of Edinburgh (2023).

Gilmore, Nadine. "Gay Activism in Northern Ireland, 1970s-1990s." PhD thesis submitted to Queen's University Belfast (2023).

Griffin, Brian. "The Irish Police, 1836–1914: A Social History." PhD thesis submitted to Loyola University (1991).

Herron, Niall. "Queer Experiences during the Troubles: The Everyday and the Erased." PhD thesis under construction at Queen's University Belfast.

Irwin, Stuart. "Belfast Corporation, 1874–1896: Managing a Mature Industrial City." PhD thesis submitted to Queen's University Belfast (2018).

Lawrence, Michael. "Quare Fellows Abroad: Homosexuality and the Irish Diaspora, 1880–1960." PhD thesis under construction at Queen's University Belfast.

Smith, Amy. "On 'the Edge of a Crumbling Continent': Poetry in Northern Ireland and the Second World War." PhD thesis submitted to Durham University (2014).

Titman, Nathan Bryan. "The Drift of Desire: Performing Gay Masculinities through Leisure, Mobility, and Non-urban Space, 1910–1945." PhD thesis submitted to the University of Iowa (2014).

Wells, Lauren Elizabeth. "Male-to-Female Cross-Dressing in Yorkshire: 1870–1939." PhD thesis submitted to University of Leeds (2021),

Web-Based Sources

"Belfast Street Directories." *Lennon Wylie*. Accessed November 6 2024. https://www.lennonwylie.co.uk.

Bengry, Justin. "The Case of the Sultry Mountie, or, We Need to Talk about Cecil." *Notches*. Accessed November 6, 2024. https://notchesblog.com/2015/05/26/the-case-of-the-sultry-mountie-or-we-need-to-talk-about-cecil.

Bengry, Justin. "Difficult Stories and Ethical Dilemmas in Family History." *History Workshop*. Accessed November 6, 2024. https://www.historyworkshop.org.uk/podcast/difficult-stories-and-ethical-dilemmas-in-family-history.

Dudgeon, Jeff. "A Century and More of Belfast Gay Life—Northern Ireland's Gay Geography, History and People: 1903–2021." *AcomsDave*. Accessed November 6, 2024. https://acomsdave.com/a-century-and-more-of-belfast-gay-life.

"Finding Aid for 'Haldeman-Julius "Little Blue Book" Collection 1919–1947.'" *Amherst College Archives and Special Collections*. Accessed November 6, 2024. https://www.amherst.edu/media/view/78748/original/little%20blue%20books.pdf.

Froggatt, Richard. "Sir Daniel Dixon (1844–1907)." *Dictionary of Ulster Biography*. Accessed November 6, 2024. http://www.newulsterbiography.co.uk/index.php/home/viewPerson/1809.

Hall, Dickon. "New Visions of Belfast in the 1930s and 40s: Modernism among the Ruins." *Art UK*. Accessed November 6, 2024. https://artuk.org/discover/stories/new-visions-of-belfast-in-the-1930s-and-40s-modernism-among-the-ruins.

"Living Queer in Northern Ireland." *BBC*. Accessed November 6, 2024. https://www.bbc.co.uk/programmes/articles/1fwF0x0BSBFDPSXV8thp6Nb/living-queer-in-northern-ireland.

Lynch, Charlie. "The Schoolteacher Who Spawned a Highland Literary Hoax." *The National*. Accessed November 6, 2024. https://www.thenational.scot/culture/24269187.schoolteacher-spawned-highland-literary-hoax.

Martin, Kenneth. "Being Irish Part Two—Trains." *Kenneth Martin Writer*. Accessed November 6, 2024. https://kennethmartinwriter.com/2013/06/03/being-irish-part-two-trains.

McCullough, Joseph Wilson. Memorial ID: 244495024. *Find a Grave*. AccessedJanuary 10, 2025. https://www.findagrave.com/memorial/244495024/joseph-wilson-mccullough.

Shaw, William. Memorial ID: 225195833. *Find a Grave*. Accessed November 6, 2024. https://www.findagrave.com/memorial/225195833/william-shaw.

Smyth, Damian. "Obituary: Joseph Tomelty." *The Independent*. Accessed November 6, 2024. https://www.independent.co.uk/news/people/obituary-joseph-tomelty-1586249.html.

"Was Orangeman Edward de Cobain jailed for a crime he didn't commit?" *BBC*. Accessed November 6, 2024. https://www.bbc.co.uk/news/uk-northern-ireland-14941512.

Weir, Anthony. *Twenty Years A-Coming Out*. Unpublished, 2002.

INDEX

Page numbers followed by *f* refer to figures.

acceptance, of queer family members, 149–52, 235nn115,121
Adair, James, 201n46
Addington, John, 81
age
 and prosecution of same-sex crimes, 164–65, 240n49
 and shift to female partners, 115–23
age of consent, 109, 228n12
Aicken, Frederick "Howard," 106–8, 116, 117*f*, 118*f*, 235n115
Aicken, Louie, 235n115
alcohol, and prosecution of same-sex crimes, 165–66, 173–74
Aleko (Matthews), 22
American GIs, 76
Ancient Greeks, 98–99
Anderson, Joseph, 201n46
Andrews, Archibald, 65–66, 208n51
Apprentice, The (Tomelty), 109–10
Arnold, Alfred, 221n19
arrest, for same-sex crimes
 churches' responses to, 153
 in early twentieth century, 18
 of George Hogg, 134
 of John Leeburn Knox, 62
 media reports on, 153–54
 of middle-aged husbands, 121, 122
 of middle- or upper-class men, 48, 140–48
 statistics on, 196n58
 of Thomas Henry Gibney, 1
 See also criminal archive; moral vigilantes; prosecution, for same-sex crimes
Ashfield, John Ernest, 166
Aylmer, James, 201n46

bachelorhood, 131–32, 227n123
bail money, 145–47, 232n86, 234n110
Baker, Paul, 71
Barbour, Harold, 182
Barbour, Patrick, 181
Barbour, Sir John Milne, 182
bars. *See* pubs
bathhouses, 54, 205n122
Beemyn, Genny, 211n113
Belfast
 city center, 9, 31*f*, 37
 conservatism of, 39
 docklands, 64–68
 economic and demographic growth of, 24–26
 founding of, 10
 sectarian conflict in, 10–11
 study of, as historical urban sex scene, 9–13
Belfast Custody Court, 142–43
Belfast Entries, 30–33, 34*f*, 47, 200n34
Belfast Scandal (1890), 19–20, 37, 38, 88, 201n46
Belfast Telegraph, 124
Belfast Union Workhouse, 61
Benson, E. F., 99
Bérubé, Allan, 209n78
Black, Archibald, 158–59, 164, 224n71
blackmail, 161–62, 169, 228n18
Blair, Henry, 75–76
Blakeway, Denys, 8
boarding hostels / boardinghouses, 52–53, 60–61
Bolland, Charles, 136–37
Bond, Cecil, 39, 54, 125–26, 127, 204n112
bookshops, 101–3
Boulton, Thomas Ernest, 213n22
Boyd, John, 150–51
Britain
 colonial and postcolonial relationship between Ireland and, 14–15
 Irish migration to, 62–64
British Society of the Study of Sex Psychology, 212n14
Brooke, Basil, 154
Buckland, Patrick, 180
Burton, Richard Francis, 86

cafés, 50–51
Caldwell, George, 232n86
camp, 129, 216n76
Campbell, Thomas Joseph, 157
Carpenter, Edward, 80–81, 84, 94, 97, 98, 196n51, 212nn6,14, 217n102
Carrick, Thomas, 156, 157, 201n48
Casement, Roger, 30, 49, 108, 197n60, 200n28, 234n113
Cassidy, Vincent, 73, 224n64, 238n25
Castle Junction, 28*f*, 29*f*
Castle Place, 125
Catholicism, 10–11, 17, 37–39, 92–93, 217n97, 244n125
Cauldwell, William, 165
Ceylon, 141
Chambers, James, 179
character / character references, 158–59, 160, 169–71, 173–74, 239n43
Chauncey, George, 60
Chichester, Sir Arthur, 10
children
  and age of consent, 109, 228n12
  sexual abuse of, 110, 150–51, 221n21
  See also age; working-class youths
Christie, Joseph, 199n16
Christie, William, 25, 199n16
Church of England, 95
Church of Ireland Young Men's Society, 52, 53*f*, 54, 89
cinemas, 49–50
Classic, The, 50
Classic Café, 50, 51*f*
classics, literary, 97, 98–99
classified adverts, 124–25
Cleveland Street Scandal (1889), 15
Cocks, H. G., 242n85
colonialism, 14–15
coming-of-age stories, 99
commercial scene, 43–54
communal support, 3, 144–49
Conley, Mary, 244n120
consent, age of, 109, 228n12
conservatism, 39
Cook, Matt, 196n58
County Antrim, 60
courts. *See* prosecution, for same-sex crimes
Craig, James, 182
criminal archive, 5–6, 27. *See also* arrest, for same-sex crimes; prosecution, for same-sex crimes
Criminal Law Amendment Act (1885), 15, 109, 113, 169
Crisp, Quentin, 58–60, 71, 78, 79
critical queer history, 4
cross-dressing, 85, 144, 146, 147, 213n22, 231n74. *See also* gender transgression
Crown Entry, 33, 34*f*
cruising
  and commercial scene, 43–54
  in docklands, 65–67
  and Irish migration, 61–62
  of married men, 119, 121
  and moral vigilantes, 135–36, 138–39
  opportunities and patterns for, 39–43
  in outdoor public spaces, 27–37, 54
  for soldiers, 75–76, 181–82
  troubles associated with, 140–44
Cunningham, Minnie, 48–49
Currie, Samuel, 61

daily routines, as opportunity for cruising, 39–41
dancing, 204n112
David (biblical figure), 93–94
de Cobain, Edward Samuel Wesley, 66, 141, 169–72, 204n96
Delaney, Enda, 206n12
D'Emilio, John, 13
Denvir, John, 168
Dillon, Gerard, 67, 93, 149, 208n40
Dillon, Joseph, 93, 149, 208n40, 233n97
Dillon, Molly, 149
Dixon, Sir Daniel, 172–73, 176
Dixon, Thomas, 173
Doan, Laura, 225n84
docklands, 64–68
Dolcis Shoes, 43, 44*f*
Dolly Sisters, 67
Donovan, Charles, 137
Douglas, James, 10, 65–66
du Barry, Jeanne Bécu, Comtesse, 66–67
Du Barry's, 66–67
Dublin Castle Scandal (1884), 15, 16, 168
Dudgeon, Jeff, 67
Dunlop, Hugh, 136–37, 209n75, 228n21, 240n56

Earls, Averill, 12, 137
Edgeworth, William, 178
effeminacy, 84–85, 129–30, 170. *See also* gender transgression
Ellis, Havelock, 81, 83, 86, 212n14
Elmwood Association, 245n5
Emerald Minstrels, 37, 168
Empire Hotel, 48–49

entrapment, of cruisers, 138
Entries, 30–33, *34f*, 47, 200n34
Erskine, Alexander, 178–79, 181, 234n110
Erskine, John, 178
Erskine, William, 61
Erskine Mayne's, 101, *102f*
Ervine, St. John, 26
exposure, public, 13, 17, 100, 121, 122–23, 140–44

familiarity, as cruising tactic, 42–43
family support, 1–3, 134, 144–49
fear, of public exposure, 140–44
Fearon, Jack, 73
female morality, religious obsession with, 17
feminine affectations, 84–85, 129–30, 170. *See also* gender transgression
Ferrer, John, 228n20
Fielding, William J., 103
Finnane, Mark, 213n33
First World War, 73, 179
Fitzgibbon, Gerald, 176
Fitzpatrick, David, 206n12
Fitzsimons, Arthur, 126, *127f*, *128f*
Fitzsimons, Joseph, 61
Flame of Freedom, The (Underwood), 22
Flying Fish, 69, 209n72
Forster, E. M., 100, 220n142
Foucault, Michel, 82
Free, Douglas, 211n115
Free Presbyterian Church, 88
Freud, Sigmund, 81, 83, 86, 87, 90

Galway, James, 147
gay community, 123–31, 184–85
gay identity, embracing of, 123–31
gay liberation movement, 11, 12, 187, 245n5. *See also* homophile activism
gendered moral hypocrisy, 17–18
gender norms, 85, 123, 147
gender transgression, 84–85, 213n22, 231n74. *See also* cross-dressing; effeminacy
Gibney, Eliza, 1–2
Gibney, Thomas Henry, 1–3, 19–20, 201n46
Gibson, Alexander, 231n74
Gifford, James, 220n143
Gilpin, John, 63
Golden Dawn, 50, 51
Goodbody, Arthur, 216n88
Gordon, Joseph "Millar," 49
Government of Ireland Act (1920), 182
Graham, Edward, 61
Graham, John, 179
Gray, Jeannie, 57
Gray, William, 56–57, 231n74
Great Famine (1845–1852), 58
Greeks, Ancient, 98–99
Greeves, Arthur, 80–81, 94–95, 97, 98, 119, 212n6, 216n88
Gregg, John, 96
Grey, Anthony, 245n5
Griffin, Brian, 213n33
Guard, Wesley, 171
guesthouses, 48–49

Hall, Radclyffe, 103–4
Harbinson, Robin, 68, 75
Harcourt, Richard Milligen, 157
Hartman, Saidya, 6
Haslett, Sir James, 170–71
hegemonic masculinity, 158–59, 237n8
Heggie, George, 169, 170
Herron, Hugh, 27–28
Hewitt, John, 103, 218n118
Hime, Maurice C., 89
Hirschfield, Magnus, 132, 196n51
Hogg, George, 133–35
homophile activism, 3–4. *See also* gay liberation movement
homophobia, 187
homosexuality
  debates regarding, 186
  and prosecution of same-sex crimes, 163–67
  scientific frameworks of, 83–87
  See also queerness; same-sex desire; sexual inversion
hostels, 52–53, 61
hotels, 48–49, 204n97
Houlbrook, Matt, 60
housing, 60–61
Hughes, John, 77
Hutton, Henry, 173
Hyde, Montgomery, 169

ignorance, of queer family members, 149–52
immigration. *See* Irish migration
Imperial Hotel, 73, *74f*, *75f*
Inheritor, The (Benson), 99
Intermediate Sex (Carpenter), 97, 98
inversion, 84–85
Irish migration
  factors motivating, 58

Irish migration *(continued)*
social and cultural effects on Irish queerness experience, 58–64
William and Jeannie Gray as examples of, 56–58

James, Henry, 98, 218n113
Janes, Dominic, 216n76
Johnson, Nevill, 77
Jonathan (biblical figure), 93–94
Jones, Timothy Willem, 214n48

Kameny, Frank, 47–48
Kavanagh, Francis, 73
Kerr, W. S., 78
Keyes, John, 63
Kilday, Anne-Marie, 231n63
Kingston, John, 224n70
Kinkead, Robert, 157
Kirk, Thomas Sinclair, 173
Knox, William John Leeburn, 62, 63*f*
Krafft-Ebing, Richard von, 84

Labouchère, Henry, 169–70, 174–75
LGBT movement. *See* gay liberation movement
Lind, Earl, 59–60
literary classics, 97, 98–99
literature, queer, 96–104
Little Victims (Rumbold), 101
London, Irish migration to, 62–63
Lost Fields (McLaverty), 143
loyalist paramilitary organizations, 137–38
Lutton, Richard, 172–77, 236n134

MacCartan, Hugh A., 39
Magee, John, 69–70
makeup swabs, 62, 63*f*
Marlowe, Christopher, 81
marriage, 119–23, 131–32
Martin, Kenneth, 50, 208n40
masculine dominance, 60, 61
masculinity, 68, 114–15, 116
hegemonic, 158–59, 237n8
masturbation, 89, 214n52
matchmaking, 126, 128–29
Matthews, Kenneth, 22
Maurice (Forster), 220n142
McClean, Davy, 102–3
McCleery, Mary, 133
McCullough, Joseph "Wilson," 21–23, 198n8
McCutcheon, Albert, 112
McDonald, Alexander, 147
McGarry, Fearghal, 206n12
McGonigal, Daniel, 173
McGowan, Mary, 122
McGowan, Samuel, 122
McGrath, Richard, 173
McKee, Ritchie, 221n19
McLaughlin, Edward, 224n79
McLaverty, Michael, 143–44
McLoughlin, Edward, 86
McManus, Ruth, 204n97
McMeekin, Tommy, 126
Meehan, Patrick, 228n17
Mental Health Act, 87
migration. *See* Irish migration
military, 68–78, 181–82, 209n78
Millar, Tommy, 43
Milligen, Edgar, 140–41, 179
Moffett, Christopher, 163
Montaigne, Michel de, 81
Montgomery, Peter, 167
Moore, Brian, 103
Moore, Terence, 162
moral hypocrisy, gendered, 17–18
moral vigilantes, 135–40
Moriarty, John, 178
Mort, Frank, 212n14
Murray, Jack, 120, 121, 151, 222n33
Murray, John, 235n121

Nash, David, 231n63
National Health Service, 87
nationalism, 167–77, 244n125
neighborhood purity, 135–40
Neill, David, 223n51
Neill, Maurice, 117–18
Nelson, William "Billy," 71–72, 214n38
New Journalism, 142
newsboys, 111–12, 120, 128–29, 179
Niles, Blair, 100
Normoyle, Thomas, 172, 242n88
Northern Ireland
creation of, 11
politics of, 12
Northridge, William Lovell, 90–92, 119–20, 215n66
Norwood, Ethel, 120–21
Nunn, Zavier, 13

obituaries, 148–49
O'Brien, Lucius Frederick, 216n88
O'Byrne, Cathal, 26
O'Connor, Thomas, 141–42

Offences against the Person Act (1861), 196n58
O'Hanlon, W. M., 30
O'Hara, Charles, 22, 23, 198n8
O'Hara, Peter, 66
O'Neill, James, 146–47
open secret, queerness as, 152–54, 186–87, 235n115, 236n134
Ormeau Park, 34–35
Out of Step (Smith), 99
Oxford Group, 53–54

Paisley, Ian, 12, 88
Palace Barracks (Holywood), 181–82
Park, Frederick William, 213n22
parks, 34–35
Patterson, Arthur, 111
personal adverts, 124–25
Pim, Terence, 103
police
  approach to same-sex activity, 17–19
  and moral vigilantes, 137–38
  as witnesses in trials, 163
  See also arrest, for same-sex crimes
Presbyterian Church of Ireland, 96
press, and public exposure, 141–43
Prime-Stevenson, Edward Irenaeus, 70–71, 73, 210n92
prison registers, 5
Progressive Bookshop, 102–3
prosecution, for same-sex crimes, 156–58, 182–83
  and avoiding scandal, 177–82
  and character and respectability of defendant, 158–60, 239n43
  of elite queer men, 167–77
  outcomes of, 162–63, 240n49
  and sexuality and the law, 163–67
  unionism and nationalism and, 167–77
  witnesses in, 159, 161–62, 163
  See also arrest, for same-sex crimes
prostitution. *See* sex work
Protestantism, 10–11, 17, 37–39
psychiatry / psychoanalysis, 81, 83, 86–87, 119, 163, 212n14, 239n42
Psychology and Pastoral Practice (Northridge), 90–92
public exposure, 13, 17, 100, 121, 122–23, 140–44
public parks, 34–35
public toilets, 32–33, 200n34
public transport, 41–42
pubs, 46–48, 66–67, 204n93
Purse, David, 148–49

Quakers (Religious Society of Friends), 95
Queen's Bridge, 40*f*
Queen's Square, 29–30, 32*f*, 52
queer culture, 129
queer literature, 96–104
queerness
  culture of purposeful silence about, 17–19
  Irish cultural politics and discourse on, 15–16
  as open secret, 152–54, 186–87, 235n115, 236n134
  scholarship on, in Ireland before 1950s, 16–17
  See also homosexuality; same-sex desire; sexual inversion
queer theory, 4, 212n11

Ramsey, Samuel, 156, 157, 201n48, 236n134
Rea, Joseph, 138–39, 224n71, 239n43
Reid, Forrest, 98, 218n113, 220n142
Reilly, Wesley, 138
religiosity
  and conceptions of respectability, 159
  and queerness as open secret, 152–53, 236n134
  as shaping experiences and understandings of same-sex desire, 88–96
  See also Catholicism; Protestantism
religious meetings, 53–54
Religious Society of Friends (Quakers), 95
remorse, ambiguities of claimed, 86
rent boys, 168. *See also* Dublin Castle Scandal (1884); sex work
Richardson, Ernie, 46–47
Ritchie, Harry, 100, 224n64
Ritchie, William, 228n20
Robins, Cecil, 182
Robinson, Charles B., 87
Rosemary Bar, 47
Royal Avenue, 26, 27*f*
Royal Avenue Hotel Bar, 48, 204n93
Royal Avenue Picture House, 50
ruin, 140–41, 172
Rumbold, Richard, 101
Rutledge, James, 33
Ryan, Paul, 196n54

sailors, 68–72, 209n78. *See also* soldiers
Sailortown, 64, 233n95
Salvation Army Home, 52–53

same-sex desire
  culture of purposeful silence about, 17–19
  Irish cultural politics and discourse on, 15–16
  and rapid demographic growth, 25
  scholarship on, in Ireland before 1950s, 16–17
  See also homosexuality; queerness; sexual inversion
Save Ulster from Sodomy campaign, 12
Seaton, William, 148
Second World War, 73–78, 211n113
sectarianism, 9, 11, 12, 14, 37–39
self-loathing, 86
servicemen, 68–78, 181–82, 209n78
sexology, 81–82, 83, 197n65
sexual inversion, 84–85. *See also* homosexuality; queerness; same-sex desire
Sexual Inversion (Ellis), 83
sex work
  at Du Barry's, 67
  of Irish migrants, 59
  military, 69, 73
  and moral vigilantes, 138–39
  and prosecution of same-sex crimes, 161, 165
  working-class youths and, 108–15, 138–39, 222n33
  See also Belfast Scandal (1890); rent boys
shame, 140–42, 231n63
Shaw, Alfred, 223n59
Shaw, Allen, 25
Shaw, William, 234n110
Sheehan, Hugh, 73, 121–22, 150, 240n51
shock cities, 24, 199n12
Sinton, James, 144, 160, 238n21
Smith, Alexander, 71–72
Smith, Derek Walker, 99
Smith, Robert, 139
Smith, Walter, 39, 98, 125, 126, 127*f*, 235n128
Smyth, Ernie, 97–98, 124
Smyth, George, 156
social constructionism, 4
social spaces, 43–54
soldiers, 72–78, 181–82. *See also* sailors
Sotadic Zone, 86
Standing, William, 216n88
Stanley, Jo, 71
Stevenson, Sharman, 153, 235n132
Stitt, Hugh, 26
Strain, David Harbison, 7–8
  and acceptance of queer relationships, 150, 151–52, 235n121
  with Arthur Fitzsimons, 128*f*
  commercial and social sites used by, 45–46, 50–51, 52
  cruising tactics of, 27–28, 33, 40, 41–42, 48
  dates woman, 120–21
  on David and Jonathan, 94
  diaries of, 195n32
  and Du Barry's, 67
  on effeminacy, 130
  experience with servicemen, 68–70, 77–78
  and gay community, 126, 127, 128–29
  and matchmaking, 126
  personal adverts used by, 125
  picks up McCullough, 21–22
  and queer literature, 97, 99, 100, 101
  relationship with Aicken, 106–7
  risks faced by, 167
  and sectarianism in queer relationships, 38–39
  sexuality of young partners of, 116, 117–18
  and working-class sex workers, 113, 114–15
Strange Brother (Niles), 100
Summers, Edward, 46–47
Symonds, John Addington, 81, 83, 93
Syrett, Nicholas, 209n80

tabloids, 153–54, 181
television, 154
Tellier, André, 100
Third Home Rule Bill (1912), 182–83
Three Brothers, The (McLaverty), 143
Todd, Isaac, 232n86
toilets, public, 32–33, 200n34
Tomelty, Joseph, 109–10, 221n19
Tosh, John, 237n8
trams, 41–42
trials. *See* prosecution, for same-sex crimes
Troubles, the, 9, 11, 12, 140
Twilight Men (Tellier), 100

Ulster Group Theatre, 221n19
Ulster Volunteer Force, 137
Underwood, Reginald, 22
unionism, 167–77, 179–81
United States, Irish migration to, 57
Upchurch, Charles, 140, 213n22
urinals, public, 33, 138

Vagrancy Act (1824), 238n21
Vagrancy Law Amendment Act (1898), 15, 197n59, 238n21
vigilantes, moral, 135–40
violence, 139–40

Wadman, Francis, 113–14, 223n51
walking, and cruising, 40–41
Walkowitz, Judith, 175
Ward, Francis, 201n46
Warnock, James, 201n46
Weeks, Jeffrey, 155
Well of Loneliness, The (Hall), 103–4
whisper network, 47–48
White Cross Society, 88–89, 214n48
Whitman, Walt, 97, 103
Wilde, Oscar, 2, 8, 15, 93, 97, 98–99, 103, 104, 170
Williams, Raymond, 194n28
Withers, Jane, 129
Witness, 91
witness statements, 5–6, 18, 62, 134–35, 147, 159–63, 169
Wolfenden Committee, 95–96, 130, 154, 217nn96–97
Women's Volunteer Patrol, 78
Woods, Gregory, 219n121
Woolworth's, 44–46, 125
workhouses, 61
working-class youths
  and prosecution of same-sex crimes, 165
  and sex work, 108–15, 138–39, 222n33
  shift to female partners, 115–23
  See also age; children
World War I, 73, 179
World War II, 73–78, 211n113
Wright, Joseph Shekelton, 173

Young, Jimmie, 221n19
Young Men's Christian Association, 89, 205n117

www.ingramcontent.com/pod-product-compliance
Lightning Source LLC
Chambersburg PA
CBHW020829270326
41928CB00006B/474

* 9 7 8 1 5 0 1 7 8 6 4 5 7 *